QUICK

Sum & Substance

REVIEW

CONSTITUTIONAL LAW

3RD EDITION

Professor
Phil Prygoski

WEST
GROUP

ISBN 1-57793-045-2

Production Coordinator   Seth Barondess
Cover Design   Johnson Gray Advertising

ISBN   1-57793-045-2

Sum & Substance Quick Review of Constitutional Law is a publication of
Sum & Substance, a division of West Professional Training Programs, Inc.

Third Edition

This product was printed and published in the United States of America.

TABLE OF CONTENTS

CASEBOOK TABLE

Quick Review Chapters and Sections	Barron, Dienes, McCormack, & Redish Constitutional Law; Principles and Policy 1996 (5th ed)	Braveman & Banks Constitutional Law: Structure and Rights in Our Federal System 1996 (3rd ed)	Brest & Levinson Processes of Constitutional Decision-making Cases & Materials 1992 (3rd ed)	Cohen & Varat Constitutional Law Cases and Materials 1993 (9th ed)	Crump, Gessman, & Reiss Cases and Materials on Constitutional Law 1989	Gunther Constitutional Law 1991 (12th ed)	Lockhart, Kamisar, Choper, Shiffrin & Fallon Constitutional Law 1996 (8th ed)	Redlich, Schwartz, & Attanasio Constitutional Law 1996 (3rd ed)	Rotunda Modern Constitutional Law Cases and Notes 1997 (5th ed)	Stone, Seidman, Sunstein, & Tushnet Constitutional Law 1996 (3rd ed)
CHAPTER V Judicial Review, General §§20-48	11-51; 1413-1496	22-47; 142-173; 205-256	71-97; 1459-1481	24-152	35-114	2-38	1-57; 1505-1546	1-74	1-60; 1138-1184	1-146
Standing, Ripeness, and Mootnes §§49-97	1433-1495	166-173		94-133	65-71	1598-1638	1511-1546	39-58	1138-1184	90-121; 143-145
Abstention §§114-130		233-240		77-89	50	1643-1650				
Eleventh Amendment §§98-113	1422-1425	207-232	300-302	60-76	255-257				12-13; 38	
CHAPTER VI National Legislative Power, General §§131-140	89-188; 281-320	268-334	310-329; 379-423	153-250; 385-386	115-178; 237-250; 325-341	66-175; 176-209; 351-370	58-171	75-162	142-222	147-287
Commerce Power §§141-166	89-159	268-334	310-321; 379-385; 390-423	178-226	127-164; 237-250	93-175	67-120; 145-157	83-135	142-171; 186-222	182-233
Taxing and Spending §§167-183	160-175		322-329; 397-398	227-233	165-176	176-200	121-133; 141-143	136-154	172-185	237-253
War and Foreign Affairs Powers §§184-195	321-353	123-141		233-243	325-341	201-209; 351-370	134-139; 204-212	155-162	223-257	233-237; 477-493
CHAPTER VII Separation of Powers, General §§206-213; 242-245	259-372	53-92	513-544	418-467	92-98; 279-352	39-50; 311-393	172-220	269-341	223-359	285-493

Quick Review Chapters and Sections	Barron, Dienes, McCormack, & Redish Constitutional Law; Principles and Policy 1996 (5th ed)	Braveman & Banks Constitutional Law; Structure and Rights in Our Federal System 1996 (3rd ed)	Brest & Levinson Processes of Constitutional Decision-making Cases & Materials 1992 (3rd ed)	Cohen & Varat Constitutional Law Cases and Materials 1993 (9th ed)	Crump, Gessman, & Reiss Cases and Materials on Constitutional Law 1989	Gunther Constitutional Law 1991 (12th ed)	Lockhart, Kamisar, Choper, Shiffrin & Fallon Constitutional Law 1996 (8th ed)	Redlich, Schwartz, & Attanasio Constitutional Law 1996 (3rd ed)	Rotunda Modern Constitutional Law Cases and Notes 1997 (5th ed)	Stone, Seidman, Sunstein, & Tushnet Constitutional Law 1996 (3rd ed)
Legislative Veto §§215-220	283-296	87-105	516-544	433-443	294-306	322-331	183-189	269-275	298-303	424-442
Appointment/Removal Power §§221-231	302-314	106-123		444-458	349-350	333-350	189-204	276-289	304-338	442-473
Executive Privilege and Executive Immunity §§232-237	354-372	33-43		460-467	342-348	371-393	212-220	323-332	279-297	412-423
CHAPTER VIII State Power to Regulate Commerce, General §246	189-258	312-334; 334-364	153-177; 424-472	251-382	187-236; 251-254; 265-278	210-290; 305-311	221-281; 286-314	163-268	72-141	289-373
Dormant Commerce Clause §§247-287	190-242	334-364	424-472	255-348	187-236	210-279	221-274	229-268	72-118	289-331; 343-373
Privileges and Immunities Clause of Article IV §§288-298	243-250		173-177	349-361; 470-471	251-254	281-290	274-281	218-221	119-126	331-343
CHAPTER IX Preemption of State Laws	254-258		473-474	372-382	179-187	291-300	281-286	164-166; 259-268	127-133	373-384
CHAPTER X State Action Requirement	1343-1412	390-422	1301-1354	1104-1192	1099-1128	883-925	1411-1467	343-355	436-495	1693-1765

Sum & Substance QUICK REVIEW of Constitutional Law

Quick Review Chapters and Sections	Barron, Dienes, McCormack, & Redish Constitutional Law: Principles and Policy 1996 (5th ed)	Braveman & Banks Constitutional Law: Structure and Rights in Our Federal System 1996 (3rd ed)	Brest & Levinson Processes of Constitutional Decision-making Cases & Materials 1992 (3rd ed)	Cohen & Varat Constitutional Law Cases and Materials 1993 (9th ed)	Crump, Gessman, & Reiss Cases and Materials on Constitutional Law 1989	Gunther Constitutional Law 1991 (12th ed)	Lockhart, Kamisar, Choper, Shiffrin & Fallon Constitutional Law 1996 (8th ed)	Redlich, Schwartz, & Attanasio Constitutional Law 1996 (3rd ed)	Rotunda Modern Constitutional Law Cases and Notes 1997 (5th ed)	Stone, Seidman, Sunstein, & Tushnet Constitutional Law 1996 (3rd ed)
CHAPTER XI Congressional Enforcement of Civil Rights	176-188; 1395-1412; 379-380	365-422	129-132; 229-261; 1481-1523	468-513; 1104-1192	1129-1154	880-882; 926-993	105-110; 1468-1504	342-397	719-750	229-232; 253-266; 1693-1699
CHAPTER XII Retroactive Legislation, General §380			362-364	468-470; 536-552	413-432	478-490	362-369	448-453	258-263; 407-421	1627-1645
Ex Post Facto Laws and Bills of Attainder §§381-396				468-538					254; 262-263; 407-412	
Contracts Clause §§397-404		366	362-364	470-471; 536-551	413-432	478-490	362-369	448-453	412-421	1627-1645
CHAPTER XIII The Takings Clause		589-644	142-143; 284-285; 365-378	552-577	378-412	465-477	338-362	454-485	422-435	1645-1692
CHAPTER XIV Procedural Due Process - Liberty or Property Interests and Right to a Hearing	402-406	577-588; 736-750	1122-1157	1070-1092	477-511	583-600	582-613	604-616	380-406	1048-1072
CHAPTER XV Substantive Due Process, General §§465-480	407-558	577-588; 623-735	943-1053; 1211-1247	939-1048	353-376; 517-594; 688-722	432-465; 491-582; 608-635; 819-877	314-338; 389-555; 1323-1410	398-430; 486-603; 918-976	360-379; 607-718	813-1048
Economic and Social Legislation §§469-483	408-433	577-623	262-284; 554-580	686-707	353-376	433-465	314-338	431-453; 964-976	360-379	813-842

Quick Review Chapters and Sections	Barron, Dienes, McCormack, & Redish Constitutional Law; Principles and Policy 1996 (5th ed)	Braveman & Banks Constitutional Law; Structure and Rights in Our Federal System 1996 (3rd ed)	Brest & Levinson Processes of Constitutional Decision-making Cases & Materials 1992 (3rd ed)	Cohen & Varat Constitutional Law Cases and Materials 1993 (9th ed)	Crump, Gessman, & Reiss Cases and Materials on Constitutional Law 1989	Gunther Constitutional Law 1991 (12th ed)	Lockhart, Kamisar, Choper, Shiffrin & Fallon Constitutional Law 1996 (8th ed)	Redlich, Schwartz, & Attanasio Constitutional Law 1996 (3rd ed)	Rotunda Modern Constitutional Law Cases and Notes 1997 (5th ed)	Stone, Seidman, Sunstein, & Tushnet Constitutional Law 1996 (3rd ed)
Fundamental Rights §§484-529	434-558; 806-886	623-735	943-1053; 1211-1235; 1235-1247	577-678; 939-1048	517-594; 688-722	481-582; 819-877	389-555; 1323-1410	486-603; 918-963	607-718	842-1048
CHAPTER XVI Equal Protection, General §§530-547	559-886	423-576; 716-723; 1099-1126	229-261; 474-480; 581-889; 1073-1110; 1248-1276	679-1069; 1093-1103	595-688; 693-708; 723-778	601-818; 820-839; 871-877	1147-1410	617-976	496-718	495-784; 842-940
Race and Ethnicity §§548-582	584-727	423-439; 474-530; 1099-1126	229-261; 474-480; 581-804	710-769; 801-829; 840-905	603-683	636-656; 704-750; 757-818	1163-1270	617-746; 798-889; 939-956	502-558	495-561; 595-697
Alienage, Gender, Age, Wealth, Illegitimacy §§583-649	728-805	530-576	805-899; 1248-1276	770-800; 801-839; 906-938; 1049-1069	684-687; 723-774	656-703; 751-818; 820-839; 871-877	1270-1323; 1390-1408	747-797; 890-936	559-606	697-784; 842-940
CHAPTER XVII Freedom of Speech, General §§658-684	887-1232	825-938; 980-1001; 1039-1098; 1126-1143	57-68; 889-942; 1158-1186	1194-1536	779-893; 927-1026	994-1454; 1459-1469	614-936; 963-1038	977-1527	751-1045	1073-1530
Time, Place, and Manner Restrictions §§685-710	1010-1013	926-938	920-935	1352-1428	927-941	1211-1216	789-809	1252-1271	777-832; 977-994	1323-1334
Content-Based Restrictions §§711-769	887-1052	829-926	895, 912, 913, 921	1194-1237; 1256-1351; 1429-1447	785-812; 821-882; 959-972	1008-1189; 1217-1249	614-850	977-1010; 1212-1251; 1498-1527	751-776; 832-852; 890-947; 1011-1028	1087-1172; 1196-1323
Defamation and Privacy §§770-788	1132-1167	896-911		1256-1281	862-882	1075-1094	661-696	1167-1211	917-947	1197-1226

Quick Review Chapters and Sections	Barron, Dienes, McCormack, & Redish Constitutional Law; Principles and Policy 1996 (5th ed)	Braveman & Banks Constitutional Law; Structure and Rights in Our Federal System 1996 (3rd ed)	Brest & Levinson Processes of Constitutional Decision-making Cases & Materials 1992 (3rd ed)	Cohen & Varat Constitutional Law Cases and Materials 1993 (9th ed)	Crump, Gessman, & Reiss Cases and Materials on Constitutional Law 1989	Gunther Constitutional Law 1991 (12th ed)	Lockhart, Kamisar, Choper, Shiffrin & Fallon Constitutional Law 1996 (8th ed)	Redlich, Schwartz, & Attanasio Constitutional Law 1996 (3rd ed)	Rotunda Modern Constitutional Law Cases and Notes 1997 (5th ed)	Stone, Seidman, Sunstein, & Tushnet Constitutional Law 1996 (3rd ed)
Public Forum Analysis §§806-828	993-1026	1039-1055		1352-1416	927-941; 948-958	1249-1356; 1385-1387	892-910	1212-1379	777-832	1334-1386
Speech and the Electoral Process; Government Employees; Right Not to Speak or Associate §§829-863	1209-1232	1056-1073; 1126-1143	1158-1186	1448-1546	973-1005	1351-1375; 1399-1454	963-1038	1011-1082; 1404-1437	948-976; 994-1010	1407-1434; 1440-1486
CHAPTER XVIII Freedom of the Press	1131-1208	907-928; 1093-1099		1537-1589	894-926	1455-1458; 1470-1500	809-891; 937-963	1083-1211	853-889	1486-1530
CHAPTER XIX The Religion Clauses of the First Amendment §911	1233-1342	752-824; 938-979; 1003-1038	1276-1289; 1405-1458	1590-1692	1027-1098	1051-1589	1039-1146	1528-1691	1046-1137	1531-1626
Establishment Clause §§912-960	1233-1296	791-824	1277-1286; 1422-1439	1590-1673	1028-1076	1503-1555	1039-1105; 1132-1146	1550-1650	1046-1110	1547-1590; 1612-1626
Religion and Public Schools §§917-942	1233-1276	938-979; 1003-1039	1276-1289	1590-1673	1028-1070	1503-1536	1039-1085	1550-1578	1050-1092	1531-1590; 1612-1626
Free Exercise §§961-1005	1297-1342	752-791	1439-1458	1674-1692	1077-1098	1556-1589	1105-1146	1651-1691	1111-1137	1590-1626

Quick Review Chapters and Sections	Barron, Dienes, McCormack, & Redish Constitutional Law; Principles and Policy 1996 (5th ed)	Braveman & Banks Constitutional Law; Structure and Rights in Our Federal System 1996 (3rd ed)	Brest & Levinson Processes of Constitutional Decision-making Cases & Materials 1992 (3rd ed)	Cohen & Varat Constitutional Law Cases and Materials 1993 (9th ed)	Crump, Gessman, & Reiss Cases and Materials on Constitutional Law 1989	Gunther Constitutional Law 1991 (12th ed)	Lockhart, Kamisar, Choper, Shiffrin & Fallon Constitutional Law 1996 (8th ed)	Redlich, Schwartz, & Attanasio Constitutional Law 1996 (3rd ed)	Rotunda Modern Constitutional Law Cases and Notes 1997 (5th ed)	Stone, Seidman, Sunstein, & Tushnet Constitutional Law 1996 (3rd ed)
CHAPTER XX Cruel and Unusual Punishment/Death Penalty			960-961	513			555-581		379	

I. INTRODUCTION

II. 10-5-2 HOUR STUDY GUIDE FOR CONSTITUTIONAL LAW

III. ANALYTICAL AND EXAM APPROACH

A. ANALYSIS OF CONSTITUTIONAL QUESTIONS. [§1]

Read the Constitution and the assigned cases. Be sure to consider the "real-life" implications of the cases.

B. BASE ALL YOUR ARGUMENTS IN THE CONSTITUTION. [§5]

Every constitutional argument must be grounded in the Constitution. Keep in mind that while the Constitution is the supreme law of the land, the Supreme Court is the ultimate arbiter of the Constitution.

IV. OVERVIEW OF CONSTITUTIONAL LAW: A SUMMARY OF THE MAJOR AREAS OF CONSTITUTIONAL LAW

A. TYPES OF CONSTITUTIONAL QUESTIONS. [§8]

Any constitutional analysis is likely to fall into one or more general categories: judicial review, separation of power, federalism, or individual rights.

B. JUDICIAL REVIEW. [§9]

A federal court may hear a case only if it involves a "case or controversy" under Article III of the Constitution.

C. SEPARATION OF POWERS. [§10]

A separation of powers question involves the relationship between or among branches of the federal government.

D. FEDERALISM. [§11]

A federalism question involves the relationship between the federal government and the states.

E. INDIVIDUAL RIGHTS. [§12]

These questions typically involve a government, federal or state, taking some action which abridges a right of an individual. An analysis should include the following steps: 1) Determine which government is acting; 2) Identify the interest that has been abridged; 3) Place the abridged interest in the Constitution; 4) Ascribe constitutional weight to the interest abridged; and 5) Set the appropriate level of scrutiny.

V. JUDICIAL REVIEW AND LIMITATIONS ON JUDICIAL REVIEW: THE CONSTITUTIONAL BASIS FOR THE EXERCISE OF FEDERAL JUDICIAL POWER

A. ARTICLE III OF THE CONSTITUTION ESTABLISHES FEDERAL COURTS. [§20]

It provides the basis for and the scope of federal judicial power.

1. ORIGINAL JURISDICTION OF THE SUPREME COURT. [§21]

The Supreme Court has original jurisdiction in all cases affecting Ambassadors, other public Ministers and Consuls, and those in which a State is a party.

2. APPELLATE JURISDICTION OF THE SUPREME COURT. [§22]

The Supreme Court has appellate jurisdiction in all other cases, with exceptions and regulations as Congress shall make.

3. WAYS TO APPEAL TO THE SUPREME COURT. [§23]

There are two ways to appeal to the Supreme Court: 1) Mandatory appeal as of right (only from decisions of three-judge federal courts); and 2) Discretionary appeal, in all other cases arising in lower federal courts, as well as all cases arising in state court.

B. DOES A FEDERAL COURT HAVE JURISDICTION? WILL IT EXERCISE IT? [§26]

Make sure that a federal court has jurisdiction: Is there a federal question in the case, or is there diversity of citizenship between the parties. Ask whether there is any "prudential" reason for a court not exercising its jurisdiction.

C. SUPREME COURT ESTABLISHMENT OF THE POWER OF JUDICIAL REVIEW. [§32]

1. JUDICIAL REVIEW OF CONGRESSIONAL LAWS AND EXECUTIVE ACTS. [§33]

Marbury v. Madison established the power of judicial review over the other branches of the federal government.

2. SUPREME COURT REVIEW OF STATE COURT CASES. [§34]

As long as a federal question is present, the Court may review civil and criminal cases from state courts.

D. LIMITATIONS ON JUDICIAL REVIEW. [§35]

There are both constitutional and prudential limitations on a federal court's power of judicial review.

1. FEDERAL COURTS MAY NOT ISSUE ADVISORY OPINIONS. [§36]

These are not within the Article III definition of a case or controversy.

2. POLITICAL QUESTIONS ARE NON-JUSTICIABLE. [§37]

There are two kinds of political questions.

a. Political Questions That The Constitution Says Are To Be Decided By Congress Or The President. [§38]

(1) Guarantee Clause Cases. [§39]

(2) Expulsion of a Member of Congress. [§40]

(3) Procedures for Impeachment. [§41]

(4) President's Power To Terminate a Treaty [§41.1]

b. Political Questions That Are "Too Hot To Handle." [§42]

(1) Lack of judicially discoverable or manageable standards.

(2) Need for an initial policy decision by another branch.

(3) Deference for decisions of another branch.

(4) Need to adhere to political decision already made.

(5) Potential embarrassment from multiple pronouncements.

3. QUALIFICATIONS CLAUSES. [§43]

Neither Congress nor a state may add requirements to the list of qualifications for members of Congress contained in the Constitution.

4. ADEQUATE AND INDEPENDENT STATE GROUNDS. [§46]

Look for a case involving both state and federal questions, coming out of state court. If the state decision is clearly based solely on state law, and the U.S. Supreme Court cannot change the result, it will not take the case.

a. Steps in an "Adequate and Independent State Grounds" Analysis. [§47]

(1) Has the highest appellate court of a state ruled on the case?

(2) Does the case involve questions of both federal and state law?

(3) Can the Supreme Court change the result of the case by ruling on the federal question?

b. State Constitution Confers Greater Protection Than The Federal Constitution. [§48]

This is a frequent scenario in the adequate and independent state grounds area because the Supreme Court cannot change the result in the case.

5. RIPENESS, STANDING, AND MOOTNESS: THE "BIG THREE" LIMITATIONS ON FEDERAL JUDICIAL POWER. [§49]

a. Ripeness. [§50]

Has anyone suffered actual or threatened harm as a result of government action?

b. Standing. [§53]

Has the plaintiff suffered an actual or threatened injury as a result of government action?

(1) Constitutional Aspects of Standing. [§54]

(a) Injury-In-Fact. [§55]

There must be an actual injury or a specific threat of injury to the plaintiff.

(b) Traceability. [§56]

The court must be able to issue a decree that will directly redress the injury.

(2) Prudential Aspects of Standing. [§57]

These are judge-made barriers to standing. The two main ones are the third-party standing rules, and the general bar to federal taxpayer standing.

(3) Examples of Injuries-In-Fact. [§58]

(a) Injuries That Do Qualify Under Article III. [§59]

There can be both economic and non-economic injuries that qualify under Article III. Non-economic injuries would include aesthetic or environmental injury, as well as religious injuries.

(b) Injuries That Do Not Qualify Under Article III. [§64]

The following injuries do not qualify under Article III: 1) general citizen standing; 2) standing of public interest organizations; 3) standing to assert stigmatic injury to a racial group.

(4) The Traceability Requirement. [§69]

An injury-in-fact must be fairly traceable to the government action complained of.

(5) Federal Taxpayer Standing. [§73]

A federal taxpayer has standing to challenge an incorrect tax bill, or to try to recover taxes paid under protest.

(a) Federal Taxpayer Standing to Challenge a Spending Measure. [§74]

In general, a federal taxpayer does not have standing to challenge a spending measure.

(b) Federal Taxpayer Standing to Challenge a Spending Measure that Establishes Religion. [§75]

A federal taxpayer does having standing to challenge a congressional spending measure that establishes religion.

Sum & Substance QUICK REVIEW of Constitutional Law

(c) State Taxpayers. [§78]

State taxpayers are treated the same as federal taxpayers in terms of not having standing to challenge a spending measure.

(d) Municipal Taxpayers. [§79]

A municipal taxpayer does have standing in federal court to challenge a municipal expenditure that violates federal rights.

(6) Third Party Standing. [§80]

In general, a person may not acquire standing by asserting the rights of a third party.

(a) Requirements for Individual Third Party Standing. [§81]

The following requirements are necessary to assert third party standing: 1) A relationship between the plaintiff and the right holder; 2) A genuine obstacle to the right holder asserting his or her own rights; and 3) The right holder's rights will be diluted if not asserted by the plaintiff.

(b) Associational Standing to Represent Members. [§85]

An association may have standing to assert the rights of its members under the following conditions: 1) The association can only represent members who have not filed suit on their own behalf; 2) Any member who is to be represented must have suffered an injury in fact; 3) Joinder of the individual members is not necessary to the disposition to the lawsuit; and 4) The interests of the members are germane to the purpose of the organization.

(7) Associational Standing to Represent Itself. [§86]

An association may have standing to vindicate an injury to itself. An association can be injured two ways: 1) The government acts directly against the association; and 2) The government takes some action that causes members to quit the organization.

(8) Congressional Power to Create Standing. [§89]

Congress may confer standing on parties who meet the Article III injury-in-fact requirement. [§54-56]

c. Mootness. [§92]

Mootness goes to the requirement that a case or controversy must exist throughout the entire litigational process.

(1) Theory Underlying the Mootness Doctrine. [§93]

A federal court will exercise its jurisdiction only if it is able to provide relief to a litigant in a contested lawsuit.

(2) Exceptions to the Mootness Doctrine. [§94]

(a) Capable of Repetition, Yet Evading Review. [§95]

This exception involves cases where the injury-in-fact will always be over by the time the lawsuit is completed (abortion laws, election laws, or age limitations).

(b) Voluntary Cessation of Illegal Activity. [§98]

This will be insufficient to make a case moot.

(c) Collateral Consequences. [§99]

Some claims contain collateral issues that will continue to affect a litigant even though the main issues have been resolved.

6. ELEVENTH AMENDMENT. [§100]

The Eleventh Amendment limits the ability of federal courts to hear cases in which an individual sues a state.

a. An Individual Cannot Directly Sue A State In Federal Court. [§101]

This rule does not apply to other states or the federal government as plaintiff.

b. How To Get Around The Eleventh Amendment Bar To The Exercise of Federal Court Jurisdiction When an Individual Sues a State. [§102]

(1) Name the state officer as an individual, not as an officer of the state.

(2) Allege that the state officer acted outside the scope of his or her authority by violating your rights.

(3) Allege that the state officer violated your federal rights.

c. Relief Available Against a State. [§103]

A plaintiff cannot obtain retroactive money damages, but may obtain prospective injunctive relief (including any money it takes for the state to comply with the injunction).

d. The Eleventh Amendment Only Applies in Federal Court. [§109]

The Eleventh Amendment does not affect a person's ability to sue a state in state court. However, issues of sovereign immunity will arise in such a suit.

e. The Eleventh Amendment Only Protects States and Statewide Departments. [§110]

An individual can sue political subdivisions of a state in federal court (such as cities, counties, or school boards).

f. Congress May Abrogate a State's Eleventh Amendment Immunity. [§111]

Congress may do this by acting pursuant to 5 of the Fourteenth Amendment.

g. Congress May Not Abrogate a State's Eleventh Amendment Immunity By Acting Under the Commer Clause. [§112]

h. A State May Waive Its Eleventh Amendment Immunity in Federal Court. [§114]

A state must clearly state its intent to waive its Eleventh Amendment immunity.

i. The Eleventh Amendment Does Not Apply When the Federal Government Sues a State in Federal Court. [§115]

j. An Individual May Sue a Public Official in Federal Court If the Official Will Pay the Damages Out of His or Her Personal Assets. [§116]

Such a suit presents no danger of depleting the state treasury.

k. The Eleventh Amendment Provides No Immunity to the Railway Subsidiary of the Port Authority of New York and New Jersey. [§117]

7. ABSTENTION. [§118]

Federal courts may abstain from deciding certain federal questions that also fall under the jurisdiction of state courts.

a. *Pullman* Abstention. [§119]

Pullman abstention arises when a lawsuit is filed in federal court, the case involves issues both of federal and state law, and the issue of state law is ambiguous, uncertain, or unsettled. A plaintiff who is sent to state court may litigate both state and federal claims in state court. Once in state court, the plaintiff may choose to reserve the right to return to federal court to litigate the federal issues in the case.

b. *Younger* Abstention. [§122]

Younger abstention arises when a defendant in a pending state proceeding files a lawsuit in federal court seeking to enjoin the state proceeding.

(1) Theory Underlying *Younger* Abstention. [§123]

Federal courts may abstain in these cases to show respect for state courts and to avoid crowding of the federal docket.

(2) Exceptions to *Younger* abstention. [§124]

A federal court may choose not to abstain if a state prosecution is brought in bad faith or for purposes of harassment.

(3) Reversal of Usual Order of Filing. [§127]

Younger abstention rules apply when a person has sued in federal court to enjoin a threatened prosecution, but the state begins its prosecution before anything of substance on the merits takes place in federal court.

(4) *Younger* Abstention Has Been Applied to Some Non-Criminal Cases. [§128]

Younger abstention has been applied in some civil cases where an important state interest is involved in the pending state proceeding.

(5) *Younger* Abstention Applies to Declaratory Relief. [§136]

VI. NATIONAL LEGISLATIVE POWER: SOURCES OF AND LIMITATIONS ON CONGRESSIONAL POWER.

A. ANY ACT OF CONGRESS MUST BE GROUNDED IN A SPECIFIC PROVISION OF THE CONSTITUTION. [§137]

Congress has no general power to pass laws for the general welfare. Ask yourself what the specific constitutional provision is that justifies the law.

B. TWO NOTES ON GOVERNMENT POWER. [§138]

Beware of these two principles when analyzing any government action.

1. GOVERNMENT POWER AS SWORD AND SHIELD. [§139]

Any provision of the Constitution which is a source of power for a particular government may also be a defense against action by another government.

2. TWO WAYS TO INVALIDATE A STATUTE. [§140]

a. Eliminate the Constitutional Power Source Relied On By Congress To Justify The Law. [§141]

The plaintiff asserts that the legislature exceeded the scope of the constitutional provision on which it relied to pass a law.

b. Balance. [§142]

Even if a law is within a constitutional power source, it may be invalid because it contravenes some other constitutional provision.

C. SPECIFIC CONGRESSIONAL POWERS. [§143]

You must be able to identify which constitutional provision Congress relies on when it passes a law. The main enumerated congressional powers are:
1. Power to tax;
2. Power to spend for the general welfare;
3. Power to regulate commerce among the several states, with foreign nations, and with the Indian Tribes;
4. Power to regulate immigration and naturalization;
5. Power to pass uniform laws dealing with bankruptcy;

6. Power to coin money;
7. Power to establish a postal service;
8. Power to set up a system of copyrights;
9. Power to set up federal courts;
10. Power to declare war;
11. Power to raise and maintain armies;
12. Power to regulate and dispose of federal property;
13. Power to acquire private property for a public use;
14. Power to pass regulations for the District of Columbia.

1. NECESSARY AND PROPER CLAUSE. [§144]

Congress has the power to pass laws for itself or any other branch or officer of the federal government. Congress may choose any reasonable means to carry out some power of government. The Necessary and Proper Clause cannot be used itself as a source of power.

2. COMMERCE POWER. [§147]

Congress has the power to regulate Commerce with foreign nations, among the several States, and with the Indian Tribes.

a. Two Main Issues Arise In The Commerce Clause Area. [§148]

(1) What is the Scope or Reach of the Commerce Power? [§149]

What people or activities fall within the definition of interstate commerce?

(2) Does A Congressional Act Unduly Abridge States' Rights? [§150]

Even if someone or something is within the reach of Congress' Commerce Power, does the federal law on balance violate the Tenth Amendment rights or powers of the states?

b. Scope Of The Commerce Power. [§151]

Today, most persons and activities are within the scope of the Commerce Power (except for the private possession of handguns).

c. Commerce Power And Federalism. [§165]

When Congress passes a law which interferes with some attribute of state sovereignty, a state may assert the Tenth Amendment as a defense against congressional action.

(1) Tenth Amendment. [§166]

The Court has interpreted the Tenth Amendment to mean that there are certain aspects of sovereignty that a state must have to function as a state and to occupy its proper place in a federal system.

(2) Major Cases in the Development of the Commerce Power and the Tenth Amendment. [§167]

(3) Present State of the Law When Congress Regulates Under the Commerce Power. [§172]

If Congress passes a law that regulates both private and governmental actors, the only protection a state receives from congressional interference is from its participation in the national legislative process. If only a state is regulated, and Congress is effectively commandeering a state legislature **or executive officer**, the Tenth Amendment may be asserted as a defense against congressional action.

3. TAXING POWER. [§173]

Congress has the power to lay and collect taxes, imposts, and excises.

a. Two Ways A Tax Can Be Valid. [§174]

A tax passed by Congress can be valid as a revenue-raising measure, or as a means to achieve a valid regulatory goal of Congress.

(1) Tax As Revenue-Raiser. [§175]

As long as a taxing measure raises money, it will be upheld.

(2) Tax as a Means to Achieve a Valid Regulatory Goal of Congress. [§176]

If Congress can regulate an activity under its Commerce Power, it may tax that activity as a means to achieve its permissible regulatory purpose.

b. Constitutional Limitations On The Taxing Power. [§177]

The federal taxing power may not be used to contravene other constitutional protections.

(1) Fifth Amendment Privilege Against Self-Incrimination. [§178]

A federal tax may be invalid if one of its reporting provisions requires a taxpayer to incriminate himself or herself in violation of the privilege against self-incrimination.

(2) Tenth Amendment. [§179]

It is possible that if a tax unduly impairs a state's ability to deliver traditional governmental services, the tax may be invalid under the Tenth Amendment.

4. SPENDING POWER. [§180]

Congress has the power to spend "for the general welfare." Remember that Congress does not have any power to regulate for the general welfare.

a. Regulation Through The Spending Power. [§181]

Congress may effectively regulate certain activities by imposing conditions on the receipt of federal money. So long as the recipient has

Sum & Substance QUICK REVIEW of Constitutional Law

a theoretical choice to accept or reject the federal money, the court will uphold the spending measure.

(1) Is the Law Voluntary? [§182]

If the law leaves the recipient with a theoretical choice to accept or reject the federal "strings" accompanying the grant, the law will be upheld.

(2) Is the Condition on the Receipt of Money Related to the General Purpose of the Federal Grant? [§183]

It is possible that conditions on federal grants may be invalid if they are unrelated to the federal purpose in passing the spending measure.

(3) Are There Any Other Constitutional Provisions Which Would Limit Congress' Ability to Impose a Condition on the Receipt of Money? [§184]

For example, the Tenth Amendment or one of the individual rights provisions may limit Congress' ability to impose a condition on the receipt of money.

5. WAR POWER. [§190]

Congress has the power to declare war, raise armies and navies, and provide for the national defense. Congress may prepare for future wars, wage war once it has begun, and deal with the social and economic consequences of past wars.

6. FOREIGN AFFAIRS POWERS. [§191]

Congress and the President have very broad powers in the area of foreign affairs.

a. Congress May Delegate To The President The Power To Act In Foreign Affairs. [§192]

Congress has a very broad power to vest discretion in the President to implement congressional policy on foreign affairs.

b. Treaties And Executive Agreements. [§193]

(1) Treaties. [§194]

The President has the power to enter into treaties with other countries. A treaty must be ratified by two-thirds of the Senate.

(2) Executive Agreements. [§195]

An executive agreement is an agreement between the President and the chief executive of another country. Executive agreements do not require Senate ratification.

c. Relationships Among Treaties, Executive Agreements, Federal Statutes, And State Laws. [§196]

(1) Under the Supremacy Clause of Article VI, Treaties and Executive Agreements Always Take Precedence Over Conflicting State Laws. [§197]

(2) Operative Treaties Are on a Parity With Federal Statutes. [§198]

If there is a conflict a between an operative treaty and a federal statute, the most recent enactment wins.

(3) An Operative Treaty or a Federal Statute Take Precedence Over a Conflicting Executive Agreement. [§199]

(4) A Treaty May Be a Source of Legislative Power. [§200]

The ability of Congress to pass a law to implement a treaty constitutes an independent source of congressional power.

(5) A Treaty or Executive Agreement Cannot Violate the Constitutional Rights of Individuals. [§201]

7. PROPERTY POWER. [§202]

Congress has the power to dispose of and make all necessary rules respecting any property belonging to the United States. Congress may also dispose of surplus government property on whatever terms and conditions it chooses.

a. Congress May Regulate Wild Animals On Federal Property. [§203]

Congress may regulate wild animals on federal land, and can probably regulate them if they wander off federal land.

b. Congress Has The Power to Pass Laws to Govern the Territories of the United States. [§204]

Congress has the power to pass laws for territories such as Guam, American Samoa, or the Virgin Islands.

8. POWER TO REGULATE IMMIGRATION AND NATURALIZATION. [§205]

Congress has the power to establish a uniform rule of naturalization. Congress also has a plenary power to regulate immigration, including determining the status and conditions of aliens in the country, as well as the terms and conditions for deportation.

a. Immigration Laws Receive Rationality Review. [§206]

The Court defers to Congress regarding the terms and conditions of immigration.

b. Congress' Power Over Immigration May Trump First Amendment Rights. [§207]

Congress' power to regulate immigration is a compelling government interest which may justify an abridgement of individual rights.

c. Loss Of Citizenship. [§208]

Congress may impose some conditions on the retention of citizenship, but may not involuntarily revoke a person's citizenship.

(1) A Citizen Must Voluntarily and Intentionally Relinquish Citizenship. [§209]

The government must prove a voluntary relinquishment of citizenship.

(2) Congress May Not Involuntarily Revoke Citizenship. [§210]

(3) Congress May Impose Some Conditions on Retention of Citizenship. [§211]

VII. SEPARATION OF POWERS: RELATIONSHIPS BETWEEN BRANCHES OF THE FEDERAL GOVERNMENT.

A. OVERVIEW OF SEPARATION OF POWERS. [§212]

The first three Articles of the Constitution set forth the powers of the respective branches: Article I deals with the powers of Congress; Article II deals with the powers of the President and the Executive Branch; and Article III deals with the powers of the Judiciary. Run through the following steps in any separation of powers analysis: 1) Determine which branch of the federal government is acting and which branch is being affected by the law; 2) Determine whether any specific constitutional provision applies to the transaction at issue; and 3) If no specific constitutional provision applies, use a balancing approach.

B. EXECUTIVE AND LEGISLATIVE POWERS. [§215]

1. THE SPECIFIC POWERS OF THE PRESIDENT. [§216]

The President is vested with the executive power (the power to take care that the laws be faithfully executed). The President has the power to make treaties, appoint officers of the federal government, veto congressional enactments, and grant pardons or reprieves for federal offenses, except in cases of impeachment. Finally, the President is Commander-in-Chief of the armed forces.

2. PRESIDENTIAL ACTION AFFECTING THE POWERS OF CONGRESS. [§217]

Generally, the President may not take action unless it falls within one of the Article II powers.

a. The President Does Not Have the Power to Seize Private Property. [§218]

The Court held it violated separation-of-powers principles for the President to seize private property to keep the Korean police action going. Only Congress can pay for the seizure of property, so only Congress can seize it.

(1) **Justice Jackson's concurrence.** There are three scenarios of presidential power:

(a) When the President acts pursuant to an express or implied authorization from Congress, Presidential power is at its maximum;

(b) When the President acts in the absence of a congressional grant or denial of authority, the President's action is in a "twilight zone" of concurrent Presidential and congressional authority;

(c) When the President acts contrary to the express or implied will of Congress, Presidential power is at its minimum.

b. Congress May Explicitly or Implicitly Authorize Presidential Action. [§219]

Congress may explicitly authorize the President to take an action, or it may implicitly authorize the action by a history of acquiescence.

3. CONGRESSIONAL ACTION AFFECTING THE POWERS OF THE PRESIDENT. [§220]

Congress may not take any action which unduly interferes with a power of the President.

a. Legislative Vetoes. [§221]

When Congress passes a law, it must comply with constitutional requirements (bicameralism and presentment), and must not retain control over the execution of the law.

(1) Delegation of Power to the Executive Branch. [§222]

As a general matter, Congress may delegate to the President or some other executive branch entity the power to promulgate rules and regulations to implement congressional goals. A delegation will be valid if:

(a) Congress has not attempted to give away some nondelegable power;

(b) Congress has stated the objective of the law; and

(c) Congress has provided specific standards for the executive branch official or independent commission to follow.

(2) A Legislative Veto May Invalidate an Otherwise Valid Delegation. [§223]

Whenever Congress passes a law, it must meet both the bicameralism and presentment requirements of Article I. Bicameralism means that both the House and the Senate must pass the bill. Presentment means that the bill must be presented to the President for signature. If a law fails either the bicameralism or presentment requirement, it will be unconstitutional.

b. Appointment Power of the President. [§227]

Under Article II, the President nominates, with the advice and consent of the Senate, all principal officers of the United States. The President also nominates, with Senate consent, all inferior officers, unless

Sum & Substance QUICK REVIEW of Constitutional Law

Congress has vested the appointment of a specific inferior officer in the President alone, a court of law, or a head of a department.

> **STUDY TIP:** A law school exam is likely to test an appointment in which Congress vests the appointment of an inferior officer in some court or person in the federal government. Two issues you should be aware of are whether the appointee is an inferior officer, and whether Congress has vested the appointment in an appropriate person or court.

c. Congressional Restrictions on the President's Power to Remove Executive Branch Officers. [§230]

There is no specific constitutional provision which gives the President power to remove executive branch officials, nor is there any provision which deals with the ability of Congress to impose limits on the President's removal power.

(1) Analysis of Congressional Restrictions on the President's Power to Remove an Executive Branch Officer. [§231]

The Court will determine if the restrictions on removal imposed by Congress unduly interfere with an essential attribute or power of the presidency.

(2) Evolution of Caselaw Dealing With Congress Restricting the President's Removal Power. [§232]

The Court uses a balancing approach to determine whether the removal restrictions imposed by Congress impermissibly interfere with presidential power. In determining whether there is an impermissible interference with presidential power, look at the nature of the functions being performed by the person whom the President wants to remove. Restrictions on the removal of a purely executive officer are more likely to be unconstitutional. Restrictions on the removal of a quasi-legislative or quasi-judicial officer are more likely to be constitutional.

4. EXECUTIVE PRIVILEGE. [§238]

Executive privilege has to do with non-disclosure by the President of materials, documents, or communications that are generated during the President's tenure in office. It is a presumptive privilege which may be overridden by a sufficiently weighty reason for disclosure. Be careful to balance the specific argument for disclosure against the specific presidential argument for maintaining the secrecy of the requested materials.

5. EXECUTIVE IMMUNITY. [§241]

Executive immunity deals with the President's being immune from liability for damages in a civil suit. A President has absolute immunity from damages liability for his or her official acts as long as the President was acting within the outer perimeter of the duties of the office. Executive branch officials other than the President have qualified immunity. The test for qualified immunity is whether a reasonable person in an official capacity knew or should have known that his or her actions were violating clearly established constitutional rights.

6. LEGISLATIVE IMMUNITY. [§244]

Under the Speech or Debate Clause, Senators and Representatives are immune from civil or criminal suit for any conduct or words that are an integral part of the legislative process.

C. CONGRESSIONAL ACTION AFFECTING THE JUDICIARY. [§248]

Whenever Congress takes an action that affects the judiciary, determine whether the law is unduly interfering with an essential attribute of the judiciary, or is undermining the integrity of the judicial branch.

1. Congress' Ability to Determine the Scope of Federal Judicial Power. [§249]

The Supreme Court has original jurisdiction in a specific set of cases, enumerated in Article III of the Constitution. The Supreme Court has appellate jurisdiction in all other cases, with such exceptions and regulations as Congress shall make.

a. Jurisdiction Stripping. [§250]

Theoretically, Congress has the power to withdraw certain classes of cases from the appellate jurisdiction of the Court. Such a jurisdiction-stripping law could be challenged as violating separation of powers, procedural due process, and the substantive right that goes unprotected because the litigant has no appellate forum.

b. Developing Sentencing Guidelines. [§251]

Federal judges may be appointed to sit on a commission which develops sentencing guidelines for federal courts.

VIII. STATE POWER TO REGULATE COMMERCE: CONSTITUTIONAL LIMITATIONS

A. INTRODUCTION. [§252]

States have a very broad police power to regulate for purposes of health, safety and welfare. A problem arises when a state police power regulation interferes with the flow of interstate commerce or treats out-of-staters differently from instaters. The three main analyses you should know are the Dormant Commerce Clause, the Privileges and Immunities Clause of Article IV, and the Equal Protection Clause.

B. DORMANT COMMERCE CLAUSE - NEGATIVE IMPLICATIONS OF THE COMMERCE CLAUSE. [§253]

The Dormant Commerce Clause doctrine applies when a state, in the absence of any preempting federal action, passes a law which interferes with interstate commerce. There are two ways that a state may interfere with the free flow of commerce: discriminate against interstate commerce, or burden interstate commerce.

1. STATE DISCRIMINATION AGAINST INTERSTATE COMMERCE. [§254]

Determine if a state law, by purpose or effect, treats out-of-staters differently from instaters.

a. Analysis of a State Law That Discriminates Against Out-of-Staters. [§255]

(1) Identify the Discrimination. [§256]

Show that the state law, by purpose or effect, classifies along state lines.

(2) Identify the Reason for the Discrimination. [§257]

You have two choices: local economic protectionism; or some valid police power reason such as health or safety. Discrimination against interstate commerce for the purpose of favoring local business interests is **per se** invalid. If the discrimination is justified by a valid police power interest, and there are no other means to achieve that interest, the law may be valid.

b. Aspects of Discrimination Analysis Under the Dormant Commerce Clause. [§258]

(1) Strict Scrutiny of Facially Discriminatory Laws. [§259]

Facial discrimination against out-of-staters invokes strict scrutiny.

(2) Similarly Situated Entities [§259.1]

To violate the Dormant Commerce Clause, the discrimination must be between similarly situated entities

(3) Risk of Multiple Burdens. [§263]

If a state law creates a risk of multiple burdens on interstate commerce, it may be unconstitutional.

(4) Reciprocity Requirements. [§264]

Reciprocity requirements violate the Dormant Commerce Clause.

(5) Requiring Business to be Performed Instate. [§267]

A state cannot require business to be performed instate.

(6) Discrimination by Political Subdivision of a State; Less Drastic Means. [§268]

City or county discrimination against persons who live outside of the jurisdiction counts as discrimination against out-of-staters.

(7) Subsidy for Instate Economic Interests. [§269]

A state may not set up a system under which it subsidizes instate economic interests.

(8) Protecting Privacy Rights of Residents. [§270]

A municipality may protect the privacy rights of its citizens, even if interstate commerce is indirectly affected by the regulation.

(9) Waste Disposal Cases. [§271]

A state may not discriminate against out-of-staters in attempting to regulate waste disposal.

(10) No Distinction Between Non-Profit and For-Profit Enterprises [§271.1]

Discrimination against interstate non-profit organizations violates the Dormant Commerce Clause.

(a) Banning the Importation of Solid Waste. [§272]

A state may not prohibit the importation of waste into the state.

(b) Extra Fee on Out-of-State Waste. [§273]

A state may not charge out-of-staters an extra fee for dumping waste.

(c) County Approval for Dumping Waste from Outside the County. [§274]

A ban by a county on out-of-county waste violates the Dormant Commerce Clause.

(d) Higher Fee for Dumping Out-of-State Waste. [§275]

A higher fee for out-of-state dumpers of waste fails strict scrutiny.

(e) Requiring Waste to be Processed Locally. [§276]

A town cannot require waste to be processed locally when it could be processed more cheaply elsewhere.

2. STATE LAWS THAT ONLY BURDEN INTERSTATE COMMERCE. [§277]

A state law that treats instaters and out-of-staters the same will be considered a burden on interstate commerce and will be analyzed under a balancing test. Such a law will be upheld if it is supported by a legitimate state interest and only incidentally affects interstate commerce, unless the burden on interstate trade is clearly excessive in relation to the local benefits.

a. Steps to Follow In Determining the Constitutionality of a State Law That Burdens Interstate Commerce. [§278]

(1) Make sure there is no discrimination, by purpose or effect, against out-of- staters.

(2) Identify the local interests advanced by the law. Economic protectionism is never a valid state interest.

(3) See if the law only incidentally affects interstate commerce.

(4) Balance the adverse impact on interstate commerce against the extent to which the state's goals are advanced by the law.

(5) See if there are any less drastic means by which the state could achieve its goals.

(6) See if the law, if upheld, would create too great a risk of multiple burdens.

b. Issues to Look For When Applying Dormant Commerce Clause Analysis to a State Law That Burdens Interstate Commerce. [§279]

(1) Determine Whether the Subject Matter Regulated Is Local Or National In Nature. [§280]

If the subject matter regulated is national in scope, requiring uniform regulation, a state law will be harder to uphold. If a state regulates a local subject matter, the court will be more disposed to uphold the law.

(2) Determine Whether the Law Creates a Risk of Multiple Burdens. [§284]

If a state law creates the potential for conflicting laws to be enacted by other states, that may be enough to invalidate the law.

(3) Determine Whether a Price Affirmation Law Has Extraterritorial Effects. [§285]

A state may not pass a law which effectively sets prices in other states.

(4) Determine Whether the State Law Causes Business to Shift From One Out-of-Stater to Another. [§286]

An incidental effect of business shifting from one out-of-state supplier to another does not violate the Dormant Commerce Clause as long as the total flow of goods in interstate commerce is not diminished.

(5) Determine Whether the State Law Simply Prefers One Kind of Container Over Another. [§287]

It is not unconstitutional for a state to distinguish between kinds of containers, even though there may be an incidental effect on out-of-state suppliers.

3. MARKET PARTICIPANT EXCEPTION TO DORMANT COMMERCE CLAUSE ANALYSIS. [§288]

When a state acts as a market participant, rather than a market regulator, it may discriminate against out-of-staters for any reason, including local economic advantage. A state is a market regulator when it acts in its sovereign capacity to regulate what other parties can do within their contractual relationships. It is a market participant when it is a party to a contract.

STUDY TIP: "The Market Participant Exception" frees a state only from Dormant Commerce Clause analysis. It does **not** immunize a discriminating state from a Privileges and Immunities Clause of Article IV analysis, or from an equal protection analysis.

a. Examples of "Market Participant" Cases. [§289]

A court has upheld the ability of a state to prefer local economic interests over those of out-of-staters, so long as the state is participating in the relevant market.

(1) State-Owned Auto Salvage Business. [§290]

A state may discriminate against out-of-staters in the operation of a state-owned auto salvage business.

(2) State-Owned Cement Company. [§291]

A state may discriminate against out-of-staters in the sale of cement by a state-owned cement company.

(3) State As Party to Construction Contracts. [§292]

A city may discriminate against non-residents of the city in the awarding of city-funded construction contracts.

b. Limits of the Market Participant Doctrine. [§293]

A state will be treated as a market participant as long as it is making purchase or sales decisions in relation to a contract to which it is a party. When it tries to control the terms of a contract to which it is not a party, it is acting as a market regulator.

C. THE PRIVILEGES AND IMMUNITIES CLAUSE OF ARTICLE IV. [§294]

As a general matter, the Privileges and Immunities Clause of Article IV prohibits a state from denying to out-of-staters privileges that it grants to its own citizens. This clause only protects individuals, not corporations, and applies only when a state is discriminating against out-of-staters in relation to the exercise of a basic or fundamental right. Basic rights protected are the right to pursue an occupation, the right to own or dispose of property within the state, the right of access to state courts, and the right to come into the state to exercise a fundamental right.

1. STANDARD OF REVIEW IN PRIVILEGES AND IMMUNITIES CLAUSE OF ARTICLE IV CASES. [§295]

A state must show that it has a substantial reason for treating out-of-staters differently from its own citizens, and that the discrimination is substantially related to achieving the state's goals.

2. ARTICLE IV PRIVILEGES AND IMMUNITIES CLAUSE DOES NOT APPLY TO NON-BASIC RIGHTS. [§304]

The protections of the clause only apply when an out-of- stater is being discriminated against in the exercise of a basic right.

D. CONGRESSIONAL POWER TO AUTHORIZE STATE DISCRIMINATION AGAINST INTERSTATE COMMERCE. [§305]

If Congress authorizes a state to impose a discriminatory tax on out-of-state entities, such a tax will be immune from a Dormant Commerce Clause challenge, but will be invalid under the Equal Protection Clause if the only reason for the law is local economic protectionism.

E. STATE POWER TO TAX INTERSTATE COMMERCE. [§308]

The main limitations on a state's power to tax come from the Dormant Commerce Clause, the Due Process Clause, and the Equal Protection Clause.

1. DORMANT COMMERCE CLAUSE LIMITATIONS ON A STATE'S POWER TO TAX INTERSTATE COMMERCE. [§309]

The Court has adopted a four-part test by which to analyze a state tax that is challenged under the Dormant Commerce Clause. Under this test a state tax will survive a Commerce Clause challenge if the tax: 1) is applied to an activity with a substantial nexus to the taxing state; 2) is fairly apportioned; 3) does not discriminate against interstate commerce; and 4) is fairly related to the services provided by the state.

2. DUE PROCESS LIMITATIONS ON A STATE'S POWER TO TAX INTERSTATE COMMERCE. [§322]

The two main due process limitations on a state's power to tax interstate commerce are that there be "minimal contacts" between the entity taxed and the taxing state, and that there be a rational relationship between the income attributed to the taxing state and the intrastate values of the enterprise taxed.

3. EQUAL PROTECTION LIMITATIONS ON A STATE'S POWER TO TAX INTERSTATE COMMERCE. [§324]

A state may not impose a higher tax on out-of-staters than on instaters if the only reason is to prefer local business interests.

4. CONSTITUTIONAL LIMITATIONS ON A STATE'S POWER TO TAX IMPORTS OR EXPORTS. [§325]

The Constitution prohibits a state from laying "any Imposts or Duties on Imports or Exports. . .." Once goods have arrived at their destination for sale or distribution in a state, they are no longer in foreign commerce and are outside the restrictions of the Import-Export Clause.

5. STATE-IMPOSED COMPENSATING USE TAXES ARE CONSTITUTIONAL DESPITE THEIR IMPACT ON INTERSTATE COMMERCE. [§326]

A state may impose a use tax, up to the amount of the state sales tax, on goods purchased out-of-state (where there is no sales tax, or one lower than that of the state imposing the use tax), and brought into the state for use. The reason is to put instate sellers on the same footing with out-of-state sellers. A use tax is invalid if it discriminates against interstate commerce by imposing a use tax on out-of-state goods that is higher than the sales tax imposed on instate sales of goods.

IX. FEDERAL PREEMPTION OF STATE LAWS

A. INTRODUCTION. [§329]

Under the Supremacy Clause, the Constitution and federal laws take precedence over contrary state constitutional provisions or laws. The "preemption bell" should go off whenever you see a fact pattern including both a federal and a state law.

1. A PREEMPTION QUESTION EXISTS WHEN BOTH CONGRESS AND A STATE HAVE REGULATED THE SAME ACTIVITY. [§330]

2. PREEMPTION MAY OCCUR IN THREE WAYS. [§331]

a. Conflict between federal and state laws — federal law wins.

b. Congress expressly says it intends to occupy an entire area of regulable activity — federal law wins.

c. Congress has regulated an area so pervasively that a court may reasonably infer that Congress intended to occupy the entire field of regulable activity — federal law wins.

B. CONFLICTING LAWS. [§332]

This kind of preemption involves two kinds of cases: In one, it is physically impossible to comply with both laws; in the other, it is possible to comply with both, but compliance with the state law frustrates the purpose of the federal law.

C. EXPRESS STATEMENT OF CONGRESS' INTENT TO PREEMPT. [§335]

Congress may, through a federal statute, expressly preempt a particular field of regulation.

D. PERVASIVE REGULATION BY CONGRESS. [§337]

If Congress regulates an area very comprehensively, a court may draw the inference that Congress intended to occupy that area exclusively.

X. STATE ACTION REQUIREMENT FOR THE APPLICATION OF CERTAIN CONSTITUTIONAL PROTECTIONS

A. INTRODUCTION. [§339]

Most of the provisions of the constitution which protect individual rights are limitations on government action. The "state action" requirement becomes an issue when a private actor harms someone in such a way that a constitutional issue would arise if the harm were inflicted by a government actor. To be able to assert constitutional protection against the actions of the private party, a plaintiff must be able to argue that the private party's actions are sufficiently imbued with state action to make the constitution applicable.

B. GENERAL ANALYSIS OF STATE ACTION QUESTIONS. [§340]

There are three main factors the Court considers when deciding whether to impute state action to a private party: 1) To what extent does the private actor rely on governmental assistance and benefits; 2) whether the actor is performing an exclusive, traditional governmental function; and 3) whether the injury caused is aggravated in a unique way by government intervention.

C. RELIANCE ON GOVERNMENTAL ASSISTANCE AND BENEFITS. [§341]

The plaintiff argues every possible connection between the private actor and the state, and the court looks at the totality of circumstances to see if there is enough of a connection between the private actor and a government to apply constitutional protections.

1. Symbiotic Relationship Between Government and Private Actor. [§342]

Numerous relationships between a private actor and a government may be enough to impute state action to the private actor.

2. Government Involvement in a Racially Discriminatory Bequest. [§343]

There is state action if government officials act as trustees of a racially discriminatory private will. State action may also be present if there are enough connections between a city and land devised for use as a whites-only park.

3. State Constitutional Authorization of Racial Discrimination. [§344]

State action existed when a private party, relying on a state constitutional provision (since repealed), refused to rent an apartment because of the race of the lessee.

4. Liquor License. [§345]

A state granting a liquor license to a private bar or club does not make the bar or club a state actor.

5. Relationships Between a State and a Private School. [§346]

Extensive funding, heavy regulation, and large student referral by the state are not enough to confer state action on a private school.

6. State Help in Executing an Attachment. [§347]

Active participation by state officials in executing a prejudgment attachment will constitute state action.

7. United States Olympic Committee is Not a State Actor. [§348]

There was no government action by virtue of Congress giving the United States Olympic Committee the power to control the use of the word "Olympic."

8. National Collegiate Athletic Association is Not a State Actor. [§349]

The NCAA is not a government actor; it is a voluntary organization made up of both private and public institutions.

D. PERFORMING AN EXCLUSIVE, TRADITIONAL GOVERNMENTAL FUNCTION. [§350]

The Court will find state action when a private party is performing a function that has traditionally been performed by government. The Court also insists that the function be one that has been performed exclusively by government.

1. Elections. [§351]

Any pre-primary election that feeds into a general election will be considered state action.

2. Company Town. [§354]

If a company town performs the traditional functions of a municipality, it will be treated as a state actor.

3. Privately-Owned Shopping Center. [§355]

No state action is involved when the owner of a privately-owned shopping center excludes speakers from the shopping center.

4. Peremptory Challenges to Jurors. [§356]

The use of peremptory challenges, in a criminal or civil case, involves state action.

5. Public Defenders. [§357]

Public defenders are not considered state actors, even though they are paid by the state.

6. State Granted Monopolies. [§358]

A public utility, even if granted monopoly status by a state, is not a state actor.

7. Statutory Warehouseman's Lien. [§359]

No state action exists when a state authorizes an owner of a warehouse to sell the belongings of someone who did not pay his or her bill.

E. STATE-COURT INTERVENTION WHICH AIDS PRIVATE DISCRIMINATION. [§360]

This kind of state action analysis has been limited to restrictive covenant cases in which a court decree would directly result in discrimination against a black buyer, or would, by assessing monetary damages against a white seller who breached a restrictive covenant, encourage racial discrimination in the sale of real property.

1. STATE-COURT INJUNCTION. [§361]

The Court has held that state action would exist if a state-court judge ordered the parties to a restrictive covenant to comply with the terms of that covenant.

2. STATE-COURT AWARD OF MONEY DAMAGES. [§362]

The Court has held that state action would exist if a state-court judge awarded money damages against a white seller who breached a restrictive covenant.

F. NO STATE ACTION WHEN INJURIES ARE INFLICTED BY PRIVATE PARTIES. [§363]

Generally, there is no state action when a private party inflicts injuries on someone. The government has no obligation to protect a person from harm by another person. There will be state action if the harmed person is under the custody or control of the state when the harm occurs.

G. A CORPORATION THAT IS CREATED AND CONTROLLED BY THE GOVERNMENT IS SUBJECT TO CONSTITUTIONAL RESTRICTIONS. [§364]

Amtrak is a government actor, despite a statutory declaration that Amtrak is not an agency of the federal government.

XI. CONGRESSIONAL ENFORCEMENT OF CIVIL RIGHTS

A. INTRODUCTION TO CIVIL RIGHTS LEGISLATION. [§365]

Each of the Civil War Amendments (13th, 14th, and 15th) has an enabling clause which gives Congress the power to pass legislation to enforce the substantive guarantees of that amendment. Congress has passed both criminal and civil legislation to implement the protections of the Civil War Amendments.

B. CONGRESSIONAL IMPLEMENTATION OF THE CIVIL WAR AMENDMENTS. [§368]

1. Congressional Regulation Of Private Actions Under the Thirteenth Amendment. [§369]

The Thirteenth Amendment does not require state action; all slavery is prohibited, whether engaged in by private or governmental entities. Congress has passed numerous laws which make actionable private acts which perpetuate certain aspects of the institution of slavery.

2. Congressional Enforcement of The Fourteenth Amendment. [§375]

The Fourteenth Amendment limits only states and political subdivisions of states; it does not apply to the actions of private parties. Congress has passed numerous laws which prohibit racial discrimination and the abridgement of individual rights.

3. Congressional Enforcement of The Fifteenth Amendment. [§382]

The Voting Rights Act of 1965 was directed at forcing governmental entities to comply with congressional mandates to ensure fairness in voting. This law was designed to eliminate all vestiges of racial discrimination in the voting process.

XII. RETROACTIVE LEGISLATION.

A. CONSTITUTIONAL STATUS OF LAWS THAT OPERATE RETROACTIVELY. [§386]

The Constitution has a number of provisions that prohibit the state and federal governments from passing laws that retroactively impair substantive rights.

B. EX POST FACTO LAWS. [§387]

An ex post facto law imposes criminal punishment for an act that was not a crime when it was done, or increases the punishment for a crime over and above the punishment prescribed at the time the crime was committed. For a law to be an ex post facto law, it must operate to the detriment of the defendant.

There are two ex post facto provisions in the constitution, one limiting states, and the other limiting the federal government.

1. NON-VIOLATIONS. [§388]

The following laws do not violate the ex post facto provisions of the Constitution.

a. Sentencing of Habitual Offenders. [§389]

Increased punishment for recidivists does not violate the prohibition against Ex Post Facto laws.

b. Deportation of Aliens. [§390]

Deportation of aliens has been held not to constitute punishment for purposes of the Ex Post Facto Clause.

c. Reducing A Sentence. [§391]

Reducing the penalty for a crime does not violate the Ex Post Facto Clause because it does not hurt the defendant.

2. VIOLATIONS. [§392]

The following laws violate the Ex Post Facto Clause.

a. Reduction of "Good Time" A Prisoner May Earn. [§393]

Reducing the amount of "Good Time" a prisoner may earn violates the Ex Post Facto Clause because it adversely affects the prisoner's rights.

b Retroactive Cancellation of Early Release Credits [§393.1]

Retroactively cancelling a person's early release credits violates the Ex Post Facts Clause because it effectively increases the prisoner's punishment.

c. Revising a Sentencing Statute. [§394]

Application of a revised sentencing statute to pre-revision crimes violates the Ex Post Facto Clause where the result is an increased sentence.

d Involuntary Civil Commitment of Dangerously Mentally Ill Persons [§394.1]

Involuntary commitment of a mentally ill person after that person has served a prison sentence for a crime does not violate the Ex Post Facto Clause.

C. BILLS OF ATTAINDER. [§395]

A Bill of Attainder is a legislative act imposing punishment on an individual or an easily identifiable group of individuals without the benefit of a judicial trial. There are two Bill of Attainder clauses in the Constitution, one limiting the states, the other limiting the federal government.

1. FACTORS TO CONSIDER TO DETERMINE IF A LAW IS A BILL OF ATTAINDER. [§396]

The Court has identified three questions to ask in deciding whether a law is a Bill of Attainder: 1) Does the law fall within the historical meaning of legislative punishment?; 2) Can the law reasonably be said to further only punitive legislative purposes?; and 3) Does the legislative record reveal a congressional intent to punish?

2. LAWS THAT ARE BILLS OF ATTAINDER. [§397]

a. Forbidding Salary Payments. [§398]

A federal law that forbade salary payments to named federal employees violated the prohibition against Bills of Attainder.

b. Exclusion of Communists From Union Positions. [§399]

Prohibiting communists from being union officers violates the prohibition against Bills of Attainder.

3. LAWS THAT DO NOT CONSTITUTE BILLS OF ATTAINDER. [§400]

a. Disposition of Presidential Papers. [§401]

A federal law taking custody of presidential materials does not constitute a Bill of Attainder.

b. Denial of Education. [§402]

Denial of education grants for failure to register for the draft was held not to constitute a Bill of Attainder.

D. CONTRACTS CLAUSE. [§403]

The Constitution prohibits a state from passing a law which impairs the obligations of existing contracts. The Contracts Clause only limits states; if the federal government passes a law impairing the obligations of a contract, an attack would be based on the Due Process Clause of the Fifth Amendment.

1. CONTRACTS CLAUSE ANALYSIS. [§404]

If a state (or the federal government) impairs the obligations of an existing contract, the Court uses a three-part test:

a. Has the state law substantially impaired an obligation of an existing contract?;

b. Does the state have a significant and legitimate reason for the impairment?; and

c. Is the law based on reasonable conditions and is it appropriate to the public purpose underlying the law?

> **STUDY TIP:** Be careful about a state impairing the obligations of a contract to which it is a party. The same three-part test applies, but a court will apply it more stringently to ensure that a state is not changing the contract simply to advantage itself.

2. APPLICATION OF CONTRACTS CLAUSE ANALYSIS. [§406]

a. Mortgage Moratorium Law. [§407]

A state law imposing a temporary moratorium on mortgage foreclosures does not violate the Contracts Clause.

b. Altering a State's Own Obligation. [§408]

A state law altering the obligations of a contract to which the state is a party may violate the Contracts Clause.

c. Adding Obligations To a Contract. [§409]

A state law adding obligations to a contract is subject to Contracts Clause analysis.

d. Limiting Prices. [§410]

A state law limiting price increases which a natural gas supplier could charge a public utility under a price-escalator clause of a pre-existing contract does not violate the Contracts Clause.

XIII. THE TAKINGS CLAUSE

A. INTRODUCTION. [§411]

The Fifth Amendment provides that the federal government may take private property for public use only if just compensation is paid to the property owner. This protection also applies against the states.

1. THE TAKINGS CLAUSE IS NOT AN INDEPENDENT SOURCE OF LEGISLATIVE POWER. [§412]

The Takings Clause is not an independent source of power. It must be exercised in conjunction with some other enumerated power of Congress, or with the Tenth Amendment police power of a state.

2. KEY CONCEPTS IN TAKINGS CLAUSE ANALYSIS. [§413]

a. Eminent Domain. [§414]

This is the power of a government to force the owner of real or personal property to transfer that property to the government.

b. Taking of Private Property. [§415]

A government may only acquire private property if it pays just compensation to the owner. Just compensation is fair market value at the time of the taking.

c. Public Use Requirement. [§416]

A public use is any use that advances a legitimate power of the government and accrues to the benefit of the general public.

B. "PUBLIC USE" REQUIREMENT. [§417]

When a legislature exercises its power of eminent domain, it must be for a public use. If a legislature says a taking is for a public use, a court will almost always agree, even if the condemned property is transferred to another private party.

1. ELIMINATING URBAN BLIGHT. [§418]

Eliminating urban blight is considered a public use.

2. DISPERSING LAND OWNERSHIP. [§419]

A transfer of private property from one party to another in an effort to reduce the concentration of land ownership will be considered a public use.

3. TRANSFER OF PROPERTY FROM ONE PRIVATE OWNER TO ANOTHER. [§420]

A condemnation may be for a public use even though the property is transferred from one private party to another.

C. WHEN SHOULD A REGULATION BE TREATED AS A TAKING? [§421]

When a government regulation severely affects the use of property, or diminishes its value, a court may treat the regulation as a taking and require the government to compensate the affected parties.

1. PHYSICAL OCCUPATION OR INVASION OF PROPERTY WILL BE CONSIDERED A TAKING. [§422]

A general regulation that effects a physical occupation or invasion of property will be considered a taking.

2. DENIAL OF ALL ECONOMICALLY BENEFICIAL USE OF THE PROPERTY CONSTITUTES A TAKING. [§425]

Government action that deprives a property owner of all economically viable use of his or her property will be treated as a taking.

3. CONDITIONS ON THE GRANTING OF BUILDING PERMITS. [§434]

Government-imposed conditions on the granting of a building permit effects a taking.

a. Granting an Easement as a Condition of Receiving a Building Permit. [§435]

It is a taking for a government to refuse to issue a building permit unless land owners grant a public easement across their property.

b. Unconstitutional Conditions Attached to the Granting of a Building Permit. [§436]

A government may not extract private property in exchange for a discretionary benefit that the government might confer.

4. TEMPORARY TAKINGS ARE COMPENSABLE FOR THE PERIOD WHEN USE OF THE PROPERTY WAS DEPRIVED. [§437]

Temporary takings are compensable if the property owner is deprived of all economically viable use of the property during the period of the taking.

D. "JUST COMPENSATION" EQUALS FAIR MARKET VALUE AT THE TIME OF THE TAKING. [§438]

XIV. PROCEDURAL DUE PROCESS

A. INTRODUCTION. [§439]

Under the Fifth and Fourteenth Amendments, a government may not deprive a person of life, liberty, or property without due process of law. The due process clauses are intended to ensure that fair procedures are used when a government singles out an individual for a deprivation of life, liberty, or property. The due process clauses only protect against intentional deprivation of life, liberty, or property.

1. Main Requirements of a Procedural Due Process Analysis. [§440]

The three major requirements of procedural due process are: (1) an impartial decisionmaker; (2) notice; and (3) a hearing.

2. Three-Prong Balancing Analysis. [§441]

To determine how much procedural protection is required, the court looks at three factors:

a. The private interest affected by the government action;

b. The risk of erroneous deprivation of that interest through the procedure presently in place; and

c. The government interest, including the added fiscal and administrative burdens that the new procedure would entail.

B. GOVERNMENT ACTION REQUIREMENT. [§442]

Procedural due process guarantees protect only against government action.

C. INTENTIONAL DEPRIVATION. [§443]

Procedural due process analysis only applies to intentional deprivation of liberty or property.

D. DEPRIVATION OF LIBERTY OR PROPERTY. [§444]

You must have a cognizable liberty or property interest that it is being deprived by the intentional government action.

1. LIBERTY INTERESTS. [§445]

Procedural due process protects individuals when they are arrested or incarcerated. It also applies in a number of civil contexts where freedom of movement or the exercise of a fundamental right is curtailed.

a. Commitment to Mental Institutions. [§446]

Involuntary commitment to a mental institution involves a cognizable liberty interest.

b. Parolees' Interests. [§451]

A parolee has a liberty interest involved when a state revokes parole.

Sum & Substance QUICK REVIEW of Constitutional Law

c. Prisoners' Interests. [§452]

A prisoner has no liberty interest in not being transferred from one prison to another, or in not being placed in administrative segregation.

d. Liberty Interests of Children. [§455]

Corporal punishment in public schools does involve a liberty interest of the child.

e. Termination of Parental Rights. [§456]

A liberty interest is involved when a state acts to terminate parental rights.

f. Reputation. [§459]

Injury to reputation alone is not a liberty interest protected under procedural due process.

2. PROPERTY INTERESTS. [§460]

Procedural due process is required when the governmental intentionally deprives an individual of real or personal property. Government benefits will be considered property for procedural due process purposes if the recipient is "entitled" to receive the benefit. An entitlement exists when, under the law granting the benefit, the recipient is entitled to receive the benefit as long as specified conditions of eligibility are met.

a. Government Employment. [§461]

Government employment will not be a property interest if the employee can be fired at will; it will be a property interest if the employee can be fired only "for cause."

b. Government Benefits. [§464]

When a government seeks to terminate a benefit which it has conferred, the court will look to the importance of that benefit to the recipient and whether the recipient's interest in avoiding the loss outweighs the government's interest in terminating the benefit without providing notice or a hearing.

c. Public School Education. [§467]

A public school student has a property interest in his or her education which may not be taken away without due process. Be sure to distinguish between a disciplinary suspension, as opposed to an academic dismissal.

d. Judicial Review of Punitive Damages Award. [§470]

Limiting judicial review of the amount of a punitive damages award may violate procedural due process guarantees.

XV. SUBSTANTIVE DUE PROCESS AND FUNDAMENTAL RIGHTS

A. INTRODUCTION. [§471]

Under substantive due process analysis, the court reviews the substance of legislation to see if it unduly interferes with an individual's rights or interests protected by the due process clauses of the Constitution. The Fifth Amendment limits the federal government, and the Fourteenth Amendment limits states.

> **NOTE**: The Privileges and Immunities Clause of the Fourteenth Amendment precludes a state from making or enforcing any law which shall abridge the privileges or immunities flowing from the federal government. The Court has interpreted this clause to be a virtual nullity in terms of providing an effective challenge to a state law.

B. SUMMARY OF STEPS IN A SUBSTANTIVE DUE PROCESS ANALYSIS. [§473]

1. IDENTIFY WHICH GOVERNMENT IS ACTING, FEDERAL OR STATE. This will determine whether the Fifth Amendment (federal) or Fourteenth Amendment (state) applies.

2. DESCRIBE IN LAYPERSON'S TERMS THE RIGHT THAT HAS BEEN ABRIDGED. In what way has the plaintiff been hurt?

3. PLACE THE ABRIDGED RIGHT IN THE CONSTITUTION. Assert that the right is an aspect of liberty under the appropriate due process clause.

4. ASCRIBE CONSTITUTIONAL WEIGHT TO THE INTEREST ABRIDGED. Is the right a fundamental right, or just a low-level liberty interest?

5. SET THE APPROPRIATE LEVEL OF SCRUTINY. A law abridging a fundamental right receives strict scrutiny, whereas a law abridging a low-level liberty interest receives only rationality review.

6. BALANCE THE ABRIDGEMENT OF THE INDIVIDUAL RIGHT AGAINST THE PROFFERED GOVERNMENT INTEREST. Be specific when articulating the government interest and the individual right being balanced against each other.

C. LEVELS OF SCRUTINY UNDER SUBSTANTIVE DUE PROCESS. [§474]

A court must determine if the interest abridged is simply a low-level liberty interest or a fundamental right. The importance of the right being abridged sets the level of scrutiny that a court will use. Setting the level of scrutiny determines who has the burden of proof — the plaintiff or the government. At rationality review, the plaintiff always has the burden of proving that the law is irrational. At strict scrutiny, the burden shifts to the government to show a compelling reason for the law and narrowly tailored means.

D. SUBSTANTIVE DUE PROCESS REVIEW OF ECONOMIC LEGISLATION. [§475]

Under modern analysis, the court virtually always upholds state laws which regulate economic matters. For substantive due process purposes, the right to contract and the right to pursue employment are low-level liberty interests, the abridgement of which receives only rationality review.

E. SUBSTANTIVE DUE PROCESS REVIEW OF SOCIAL LEGISLATION. [§487]

The court uses low-level rationality review when a law is challenged as violating some non- fundamental social interest.

F. SUBSTANTIVE DUE PROCESS REVIEW OF FUNDAMENTAL RIGHTS. [§490]

Whenever a government regulation abridges a fundamental right, the court will use strict scrutiny to review the law: the state will have to show a compelling interest and means that are narrowly tailored to achieve that interest.

1. TWO TYPES OF FUNDAMENTAL RIGHTS - ENUMERATED OR UNENUMERATED. [§491]

Fundamental rights may be enumerated or unenumerated. The Court has incorporated certain Bill of Rights provisions by declaring them to be aspects of liberty under the Due Process Clause of the Fourteenth Amendment. Enumerated rights are specifically mentioned in the Constitution (such as the right to free speech), while unenumerated rights are not (right of privacy).

a. The Bill of Rights provisions that have been incorporated are:

(1) All First Amendment rights: speech, both religion clauses, press, to peaceably assemble, and to petition the government for the redress of grievances.

(2) The Fourth Amendment prohibition against unreasonable searches and seizures.

(3) All provisions of the Fifth Amendment, except the requirement that all criminal prosecutions be started only on a grand jury indictment.

(4) All Sixth Amendment rights.

(5) All Eighth Amendment rights.

b. Unenumerated fundamental rights are:

(1) The right to privacy.

(2) The right to interstate travel.

(3) The right to vote.

(4) The right of political association.

2. ALTERNATIVE TO SUBSTANTIVE DUE PROCESS: FUNDAMENTAL RIGHTS STRAND OF EQUAL PROTECTION. [§492]

A substantive due process analysis is called for when a legislature passes a mandatory law (a requirement or a prohibition) which affects all persons within the relevant population (like a state law prohibiting abortions to all women). A fundamental rights strand of equal protection analysis is called for when the legislature sets up a classification system which deprives only a certain group of persons of a fundamental right (a poll tax classifies along wealth lines, and deprives poor people of the right to vote). Under the fundamental rights strand of equal protection, there is nothing about the classification itself that raises the level of scrutiny, but the fact that the classification system operates to deprive a class of persons of a fundamental right raises the scrutiny.

3. SPECIFIC FUNDAMENTAL RIGHTS. [§493]

The Court has recognized fundamental rights in the areas of procreational and family autonomy, interstate travel, voting, and political association.

a. Right to Direct the Educational Upbringing of Your Children. [§494]

Parents have a fundamental right to decide where and how to educate their children.

(1) Choice of School. [§495]

Parents have a right to determine which school their children will attend.

(2) No Right To a Public School Education. [§498]

There is no right to a public school education. State methods of funding public education receive rationality review.

b. Right to Privacy. [§502]

There is no right to privacy enumerated in the Constitution. Today, the right to privacy is accepted as an aspect of liberty protected by the Due Process Clauses.

(1) Abortion and Reproductive Freedom. [§503]

The Court has held that the following areas involve privacy rights protected by the Due Process Clauses of the Constitution.

(a) Right to marriage and procreation. [§504]

(b) Right to marry. [§505]

(c) Right of married couples to receive information about contraceptives. [§506]

(d) Right of unmarried persons to receive contraceptives. [§507]

(e) Right of minors to purchase non-prescription contraceptives. [§508]

(f) Abortion rights. [§509]

The Court has held that a woman has a fundamental right to decide whether or not to terminate her pregnancy.

####### (i) Spousal consent laws invalid. [§510]

A state may not require a woman to obtain the consent of her spouse before she may have an abortion.

Sum & Substance QUICK REVIEW of Constitutional Law

(ii) Judicial bypass procedure when a minor wants an abortion. [§511]

Parental consent laws are invalid unless accompanied by a judicial bypass procedure through which a pregnant minor can go to court to obtain authorization for an abortion.

(iii) Government funding of abortion. [§512]

The government has no duty to fund abortions for indigent women.

(iv) Use of public facilities or employees to perform abortions. [§513]

The government may deny the use of public facilities or employees to perform abortions.

(v) Two parent notification; forty-eight hour wait for a minor seeking an abortion. [§514]

The Court has upheld state laws requiring a minor to notify both parents as long as an appropriate judicial bypass was available. Two-parent notification without an accompanying bypass procedure is unconstitutional. A state may also require a minor to wait 48 hours after notifying one parent.

(vi) Federally funded family planning clinics; conditions on receipt of federal money. [§515]

The Court has held that Congress may properly withhold federal funds from family planning clinics that mention abortion as a method of family planning.

(vii) "Undue burden" analysis in abortion cases. [§516]

Post-viability, a state may restrict or prohibit abortion. Pre-viability, a state may not pass a law which, by purpose or effect, imposes an undue burden on a woman's decision to terminate her pregnancy.

(2) No Right to Adult, Consensual Homosexual Activity. [§517]

The court refused to extend the fundamental right of privacy to protect the ability of consenting adults to engage in homosexual activity.

(3) Liberty Interest in Refusing Unwanted Medical Treatment. [§518]

A majority of the court has recognized a liberty interest in refusing medical treatment. So far, this is not a fundamental right.

(4) No Fundamental Right to Physician-Assisted Suicide. [§519]

The Due Process Clause of the Fourteenth Amendment does not create or protect a fundamental liberty interest in physician-assisted suicide.

(5) A State May Allow Refusal of Unwanted Medical Treatment But Prohibit Physician-Assisted Suicide. [§519.1]

Under the Equal Protection Clause, there is a rational distinction between refusing unwanted medical treatment and receiving assistance in committing suicide.

c. Right to Interstate Travel. [§522]

The court has recognized a fundamental right to interstate travel. Laws that inhibit interstate travel must meet strict scrutiny.

d. Right to Vote. [§523]

While the right to vote is not enumerated in the Constitution, the court considers it a fundamental right. Many of the cases use the Equal Protection Clause to invalidate restrictions on voting.

e. Right to Political Association. [§528]

The court has deemed the right to political association to be fundamental because it is essential to our system of government. This right comes into play whenever a government makes it difficult for a person or a political party to gain access to the ballot.

f. Right of Access to Courts. [§531]

The Court has recognized the importance of access to state and federal courts as a means of protecting individual rights. The importance of the right affected determines when a state must waive court costs.

XVI. EQUAL PROTECTION

A. INTRODUCTION. [§536]

Under equal protection analysis, the court reviews legislation to see if a government has intentionally discriminated against a class of people entitled to special constitutional protection. The Equal Protection Clause only pertains to states; if the federal government discriminates, the argument is based in the Due Process Clause of the Fifth Amendment. At rationality review, the plaintiff has the burden of proof all the way through the case. At intermediate or strict scrutiny, the burden of proof shifts to the government once the plaintiff shows that a quasi-suspect or suspect class has been disadvantaged.

B. LEVELS OF SCRUTINY. [§537]

The suspectness of the class determines the level of scrutiny (and who has the burden of proof).

1. RATIONAL BASIS REVIEW. [§538]

If a government intentionally discriminates against a non-suspect class (such as age), a court will use rational basis review: there must be a legitimate government interest and the measurement be rationally related to the goal sought. At rationality review, the plaintiff has the burden all the way through the case — it never shifts to the government.

2. INTERMEDIATE SCRUTINY. [§539]

If a government intentionally discriminates against a quasi-suspect class (gender or illegitimacy), a court will use intermediate scrutiny: there must be an important or significant government interest and the means must be substantially related to the goal sought. At intermediate scrutiny, the burden of proof shifts to the government once the plaintiff shows that a quasi-suspect class has been disadvantaged.

3. STRICT SCRUTINY. [§540]

If a government intentionally discriminates against a suspect class (race), a court will use strict scrutiny: there must be a compelling government interest and the means must be narrowly tailored to achieve that goal. At strict scrutiny, the burden of proof shifts to the government once the plaintiff shows that a suspect class has been disadvantaged.

C. INTENT REQUIRED TO MAKE AN EQUAL PROTECTION ARGUMENT. [§541]

The Constitution prohibits only intentional discrimination. To make out a prima facie equal protection argument, a plaintiff must show both disparate impact and intent. Intent to discriminate may be evident in the language of the statute (facial discrimination), or it may be inferred from the circumstances surrounding the passage or application of a facially neutral statute (as applied discrimination).

1. EXAMPLES OF CASES DEALING WITH THE INTENT REQUIREMENT. [§542]

The following general rules apply when dealing with the intent requirement: (1) intent may be shown by the manner in which a facially neutral law is applied; (2) statistical evidence alone is insufficient to prove intent; and (3) the degree and foreseeability of disparate impact are relevant to proving intent.

2. INTENT IN JURY SELECTION CASES. [§547]

In jury selection cases, the rule is that once a litigant shows substantial underrepresentation of a certain racial or gender group, he or she has made a prima facie case of showing discriminatory purpose, and the burden of proof shifts to the government.

3. INTENT IN RACIAL GERRYMANDERING CASES. [§550]

The shape and size of voting districts may be relevant to showing intent. Usually the plaintiff merely needs to show that race was the predominant factor underlying the drawing of distinct lines.

D. REVIEW OF LAWS THAT DISCRIMINATE ON THE BASIS OF RACE OR ETHNICITY. [§554]

Generally, any racial classification will receive strict scrutiny. State or federal laws that invidiously discriminate on the basis of race receive strict scrutiny. State and federal race-based affirmative action laws also receive strict scrutiny.

1. SEPARATE BUT EQUAL. [§555]

From 1896 to 1954, the court upheld the "Separate But Equal" doctrine. In 1954, the court ruled that separate educational facilities are inherently unequal and violative of the Equal Protection Clause.

2. POST-*BROWN* REMEDIES FOR SCHOOL SEGREGATION. [§560]

Post-*Brown*, when deliberate (intentional) segregation was found, courts would order remedial steps to be taken. Intentional segregation would be found if a school district was operating a dual school system (primarily one-race schools), and was under a statutory mandate to segregate at the time of *Brown I*. If there was no statutory mandate to segregate schools as of 1954, a plaintiff would have to make the normal showing of intent under equal protection analysis. Remedial powers of district courts are very broad, including busing, reassignment of teachers and students, and altering of attendance zones.

a. Post-*Brown* Cases Involving School Desegregation. [§561]

The Court has rejected attempts to nullify the holding in *Brown*. For example, the Court has held that officials cannot use the fear of public hostility to justify segregated schools. In addition, the Court has recognized the broad power of federal courts to require local school districts to comply with the mandate to desegregate local schools.

b. Post-*Brown* Cases Dealing with the Remedial Power of the Federal Courts. [§567]

Federal courts have extremely broad equitable powers to remedy unconstitutional school segregation by ordering busing, redrawing district lines, or assigning teachers or students based on race. One question that has frequently arisen is: When should a federal court end its supervision of a school district?.

Three factors are considered when deciding to terminate a desegregation plan: 1) whether there has been full compliance with the decree; 2) whether retention of judicial control is necessary or practicable to achieve compliance with the decree; and 3) whether the school district has demonstrated a good-faith commitment to complying with the decree.

3. AFFIRMATIVE ACTION. [§574]

An affirmative action program is a government program that gives a preference to members of specified racial or ethnic groups. These programs are most common in the areas of education and employment. Generally, for an affirmative action program to be constitutional it must be a remedy for a past violation. Also, the scope of the affirmative action plan must be proportionate to the scope of the violation.

a. State Race-Based Affirmative Action Plans. [§575]

State race-based affirmative action programs receive strict scrutiny. Societal discrimination does not count as a violation that would justify a state raced-based affirmative action plan. To have a voluntary affirmative action plan based on race, a state must show at least that it was a passive participant in some prior discrimination against a racial group.

b. Federal Race-Based Affirmative Action Plans. [§580]

Federal race-based affirmative action plans also receive strict scrutiny. Today, the rules for federal affirmative action programs based on race are the same as the rules for state affirmative action programs based on race.

4. INTERRACIAL SEXUAL RELATIONS. [§585]

A number of states have had laws prohibiting sexual relations between persons of different races. The state usually argued that there was not an equal protection problem because black people and white people were treated the same — neither could associate with the other. These anti-miscegenation laws have been consistently struck down by the Court.

E. REVIEW OF LAWS THAT DISCRIMINATE ON THE BASIS OF ALIENAGE. [§590]

Be careful about which government (federal or state) is discriminating against aliens. A federal law discriminating against aliens will receive only rational basis review. A state law discriminating against aliens will receive strict scrutiny, unless the state is excluding aliens from politically sensitive positions — then rational basis review will apply. This "political function" exception applies when a state (or city) excludes aliens from elected positions, important non-elected positions, or employment as public school teachers, police officers, or probation or parole officers.

1. FEDERAL LAWS THAT DISCRIMINATE AGAINST ALIENS. [§591]

Because of Congress' power to regulate immigration and naturalization, the court is extremely deferential to federal laws regulating aliens: rationality review is the appropriate level of scrutiny.

2. STATE LAWS THAT DISCRIMINATE AGAINST ALIENS. [§594]

When a state discriminates against aliens, strict scrutiny applies unless the alien is being excluded from a politically sensitive position; then rationality review applies. The positions that the Court has recognized as being politically sensitive are: police officers, public school teachers, and probation or parole officers.

> **STUDY TIP:** If you get an alienage question in which a state is discriminating against aliens, the professor is probably asking about the political function exception.

3. INTERPLAY BETWEEN PREEMPTION AND ALIENAGE ANALYSIS. [§601]

When a state law discriminating against aliens imposes requirements on aliens over and above those mandated by Congress, there may be a preemption problem in that the state law frustrates the purpose of the federal law.

F. REVIEW OF LAWS THAT DISCRIMINATE ON THE BASIS OF GENDER. [§604]

Federal or state laws which discriminate on the basis of gender receive intermediate scrutiny: the government must show a significant or important reason for the classification, and means that are substantially related. A government must treat equally those persons who are similarly situated in terms of the purpose of the law. In some cases, the court has said that there are constitutionally relevant differences between women and men.

1. TRACING THE DEVELOPMENT OF GENDER ANALYSIS UNDER EQUAL PROTECTION. [§605]

The Court has gone from affording women virtually no constitutional protection, to almost making gender a suspect classification, to holding that gender is a quasi-suspect class entitled to intermediate scrutiny review. Today, gender is a quasi-suspect class entitled to intermediate scrutiny review.

2. DISCRIMINATION BASED ON PREGNANCY IS NOT GENDER DISCRIMINATION UNDER THE EQUAL PROTECTION CLAUSE. [§613]

Under the Equal Protection Clause, it is not gender discrimination for a state to discriminate on the basis of pregnancy. Pregnant persons are all female, but non-pregnant persons are both male and female. Remember that Congress has passed the Pregnancy Discrimination Act, which includes discrimination based on pregnancy within the definition of gender discrimination under Title VII.

3. REMEDIAL DISCRIMINATION IN FAVOR OF WOMEN. [§614]

The court usually upholds laws which compensate women for past economic discrimination against them as a class. For example, the Court has upheld the following laws: (1) a state law providing property tax exemptions for widows but not widowers; and (2) a federal law providing higher old-age benefits to females. However, the Court struck down a state exempting women from paying alimony.

4. IN SOME CASES, WOMEN AND MEN ARE NOT SIMILARLY SITUATED IN RELATION TO THE PURPOSE OF A LAW. [§618]

There may be constitutionally relevant differences between women and men in relation to the purpose of the law. The Court has held that, in certain cases, biological differences between the sexes may be a basis for treating men and women differently.

a. Women as Prison Guards. [§619]

The Court upheld a state law that excluded women from positions as guards in all-male prisons.

b. Different Treatment of Males and Females Under a Statutory Rape Law. [§620]

Statutory rape laws that punish males for having sex with underage females, but do not punish the underage female, are permissible.

c. Male-only Registration for the Draft. [§621]

The federal government may require males only to register for the draft.

G. REVIEW OF LAWS THAT DISCRIMINATE ON THE BASIS OF ILLEGITIMACY. [§622]

When a government discriminates against illegitimate children, intermediate scrutiny applies — the government must show a significant or important reason for the law, and the means must be substantially related to achieving that goal. It is not a legitimate purpose for the government to try to punish illegitimate children for the actions of their parents.

H. REVIEW OF LAWS THAT DISCRIMINATE ON THE BASIS OF AGE. [§636]

Laws that discriminate based on age receive rational basis scrutiny — the plaintiff must show that there is no legitimate reason for the law, or that the means are not rationally related to the asserted government interest. Remember, however, that if an age classification is used to abridge a fundamental right, the scrutiny may go up because of the impact of the classification system on the right.

I. REVIEW OF LAWS THAT DISCRIMINATE ON THE BASIS OF MENTAL STATUS. [§641]

Laws that discriminate against the mentally retarded or mentally ill receive rational basis review — the plaintiff has the burden of showing that there is no legitimate reason for the law, or that the means are not rationally related to the asserted government interest. It is constitutional for states to distinguish between mentally ill and mentally retarded persons.

J. REVIEW OF LAWS THAT DISCRIMINATE ON THE BASIS OF SEXUAL ORIENTATION. [§644]

Laws that discriminate on the basis of sexual orientation receive rational basis review - the plaintiff must show that there is no legitimate reason for the law, or that the means are not rationally related to the asserted government interest. A voter-initiated state constitutional amendment prohibiting state or local governments from passing laws to protect persons of homosexual, lesbian, or bisexual orientation fails rational basis scrutiny under the Equal Protection Clause.

K. REVIEW OF LAWS THAT DISCRIMINATE ON THE BASIS OF SOCIAL OR ECONOMIC INTERESTS. [§645]

Laws that discriminate on the basis of social or economic interests receive rational basis review — the plaintiff must show that there is no legitimate reason for the law, or that the means are not rationally related to the asserted government interest. For instance, laws that discriminate between classes of people in relation to pursuing an occupation, receiving unemployment benefits, or receiving welfare payments will receive only rational basis review.

L. IRREBUTTABLE PRESUMPTIONS USED TO DEPRIVE A PERSON OF A GOVERNMENTAL BENEFIT OR THE EXERCISE OF A RIGHT. [§653]

Under this doctrine, a government sets up a conclusive presumption (no hearing provided) of disability or unfitness to perform a function or exercise a right. This analysis shares aspects of procedural due process and equal protection analysis. The cases present the procedural due process problem of not providing a hearing for those who are disadvantaged; they present the equal protection problem of classifying too broadly — too many people are disadvantaged by the classification.

1. Presumption that Unmarried Fathers are Unfit Parents. [§654]

States may not conclusively presume that all unmarried fathers are unfit parents.

2. Presumption that Certain College Students are Not State Residents. [§655]

States may not conclusively presume that certain classes of college students are not state residents.

3. Presumption of Ineligibility for Food Stamps. [§656]

Federal laws may not conclusively presume ineligibility for food stamps.

4. Presumption that Pregnant Teachers Cannot Teach Beyond a Certain Time. [§657]

A state may not conclusively presume that a pregnant teacher is unable to teach beyond a certain time in her pregnancy.

5. Presumption that Spouses of Stepchildren Do Not Qualify for Death Benefits. [§658]

A state may presume that spouses of stepchildren do not qualify for death benefits.

6. Presumption that Certain Workers are Disabled. [§659]

The Court upheld a federal law that provided for a presumption of total disability for coal miners with black-lung disease.

7. Presumption that a Child Born to a Married Woman is a Child of Her Marriage. [§660]

A state may presume that a child born to a married woman is a child of her marriage.

XVII. FREEDOM OF SPEECH

A. OVERVIEW OF FREE SPEECH ANALYSIS. [§661]

Freedom of speech is a fundamental right which has been incorporated to apply against the states. The First Amendment says that Congress shall make no law abridging the freedom of speech. Speech includes oral, written, or symbolic communication. Make sure that a court is willing to characterize activity as speech.

Sum & Substance QUICK REVIEW of Constitutional Law

1. PROCEDURAL ISSUES. [§662]

Check for vagueness. Does the law contain sufficiently narrow standards for its enforcement? A vague law presents two problems: 1) no notice to the person to whom the law may be applied; and 2) too much discretion on the part of the government official applying the law. Also, see if the law is overbroad in the sense that it is capable of punishing too much protected speech. Finally, remember that for a licensing system for movies or books to be constitutional, the government has the burden of justifying a refusal to grant a permit.

2. IS THE GOVERNMENT PROHIBITING SPEECH OR MERELY CHANNELING IT? [§666]

See if the government is trying to prohibit the speech entirely, or just move it around. If the government is just trying to move the speech around, you apply the rules for what are called "time, place, or manner restrictions." To be a valid time, place, or manner restriction, a law must be content neutral, narrowly tailored to achieving a significant government interest, and leave open ample alternative channels of communication. If the government is prohibiting the speech, you will probably use one of the specific tests, such as clear and present danger, fighting words, obscenity, commercial speech, or defamation.

B. DUE PROCESS CONCERNS THAT ARISE WITH LAWS THAT REGULATE SPEECH. [§667]

1. VAGUENESS. [§668]

Vagueness problems arise when a statute or regulation has no standards, or insufficient ones, to guide the government official applying the law. Absence of specific standards equals absence of notice to the person to whom the law might be applied. It also means that the government official gets to make up standards as he or she goes along.

2. OVERBREADTH. [§673]

Under an overbreadth analysis, the question is whether too much protected speech is being regulated under the law. Remember that these concepts may both arise in the same question: a vague law, because of its absence of standards, may be used to punish protected speech.

C. PRIOR RESTRAINTS. [§677]

A prior restraint is any government action that stops speech before it is able to be communicated. Constitutional Law courses usually treat two kinds of prior restraints: 1) those imposed by an injunctive order of the court; and 2) those imposed by the application of a licensing system.

1. INJUNCTIVE ORDERS IMPOSING PRIOR RESTRAINTS. [§678]

Court orders imposing prior restraints are presumed unconstitutional, and the government has a heavy burden of justifying such a restriction on speech. To justify such an injunction, the government must assert some compelling interest, such as national security or military secrets.

2. LICENSING SYSTEMS AS PRIOR RESTRAINTS: CASES INVOLVING REVIEW OF FILMS BEFORE EXHIBITION. [§682]

If properly drafted, a permit system for movies is constitutional. For such a system to be constitutional, the government must have the burden of proving the work is obscene, must promptly go to court or issue the permit, and must ensure that there is a prompt, final judicial decision regarding the alleged obscenity of the work.

3. "INFORMAL" PRIOR RESTRAINTS. [§686]

Informal government action, short of passing a statute, may operate as a prior restraint. For example, it is unconstitutional for a state commission to threaten obscenity prosecutions against booksellers who sell books from a state-compiled list of objectionable books.

4. CONTRACTUALLY AGREED UPON PRIOR RESTRAINTS. [§687]

It is permissible for the CIA to require that its employees get agency approval before publishing a book.

D. TIME, PLACE, OR MANNER RESTRICTIONS. [§688]

If the government is simply moving speech around, the court uses the following four-part analysis: is the restriction content neutral, is it narrowly tailored to achieve a significant government interest, and does it leave open ample alternative channels of communication? The government's argument is that the medium or method of communication creates certain secondary effects which it has the power to regulate. Remember that a government may never regulate speech just because it dislikes or disapproves of the speech; such a regulation would be content based, and would be invalid under a strict scrutiny analysis.

1. REQUIREMENTS FOR A VALID TIME, PLACE, OR MANNER RESTRICTION. [§689]

a. The Restriction Must Be Content-Neutral. [§690]

A law can be content neutral one of two ways: 1) the government does not even look at the content of the speech when it regulates; or 2) the government looks at content, not to approve or disapprove of it, but to see if the content causes some "secondary effect" which the government has the power to regulate.

b. The Restriction Must Be Narrowly Tailored. [§693]

The regulation does not have to be the least drastic means of achieving the government's goal. A law will be valid as long as the means are not substantially broader than necessary to achieve the government's goal.20 A court will not invalidate a law simply because it is able to conclude that the government could have chosen some alternative means that might have been less restrictive.

c. The Restriction Must Advance a Significant Government Interest. [§694]

The government does not need a compelling interest to support a time, place, or manner restriction. A significant or important interest will suffice.

Sum & Substance QUICK REVIEW of Constitutional Law

d. The Restriction Must Leave Open Ample Alternative Channels of Communication. [§695]

If there are no ample alternative channels of communication for the speaker, the regulation will be tantamount to a prior restraint, and strict scrutiny will apply.

2. TIME, PLACE, OR MANNER RESTRICTIONS IN A PUBLIC FORUM. [§696]

Time, place, manner rules developed in the public forum area. A public forum is any government-owned property that is used for speech purposes. The concept in this area is that certain public places have been used for speech purposes for so long that the public has a right of access to them for speech purposes. This guaranteed right of access means that the government may not prohibit persons from speaking in these places; it may only impose time, place, or manner restrictions. The purpose of time, place, or manner analysis in public forum cases is to strike a balance between the speaker's right of access and the government's ability to maintain the use of the place for its intended purpose.

3. TIME, PLACE, OR MANNER RESTRICTIONS IMPOSED THROUGH AN INJUNCTION, RATHER THAN A GENERALLY APPLICABLE ORDINANCE. [§711]

A time, place, or manner restriction imposed by an injunctive order is subject to more stringent review than one effected by a general ordinance. The test for a content-neutral injunction is whether it burdens no more speech than is necessary to serve a significant government interest.

E. CONTENT-BASED RESTRICTIONS ON SPEECH. [§714]

There are certain times when the government looks at the content of speech to determine whether and how to regulate the speech. Be aware of the evil that the government is trying to prevent or punish.

> **STUDY TIP:** When you get a free speech question, focus on the evil the government is trying to prevent. Once you identify the evil, it will take you directly into the appropriate analysis.

1. CLEAR AND PRESENT DANGER ANALYSIS. [§715]

Under clear and present danger analysis, the government tries to punish a speaker for inciting a listener to engage in illegal activity. This determination looks at all the circumstances surrounding the speech to see if there is a high enough probability that the speaker would have incited or did incite a listener or listeners to break the law. The modern test asks whether the speaker's advocacy of illegal action is directed to inciting or producing imminent lawless action and is likely to incite or produce such action by the audience.

2. FIGHTING WORDS, OFFENSIVE SPEECH, HATE SPEECH. [§727]

Each of these three kinds of speech involves nasty, scurrilous language that is intended or likely to offend some people or hurt some feelings. Preventing hurt feelings, or psychic trauma, is not a legitimate government interest. There must be more, such as a breach of the peace.

a. Definition of Fighting Words. [§728]

Fighting words are scurrilous epithets, delivered in person to the listener, which are likely to cause an average addressee to retaliate against the speaker. Statutes which attempt to proscribe fighting words are frequently vague and overbroad, and are very susceptible to attacks on these bases. Remember that only speech that creates a probability of violence can be prohibited.

b. Offensive Speech. [§732]

Offensive speech is speech that is usually sexually oriented (but not obscene) and is offensive to mainstream sensibilities. The general rule is that government cannot regulate the speech just because it doesn't like it, or because it offends the sensibilities of adults. This speech may be regulated to protect children, or if it falls within one of the other proscribable categories.

c. Hate Speech. [§737]

Hate speech is offensive speech that is derogatory toward racial or ethnic groups. This speech is punishable under other established tests, but is not independently punishable based on the emotional injury it inflicts on the targeted group. However, a state may increase the sentence for an assaultive crime if the criminal chose his or her victim based on race or ethnicity.

3. OBSCENITY. [§741]

Obscenity is sexually oriented speech that fails the test of *Miller v. California*: 1) whether the average person, applying contemporary community standards, would find that the book or movie appeals to prurient interests; 2) whether the work depicts, in a patently offensive way, sexual conduct that is specifically defined by state law; and 3) using a reasonable person standard (not contemporary community standards), whether the work, taken as a whole, lacks serious literary, artistic, political, or scientific value. A state may not criminalize the private possession of obscenity by an adult, but may criminalize the private possession of child pornography by an adult (if child pornography is defined as a videotape or film of children in explicit sex scenes).

a. Development of the Obscenity Doctrine. [§742]

Under the Court's prevailing interpretation of the *Miller* test, the first two prongs are evaluated by considering the average person applying contemporary community standards. However the third prong of *Miller* (whether the work as a whole lacks serious literary, artistic, political, or scientific value) is judged by a reasonable person standard.

b. Right to Possess Obscenity and the Right to Receive Information. [§747]

A person has a constitutionally protected right to possess adult obscenity in the privacy of the home. There is no constitutional protected right to watch obscene movies in a theater, even if the theater restricts its clientele to consenting adults.

c. Child Pornography — No Right to Sell or Privately Possess Child Pornography. [§750]

A state's interest in preventing the sexual exploitation of children is so great that it overrides a person's interests in the possession of child pornography.

d. Factoring Children into the Obscenity Equation. [§753]

A state may not generally prohibit the sale of sexually oriented material that is not suitable for consumption by children. The result would be that the adult population would have its reading or viewing choices reduced to a level appropriate for children.

e. Pornography as Sex Discrimination: The Feminist Perspective. [§757]

Feminist scholars have drafted a statute based on the premise that pornography is sex discrimination (it does not matter whether the work passes *Miller*). The problems with this kind of ordinance are that it is viewpoint based, and does not fit into any traditional method of First Amendment analysis. The government may not prohibit pornography merely because it depicts women in a certain way.

4. COMMERCIAL SPEECH. [§758]

Commercial speech is speech that advertises a product or service, usually for profit. Commercial speech receives an intermediate level of protection under the First Amendment. The main reason commercial speech is protected is to benefit consumers. When analyzing a commercial speech question, first ask whether the commercial speech concerns a lawful activity, and is not misleading. If it is a non-misleading advertisement for a lawful product or service, apply the following three-part test: 1) Does the government have a substantial (not compelling) reason for the regulation?; 2) Does the restriction directly advance the government interest?; and 3) Is the restriction narrowly tailored to achieve the government interest?

a. Development of Commercial Speech Doctrine. [§759]

Up until the mid-1970's, commercial speech was not protected under the First Amendment, but was simply a kind of economic transaction which a government could regulate for any rational reason. Today, commercial speech is protected under the First Amendment, but receives only an intermediate level of protection. Remember that, in the commercial speech area, the power to prohibit activity includes the power to channel its advertising.

b. Advertising by Lawyers and Certified Public Accountants. [§767]

The general rule is that a state bar association may discipline an attorney for violating a ban on in- person solicitation of clients for money. However, a state bar association may not completely prohibit targeted mail solicitation of clients (although some restrictions may be proper). Certified public accountants cannot be prohibited from engaging in in-person solicitation of clients for money.

5. DEFAMATION. [§775]

State common law rules pertaining to the torts of slander and libel are limited by the First Amendment guarantee of freedom of speech. The Court has attempted to balance the rights of free speech and press against the right of a person not to have his or her reputation injured. Be careful about whether the plaintiff in a defamation action is a public official or public figure, or whether the allegedly defamatory statement involves a matter of public concern.

a. First Amendment Limitations on the Law of Defamation. [§776]

(1) Rules for Defamation of Public Officials. [§777]

Under *New York Times v. Sullivan*, if the defamatory speech is directed at a public official or public figure, the plaintiff must prove: (a) all the elements of defamation required by state law; (b) that the statement includes a false statement of fact; and (c) by clear and convincing evidence that the statement was made with actual malice - the speaker knew that the statement was false, or acted with reckless disregard of its truth or falsity.

(2) Rules for Defamation of Public Figures (as opposed to public officials). [§778]

The rules for defamatory speech directed at public figures are the same as for defamatory speech directed at public officials.

(3) Constitutional Limitations on Defamation Actions When A Private Individual is the Plaintiff. [§781]

If a private individual is the plaintiff in a defamation action, the plaintiff must prove: (a) all the elements of defamation required by state law; (b) that the statement includes a false statement of fact; and (c) that the speaker was at least negligent in not determining the falsity of the allegedly defamatory statement. If the speech is on a matter of public concern, a private-figure plaintiff must show actual malice to be able to recover punitive or presumed damages. If the speech is about a purely private matter, a private-figure plaintiff does not need to show actual malice to be able to recover punitive or presumed damages.

(4) Speech That Involves Matters of Public Concern. [§782]

When speech involves a matter of public concern, no punitive damages may be awarded without a showing of "actual malice." A state may set its own standards for liability, but may not permit the recovery of punitive or presumed damages unless there is a showing of "actual malice."

(5) Speech That Does Not Involve Matters of Public Concern. [§783]

When speech does not involve a matter of public concern, punitive damages may be awarded even without a showing of "actual malice."

(6) Newsworthy Persons. [§784]

All newsworthy persons are not public figures for First Amendment purposes. Newsworthy persons are not "public figures" unless they thrust themselves to the forefront of particular public controversies.

(7) Defamation Actions by Private Figures Against Media Defendants for Statements of Public Concern. [§785]

A private-figure plaintiff who files a defamation action against a media defendant for statements of public concern has the burden of proving the falsity of those statements.

(8) Recovery For Intentional Infliction of Emotional Distress by Public Officials or Public Figures. [§786]

Public officials or public figures may not recover for intentional infliction of emotional distress unless they can show that the publication contains a false statement of fact and was made with knowledge of the falsity or with reckless disregard as to whether it was true.

(9) Erroneous Reports About Private Individuals Involved in a Matter of Public Interest. [§787]

The *New York Times* standard of actual malice must be met in cases involving false reports of matters of public interest. This standard applies even though the plaintiffs did not voluntarily place themselves in a position of notoriety or celebrity.

(10) Use of Quotation Marks to Attribute Words to a Speaker. [§788]

The use of quotation marks to attribute words to a speaker may constitute "actual malice" if the alteration results in a material change in the meaning of what the speaker actually said. Making up quotations does not always provide evidence of actual malice.

(11) No Defamation Exception for Statements Labeled "Opinions." [§789]

Speech is not necessarily exempt from a defamation action because it is phrased in terms of being an opinion. Some opinion statements will be protected if they are on a matter of public concern, and are purely statements of opinion that do not imply false or defamatory facts.

(12) Publication of Names of Rape Victims. [§790]

A newspaper cannot be held civilly liable for the publication of the name of a rape victim when the name was lawfully obtained.

(13) Lawsuits by Performers Against Television Stations for Copyright Infringement. [§791]

The First Amendment does not prohibit a performer from suing a television station for broadcasting his entire act. Airing a videotape of an entire act is actionable in the same sense as using a copyrighted work without the permission of the copyright owner.

b. First Amendment Limitations on Defamation of Groups. [§792]

The court has upheld a group libel law which defamed a group of people, rather than an individual.

F. SYMBOLIC SPEECH. [§793]

Symbolic speech is communication effected through conduct; there are no words involved. Symbolic speech always involves both a communicative element and a conduct element. The government has the power to regulate the conduct component of symbolic speech, and thereby impose some incidental burden on the communicative aspect of that conduct. Determine whether the government is totally prohibiting the symbolic speech, or just moving it around.

1. PROHIBITION OF SYMBOLIC SPEECH. [§794]

If a government is prohibiting symbolic speech, use the four-part test from *U.S. v. O'Brien*: (a) Is the law within a constitutional power of the government?; (b) Does the law further an important or substantial government interest?; (c) Is the government interest unrelated to the suppression of free expression?; and (d) Is the incidental restriction on speech no greater than essential to furthering the government interest? (Are the means narrowly tailored?)

2. TIME, PLACE, OR MANNER RESTRICTIONS ON SYMBOLIC SPEECH. [§795]

If a government is simply trying to channel the symbolic speech in some way, use the four-part test for evaluating time, place, or manner restrictions: (a) Is the law content- neutral?; (b) Does the government have a significant or important reason for the law?; (c) Are the means narrowly tailored to achieve the asserted interest?; and (d) Are there ample alternative channels of communication available?

> **STUDY TIP:** The only difference between the *O'Brien* test and the time, place, manner analysis is that the latter has the requirement of "ample alternative channels."

G. SPEECH IN PUBLIC SCHOOLS. [§804]

If you see a speech question in a public school setting, be careful of the role the school plays in the communicative process. Are the school officials simply allowing students to come onto school grounds and express themselves, or is the school in some way sponsoring the speech (paying for it or providing a forum)?

1. NON-SCHOOL-SPONSORED SPEECH. [§805]

If the school officials are simply allowing students to come in from the outside and speak, without school sponsorship of the speech, the test is whether the student's speech materially and substantially interferes with the functioning of the school, or disrupts the discipline of the school.

2. SCHOOL-SPONSORED SPEECH. [§806]

If the school sponsors the student's speech, content-neutral restrictions may be imposed if they are reasonably related to a legitimate educational interest, such as teaching students journalistic ethics, or the ability to engage in civil discourse.

3. REMOVAL OF BOOKS FROM A SCHOOL LIBRARY. [§809]

If a school board removes books from a school library, its decisions will be upheld if content-neutral, and reasonably related to a legitimate educational goal, such as ensuring that vulgar or grade-inappropriate books are not available to students.

H. PUBLIC FORUM ANALYSIS. [§810]

Public forum analysis is called for whenever a person is speaking on or by means of public property. The goal is to balance a person's right to use public property for speech purposes against the government's right to maintain the property for its intended use. There are three ways that public forums may come into existence: (1) By tradition, some public places have become forums for speech purposes; (2) The government may designate publicly owned property as a forum; and (3) Speakers may commandeer publicly owned property for use as a forum.

1. TRADITIONAL PUBLIC FORUM. [§811]

In a traditional public forum, the government may not prohibit all communicative activity. Speakers have a presumptive right of access to traditional public forums. In these forums, a government usually imposes time, place, or manner restrictions.

2. DESIGNATED PUBLIC FORUM. [§812]

A state may designate property to be a public forum. It may also un-designate it as a public forum, returning the property to its prior, non-speech use.

a. Designated Open Forum. [§813]

If the government designates the property as an open public forum, the same rules apply as in traditional public forum cases.

b. Designated Limited Forum. [§814]

If the government designates the property as a limited or non-public forum, the following rules apply: 1) properly drawn time, place, or manner restrictions are permissible; 2) content-based restrictions get strict scrutiny; and 3) total or selective restrictions of speakers are permissible if rationally related to a legitimate government interest.

3. COMMANDEERED PUBLIC FORUM. [§815]

A commandeered public forum exists when a speaker goes on to public property to speak even though the property is not a traditional public forum, and the government has not designated the property to be a forum for speech purposes. The analysis in these cases is whether the particular speech engaged in is compatible with the normal functioning of the place.

4. APPLICATION OF PUBLIC FORUM ANALYSIS. [§816]

a. Government Power to Regulate Public Places. [§817]

The government does not have the same power to exclude speakers from public property that owners of private property enjoy.

b. Handbilling on Public Streets. [§818]

A city may not totally prohibit handbilling on public streets.

c. Protesting on Jail Grounds. [§820]

A state may prohibit protesting on jail grounds.

d. Picketing Near Schools. [§821]

A city may not selectively prohibit picketing near a school.

e. Noise Near Schools. [§822]

A state may impose a generally applicable ban on noise near schools.

f. Access to School Mailbox Systems. [§823]

A school board may grant selective access to a school mailbox system.

g. Signs Near Embassies. [§824]

The District of Columbia may not prohibit signs near embassies merely because the messages on the signs may be offensive to persons in the embassies.

h. Picketing in Front of a Residence. [§825]

A city can prohibit focused picketing in front of a residence.

i. Fees for Use of Public Property. [§826]

A city cannot require payment of a fee to use public property.

j. Airport Terminals. [§827]

Government-owned airport terminals are not public forums for speech purposes; therefore, the government may prohibit activities that are inconsistent with the use of the terminals.

5. DESIGNATED FORUMS AND RELIGIOUS SPEAKERS. [§828]

If a government entity opens its facilities to speakers, it may not exclude religious speakers from using the forum. It does not establish religion to allow religious speech along with other kinds of speech.

I. THE FIRST AMENDMENT AND THE ELECTORAL PROCESS: REGULATION OF BALLOT ACCESS, AND LIMITATIONS ON CONTRIBUTIONS AND EXPENDITURES. [§833]

Participation in the electoral process, by voting, becoming a candidate, or spending money to influence an election, involves the fundamental rights of free speech and freedom of political association. The government interests in regulating these activities are to enhance equality of access to the electoral system and to prevent corruption or the appearance of corruption in the electoral process.

1. RESTRICTIONS ON VOTING AND BECOMING A CANDIDATE. [§834]

The court scrutinizes very carefully any state or local law which interferes with a person's right to become a candidate, or a political party's right to set the qualifications to participate in party primaries.

2. LIMITATIONS ON CAMPAIGN CONTRIBUTIONS AND EXPENDITURES. [§838]

Be very careful to distinguish a contribution to a candidate from an independent expenditure on behalf of the candidate. Even though you may spend your own money to help someone get elected, the government has an important interest in avoiding the appearance of a contributor buying a candidate. The court allows greater limitations on contributions to candidates than it does on expenditures. The court also distinguishes between contributions to a candidate (restrictions allowed) and contributions to a Political Action Committee supporting a ballot referendum (restrictions not allowed). While you can (appear to) own a candidate, you cannot own an idea.

J. RESTRICTIONS ON THE SPEECH OF GOVERNMENT EMPLOYEES. [§845]

The court balances the free speech rights of a government employee against the interest of the government as employer in maintaining the functioning of the work place. You must distinguish between speech on matters of public concern and speech that is purely private. Speech on matters of public concern is more important than purely private speech; disciplining or firing government employees for public speech carries the danger of censorship.

1. LOYALTY OATHS. [§846]

Loyalty oaths will be upheld as long as they simply require an affirmation by the employee to abide by the Constitution. They will be suspect if they are used to punish someone for membership in a subversive organization; that kind of oath would infringe upon the employee's freedom of political association.

2. POLITICAL ACTIVITY AND POLITICAL PATRONAGE IN PUBLIC EMPLOYMENT SITUATIONS. [§849]

Two issues run through these cases: 1) the ability of a government employer to make employment decisions based on the political affiliation of an employee; and 2) the ability of a government employer to discipline employees for their speech.

a. Political Activity of Government Employees. [§850]

The court has upheld some restrictions on the political activity of government employees on the theory that such limitations are needed to prevent corruption or the appearance of corruption in government. However, remember that a public employee's speech will be protected if it is on a matter of public concern, and does not disrupt the work place. Speech on a matter of private concern will not be protected in the same manner; discipline or dismissal for private speech is simply an ordinary employment decision, requiring no special constitutional analysis.

b. Political Patronage in Government Employment. [§858]

Employment decisions based on political affiliation will be upheld if the government can show that they are necessary to the effective performance of the job. As a general matter, employment decisions based on political affiliation are more likely to be upheld in relation to high- level government positions, as opposed to low-level positions which do not concern the formulation or implementation of public policy.

K. THE RIGHT NOT TO SPEAK: FREEDOM FROM GOVERNMENT COERCION, SUBSIDIES, OR TAXES. [§864]

While there is no enumerated right not to speak, the court has said that there is a right to be free from government compelled speech, whether by a regulation, a subsidy, or a tax.

1. THE RIGHT TO BE FREE FROM COMPELLED SPEECH. [§865]

The government may not force a person to speak, or to affirm any prescribed belief or idea. Remember that if a person has religious objections to expressing a prescribed idea, the religion clauses of the First Amendment are also relevant.

2. GOVERNMENT SUBSIDIES OF SPEECH. [§871]

Generally, government subsidies are constitutional if they are rationally related to a legitimate government interest. However, a government may not use its virtually unlimited economic power to require or control speech.

3. TAX EXEMPTIONS AS DE FACTO SUBSIDIES FOR CERTAIN KINDS OF SPEECH. [§875]

General taxes applied to the media will be constitutional. However, a government may not discriminatorily tax the media. Also, a state may not grant a sales tax exemption to certain publications based on the content of their message.

L. FREEDOM OF ASSOCIATION. [§878]

Although there is no right of association enumerated in the Constitution, the Court has afforded constitutional protection to different kinds of associational rights.

1. ASSOCIATION FOR BUSINESS PURPOSES. [§879]

If people associate for business or commercial purposes, no fundamental right is involved, and a government regulation will be valid if rationally related to a legitimate government interest.

2. ASSOCIATION FOR PERSONAL REASONS. [§880]

If people associate for purely personal reasons the court may recognize a fundamental right of intimate association. The court looks at three factors to decide whether the right of intimate association exists: (1) Is it a relatively small group?; (2) Is there a high degree of selectivity in decisions to begin and to maintain the affiliation?; and (3) Is there seclusion from others in critical aspects of the relationship?

3. ASSOCIATION FOR FIRST AMENDMENT PURPOSES. [§881]

If people associate for First Amendment purposes (speech, assembly, religion), the court may recognize a fundamental freedom of expressive association. This right is not absolute, and a government may abridge it to advance a compelling government interest.

4. RIGHT NOT TO ASSOCIATE, OR BE ASSOCIATED, WITH CERTAIN IDEAS. [§882]

The court has recognized an unenumerated right not to be associated with certain ideas or speech. Be aware of cases involving a union or a bar association which uses member's dues for political purposes. The member has a right to not be associated with political speech with which he or she disagrees. Members may be forced to pay dues to cover the union's cost of performing essential union or bar association functions, but may not be forced to contribute to the dissemination of speech that is extraneous to the union's or bar association's function as a representative entity.

5. CASES INVOLVING THE RIGHT OF ASSOCIATION, AND THE RIGHT NOT TO ASSOCIATE. [§883]

a. Membership Lists. [§884]

A state cannot compel the disclosure of the membership list of a political organization.

b. Union Dues. [§885]

Union dues may not be spent to advance political views opposed by a union member.

c. Bar Association Dues. [§886]

Bar association dues may not be spent to advance political views opposed by a member of the bar.

d. Contributions to Generic Advertising For An Industry. [§886.1]

Forced contributions to generic advertising for an industry do not implicate the First Amendment.

e. Privately Owned Shopping Centers. [§887]

A state constitution may confer a right of access by speakers to privately owned shopping centers for speech purposes.

f. Consumer Boycotts. [§888]

Consumer boycotts are protected as an aspect of the associational rights of the group organizing the boycott.

g. Gender Discrimination by Private Associations. [§889]

A state may require private associations to accept women as members.

h. Welfare Benefits. [§890]

The federal government can reduce the welfare benefits of family members and striking workers.

i. Social Association With Older Persons. [§891]

A city may prohibit persons over the age of 18 from using certain dance halls frequented by minors.

XVIII. FREEDOM OF THE PRESS

A. INTRODUCTION. [§892]

Under the First Amendment, neither Congress nor a state may pass a law abridging freedom of the press. Remember that the press does not have any special immunity from laws that bind the rest of us, nor does the institutional status of the press confer any special privileges on the media.

B. FREEDOM OF THE PRESS AND THE RIGHT TO A FAIR TRIAL. [§893]

A potential conflict exists between the right of the media to gather and report news and the right of a defendant to a fair trial. When considering what steps a judge may take to ensure a fair trial, remember that prior restraints are presumed unconstitutional, and the government has a heavy burden of justification for any such restriction on the media.

C. ACCESS OF THE PRESS TO PRISONERS AND COURTROOMS. [§896]

Members of the media do not have any special right of access to courtrooms or jails. Their rights are the same as those of the general public. There is a presumptive First Amendment right of the public and the press to attend criminal trials and voir dire of potential jurors in a criminal case.

D. NO REPORTER'S PRIVILEGE. [§903]

Members of the media are no different from the rest of us. If you want to know if a reporter must do something (or is prohibited from doing it), ask whether if you must do it (or are prohibited from doing it). For example, reporters do not have any special privilege that exempts them from testifying before a grand jury, from complying with search warrants, from testifying in depositions, or from being held accountable for breaching promises of confidentiality.

E. ACCESS BY INDIVIDUALS TO THE MASS MEDIA. [§908]

When may the government require the media to disseminate certain messages? The print and electronic media are treated differently.

1. FEDERALLY MANDATED REPLY TIME ON TELEVISION OR RADIO. [§909]

The federal government may require a radio or television station to give reply time to answer personal attacks or political editorials.

2. NO RIGHT TO REPLY IN NEWSPAPERS. [§910]

A newspaper may not be forced to provide a "right to reply."

3. PAID EDITORIAL ADVERTISEMENTS. [§911]

Broadcasters may not be forced to accept paid editorial advertisements.

4. HELP-WANTED ADVERTISEMENTS. [§912]

A city can prohibit gender-specific help-wanted advertisements.

5. CABLE TELEVISION FRANCHISES. [§913]

A city's refusal to grant a cable television franchise implicates the First Amendment.

F. SPECIAL TAXES ON THE PRESS. [§914]

Generally applicable laws, including taxes, may be imposed on the press. However, taxes which single out the press for discriminatory treatment will be invalidated.

XIX. THE RELIGION CLAUSES OF THE FIRST AMENDMENT

A. INTRODUCTION. [§918]

The First Amendment has two religion clauses: the Establishment Clause and the Free Exercise Clause. Both clauses have been incorporated, so that neither Congress nor a state may establish religion or violate a person's right to the free exercise of religion.

B. THE ESTABLISHMENT CLAUSE. [§919]

The First Amendment says that Congress may not pass any law respecting the establishment of religion. The Establishment Clause prohibits a government from setting up or recognizing an official state church. It also prohibits government from forcing people to go to church or refrain from going to church. The question usually is how much and what kind of government aid to religion is constitutionally permissible.

1. ESTABLISHMENT CLAUSE TESTS. [§920]

The court has set forth two tests to use in Establishment Clause cases.

a. The *Lemon* Test. [§921]

The test from *Lemon v. Kurtzman* is used when government acts in such a way as to prefer or advance religion over non-religion. For a law to be valid under a *Lemon* analysis:

(1) The law must have a secular legislative purpose;

(2) Its principal or primary effect must be one that neither advances nor inhibits religion; and

(3) It must not foster an excessive government entanglement with religion.

> **STUDY TIP:** The law must pass all three prongs of the *Lemon* test to be constitutional.

b. The *Larson* Test. [§922]

The test from *Larson v. Valente* is used when government prefers one religion over another. In such a case, use a compelling interest balancing test to analyze the law. Strict scrutiny is called for because preferring one religion over another goes to the heart of Establishment Clause concerns.

> **STUDY TIP: THE "ADD OTHER STUFF" THEORY. [§923]**
> If the government does something that arguably advances religion, the way for the government to immunize its action from constitutional attack is to "add other stuff." In other words, the government must secularize the program by making it apply to non-religious as well as religious beneficiaries, or include non-religious items or activities in the display or program.

2. RELIGION AND SCHOOLS. [§924]

The Court has been very sensitive to the fact that school children are impressionable and present a captive audience.

a. Financial Aid to Parochial School Students or Their Parents. [§925]

Generally, state financial aid to religious school students or parents will be upheld if the aid is also given to students or parents in non-religious schools. Whenever the government gives financial aid that benefits religion, the grant or benefit will probably be constitutional if it goes to an individual who, in turn, makes the decision to direct the money or benefit to a religious institution. This is so because the person, not the government, is choosing to prefer religion. Also, the aid will probably be constitutional if both religious and non-religious entities are the ultimate beneficiaries.

(1) Transportation. [§926]

A state can reimburse parents for transportation to and from school.

(2) Textbooks. [§927]

A state can loan textbooks to religious and private non-religious schools.

(3) Salaries. [§928]

A state cannot supplement the salaries of religious school teachers.

(4) Maintenance Grants, Tuition Reimbursement, and Tax Benefits. [§928.1]

A state cannot provide these benefits solely to nonpublic schools and nonpublic school parents.

(5) Special School Districts For Religious Groups. [§929]

A state cannot create a special school district for a religious group.

(6) Aid For Handicapped Students. [§930]

A state may provide money grants for handicapped students for use at religious institutions.

(7) Sign-Language Interpreter. [§931]

A state may provide sign language interpreters for religious school students.

b. Released Time, Religious Instruction in Public Schools, and Enrichment Classes in Religious Schools. [§932]

Religious instruction in public school buildings violates the Establishment Clause because it has the effect of endorsing religion and creates a symbolic union between church and state.

(1) Religious Instruction in Public School Buildings. [§933]

Religious teachers cannot hold classes in a public school building.

(2) Released Time. [§934]

Public school students can **leave** school to go to religious education programs conducted in religious centers.

(3) Public School Teachers in Religious Schools. [§935]

Public school teachers can provide supplemental remedial instruction on the premises of religious schools if safeguards are in place to prevent the endorsement of religion.

c. Prohibiting the Teaching of Evolution and the Teaching of Creation Science. [§937]

A state may not prohibit the teaching of evolution in public schools, nor may it require the teaching of creation science.

d. Posting the Ten Commandments in Public Schools. [§940]

A state may not require the posting of the Ten Commandments in public school classrooms.

e. School Prayer, Moments of Silence, and Invocations at Graduation. [§941]

The court has consistently invalidated any form of government sponsored or coerced prayer in public schools.

(1) Official School Prayer. [§942]

A state cannot require that an official school prayer be said in public school classrooms.

(2) Minute of Silence. [§943]

A state may not require a minute of silence in public schools for mediation or voluntary prayer if the sole purpose is to endorse religion.

(3) Graduation Ceremonies. [§944]

Clergy cannot offer the invocation and benediction at graduation ceremonies for junior or senior high school.

(4) Legislative Sessions. [§945]

A chaplain can open a legislative session with a prayer.

f. Government Aid to Colleges and Universities. [§946]

Government financial aid to church affiliated colleges and universities is analyzed under the *Lemon* standards. The court is usually willing to assume a secular purpose (educating as many students as possible), and there will not be a primary effect of advancing religion if there is a guarantee by the college or university that the money will be used only for secular purposes.

3. RELIGIOUS SYMBOLS DURING THE HOLIDAY SEASON. [§950]

Government-sponsored Christmas displays will be constitutional if they are sufficiently secular to avoid the appearance of the government endorsing religion. This means that it is necessary to include non-religious symbols in any Christmas display. ("Add other stuff.")

4. TAX EXEMPTIONS AND DEDUCTIONS FOR RELIGIOUS ORGANIZATIONS. [§955]

These will be constitutional if both religious and non-religious taxpayers are able to claim them.

5. DELEGATION OF SOVEREIGN POWER TO A CHURCH. [§958]

A state may not delegate a sovereign function to a church. For example, a state may not give a church the power to veto a liquor license.

6. RESOLVING CHURCH DISPUTES ON THE BASIS OF CHURCH DOCTRINE. [§959]

Civil courts may not decide disputes on the basis of religious doctrine. To do so would implicate both the Free Exercise and Establishment Clauses. A civil court may apply "neutral principles" of secular law to decide matters such as property or trust disputes, but it must not entangle itself with religious doctrine.

7. GRANTS TO RELIGIOUS SOCIAL WELFARE AGENCIES. [§960]

Religious entities may be recipients of governmental aid if they are not pervasively religious, and are among a group of beneficiaries which includes non-religious institutions.

8. ESTABLISHMENT CLAUSE ISSUES IN A DESIGNATED PUBLIC FORUM. [§961]

If a government opens its property to a wide range of speakers, it does not violate the Establishment Clause to allow religious speakers to use the property.

> **STUDY TIP:** Be aware of how the Establishment Clause argument gets raised here. A government is excluding speakers from a forum based on the content of their speech. This requires strict scrutiny. The government says its compelling interest is to avoid the establishment of religion that would result from allowing the religious group to speak. The court applies Lemon to see if inclusion of religious speakers would establish religion. It does not, so the government has no compelling interest in excluding the religious speakers.

a. Religious Student Groups in a University. [§962]

A state university may not exclude a religious student group from a designated public forum.

b. Religious Student Groups in High School. [§963]

Public schools may not exclude a religious student group from a designated public forum.

c. Religious Speakers. [§964]

A school may not exclude religious speakers from a designated public forum open to the public.

d. Religious Student Publications. [§965]

A school may not deny funding to a religious student publication if it funds other student journals.

e. Display of Religious Symbols. [§966]

A state may not prohibit a private, unattended display of a religious symbol in a public forum.

9. GOVERNMENT PREFERENCE FOR ONE RELIGION OVER ANOTHER. [§967]

In this kind of case, the court uses the strict scrutiny compelling interest balancing test.

C. THE FREE EXERCISE CLAUSE. [§968]

Neither Congress nor a state may make any law which abridges the free exercise of religion. Government may never regulate religious beliefs, just actions. Government may never inquire into the truth of a religious belief, but it may examine the sincerity with which a person claims to hold a religious belief.

1. OVERVIEW OF FREE EXERCISE ANALYSIS. [§969]

Be very careful about two factors in this area. First, is the law generally applicable, or does it have exceptions or exemptions built into it. Second, is the challenge to the law based solely on the Free Exercise Clause, or on the Free Exercise Clause plus some other constitutional right, such as freedom of speech, or the right to direct the education of your children. The court applies a different analysis in each area.

a. Generally Applicable Laws. [§970]

Laws that apply equally to all persons (such as a criminal statute) are considered to be generally applicable.

(1) Challenges Based Solely on the Free Exercise Clause. [§971]

If a government has passed a generally applicable law, and the plaintiff's challenge to the law is based solely on the Free Exercise Clause, the law is good. There is no heightened scrutiny used.

(2) Challenges Based on the Free Exercise Clause Plus Some Other Constitutional Right. [§972]

If a government has passed a generally applicable law, and the plaintiff's challenge to the law is based on the Free Exercise Clause and some other constitutional right, strict scrutiny applies, and the government must show that the law is narrowly tailored to achieve a compelling government interest.

b. Laws That Are Not Generally Applicable. [§973]

If a government has passed a law that is not generally applicable, strict scrutiny applies. Look for two kinds of laws that are not generally applicable: unemployment compensation laws that provide individualized hearings on eligibility; and laws which have built-in exceptions or exemptions.

c. Types of Free Exercise Clause Analysis. [§974]

Employment Division v. Smith is the leading free exercise case. The court upheld a state's power to criminalize the sacramental use of peyote by Native Americans as an essential part of their religion. Oregon had a generally applicable drug law which was challenged solely on the basis that it violated the free exercise rights of two drug counselors who had been fired for peyote use. The court said that a general applicable law which has only an incidental effect of burdening religion does not violate the Free Exercise Clause. No heightened scrutiny is called for.

> **STUDY TIP:** Be aware that Congress, through the Religious Freedom Restoration Act of 1993, has effectively overruled *Smith*. Under the act, a government may not substantially burden a person's free exercise of religion, even through a law of general applicability, unless it has a compelling interest for the law and has chosen the least restrictive means of achieving that goal. Be very careful about what your professor is asking for if you get a free exercise question. If you are asked to discuss constitutional principles, *Smith* is the prevailing analysis. If the question asks you, in more general terms, "what the law is," then you should mention the Religious Freedom Restoration Act.

(1) Examples of Generally Applicable Laws Challenged Solely on Free Exercise Grounds. [§976]

These laws receive no heightened scrutiny.

(a) Anti-Polygamy Laws. [§977]

A federal law prohibiting polygamy is constitutional.

(b) Dress Codes. [§978]

An Air Force regulation prohibiting wearing a yarmulke on duty is constitutional.

(2) Examples of Generally Applicable Laws Challenged on the Basis of the Free Exercise Clause and Another Constitutional Right. [§979]

Strict scrutiny is used when a generally applicable law is challenged on the basis that it violates the Free Exercise Clause plus some other constitutional right, such as freedom of speech or the right of parents to educate their children.

(a) Mandatory Education Laws. [§980]

A state cannot apply a mandatory education law to the Old Order Amish.

(b) State Law Requiring A Motto On a License Plate. [§981]

A state may not force a person to use license plates which carry a message to which the person objects on religious grounds.

(3) Examples of Laws That Are Not Generally Applicable. [§982]

In these cases, strict scrutiny applies, even though the law is challenged solely on free exercise grounds.

(a) Unemployment Compensation Cases. [§983]

These cases arise when benefits are denied to a person who has lost a job, but the government provides an individualized hearing to determine eligibility for benefits.

(b) Examples of a Law That Is Not Generally Applicable Because It Has Exception Built Into It. [§987]

If statutes operate to prohibit activity only when engaged in by a specific religious group, strict scrutiny applies, and the law will be unconstitutional.

2. WHAT COUNTS AS "RELIGION" FOR FREE EXERCISE CLAUSE PURPOSES? [§989]

If someone is a believer in or a member of an accepted mainstream religion, he or she will be able to make a free exercise challenge to a law. When someone is not an adherent of a mainstream religion, the court has asked whether the non-mainstream believer's religious beliefs fill the same place in a person's life as an accepted religion does in the life of a member of that mainstream religion.

a. Religious Belief As a Basis for Conscientious Objector Status. [§990]

The court looks to the importance of religion in the life of a recognized, mainstream believer to evaluate the religion claims of conscientious objectors.

b. Sincerity of Religious Beliefs. [§993]

The government may not inquire into the truth or falsity of religious beliefs. It may, however, question the sincerity of a person's claimed religious belief.

3. RELIGION AND POLITICAL OFFICE. [§996]

Religion may not be used to qualify or disqualify a person from holding political office. Article VI of the Constitution prohibits any religious tests from being required as a qualification for federal office. The court has applied the same rule to protect the Free Exercise Clause rights of those seeking public office.

4. TAXES ON RELIGIOUS INSTITUTIONS. [§999]

Generally applicable taxes may be imposed on religious institutions. Churches may not be singled out for discriminatory taxation. The federal government can deny tax-exempt status to schools that discriminate on the basis of race, and can deny tax deductions for expenses for mandatory church programs.

5. SUNDAY CLOSING LAWS. [§1004]

A state law which requires businesses to close on Sundays does not violate the First Amendment. Just because a law happens to coincide with the tenets of a religion does not mean that the law is unconstitutional.

6. LAWS AFFECTING THE FREE EXERCISE RIGHTS OF NATIVE AMERICANS. [§1007]

The Court has not been sympathetic to the free exercise claims of Native Americans. Government action frequently makes it impossible for Native Americans to practice essential aspects of their religion.

a. Social Security Numbers. [§1008]

Forcing Native Americans to submit and use an identification number does not violate the Free Exercise Clause.

b. Destruction of Sacred Sites. [§1009]

Federal land may be used in a way that necessitates the destruction of sacred sites.

c. Sacramental Use of Peyote. [§1010]

A state may criminalize the sacramental use of peyote by Native Americans.

D. ACCOMMODATION BETWEEN THE RELIGIOUS BELIEFS OF EMPLOYEES AND THE INTERESTS OF EMPLOYERS: TENSION BETWEEN THE FREE EXERCISE CLAUSE AND THE ESTABLISHMENT CLAUSE. [§1011]

When a government accommodates the religious beliefs of employees (by forcing employers to recognize a chosen sabbath), it runs the risk of establishing religion. The court balances the religious beliefs of employees against the degree of hardship imposed on the employer by the accommodation.

1. REFUSAL TO WORK ON THE SABBATH. [§1012]

Employees have no absolute right to a day off on their chosen sabbath.

2. EXEMPTION OF RELIGIOUS ORGANIZATIONS FROM LAWS BANNING DISCRIMINATION BASED ON RELIGION. [§1013]

Congress may exempt religious organizations from laws banning discrimination based on religion.

XX. CRUEL AND UNUSUAL PUNISHMENT: THE DEATH PENALTY AND PROPORTIONALITY OF PUNISHMENT TO THE CRIME COMMITTED.

A. INTRODUCTION. [§1014]

The Eighth Amendment prohibits the infliction of cruel and unusual punishments. This protection has been incorporated to apply against the states. The Constitution prohibits only those punishments that are cruel **and** unusual.

B. DEATH PENALTY CASES. [§1015]

The death penalty is not intrinsically unconstitutional; the due process clauses refer to the deprivation of life. The issue is the manner in which the death penalty is imposed.

1. FOUNDATION CASES DEALING WITH THE DEATH PENALTY. [§1016]

The main focus of the Court's jurisprudence in the death penalty area has been to erect procedural safeguards to alleviate problems of discrimination and arbitrary imposition of the death penalty.

a. Imposition of the Death Penalty. [§1017]

Arbitrary imposition of the death penalty violates the Eighth Amendment.

b. Procedural Aspects of Imposing the Death Penalty. [§1018]

States may impose the death penalty as long as bifurcated trials are used, and aggravating and mitigating circumstances are considered.

c. Mandatory Death Sentences. [§1019]

States may not impose mandatory death sentences for certain crimes.

d. Mitigating Circumstances. [§1020]

The trial judge must be able to consider all mitigating circumstances.

e. Advisory Jury Verdicts. [§1023]

Capital sentencing statutes that require the sentencing judge to consider an advisory jury verdict need not specify the weight the judge must give to the advisory verdict.

f. Vagueness Challenge to Aggravating Factors. [§1024]

A state's definition of an aggravating factor may be subject to a vagueness challenge.

g. Vagueness Challenge to Jury Instructions. [§1025]

Reviewing courts should give deference to state court jury instructions regarding the conditions under which the death penalty should be imposed.

2. MENTAL STATE OF DEFENDANTS IN DEATH PENALTY CASES. [§1026]

The Eighth Amendment prohibits the execution of a defendant who is insane at the time of the scheduled execution. However, it does not prohibit the execution of a mildly or moderately retarded defendant, as long as the retarded defendant has the ability to prove mitigating circumstances pertaining to his or her character, record, or circumstances of the offense. In addition, the court has held that as long as proper administrative procedures are used, a psychotic inmate maybe given antipsychotic medication against his or her will, making that prisoner eligible for the death penalty.

3. EXECUTION OF JUVENILES. [§1030]

The Eighth Amendment prohibits the execution of a defendant who was fifteen years old or younger at the time of committing the offense. It does not prohibit the execution of a defendant who was sixteen years old or older at the time of committing the offense.

4. STATISTICAL EVIDENCE OF RACIAL DISPARITY IN IMPOSING THE DEATH PENALTY IS NOT ENOUGH TO PROVE AN EIGHTH AMENDMENT VIOLATION. [§1031]

The court rejected the argument that an Eighth Amendment violation can be proven by presenting statistical evidence that black defendants who murder white victims are more likely to receive the death penalty than other defendants.

5. VICTIM IMPACT STATEMENTS. [§1032]

The Eighth Amendment does not erect any **per se** bar to the introduction of "victim impact evidence" in a capital sentencing proceeding. This evidence involves the impact of the crime on the victim's family, friends, and professional associates, as well as its effect on the community.

6. JURY INSTRUCTIONS REGARDING INELIGIBILITY FOR PAROLE FROM A LIFE SENTENCE. [§1033]

A jury cannot sentence a defendant to death unless it is apprised of the fact that, under state law, the defendant would be ineligible for parole if he or she received a life sentence. It would be unfair for a jury to sentence a defendant to death on the assumption that he or she may get out on parole and create a future danger to society.

7. EVIDENCE OF A PRIOR DEATH SENTENCE. [§1034]

Even though irrelevant under state rules of evidence, it is not a constitutional violation for a sentencing jury to learn that the defendant had received the death penalty in a prior case.

C. PROPORTIONALITY. [§1035]

The court has said that the Eighth Amendment includes a proportionality requirement that should be applied in both capital and non-capital cases. The harshness of the sentence should be proportionate to the gravity of the offense.

1. Proportionality In Capital Cases. [§1036]

The court has used the proportionality principle to overturn certain death sentences.

a. Rape. [§1037]

The death penalty may not be imposed for rape.

b. Accomplice Not Present at a Murder. [§1038]

The death penalty may not be imposed on an accomplice who was not present at the murder.

c. Accomplice Present at Murder. [§1039]

The death penalty may be imposed on an accomplice who was present at the murder.

2. Proportionality In Non-Capital Cases. [§1040]

The court also uses proportionality analysis in non-capital cases.

a. Factors In Applying Proportionality Analysis. [§1041]

Asserting that proportionality analysis is applicable in non-capital cases, the court set forth three factors to consider: 1) the gravity of the offense and the harshness of the penalty; 2) the sentences imposed on other criminals in the same jurisdiction; and 3) sentences imposed for the same crime in other jurisdictions.

b. Life Sentence under Recidivist Statute. [§1042]

A state may impose a life sentence under a recidivist statute, even for fairly minor crimes.

c. Mandatory Life Sentence for Cocaine Possession. [§1043]

A state may impose a mandatory life sentence for possession of cocaine.

This book is dedicated to my wife Mary
and to
Matt, Jeff, and Alicia

I. INTRODUCTION

About the Author —

Professor Philip J. Prygoski has taught Constitutional Law at the Thomas M. Cooley Law School since 1977. He has also taught at the University of Wisconsin Law School, the University of Tennessee College of Law, and the University of Oklahoma College of Law. Professor Prygoski has received over twenty teaching awards at Cooley, and was awarded the Outstanding Professor Award by the Student Bar Association at Tennessee. He has written a number of law review articles on Constitutional Law, and is a frequent lecturer to lawyers and judges. Professor Prygoski received his J.D. and LL.M. degrees from the University of Michigan Law School. Professor Prygoski is a member of the American Law Institute.

From the Author —

The study of Constitutional Law is difficult because it is the study of a process of interpretation. A student must try to recognize and synthesize the different factors that influence the Supreme Court's interpretation of the Constitution. First of all, there is the document itself - what did the words mean when written, and do they mean the same thing today? What was the intent of the drafters of the Constitution, and to what extent does that intent (if discernible) influence or dictate constitutional interpretation today? How much should extrinsic factors such as war, national emergency, political exigencies, or changing social standards affect the interpretive process? How much do the political philosophies or personal prejudices of individual Justices affect the decision making process?

This outline tries to shed some light on these questions through its structure and its content. Each section sets forth the relevant principles and rules for a specific area of constitutional law. Then, summaries of frequently studied cases are provided to illustrate these principles and rules. I have tried to give you some ideas of both "the words and the music:" the specific rules, as well as the underlying theory. Once you understand the general rule, it is wise to see how the Court has applied that rule to accommodate the facts of a given case.

Acknowledgement —

I would like to thank Elaine Colville, a good friend and great secretary, for her efforts in producing this work. Without her, this project would not have been completed.

OUTLINE

This **Quick Review** is designed to help you maximize your performance on your Constitutional Law examination. However, these materials are not intended to be the primary source of information about Constitutional Law. Your casebook and class notes are the main source of knowledge about this subject. The **Quick Review** supplements these materials. Providing the **10-5-2 Hour Study Guide** does not mean to suggest that you begin your review 10 hours before the examination. Constitutional Law is much too complicated a subject to be reviewed in such a short period of time.

Before you begin the **10-5-2-Hour Countdown**, review your class notes carefully. This is important for two reasons: to get a handle on the big picture of Constitutional Law; and to try to figure out what will be on your exam. Pay close attention to subjects that your professor seems to like, especially those involving new issues or cases working their way up to the Supreme Court. Also, if possible, review your professor's past exams and any model answers that may be available. This may give a hint as to what subjects your professor likes to test and what kinds of questions you are likely to see.

Remember that in Constitutional Law, the primary approach of the Court is to balance. You should know the competing policy interests in a given area, and be able to balance these interests to achieve an equitable result. Also, be sure to pay attention to "the words and the music." Know the rules the Court has given us, but also know how different policy considerations would affect the decisionmaking of liberal or conservative Justices.

10 Study Hours Before the Final Examination

___ Review your class notes, with close attention to areas emphasized in class and your professor's areas of interest and opinions.

___ Review relevant constitutional provisions.

___ Review **Quick Review** to clarify and reinforce substantive rules and policies covered in class.

___ Do one more review of the major cases covered in class, filling in any gaps in your understanding by going over the section of **Quick Review** that covers your class material. In reviewing the cases, make sure you know precisely what the issue is in a given case, and what are the policy reasons underlying the Court's decision. Think about your professor's position on the rules, exceptions, and policies in a given area.

___ Answer the multiple choice questions in **Quick Review** as a means of checking your understanding of rules, policies, and cases.

___ Review the essay questions in **Quick Review** as a means of testing your substantive knowledge and your ability to spot issues in constitutional cases.

5 Study Hours Before the Final Examination

___ Quickly scan your class notes, reviewing major areas and cases covered in class that you feel need more attention to complete your understanding. Pay attention to your professor's over-all approach.

___ Pay close attention to the specific tests or analyses given by the Court in the areas you have covered in class.

___ Review and highlight the **Capsule Outline**. You may wish to annotate the **Capsule Outline** with your class notes.

2 Study Hours Before the Final Examination

___ Review your highlighting of the **Capsule Outline**.

___ Quickly review your notes for those favorite areas of your professor which you believe are most likely to be tested.

___ Get yourself into an exam frame of mind. Think of how you will set up your analysis in answering questions. A good approach is 1) to identify the issue raised in the question, 2) to identify and apply the applicable rules and law, and any qualifications or exceptions, 3) to discuss competing policies if applicable, 4) to apply all this to the facts presented in the question, and 5) to briefly state the conclusion.

___ **Relax!** Take a break at least a few minutes before exam time.

III. ANALYTICAL AND EXAM APPROACH

A. ANALYSIS OF CONSTITUTIONAL QUESTIONS. [§1]

To prepare yourself to discuss any Constitutional Law question, either in class, or on an exam, you should follow these three suggestions.

1. READ THE CONSTITUTION. [§2]

First of all, read the Constitution. You should do this before reading the cases. The reason is to become familiar with the specific powers, limitations on power, and individual rights enumerated in the document. It is also important to get a sense of the structure of the document and of the system of government it establishes. You must have some sense of the "big picture" to effectively engage in the balancing of interests analysis that your professor will inevitably require.

2. READ THE ASSIGNED CASES IN THE CASEBOOK. [§3]

Constitutional law, as taught in law school, is primarily the study of United States Supreme Court cases. While reading the cases in your casebook, you must come to know both "the words and the music." What I mean is that you must know the rule of the case, as well as the theory underlying the rule. Knowing the rule is important in reaching the correct result when analyzing a fact pattern. Knowing the theory is important in explaining why a court ruled a particular way, and in trying to determine what it might do in subsequent cases with different facts.

3. CONSIDER THE "REAL-LIFE" IMPLICATIONS OF THE CASE. [§4]

In addition to knowing the legal theory of a case, consider what would happen in the real world if the Supreme Court ruled a certain way. The primary job of the Court is to decide the case before it. However, a Supreme Court ruling on a constitutional question is controlling on all other federal or state courts which might hear a case involving the same issue. As a result, a Supreme Court ruling on a particular constitutional question might have the effect of invalidating all state laws dealing with that question. The wide-ranging implications arising from the effect of a Supreme Court ruling are factors which you should consider when analyzing why the Court ruled a certain way in a given case. Also consider the historical, political, social, or military context of a case. These factors may also influence how a court decides a case. In trying to understand why the Court ruled the way it did, a very important question to ask is: "What if the Court ruled the other way?"

B. BASE ALL YOUR ARGUMENTS IN THE CONSTITUTION. [§5]

Every constitutional argument must be grounded in the Constitution. If you are asserting that Congress has the power to pass a law, that law must fall within some constitutional power of Congress. If the President takes some action, it must be based in a constitutional power of the President. If a federal court hears a particular lawsuit, that exercise of judicial power must be based in the Constitution. If a state takes action, that action must be within the constitutional power of the state. If a person asserts an individual right as a defense to government action, that right must be based in the Constitution.

OUTLINE

1. THE CONSTITUTION IS THE SUPREME LAW OF THE LAND. [§6]

The Constitution is the supreme, overriding law of the United States. The Supreme Court has made it clear that any statute or other governmental action that conflicts with the Constitution cannot stand. If Congress or the President engages in action that conflicts with or contravenes the Constitution, the Court will invalidate such action. Under the Supremacy Clause of Article 6 of the Constitution, the Constitution takes precedence over any conflicting state law.

2. THE SUPREME COURT IS THE ULTIMATE ARBITER OF THE CONSTITUTION. [§7]

Under our system of constitutional law, the Supreme Court is the ultimate arbiter of the Constitution. In the landmark decision of *Marbury v. Madison* (see §33), Chief Justice John Marshall asserted for the Court the ultimate power to interpret the Constitution. This power has come to be accepted by the other branches of the federal government and by the states.

IV. OVERVIEW OF CONSTITUTIONAL LAW: A SUMMARY OF THE MAJOR AREAS OF CONSTITUTIONAL LAW

A. TYPES OF CONSTITUTIONAL QUESTIONS. [§8]

In general terms, any constitutional analysis is likely to fall into one or more of four general categories: judicial review, separation of powers, federalism, or individual rights. While each of these will be discussed more fully later in this book, here are some general issues to consider in each area.

B. JUDICIAL REVIEW. [§9]

The first issue in this area is whether a federal court has jurisdiction to hear a case. Under Article III of the Constitution, a federal court may hear a case only if it involves a "case or controversy," which means that the party seeking to invoke the jurisdiction of a federal court must have suffered (or be imminently in danger of suffering) an injury-in-fact which is fairly traceable to the government action complained of. An injury-in-fact will be fairly traceable to the government action complained of if a court can issue an order which will directly eliminate the injury-in-fact. If there is no Article III case or controversy, a federal court cannot hear the case.

The next inquiry is whether a federal court will decline to hear a case even though the case technically falls within its jurisdiction. The Supreme Court has created a number of "prudential" rules, under which a federal court will decline to exercise its powers. Some of these prudential rules are: a federal court will not allow a person to have standing to file a lawsuit simply because that person is a citizen who is dissatisfied with a certain government act; a federal court generally will not allow a federal taxpayer to file a lawsuit challenging an expenditure of money by Congress; and a federal court generally will not get involved in sensitive cases of foreign relations, such as declaring or conducting a war, or recognizing a particular government in a foreign country. Prudential rules do not involve constitutionally-based barriers to the exercise of a federal court's jurisdiction, but simply focus on whether it is a "bad idea" for a court to hear a case. In general, these rules reflect the idea that a federal court should decline to hear a case out of deference to another branch of the federal government or to a state. These prudential rules governing a federal court's refusal to hear a case present a prime example of the importance of understanding the theory and basic structure of our constitutional form of government, and of having a grasp of the political, social, historical, or military context of the case.

C. SEPARATION OF POWERS. [§10]

A separation of powers question involves the relationships between branches of the federal government. This "horizontal" analysis (involving co-equal branches of the same government) will arise when one branch of the federal government takes some action which interferes with an attribute or power of another branch. The analysis focuses on whether the branch that has acted has unduly interfered with what the Court has deemed to be an essential function of another branch of the federal government. This balancing approach will require answers to two questions: 1) which attribute or power of the affected government has been infringed? and; 2) has there been an "undue interference" with that attribute? In a pure separation of powers question, there will be no mention of a state, or of any individual right being abridged.

D. FEDERALISM. [§11]   **A federalism question involves the relationship between the federal government and the states.** In the typical federalism question, Congress passes a law which interferes with a state's ability to function as an independent sovereign. This "vertical" analysis (involving two separate governments, each having its own sphere of sovereignty) will frequently ask you to balance the federal interests advanced by the congressional statute against the Tenth Amendment police powers of the state. The Tenth Amendment has been interpreted to be the primary source of state power. In general terms, the police power of a state includes the state's power to regulate for the health, safety, welfare, or morals of its citizens. You may be asked to figure out which attribute or power of a state is being abridged, and whether the abridgement is so severe as to be unconstitutional.

If both the federal government and a state regulate the same subject matter, there may be an issue of preemption. Under the Supremacy Clause of Article 6, the Constitution and any federal laws passed pursuant to it take precedence over any state law that conflicts with the federal law or frustrates its purpose. A preemption question is easy to identify, because there will always be both a federal and a state law in the fact pattern.

E. INDIVIDUAL RIGHTS. [§12]   **These questions typically involve a government, federal or state, taking some action which abridges a right of an individual.** This "government action" requirement will be present in all individual rights cases, except those involving the Thirteenth Amendment, which prohibits slavery whether engaged in by government actors or private persons. An individual rights analysis should include the following steps:

1. Which government is acting? [§13]

Identify whether it is the federal government or a state which has passed the law which allegedly abridges someone's right. This is important because different constitutional provisions limit the federal government, as opposed to those which restrict states. For example, if Congress deprived someone of due process, the plaintiff's argument would be based or the Fifth Amendment due process clause. If, on the other hand, a state deprived someone of due process, the plaintiff's argument would fall under the due process clause of the Fourteenth Amendment.

2. Identify the interest that has been abridged. [§14]

Describe in layperson's terms the interest that has been abridged. For example, if a state law imposes a two-year educational requirement before someone may be licensed to drive an eighteen-wheel truck, the plaintiff would be complaining about his or her inability to pursue an occupation. Or, if a state law said that aliens may not attend college within the state, the plaintiff would be complaining about exclusion from college based on the trait of lack of U.S. citizenship.

3. Place the abridged interest in the Constitution. [§15]

The ability to pursue an occupation would be an aspect of liberty under the Fourteenth Amendment due process clause. The right not to be excluded from a benefit based upon individual or group status falls within the Equal Protection Clause of the Fourteenth Amendment.

4. Ascribe constitutional weight to the interest abridged. [§16]

If a right is abridged, you must decide whether it is a fundamental right (such as freedom of speech), or simply some low-level liberty interest under the due process clause (such as the interest of police officers in wearing their hair as they choose). If a class has been disadvantaged, you must then determine whether the class is "suspect," "quasi-suspect," or "non-suspect."

5. Set the appropriate level of scrutiny for a court to use. [§17]

The level of scrutiny used by a reviewing court corresponds to the importance of the governmental interest needed to justify the law. Whenever a court reviews a case in the individual rights area, it will look at the purpose of the law, and the means chosen to effectuate that purpose. When the government abridges an important right, or disadvantages a suspect class of people, it will have to show a very important interest to justify the law. If only a relatively unimportant interest is affected, the law may be upheld if it advances any legitimate government interest.

6. Balance. [§18]

Once you have identified the interest abridged, placed it in the Constitution, ascribed its appropriate constitutional weight, and set the level of scrutiny to be used by a court, the final step in the analysis is to balance the government interest against the intrusion into the individual's constitutional interest. For example, if a very important individual right, such as free speech, is being abridged, the government will have to show a very important or compelling reason for the abridgement. If some relatively unimportant interest is abridged, the law may be good if the government has any legitimate reason for the law.

> **LAW SCHOOL EXAM TIP. [§19]** Your exam will probably have essay questions, multiple choice questions, or a combination of both. Think about what kinds of issues are testable under each format. With essay questions, you are most likely to be tested on the "gray areas" of law. In this instance the professor tries to draft questions which will distinguish those students who know the theory, as well as the black-letter rules, from those who don't. If that is the goal of the exam, it makes little sense to give a question which has a clear-cut right answer. Such questions are not good evaluative tools, because they result in top-heavy grading curves. Essay questions are used to test the depth of a student's knowledge. Multiple choice questions, on the other hand, are frequently used to test the breadth of a student's knowledge. Multiple choice questions are much more likely to test rules than theory. This is where specific constitutional requirements are likely to show up (i.e., how many Senators does it take to ratify a treaty). As you go through the semester, be sensitive to what material is susceptible to each of these testing techniques.

A. ARTICLE III OF THE CONSTITUTION ESTABLISHES FEDERAL COURTS. [§20]

Article III of the Constitution provides the basis for and the scope of federal judicial power. Under Article III, "[t]he judicial power of the United States shall be vested in one Supreme Court, and in such inferior Courts as the Congress may from time to time ordain and establish. . . ."

1. ORIGINAL JURISDICTION OF THE SUPREME COURT. [§21]

Under Article III, the Supreme Court has original jurisdiction in all cases ". . . affecting Ambassadors, other public Ministers and Consuls, and those in which a State shall be a party . . . ." Under present statutes, the Supreme Court has exclusive original jurisdiction only when a state sues a state; in all other cases involving the Supreme Court's original jurisdiction, Congress, under its power to ordain and establish inferior federal courts, has conferred concurrent original jurisdiction on federal district courts. The original jurisdiction of the Supreme Court can be neither expanded nor diminished by statute.

2. APPELLATE JURISDICTION OF THE SUPREME COURT. [§22]

Under Article III, the Supreme Court has original jurisdiction in a very limited category of cases. (See §21) In all cases other than those listed under its Article III original jurisdiction, the Supreme Court has appellate jurisdiction, with such exceptions and regulations as Congress shall make. Under this grant of appellate jurisdiction, the Court has appellate jurisdiction over all cases coming from lower federal courts, and from cases coming from state courts, as long as those state-court cases involve a federal question.

3. WAYS TO APPEAL TO THE SUPREME COURT. [§23]

By statute, the Supreme Court is authorized to review some lower court decisions as a matter of right (by appeal) and others as a matter of judicial discretion (by writ of certiorari).

a. Appeal. [§24]

Under present statutes, an appeal as a matter of right may only be taken to the Supreme Court from decisions of three-judge courts. Federal law allows such appeals in only a small number of cases. 28 U.S.C.A. §§2281 and 2284.

b. Certiorari. [§25]

All federal cases not brought in three-judge courts go to **the Supreme Court by a petition for a writ of certiorari.** All cases from state courts go to the Supreme Court via a petition for a writ of certiorari. The Supreme Court will only review a final order of the highest appellate court of a state. The theory underlying the exceptionally broad scope of the certiorari jurisdiction of the Supreme Court is to give the Court the discretion to control its own docket. The Court's refusal to grant a petition

OUTLINE

for a writ of certiorari is of no precedential value, and should not be cited as precedent.

B. DOES A FEDERAL COURT HAVE JURISDICTION? WILL IT EXERCISE IT? [§26]

Under Article III, a court must have jurisdiction over a case before it may act. However, in some cases where a court has jurisdiction, it may choose not to exercise it out of deference to another branch of the federal government or to a state.

1. DETERMINE JURISDICTION EXISTS. [§27]

The first thing to do when analyzing a constitutional law question is to make sure that a federal court has jurisdiction to hear the case.

a. Federal question jurisdiction. [§28]

Under Article III, federal courts have jurisdiction to hear cases involving a federal question. Article III says that the jurisdiction of federal courts shall extend to all cases, in law and equity, arising under the Constitution, the laws of the United States, and treaties entered into by the United States.

b. Diversity jurisdiction. [§29]

Under federal statutes, federal courts have jurisdiction in diversity cases - those involving a dispute between citizens of different states, or between a citizen of a state and an alien. The idea behind diversity jurisdiction is to provide a litigant with access to a federal forum so as to escape the possible prejudices that might come into play in state court, such as elected state court judges being overly concerned with their re-election, or with the political interests of their respective states.

c. Case or controversy requirement. [§30]

A lawsuit must meet the Article III definition of a "case or controversy" to fall within the jurisdiction of a federal court. For there to be a case or controversy, there must be an actual dispute before the court, brought by a plaintiff who has suffered (or is about to suffer) a specific injury as a result of an identified government action.

2. EVEN IF JURISDICTION EXISTS, SHOULD A FEDERAL COURT REFUSE TO HEAR A CASE? [§31]

Even if a case presents a justiciable case or controversy, there are some "prudential" doctrines that a court may use to avoid taking such a case. These prudential rules usually concern separation of powers or federalism issues; the court deems it wise to defer to another branch of the federal government or to the states for a decision. For example, as a practical matter, it may be unwise for a federal court to hear a lawsuit challenging the constitutionality of U.S. military action in a foreign country. While there may be serious constitutional issues involved, the question becomes whether there is anything a federal court can (or should) do about the allegedly unconstitutional commitment of troops to a foreign country. Will the President, as Commander-in-Chief, be subject to deposition during the course of the military action? Should a federal court order the termination of hostilities by a certain date, and the return of all American troops? There are some constitutional questions which are better decided by the political (elected) branches of government, rather than by the courts.

C. SUPREME COURT ESTABLISHMENT OF THE POWER OF JUDICIAL REVIEW. [§32]

In a number of cases in the early 1800's, the Supreme Court established for the judicial branch of the federal government the power to review acts of other branches of the federal government, as well as decisions from state courts. The Court declared that the judiciary is the ultimate arbiter of constitutional powers and rights.

1. JUDICIAL REVIEW OF CONGRESSIONAL LAWS AND EXECUTIVE ACTS. [§33]

In *Marbury v. Madison,* 5 U.S. 137 (1803), the Court established for the federal judiciary the power to review and, when appropriate, invalidate acts of Congress, as well as the power to issue mandatory writs (such as a writ of mandamus) to members of the Executive branch. Right before leaving office, President John Adams appointed William Marbury to be a justice of the peace. Marbury's commission was not delivered before Adams left office, and Thomas Jefferson, the new President, directed his Secretary of State, James Madison, not to deliver the commission to Marbury. Marbury sued Madison, seeking a writ of mandamus forcing Madison to deliver the commission. Marbury relied on §13 of the Judiciary Act of 1789, which, as Chief Justice Marshall interpreted it, purported to give the Supreme Court original jurisdiction to issue writs of mandamus. Analyzing Marbury's argument, Chief Justice John Marshall ruled, "It is emphatically the province and duty of the judicial department to say what the law is." Applying this principle, the Court invalidated §13, on the basis that it was a congressional attempt to enlarge the constitutionally-prescribed original jurisdiction of the Supreme Court. This part of *Marbury* established the power of the judiciary to invalidate acts of Congress.

In another part of the opinion, Chief Justice Marshall declared that an appropriate federal court could issue a writ of mandamus ordering a federal executive branch official to perform a duty that he or she had a legal duty to perform. The result of *Marbury* is that the federal judiciary has review power over the other branches of the federal government.

2. SUPREME COURT REVIEW OF STATE COURT CASES. [§34]

In two other cases, *Martin v. Hunter's Lessee,* 14 U.S. 304 (1816), and *Cohens v. Virginia,* 19 U.S. 264 (1821), the Supreme Court asserted its power to review both civil and criminal cases coming out of state courts, so long as a federal question was presented on appeal.

After *Marbury*, *Martin*, and *Cohens*, the power of judicial review was established in relation to other branches of the federal government, as well as to state courts.

D. LIMITATIONS ON JUDICIAL REVIEW. [§35]

There are both constitutional and prudential limitations on the exercise of judicial power by a federal court. Constitutional limitations derive from the document itself; certain constitutional provisions establish specific requirements for the exercise of federal judicial power. For example, under Article III, a federal court can only hear a "case or controversy." If none exists (because no one has been injured by any government action), a federal court cannot hear the case. Prudential limitations, however, are judge-made rules of restraint or avoidance, whose main purpose is to show respect for other branches of the federal government or for the states. Prudential limitations are not constitutionally required, but reflect the Court's view of the proper role of the judiciary in the federal system. An example of a prudential limitation is the Court's unwillingness to exercise its power to determine the constitutionality of a war overseas, even though the constitutional rights of soldiers may be implicated.

1. FEDERAL COURTS MAY NOT ISSUE ADVISORY OPINIONS. [§36]

An advisory opinion is an opinion requested by an executive official, or by a legislature, asking a court to rule on the constitutionality of some proposed government action before the law has been applied to anyone. There is no party who has been adversely affected by the law, so the opinion is merely advisory in nature. **Advisory opinions are not within the Article III definition of a "case or controversy," so federal courts may not issue such opinions.** *Muskrat v. U.S.*, 219 U.S. 346 (1911).

As a corollary, federal courts will not hear collusive suits because they also fail to meet the Article III requirement of a case or controversy involving parties who are truly adverse, and who have a concrete stake in the outcome of the lawsuit. Collusive suits are those in which the parties do not have conflicting interests, but are acting in concert to test the constitutionality of a law.

2. POLITICAL QUESTIONS ARE NON-JUSTICIABLE. [§37]

Some disputes are not justiciable (they are not able to be resolved in a court of law). Rather, they are to be decided by the political (elected) branches of the federal government. A political question ultimately involves separation of powers issues; a branch of the federal government other than the judiciary is the appropriate forum for resolution of a given issue. There are two kinds of political questions: Those which the Constitution explicitly gives to Congress or the President for resolution; and those which a court could hear, but are simply "too hot to handle" for some reason. With the first kind of political question, look for a specific constitutional provision which gives the decisionmaking power to Congress or the President. With the second kind, look for some separation-of- powers reason why a federal court should not hear a case, such as respect for a decision already made by Congress or the President, or risk of embarrassment to the federal government by the Court overruling some political decision made by Congress or the President (such as a decision to commit troops overseas).

a. Political Questions To Be Decided By Congress Or The President. [§38]

(1) Guarantee Clause cases. [§39]
Article IV, §4 of the Constitution says, "The United States shall guarantee to every State . . . a Republican Form of Government . . . ." Cases involving the Guarantee Clause are not within the jurisdiction of federal courts. In *Pacific States Telephone & Telegraph Co. v. Oregon*, 223 U.S. 118 (1912), the Court refused to rule on the constitutionality of an Oregon law which allowed its citizens to pass laws through the initiative and referendum process. The Court said this issue was a political question to be decided by Congress.

(2) Expulsion of a Member of Congress. [§40]

Either house of Congress may, upon a two-thirds vote, expel a member. Expulsion is the removal of a legislator after he or she has been elected, taken the oath, and taken his or her seat. As a general matter, the Constitution gives either House the power to expel one of its members (Article I, §5, cl. 2), provided that the expulsion is properly done. An interesting issue would arise if the House, for instance, exercised its power to expel a member, but did so for a constitutionally suspect reason, such as racial discrimination. The injection of an individual rights issue would then change that dispute from a political question into a justiciable one.

(a) A case which does not involve a political question, but is usually discussed in that section of a constitutional law casebook is *Powell v. McCormack*, 395 U.S. 486 (1969) (see §44). In *Powell*, the Court discussed the difference between a house of Congress expelling a member (non-justiciable as a political question), and a house of Congress excluding a member (justiciable and unconstitutional). In that case the Court invalidated a decision by the House of Representatives to exclude (rather than expel) one of its members. After a Select Committee of the House reported on certain alleged instances of malfeasance in office by Representative Powell (including allegations of lying about travel expenses and making illegal salary payments to his wife), the House passed a resolution preventing him from taking his seat. The problem was that by refusing to allow him to take his seat, despite being elected and meeting age, citizenship and residency requirements, the House was, in effect, adding a "good citizenship requirement" to those listed in the Constitution.

(3) Procedures for Impeachment. [§41]

Article 1, §3, cl. 6 gives the Senate the power to try impeachments. The Court has ruled that the Constitution gives to the Senate the exclusive power to determine the exact procedures it will use in impeachment cases.

In *Nixon v. U.S.*, 113 S.Ct 733 (1993), a federal district judge who had been convicted of perjury and given a prison sentence challenged the procedure used by the Senate in his impeachment trial. Specifically, Judge Nixon asserted that the Senate violated the Constitution by having a committee of Senators take evidence against him, and having the full Senate decide his case on the basis of a report filed by the committee. The Court held the Constitution gives the Senate, rather than the courts, the power to decide the rules for an impeachment trial.

(4) President's Power to Terminate a Treaty. [§41.1]

The issue of whether the President has the power to unilaterally terminate a treaty is a political question.

In *Goldwater v. Carter*, 444 U.S. 996 (1979), the Court summarily vacated the judgment of the Court of Appeals and directed that the case be dismissed. The case involved a dispute between the Senate and the President as to whether the President has the power to unilaterally terminate a treaty without the advice and consent of the Senate.

Although Art. II §2 of the Constitution provides for the creation of treaties by the President, with the advice and consent of the Senate, the Constitution is silent as to the termination of treaties. A plurality of the Court held that the case was a nonjusticiable political question, because it involved a dispute about the extent of Presidential authority in foreign affairs and was best left for resolution by the Executive and Legislative Branches of the Government.

b. Political Questions That Are "Too Hot To Handle." [§42]

Some disputes are deemed political questions even though the Constitution does not specifically commit these issues to the executive or legislative branch for decision. These "prudential" political questions reflect a judicial deference to decisions made by other branches of the federal government.

In *Baker v. Carr*, 369 U.S. 186 (1962), the Court lists the following factors as guidelines in determining whether a dispute is a "prudential" political question which a court should avoid hearing. Each of these factors involves the Court showing respect for a coordinate branch of the federal government:

(1) The lack of judicially discoverable or manageable standards for resolving it;

(2) The impossibility of a court deciding the case without an initial policy decision by some other branch of government;

(3) The need for a court to show proper respect for the decisions of another branch of government;

(4) The need to adhere to a political decision already made; and

(5) The potential embarrassment from multiple pronouncements on the same issue.

Issues to watch for in the "too hot to handle" area are 1) foreign relations (whether or not a treaty has been terminated), 2) dates and duration of military activities (litigating the constitutionality of Desert Storm), and 3) validity of enactments (ratification periods for proposed amendments to the Constitution).

3. QUALIFICATIONS CLAUSES. [§43]

Neither Congress nor a state may add requirements to the exclusive list of qualifications for members of Congress contained in the Qualifications Clauses of the Constitution. Article I, §2, clause 2, which applies to the House of Representatives, provides:

"No person shall be a Representative who shall not have attained to the Age of twenty five Years, and been seven Years a Citizen of the United States, and who shall not, when elected, be an Inhabitant of that State in which he shall be chosen".

Article I, §3, clause 3, which applies to the Senate, provides:

"No person shall be a Senator who shall not have attained to the Age of thirty Years, and have been nine Years a Citizen of the United States, and who shall not, when elected, be an Inhabitant of that State for which he shall be chosen."

a. Congressional attempts to add to the constitutionally prescribed requirements for membership in Congress. [§44]

Congress may not add requirements for membership over and above those listed in the Constitution.

In *Powell* (see §40), the Court invalidated a decision by the House of Representatives to prohibit Adam Clayton Powell from taking his seat, even though he had been elected and had met the age, citizenship, and residency requirements of the Constitution. The House voted to exclude Powell because of allegations of lying about travel expenses and making illegal salary payments to his wife. The Court reasoned that the House was, in effect, adding a "good citizenship" requirement to those listed in the Constitution.

b. State attempts to add to the constitutionally prescribed requirements for membership in Congress. [§45]

A state may not impose limits on the number of terms that the state's congressional delegation may serve.

In *U.S. Term Limits, Inc. v. Thornton*, 115 S.Ct. 1842 (1995), the Court invalidated a provision of the Arkansas Constitution which prohibited a candidate's name from being on the ballot for a congressional election if that person had already served three terms in the House of Representatives or two terms in the Senate. The Court ruled that the Arkansas provision violated the Qualifications Clauses of the U.S. Constitution, and that state limitations could not be justified under either the Tenth Amendment state police powers provision or under the Elections Clause of the Constitution (Article I, §1) that gives states the power to regulate the "Times, Places and Manner of holding Elections."

4. ADEQUATE AND INDEPENDENT STATE GROUNDS. [§46]

The adequate and independent state grounds analysis is a judicially-imposed limitation on the ability of the Supreme Court to review decisions by the highest appellate courts of states. The adequate and independent state grounds doctrine arises when the highest appellate court of a state decides a case involving both state and federal issues. The Supreme Court will not review such a case if the state court based its decision solely on state law, and the Supreme Court cannot change the result of the case. This is true despite the presence of a federal issue in the case. The key question in determining whether the state decision is based on adequate and independent state grounds is whether the Supreme Court can change the result of the case. If it can, by ruling on the federal question, it will take the case. If it cannot change the result, it will not take the case because its ruling would then be very much like an advisory opinion - clarifying a federal question, but with no impact on the litigants. *Michigan v. Long*, 463 U.S. 1032 (1983).

a. Steps in an "Adequate and Independent State Grounds" Analysis. [§47]

Here are the factors to look for in an adequate and independent state grounds issue:

(1) Has the highest appellate court of a state ruled on the case;

(2) Does the case involve questions of both federal and state law; and

(3) Can the Supreme Court change the result of the case by ruling on the federal question? (Remember that the Supreme Court has no business ruling on questions that solely address state law.)

If the answer to all three questions is "yes," there is no adequate and independent state basis for decision, and the Supreme Court may take the case.

b. State Constitution Confers Greater Protection Than The Federal Constitution. [§48]

The common scenario in an "adequate and independent state grounds" case is that the state constitution grants a person more rights than the federal Constitution. The litigant wins under state law, and there is nothing the Supreme Court can do about it.

Assume that a defendant is prosecuted in state court for possession of drugs. The defendant moves to exclude the drugs from evidence because the search by the police violated the Fourth Amendment to the U.S. Constitution (applied to the states through the Fourteenth Amendment), as well as the search and seizure provision of the state constitution. The state supreme court rules that the search violated the state constitution; therefore the drugs are excluded from evidence. In its opinion, however, the state supreme court misinterprets U.S. Supreme Court precedent on the Fourth Amendment, holding the drugs inadmissible under the Fourth Amendment, when they should have been admitted under federal case law. The state seeks to appeal to the U.S. Supreme Court. The Court should not take the case because its cannot change the result - the drugs are still excluded based solely on the state constitution.

SUMMARY CHART: ADEQUATE AND INDEPENDENT STATE GROUNDS

NOTE: In each of these cases, the plaintiff is challenging some state action on both state and federal constitutional grounds.

	Did the state court find the state action valid under the state constitution?	Did the state court find the state action valid under the federal constitution?	Who won in state court?	Will the Supreme Court take this Case?
Case 1	Yes	Yes	State	Yes
Case 2	Yes	No	Individual	Yes
Case 3	No	No	Individual	No
Case 4	No	Yes	Individual	No

In cases 1 and 2, the state law or action was permissible under the state constitution. That means the only remaining question (and the dispositive one), is whether the state law or action was permissible under the federal constitution. Since the federal question is the one that will ultimately determine the outcome of the case, the U.S. Supreme Court will take the case and decide the federal question. In cases 3 and 4, the state law or action is unconstitutional under the state constitution. That means that the federal constitutional question is irrelevant to the outcome, and the U.S. Supreme Court will not take the case because it cannot change the outcome.

5. RIPENESS, STANDING, AND MOOTNESS: THE "BIG THREE" LIMITATIONS ON FEDERAL JUDICIAL POWER. [§49]

There are a number of rules which limit the exercise of federal judicial power in both trial courts and appellate courts. These rules reflect both constitutional and judge-made limitations on the exercise of judicial power. The three areas of justiciability tested most frequently in law school are ripeness, standing, and mootness. These are not necessarily separate, distinct areas of analysis. Be aware that some questions may call for a discussion of more than one of these doctrines.

a. Ripeness. [§50]

The main question in the area of ripeness is whether anyone has suffered actual or threatened harm by the application of a statute. If there is no one who has suffered an actual injury, or a specific threat of injury, the case will not be ripe for decision.

(1) The Supreme Court in *Poe v. Ullman,* **367 U.S. 497 (1961), [§51],** refused, on ripeness grounds, to hear a challenge to a Connecticut law which prohibited the use of contraceptives, as well as the giving of advice about contraceptives. In over seventy-five years of the law being on the books, only one prosecution (a test case eventually dismissed at the government's request) was brought under the statute. The Court reasoned that the mere abstract, generalized threat of enforcement of the law did not create a ripe controversy.

(2) In *United Public Workers v. Mitchell,* **330 U.S. 75 (1947), [§52],** again on ripeness grounds, the Court refused, to hear a challenge by federal civil service employees to the Hatch Act, which prohibited federal executive branch employees from participating in political campaigns. Since none of the employees (save one, whose case was accepted) had actually suffered any injury other than a subjective "chilling effect on their speech," the Court refused to hear the case, asserting that to do so would be tantamount to issuing an advisory opinion.

b. Standing. [§53]

Standing has to do with whether the proper party is seeking to raise an issue in federal court. For a plaintiff, the question is whether he or she is able to invoke the jurisdiction of a court to hear a case. For a defendant, who is already in court, as in a criminal case, the question is whether he or she can raise an issue as part of a defense (does a defendant in a criminal case have standing to object to the introduction of evidence that was allegedly illegally seized?).

(1) Constitutional Aspects of Standing. [§54]

There are two requirements of standing that must always be met to satisfy the "case or controversy" requirement of Article III.

(a) Injury-in-fact. [§55]

The would-be litigant must have suffered, or be imminently threatened with suffering, an injury-in-fact as a result of the defendant's actions. In constitutional cases (because of the fact that the government is the defendant), this means that a government agent or entity must be the cause of the actual or threatened injury.

(b) Traceability. [§56]

The injury-in-fact must be fairly traceable to the government action complained of. In other words, the court must be able to issue a decree which will directly redress the injury asserted by the plaintiff.

(2) Prudential Aspects of Standing. [§57]

In addition to the constitutional requirements for standing, there are also judge-made, "prudential" barriers to standing. These prudential barriers reflect institutional concerns such as docket control and judicial insistence on the parties having a personal stake in the outcome of the controversy. Two examples of judge-made prudential barriers to standing are the bar to a federal taxpayer challenging a spending measure by Congress, and the bar to third-party standing. As a general matter, a federal taxpayer will not have standing to challenge a spending measure by Congress. Too many lawsuits would result, and the absence of any particularized injury would detract from the vigor with which the issues would be presented to a court. Under third-party standing, a plaintiff asserts the rights of another person to acquire standing (a doctor-plaintiff may assert the abortion rights of patients in order to challenge the cessation of welfare payments for abortions). The problem with third-party standing is that if the right-holder is not suing to vindicate his or her own right, the issues may not be litigated as vigorously as if the right-holder were the plaintiff.

(3) Examples of Injuries in Fact. [§58]

The Court has held that it will recognize certain kinds of injuries for standing purposes, but that other asserted injuries will not qualify as meeting the case or controversy requirement of Article III. For example, a specific economic or aesthetic injury is usually sufficient to meet Article III requirements, whereas injury to some generalized interest (such as concern about how the federal government is functioning) will not suffice to confer standing.

(a) Injuries That Do Qualify Under Article III. [§59]

(i) Economic Injury. [§60]

An economic injury clearly meets the injury-in-fact requirement of Article III. A doctor has been able to assert lost payments as the injury resulting from a government decision to stop funding abortions for indigent women. *Singleton v. Wulff,* 428 U.S. 106 (1976).

(ii) Standing to Assert a Non-Economic Injury. [§61]

A non-economic injury may qualify to confer standing if the injury is specific to the plaintiff. If the plaintiff personally is adversely affected by a government action, the injury asserted may be to an aesthetic, environmental, religious, or other non- economic interest.

a) Standing to Assert Aesthetic or Environmental Injuries. [§62]

A specific claim that members of an environmental group use a certain recreational area, and that their use will be harmed by government action (by polluting rivers or despoiling forests), will qualify as an injury-in-fact. *Sierra Club v. Morton*, 405 U.S. 727 (1972).

b) Standing to Assert a Religious Injury. [§63]

An injury to a religious interest may qualify as an Article III injury-in-fact. In *School District of Abington v. Schempp*, 374 U.S. 203 (1963), the Court held that parents had standing to challenge Bible reading in their children's public school classrooms as a violation of the Establishment Clause of the First Amendment. The Court did require that the plaintiff be personally affected by the challenged practice.

(b) Injuries That Do Not Qualify Under Article III. [§64]

(i) General Citizen Standing. [§65]

A person will not have standing to challenge a government action solely because he or she is a citizen who is unhappy about how the government is functioning. The remedy for such a grievance is through the ballot box. The Court has said that the interest of a citizen in constitutional governance is too abstract an injury to confer standing. *Schlesinger v. Reservists Committee to Stop the War*, 418 U.S. 208 (1974); *Lujan v. Defenders of Wildlife*, 112 S.Ct. 2130 (1992).

(ii) Legislative Standing. [§65.1]

Individual Members of Congress do not have standing to challenge the constitutionality of an Act on the basis that it dilutes their legislative power. An abstract institutional injury is not sufficiently concrete to meet the requirement of an injury-in-fact.

In *Raines v. Byrd*, ___ S.Ct. ___ (1997), the Court ruled that six members of Congress did not have standing to challenge the constitutionality of the Line Item Veto Act. The Act gave the President the power to cancel specific spending and tax benefit measures of Bills after he signed them into law. The injury the members of Congress asserted was that the Act diluted their voting power, and they claimed that the Act was an unconstitutional expansion of Presidential power. The legislators did not assert a personal, particularized injury, but rather an institutional injury that affected all members of Congress equally. The Court distinguished this case from *Coleman v. Miller*, 307 U.S. 433 (1939), where standing was granted to state legislators claiming an institutional injury when the Lieutenant Governor cast a tie-breaking vote to ratify a proposed federal Constitutional Amendment. There, the votes had been overridden when they were sufficient to prevent ratification, but in this case, the legislators' votes were given full effect and they simply lost the vote.

(iii) Standing of Public Interest Organizations. [§66]

Public interest organizations will not have standing unless the organization itself or at least one of its members has suffered an injury.

In *Sierra Club v. Morton*, 405 U.S. 727 (1972), the Court denied standing to the Sierra Club when it tried to challenge the construction of a recreation area in a national forest. The Sierra Club had failed to assert that it or any of its members had suffered any specific injury by the proposed construction. It was not enough to assert that the organization had an interest in the environment and that the government action would adversely affect that interest.

(iv) Standing to Assert Stigmatic Injury to a Racial Group. [§67]

A court will not grant standing if plaintiffs assert a stigmatic injury suffered by all members of a racial group.

In *Allen v. Wright*, 468 U.S. 737 (1984), parents of black school children challenged federal tax exemptions for racially discriminatory private schools. The Court refused to recognize as an Article III injury-in-fact a claim of stigmatic injury or denigration suffered by all members of a racial group. Its rationale was that to recognize such an injury would create a cause of action on behalf of any member of the racial group throughout the country. This came too close to a grant of general citizen standing.

(v) There Is No Standing to Challenge a State Legislative Redistricting Plan When the Plaintiffs Do Not Live in the District. [§68]

Voters who do not live in a congressional district that is the primary focus of their racial gerrymandering claim do not have standing to challenge a statewide reapportionment scheme as being violative of the Equal Protection Clause.

In *U.S. v. Hays*, 115 S.Ct. 2431 (1995), the Court ruled that Hays and other plaintiffs lacked standing to challenge Louisiana's congressional redistricting plan because they did not live in the specific district which they claimed had been drawn along racial lines. The Court treated their claim as a generalized grievance against allegedly illegal governmental conduct which did not meet the Article III requirement of a specific injury-in-fact suffered by the plaintiffs.

(4) The Traceability Requirement. [§69]

To meet the Article III requirements, an injury-in-fact must be fairly traceable to the government action complained of. To that end, the injury-in-fact must be redressable by a decree of the Court. Be very careful of any fact pattern in which the entity causing the injury-in-fact is not a party to the lawsuit. In that scenario, a court cannot direct the injury-causer to do anything, so there is no traceability.

(a) In *Simon v. Eastern Kentucky Welfare Rights* Organization, 426 U.S. 26 (1976), [§70] the Court refused to find standing on behalf of persons who had been denied hospital services because of their indigency. The plaintiffs challenged an IRS ruling which continued to grant tax-exempt status to hospitals, despite their failure to treat indigents. The reason for the finding of no standing was that the entity actually causing the injury, the hospital, was not a party to the lawsuit, so the Court could not direct the hospital to treat indigents. In other words, regardless of the Court's decree, it was still speculative as to whether the hospital would change its behavior.

(b) In *Allen v. Wright*, 468 U.S. 1250 (1984), [§71] the Court again refused to find standing, this time, on behalf of parents of black children who challenged an IRS ruling which gave tax-exempt status to racially discriminatory private schools. Since the private schools were not parties to the lawsuit, an order of a court could not directly change the behavior of the entity causing the injury. The white private schools could still, if they chose, exclude black children, despite the loss of their tax-exempt status.

(c) In *Linda R.S. v. Richard D.*, 410 U.S. 614 (1973), [§72] the Court again found no traceability. In that case, a mother sued to challenge a state law which authorized the prosecution of husbands who failed to pay child support, but did not authorize prosecution of non-husband fathers who did not pay child support. The Court concluded that Linda's injury (no money for her child) was not traceable to the state's not prosecuting the child's father for non-payment of support. The idea was that, even if he were prosecuted, Richard could still decide not to give Linda any money. Even if the Court ordered the state to treat both classes of fathers the same, there was no guarantee that Linda's injury would be alleviated.

(5) Federal Taxpayer Standing. [§73]

First of all, be careful about whether a federal taxpayer is challenging a tax, or is challenging a spending measure. A federal taxpayer has standing to challenge an incorrect tax bill, or to attempt to recover taxes paid under protest. The usual law school discussion, however, focuses on whether a federal taxpayer has standing to challenge how Congress spends his or her money.

(a) Federal Taxpayer Standing to Challenge a Spending Measure. [§74]

The general rule is that federal taxpayers do not have standing to challenge expenditures of money by Congress. *Frothingham v. Mellon*, 262 U.S. 447 (1923). The reason for this rule is that the interest of any one federal taxpayer in how Congress spends money is too remote and speculative to qualify as the specific injury-in-fact required for standing.

(b) Federal Taxpayer Standing to Challenge a Spending Measure that Establishes Religion. [§75]

The Court has ruled that a federal taxpayer does have standing to challenge a congressional expenditure on the basis that it violates the Establishment Clause of the First Amendment. (In general, a government may not pass a law which has the purpose or effect of endorsing or establishing religion. See §919 for a full discussion of the Establishment Clause.)

In *Flast v. Cohen*, 392 U.S. 83 (1968), federal taxpayers challenged federal expenditures for parochial schools. The Court reasoned that the Establishment Clause is a specific limitation on the taxing and spending powers of Congress. Remember that for the *Flast* exception to apply, a plaintiff must assert three things: 1. Congress is acting; 2. under the spending power; 3. to establish religion. If a plaintiff does not establish all three elements, there will be no standing.

(i) The Court Has Refused to Extend *Flast* Beyond the Area of Congressional Exercise of the Spending Power. [§76]

A federal taxpayer will not have standing based on that status unless he or she is challenging an exercise of the spending power by Congress.

(ii) Federal Taxpayer Standing to Challenge an Exercise of the Property Power. [§77]

In *Valley Forge Christian College v. American United for Separation of Church and State*, 454 U.S. 464 (1982), taxpayers did not have standing to challenge an action by the Secretary of Health, Education, and Welfare ("HEW") in giving a $500,000 piece of federal property to a church college. The Court reasoned that the taxpayers failed the *Flast* test in two respects. First, there was no congressional action (the Secretary of HEW is an executive official). Second, this was not an exercise of the spending power, but rather of Congress' Article IV, §3, clause 2 power to dispose of federal property. In other words, the plaintiffs did not go three-for-three under *Flast*, so they did not have standing.

(c) State Taxpayers. [§78]

State taxpayers are treated the same as federal taxpayers in that they do not have standing in federal court to challenge expenditures of money by their state legislature. *Asarco v. Kadish*, 490 U.S. 605 (1989). Presumably, under *Flast*, a state taxpayer would have standing in federal court to challenge a state legislature's expenditure of money to establish religion.

(d) Municipal Taxpayers. [§79]

A municipal taxpayer, on the other hand, is treated differently from a state or federal taxpayer. In *Frothingham*, (see §74 above) the Court said that a municipal taxpayer's interest in the expenditure of his or her money by a municipal legislative body is direct and immediate, unlike the interests of a state or federal taxpayer. As a result, a municipal taxpayer does have standing in federal court to challenge a municipal expenditure.

(6) Third-Party Standing. [§80]

The general rule in federal court is that a person may not acquire standing by asserting the rights of a person not in court as a party to the lawsuit. The theory underlying this rule is that the party whose rights are endangered should be in court as the most effective advocate of those rights. The bar to third-party standing is only a prudential rule, with the following exceptions.

(a) Requirements For Individual Third-Party Standing. [§81]

If certain requirements are met, an individual plaintiff (as opposed to an association) may get standing by asserting the rights of another person. The requirements are:

- A relationship between the plaintiff and the right-holder;

- A genuine obstacle to the right-holder asserting his or her own rights; and

- The right-holder's rights will be diluted if not asserted by the plaintiff.

(i) In *Barrows v. Jackson*, 346 U.S. 249 (1953), [§82] a case involving a restrictive covenant entered into by white homeowners, the Court said that a white seller did have standing to assert the equal protection rights of unidentified potential future black buyers as a defense to a breach-of-contract suit by other white homeowners. The buyer-seller relationship was close enough to persuade the Court to grant standing to the white defendant. In *Barrows*, there was no black purchaser in court, so there was a genuine obstacle to the rightholder asserting his or her own rights. Also, if the white seller was not able to assert the rights of potential black purchasers, those rights would be diluted by the decree of a court enforcing the restrictive covenant.

(ii) In *Griswold v. Connecticut*, 381 U.S. 479 (1965), [§83] the Court recognized third-party standing on behalf of doctors who were convicted of violating a state criminal statute by giving information about contraceptives to married couples. The doctor-patient relationship qualified for third-party standing purposes. The married couples were not parties to the criminal prosecution, so there was a genuine obstacle to their asserting their own rights. In addition, the privacy rights of the married couples would be diluted if the doctor were unable to assert their rights.

NOTE: In a case like *Griswold*, the criminal defendant wants to assert the fundamental privacy rights of the married couple to persuade the Court to raise the level of scrutiny it will use in reviewing the case. (See §506, below). Put simply, the doctor has a much better chancer of prevailing if he or she can inject an important constitutional interest into the case.

(iii) In *Craig v. Boren*, 429 U.S. 190 (1976), [§84] sellers of beer were granted third-party standing to assert the equal protection rights of 18-20 year-old males who were unable to buy beer in a state where females could buy beer at the age of 18. The commercial relationship was enough to grant standing.

(b) Associational Standing to Represent Members. [§85]

An association may have standing to assert the rights of its members. Even if an association has not suffered any injury to itself (for example, a fine levied directly against the association in its corporate capacity), it may have standing to represent its members if certain requirements are met.

(i) The association can only represent members who have not filed suit on their own behalf. To do otherwise would allow for duplicative suits, and would be a waste of time, money, and judicial resources.

(ii) Any member who is to be represented must have suffered, or be imminently in danger of suffering, an injury-in-fact. **Remember that any time you see a standing question, someone must have an injury-in-fact to meet the Article III case-or- controversy requirement.**

(iii) Joinder of the individual members is not necessary to the disposition of the lawsuit. Generally, the members are necessary parties when they would be entitled to differing monetary damages (for e.g., Member A gets $10,000, Member B gets $30,000). The members are not necessary or indispensable parties when all the association seeks is a declaration that the law is invalid, plus an injunction against its application. The theory is that, with a declaration or injunction, all members benefit equally, and are not needed to provide any individualized proofs as to damages.

(iv) The interests of the members are germane to the purpose of the organization. A State Carpenter's Association would not be able to challenge a restrictive state abortion law on behalf of its female carpenter members. However, the same group could assert the rights of its members to challenge a state law which set certain requirements for licensing of carpenters.

(7) Associational Standing to Represent Itself. [§86]

An association may have standing to represents its own interests. An association (corporation, association, partnership) may have standing to vindicate an injury-in-fact suffered by the association itself. *Warth v. Seldin*, 422 U.S. 490 (1975). An association can be injured in two ways.

(a) The Government Acts Directly Against the Association. [§87]

For instance, a fine levied by the Environmental Protection Agency against a polluting corporation injures the corporation because it must be paid out of the corporate funds. This is clearly an injury-in-fact that is fairly traceable to government action.

(b) Government Action That Causes Members to Quit the Organization. [§88]

In *NAACP v. Alabama*, 377 U.S. 288 (1958), the NAACP challenged a state law which required the organization to turn its membership list over to the state. For our purposes assume that members started to drop out of the organization to avoid having their names disclosed to state officials. This adverse effect on the associational ties of its members would, in turn, hurt the NAACP through a reduction in contributions, dues, and volunteers. There would be a cognizable injury suffered by the NAACP that flows directly from the impact of the law on its members.

(8) Congressional Power to Create Standing. [§89]

Congress does have the power to confer standing on parties who meet the Article III injury-in-fact requirement, and who are within the zone of interests to be protected by the statute or constitutional provision in question. *Association of Data Processing v. Camp*, 397 U.S. 150 (1970). The "zone of interests" language is a term of art which applies only to congressional grants of standing. The interests protected by Congress are not only economic ones; aesthetic, recreational, conservational, or religious values may also be protected.

(a) In *Trafficante v. Metropolitan Life Insurance* Co., 409 U.S. 205 (1972), [§90] the Court granted standing to tenants of an apartment complex to challenge the racially discriminatory leasing practices of the owner of the complex. The plaintiffs sued under the Civil Rights Act of 1968, which gave "persons aggrieved" the right to sue in federal court. The Court recognized the plaintiffs' asserted injuries of lost social benefits of living in an integrated community, missed business and professional opportunities, and embarrassment from being stigmatized as residents of a racially exclusive housing complex.

(b) *United States v. SCRAP*, 412 U.S. 669 (1973), [§91] is one of the strangest cases in which the Court granted standing. SCRAP was a group of five law students who were interested in a clean environment. They sued under the federal Administrative Procedures Act (APA) to challenge a surcharge on railroad freight rates imposed by the Interstate Commerce Commission (ICC). According to SCRAP, its members used the outdoor recreational areas in the Washington metropolitan area for hiking, camping, and other outdoor activities. The increase in freight rates, they claimed, would increase the use of non-recyclable goods, requiring more trees to be cut in certain forests to provide the raw material for the non-recyclable goods. Then, some of the non-recyclable products might be thrown away in the forests SCRAP members visit, thus ruining the beauty of the forests. The Court said this argument was sufficient to meet the standing requirements of Article III and the APA. Keep in mind that the SCRAP case is an extreme example of a fairly traceable injury, and the case is hard to reconcile with other standing cases.

c. Mootness. [§92]

Under the mootness doctrine, an Article III case or controversy must exist throughout the entire litigational process. If the plaintiff's injury-in-fact ever goes away, the case will be dismissed as moot because there is nothing more the court can do for the plaintiff.

(1) Theory Underlying the Mootness Doctrine. [§93]

The idea here is that a federal court will exercise its jurisdiction only if it is able to provide relief to a litigant in a contested lawsuit. If a court cannot redress the injury of a litigant before the court, the court's decree is tantamount to an advisory opinion.

In *DeFunis v. Odegaard*, 416 U.S. 312 (1974), a white law student challenged the University of Washington's affirmation action admissions program as a violation of his equal protection rights. His asserted injury-in-fact was his failure to be admitted to law school. However, during his lawsuit, a state court ordered him admitted to law school. When his case got to the Supreme Court, he had registered for his final term of law school. Since his only asserted injury, failure to be admitted to law school, had been taken care of, the Court dismissed his case as moot. The idea is that there was nothing that the Court could do for him — he had, in fact, received the relief he requested.

> **STUDY TIP:** What if a plaintiff such as DeFunis had asserted another injury-in-fact, such as having to spend money to treat the depression he suffered from having failed to gain admission to law school? This injury-in-fact would not be rectified by his having been admitted to law school; thus the case would not be moot under these facts. The moral of the story is to be careful about the injury alleged and the relief requested. As they change, so may a court's decision as to the mootness of a case.

(2) Exceptions to the Mootness Doctrine. [§94]

There are three main exceptions to the mootness doctrine:

- **Capable of repetition, yet evading review.**

- **Voluntary cessation of illegal activity.**

- **Collateral consequences.**

(a) Capable of Repetition, Yet Evading Review. [§95]

Under this exception, a court will not declare a dispute moot if the controversy is capable of repetition, yet evading review, in relation to the plaintiff or a member of his or her certified class. These cases always involve controversies of short duration, such as abortion, elections, or age laws. The idea is that the injury-in-fact will always go away before the lawsuit winds its way through the court system.

(i) In *Roe v. Wade*, 410 U.S. 113 (1973), [§96] the Court ruled that Jane Roe's challenge to Texas abortion laws was not moot, even though she was no longer pregnant. The Court reasoned that if the fact of non-pregnancy moots a case out, challenges to restrictive abortion laws will never survive the appellate review process.

(ii) In *Moore v. Ogilvie*, 394 U.S. 814 (1969), [§97] the plaintiffs, who were candidates for presidential and vice-presidential electors, challenged a state statute requiring a certain number of signatures on petitions from throughout the state. By the time the case got to the Supreme Court, the election was over. The Court invoked the "capable of repetition" exception because it was likely that the controversy would recur, but would never be resolved before the contested election was over.

(iii) Assume that an 18-year-old college student wants to challenge a state law setting the minimum drinking age at 21. By the time this case can get through the appellate courts, the dispute would be moot as to the plaintiff (he or she would be old enough to buy alcohol), but would be capable of repetition in relation to the other members of the plaintiff's certified class.

(b) Voluntary Cessation of Illegal Activity. [§98]

Voluntary cessation of illegal activity by the alleged wrongdoer is usually insufficient to make a case moot.

In *U.S. v. W.T. Grant Co.*, 345 U.S. 629 (1953), the federal government filed an antitrust suit to break up interlocking directorates among several companies. Interlocking directorates exist when a number of the same people are on the boards of directors of different companies. The Justice Department frowns on such arrangements, and sought to stop this practice. After the U.S. government sued, the interlocking directors resigned, and then argued that the case was moot. The Court disagreed, refusing to grant these defendants the power to have their case dismissed, then rejoin other boards of directors. The Court did say, however, that the case would be moot if there were no reasonable expectations that the wrong would be repeated.

(c) Collateral Consequences. [§99]

A claim is not moot if some collateral consequences of court action will continue even though the main issue has been resolved.

A person may attack the constitutionality of his or her criminal conviction even if the entire sentence has been served, because the conviction may cause that person to be denied the right to vote, or to be subjected to a recidivist statute at some time in the future. *Sibron v. New York*, 392 U.S. 40 (1968).

6. ELEVENTH AMENDMENT. [§100]

The Eleventh Amendment limits the ability of federal courts to hear cases in which an individual sues a state. Eleventh Amendment analysis involves some of the most arcane rules in all of constitutional law. You should focus on what the Court says the Eleventh Amendment means, rather than on what the Eleventh Amendment actually says.

a. An Individual Cannot Sue a State in Federal Court. [§101]

In general, the Eleventh Amendment prohibits an individual (not a state or federal government) from suing a state in federal court. It does not matter whether the individual plaintiff is or is not a resident of the state he or she is suing. The Eleventh Amendment applies in either case.

b. How to get around the Eleventh Amendment bar to the exercise of federal court jurisdiction when an individual sues a state. [§102]

These rules were created because it would not be acceptable for a state to be able to violate an individual's federal rights and be totally immune from federal court supervision.

(1) Name the state officer as an individual, not as an officer of the state. For instance, if Tom Smith, the Attorney General of State A, has violated your federal rights, you should name Tom Smith as the Defendant in his individual capacity, not as Attorney General. The fiction here is that you are not suing the state, but just an individual named Tom;

(2) Allege that the state officer acted outside the scope of his authority by violating your rights. This "authority stripping" is needed to maintain the fiction that you are not suing a state. In other words, for purposes of the Eleventh Amendment, Tom is just an individual who abridged your rights; and

(3) Allege that the state officer violated your federal rights. If you are only able to argue that Tom violated your state rights, the Eleventh Amendment will bar the federal court from hearing your case. *Pennhurst State School and Hospital v. Halderman*, 465 U.S. 89 (1984).

c. Relief Available Against a State. [§103]

If you are able to jump through these hoops, you are now in federal court with a lawsuit against a state official. The next question is what relief is available once these requirements are met. The Court has given the following rules regarding the relief available when a plaintiff has successfully met the requirements for suing a state official in federal court.

(1) No Retroactive Money Damages. [§104]

A plaintiff cannot receive any retroactive money damages from the state. Recovery of past debts, for instance, is totally barred by the Eleventh Amendment. The theory here is that a state could be bankrupted if ordered by federal courts to pay retroactive money damages.

(2) Prospective Injunctive Relief Permissible. [§105]

Prospective injunctive relief is permissible to force a state official to comply with federal law in the future. Under this rule, it is also permissible for a federal court to order a state to pay, in the future, any money that is needed to comply with the injunctive order.

(a) In *Edelman v. Jordan*, 415 U.S. 651 (1974), [§106] a plaintiff sued a state official, arguing that welfare benefits were withheld in violation of federal regulations. The plaintiff requested retroactive money damages (the welfare payments not received in the past), as well as a prospective injunctive order compelling state officials to pay him the correct amount in the future. The Court denied the request for retroactive money damages, but granted the injunction, despite the fact that the state would have to pay more money in the future by way of increased welfare payments.

(b) In *Milliken v. Bradley*, **418 U.S. 717 (1977), [§107]** the Court upheld a lower court ruling which ordered the desegregation of Detroit public schools. The Detroit schools would have to spend $5.8 million to comply with the court's order. This future expenditure was permissible because it operated prospectively, giving the government a chance to plan for the expenditure.

(c) If a plaintiff is able to point to specific pieces of property (artifacts from a sunken Spanish galleon) which have been unconstitutionally taken into possession by a state official, a federal court may order the state official to turn those pieces of property over to the plaintiff. *Florida Dept. of State v. Treasure Salvors, Inc.*, 458 U.S. 670 (1982). [§108]

d. The Eleventh Amendment Only Applies in Federal Court. [§109]

The Eleventh Amendment does not apply in state court. *Nevada v. Hall*, 440 U.S. 410 (1979). The Eleventh Amendment only bars federal courts from hearing suits by an individual against a state; it does not apply to the exercise of judicial power by a state court. If an individual sues a state in state court, the state will assert sovereign immunity as its defense. *Mt. Healthy City School District v. Doyle*, 429 U.S. 274 (1977).

e. The Eleventh Amendment Only Protects States and Statewide Departments. [§110]

The Eleventh Amendment does not protect political subdivisions of a state (cities counties, school boards) from being sued for damages in federal court.

f. Congress May Abrogate a State's Eleventh Amendment Immunity By Acting Under Section 5 of the Fourteenth Amendment. [§111]

Congress may, by a plain and clear statement of its intent to do so, take away a state's Eleventh Amendment immunity. This means that a state may then be sued directly in federal court for retroactive money damages. Congress may take away a state's immunity by acting under §5 of the Fourteenth Amendment, *Fitzpatrick v. Bitzer*, 427 U.S. 445 (1976).

g. Congress May Not Abrogate a State's Eleventh Amendment Immunity By Acting Under the Commerce Clause. [§112]

Congress may not take away a state's Eleventh Amendment immunity by acting under the Interstate Commerce Clause or the Indian Commerce Clause.

Seminole Tribe of Florida v. Florida, 116 S.Ct. 1114 (1996), [§113]

The Court invalidated a provision of the federal Indian Gaming Regulatory Act (IGRA) which allowed Indian tribes to sue states in federal court to enforce the IGRA. **The Court ruled that section 5 of the Fourteenth Amendment is the only constitutional provision under which Congress may unilaterally abrogate a state's Eleventh Amendment immunity from suit in federal court.** In so ruling, the Court overruled *Pennsylvania v. Union Gas Co.*, 491 U.S. 1 (1989), in

OUTLINE

which the Court said that Congress could abrogate a state's Eleventh Amendment immunity by acting under the Commerce Clause.

h. A State May Waive Its Eleventh Amendment Immunity. [§114]

A state may, by making a plain and clear statement of its intent to do so, waive its Eleventh Amendment immunity in federal court. *Della Grotta v. Rhode Island*, 781 F.2d 343 (1st Cir. 1986).

i. The Eleventh Amendment Does Not Apply When the Federal Government Sues a State in Federal Court. [§115]

The Eleventh Amendment only applies when an individual sues a state in federal court; it does not bar the exercise of federal judicial power when the United States sues a state in federal court. *U.S. v. Texas, 143 U.S. 621* (1892).

j. An Individual May Sue a Public Official in Federal Court If the Official Will Pay the Damages Out of His or Her Personal Assets. [§116]

The Eleventh Amendment bars a plaintiff from seeking damages from the public treasury, but damages are a permissible remedy against individual public office-holders if the damages are to be paid out of their assets. *Scheuer v. Rhodes*, 416 U.S. 232 (1974).

k. The Eleventh Amendment Provides No Immunity to Entities Created Pursuant to the Compact Clause. [§117]

The Eleventh Amendment does not protect an entity created pursuant to the Compact Clause unless the states intended to confer immunity on that entity. (Under Article I, §10, clause 3, "No State shall, without the consent of Congress, . . . enter into any Agreement or Compact with another State. . . . ." This provision is intended to prevent agreements between states that will increase the political power of one or both states or diminish the power of the federal government). In *Hess v. Port Authority Trans-Hudson Corp.*, 115 S.Ct. 394 (1994), the Court held that two injured railway workers could sue the Port Authority railway in federal court. The Court reasoned that even though the Port Authority was created pursuant to a compact between New York and New Jersey, those states did not structure the railway so as to confer on it the Eleventh Amendment immunity of the states. The Court focused on the fact that the railway is financially independent, and any judgment against it would not be paid out of state funds.

7. ABSTENTION. [§118]

The abstention doctrine deals with the relationship between the federal and state court systems. An abstention issue arises when a federal court has jurisdiction to hear a case, because a federal question is present, but declines to do so out of respect for state courts. Abstention is an example of a judicially-imposed limitation on the exercise of federal judicial power. The idea here is that, except in extreme circumstances, a federal court should defer to a state court for the resolution of an issue which also falls within the state court's jurisdiction.

There are two kinds of abstention that you should know:

a. *Pullman* Abstention. [§119]

Pullman **abstention arises when 1) a lawsuit is filed in federal court, 2) the case involves issues both of federal and state law, and 3) the issue of state law is ambiguous, uncertain, or unsettled.** If it chooses, the federal court may abstain from hearing this case and allow the parties to seek a state-court clarification of the unclear question of state law. The state- court ruling on the state-law question may obviate the need for a return to federal court for a ruling on the federal constitutional issue. In other words, if the plaintiff wins in state court, based on the state law issue, there is no need to return to federal court. As a matter of fact, the federal court then would not be able to entertain the federal question because to do so would be to issue an advisory opinion.

In *Railroad Commission v. Pullman Co.*, 312 U.S. 496 (1941), railroads filed suit in federal court challenging an order of the Railroad Commission of Texas that all sleeping cars in Texas be under the control of a Pullman conductor, as opposed to a Pullman porter. The railroads argued that the order was not authorized by state law, and that it was unconstitutional. If the Commission order was not valid, the result would be that more positions would be available for Pullman porters than for Pullman conductors. At the time, Pullman conductors were white and Pullman porters were black. Pullman porters intervened in the case, claiming that the order violated their equal protection rights. The federal district court heard the case, and decided that the Commission order was not authorized by the laws of Texas. The Supreme Court reversed and remanded, on the theory that the federal district court should have abstained on the question of state law and allowed the Texas courts to decide the issue. The federal district court was to retain jurisdiction, but allow the parties to go to state court for clarification of the power of the Commission.

(1) Once in State Court, the Plaintiff May Litigate All Claims in State Court. [§120]

Under *Pullman* **abstention, the plaintiff who is sent to state court for a ruling on the state-law issue may decide to litigate the entire package (both state and federal claims) in state court.** The reason to do so would be to save the time and money that would be required to return to federal court after the state-court proceedings have run their course.

(2) Once in State Court, the Plaintiff Must Reserve the Right to Return to Federal Court to Litigate the Federal Issues in the Case. [§121]

A plaintiff who has been sent to state court to clear up a state-law issue has a right to return to federal court for a resolution of the federal constitutional question. However, once in state court, the plaintiff must specifically reserve, on the record, the right to return to federal district court to litigate his or her federal claims. *England v. Louisiana State Board of Medical Examiners*, 375 U.S. 411 (1964).

b. *Younger* Abstention. [§122]

Under *Younger v. Harris*, 401 U.S. 37 (1971), abstention, in its classic form, arises when a defendant in a pending state criminal proceeding files a lawsuit in federal court seeking to enjoin the pending state criminal proceeding. **The general rule is that a federal district court will not enjoin a pending state criminal proceeding unless the prosecution is brought for purposes of bad faith or harassment.**

(1) Theory Underlying *Younger* Abstention. [§123]

The federal district court will abstain in such a case to show respect for state courts, as well as to avoid the unworkable result of having to decide a huge number of requests for injunctions by state defendants who believe their federal rights have been violated. It would wreak havoc on both the federal and state court systems if federal district courts were routinely to interfere with ongoing state criminal proceedings. Another part of the justification for *Younger* abstention is that the state criminal defendant may assert his federal constitutional rights in the state courts. As long as the state criminal defendant has a forum in which to assert his or her constitutional arguments, there is no overriding need for a federal court to get involved.

(2) Exceptions to *Younger* Abstention. [§124]

A federal court may choose not to abstain, even if there is a pending state criminal proceeding, if there is serious danger to the rights of the state criminal defendant. For e.g.;

(a) Bad Faith. [§125]

A bad-faith prosecution is one which has no reasonable chance of success. *Allee v. Medrano*, 416 U.S. 802 (1974). A federal court may decide to enjoin such a state-court prosecution.

(b) Harassment. [§126]

A prosecution brought only to harass or retaliate against a person may be enjoined, despite the general rule of *Younger*.

In *Dombrowski v. Pfister*, 380 U.S. 479 (1965), a civil rights organization, and a number of its officers sued to enjoin enforcement of two Louisiana laws regulating the activities of subversive organizations. Under these state laws, it was a felony to participate in the formation or management, or to contribute to the support, of any subversive organization. The plaintiffs asserted that the state authorities were threatening prosecution simply to harass them, and that there was no reasonable chance of a valid conviction. The Court ruled that the plaintiffs were entitled to injunctive relief to prevent their prosecution under state laws that were so vague and overbroad as to chill their right to free speech.

(3) Reversal of Usual Order of Filing. [§127]

In the typical *Younger* case, the first lawsuit is the pending state criminal proceeding, and the second is the federal request for injunctive relief. Federal courts usually abstain in these circumstances because it would wreak havoc on state criminal justice systems for federal courts to routinely enjoin pending state criminal proceedings. However, *Younger* may apply even if the order of the lawsuit is reversed.

Hicks v. Miranda, 422 U.S. 332 (1975). The Court held that *Younger* abstention may apply when a state prosecution is begun shortly after a federal lawsuit is filed. The fact pattern under *Hicks* invloves a person who is specifically threatened with prosecution under a state criminal law and files a lawsuit in federal court to enjoin the threatened prosecution. Before anything of substance on the merits (swearing-in of witnesses, taking testimony) takes place in federal court, the state prosecutes. The state may then, under *Younger*, ask the federal court to abstain from hearing the federal lawsuit pending the outcome of the state criminal trial. The rule allows a state to pull the federal plaintiff out of federal court by filing criminal charges soon after the federal lawsuit is filed.

(4) *Younger* Abstention Has Been Applied to Some Non-Criminal Cases. [§128]

Younger abstention has been extended to some, but not all, state civil and administrative proceedings. **The general principle is that *Younger* will apply to any pending civil or administrative proceeding in which an important state interest is involved.** As a result, a federal court will abstain from hearing lawsuits in which the federal plaintiff has a state forum in which to assert his or her federal constitutional rights. The Court has ruled that federal courts should abstain, under *Younger*, when the following state proceedings are pending at the time of the filing of the federal lawsuit.

(a) The application of a state public nuisance statute to a theater that allegedly showed obscene movies. *Huffman v. Pursue Ltd.*, 420 U.S. 592 (1975). [§129]

(b) An action by a state to recover fraudulently obtained welfare funds. *Trainor v. Hernandez*, 431 U.S. 434 (1977). [§130]

(c) A state contempt proceeding for failure to pay civil judgments. *Juidice v. Vail*, 430 U.S. 327 (1977). [§131]

(d) State child abuse proceedings. *Moore v. Sims*, 442 U.S. 415 (1979). [§132]

(e) State bar disciplinary hearings. *Middlesex County Ethics Committee v. Garden State Bar Association*, 457 U.S. 423 (1982). [§133]

(f) State administrative agency hearing involving an alleged civil rights violation. *Ohio Civil Rights Commission v. Dayton Christian Schools*, 477 U.S. 619 (1986). [§134]

(g) State lien provisions in support of civil judgment. *Pennzoil Co. v. Texaco, Inc.*, 418 U.S. 1 (1987). [§135]

(5) *Younger* Abstention Applies to Declaratory Relief. [§136]

Younger abstention also applies when there is a pending state proceeding and the party goes to federal court to seek declaratory (as opposed to injunctive) relief. *Samuels v. Mackell*, 401 U.S. 66 (1971).

REVIEW PROBLEMS — JUDICIAL REVIEW AND LIMITATIONS ON JUDICIAL REVIEW

PROBLEM 1. The City of Id has a criminal trespass ordinance which prohibits anyone from going onto someone else's private property, for any reason. Members of a certain religious group are upset about the employment practices of a store in a privately-owned shopping mall. They would like to go into the mall to protest, but are afraid that they might be arrested. They want to file suit to challenge the ordinance. Should a court hear this lawsuit?

> **Answer:** No. This is not a ripe controversy. The generalized threat of enforcement of a law is not enough to create a ripe controversy under Article III. If the members of the religious group had been arrested or been specifically threatened with arrest, a ripe controversy would exist and a federal court would hear their lawsuit. See §50 for review.

PROBLEM 2. The State of Oz passed a law allowing 18, 19, and 20-year old women to buy beer, but prohibiting males from buying beer until they were 21 years of age. Paul Pubmeister is the owner of a local tavern whose business is hurt by not being able to sell beer to 18, 19, and 20 year-old males. Paul wants to challenge the Oz law on behalf of his 18, 19, and 20-year-old male customers. Does he have standing?

> **Answer:** Yes. Under third-party standing rules, a seller of a product has standing to assert the rights of his or her customers in order to obtain standing to sue in federal court. See §§80, 84 for review.

PROBLEM 3. Jane Jones is pregnant and wants an abortion. The State of Oz has a law which requires an adult woman to notify a doctor of her intent to have an abortion, and then to wait seventy-two hours before having the abortion. Jane files a class action lawsuit challenging the state law. Shortly after filing the lawsuit, Jane has a miscarriage. Should the court dismiss the case as moot?

> **Answer:** No. A case will not be declared moot if the controversy is capable of repetition, yet evading review, in relation to the plaintiff or a member of her certified class. Jane may become pregnant again, or, even if she may not, another woman in the class may become pregnant and want an abortion. See §§92, 95-96 for review.

PROBLEM 4. Joe Jones is the parent of a boy attending the City of Id School District. Joe and his son, Bob, are members of the Sikh religion. Due to his religious beliefs, Bob wears a small dagger, called a kirpan, to school. The school has a "no- weapons" policy, and suspends Bob when he refuses to take off his kirpan. Joe and Bob sue the City of Id School District in federal court. Does the Eleventh Amendment bar this suit?

> **Answer:** No. The Eleventh Amendment is irrelevant to these facts. The Eleventh Amendment is a bar to an individual suing a state in federal court. Political subdivisions of states, such as cities, counties, or school boards, are not protected by the Eleventh Amendment. See §110 for review.

VI. NATIONAL LEGISLATIVE POWER: SOURCES OF AND LIMITATIONS ON CONGRESSIONAL POWER

A. ANY ACT OF CONGRESS MUST BE GROUNDED IN A SPECIFIC PROVISION OF THE CONSTITUTION. [§137]

Congress does not have a general power to pass laws for the general welfare; congressional legislation must fall within a constitutional provision which provides specific justification for the law. To analyze the constitutional validity of any law passed by Congress, ask two questions: 1) what is the specific constitutional provision which justifies the law; and 2) what is the scope of that constitutional provision (what people or activities fall within the reach of that constitutional power). For example, if Congress passes a law making carjacking a federal crime, first ask what constitutional provision might provide a basis for that law. Arguably, carjacking is within the scope of Congress' power to regulate interstate commerce. Once the Commerce Clause is identified as the provision which arguably justifies the federal carjacking law, ask whether the specific activity regulated under the statute is in interstate commerce. For instance, may Congress, under its commerce power, criminalize the theft of a car that was built, sold, stolen, and recovered, all in the same state?

B. TWO NOTES ON GOVERNMENT POWER. [§138]

There are two principles that should be applied when analyzing the constitutionality of an exercise of government power.

1. GOVERNMENT POWER AS SWORD AND SHIELD. [§139]

Any provision of the Constitution which is a source of power for a particular government may also serve as a defense against action by another government or branch of government. For instance, the Tenth Amendment is a source of power for a state when it passes a law (such as a criminal law). However, when Congress passes a law which arguably abridges a state's powers, the state may assert the Tenth Amendment as a defense against that congressional action (such as the argument that a federal law requiring local police to investigate and report on purchasers of handguns violates a state's ability to decide how to deliver police services to its citizens).

2. TWO WAYS TO INVALIDATE A STATUTE. [§140]

When analyzing the constitutionality of congressional action, there are two ways for a court to invalidate the action: 1) Eliminate the power source, or; 2) Balance.

a. Eliminate the Constitutional Power Source Relied On By Congress To Justify The Law. [§141]

Under this approach, the plaintiff asserts that the legislature exceeded the scope of the constitutional provision on which it relied to pass a law. For example, the Court has ruled that Congress exceeded its commerce power when it passed a federal criminal statute prohibiting the possession of a firearm in or within 1,000 feet of a school.

b. Balance. [§142]

Under the balancing approach, the law is presumptively within a constitutional power source, but it is invalid if it contravenes some other provision of the Constitution. For example, the Court ruled that the commerce power was broad enough to allow Congress to regulate the wages and hours of state employees, but that federally-mandated wage and hour laws unduly abridged a state's Tenth Amendment power to decide how to deliver police services to its citizens.

C. SPECIFIC CONGRESSIONAL POWERS [§143]

Whenever Congress passes a law, you must be able to identify the specific provision in the Constitution which justifies that law.

The powers of Congress are dispersed throughout the Constitution, but the main list, for law school purposes, is in Article I, §8. Here is a list of the main congressional powers listed in that section:

1. Power to tax;
2. Power to spend for the general welfare;
3. Power to regulate commerce among the several states, with foreign nations, and with the Indian Tribes;
4. Power to regulate immigration and naturalization;
5. Power to pass uniform laws dealing with bankruptcy;
6. Power to coin money;
7. Power to establish a postal service;
8. Power to set up a system of copyrights;
9. Power to set up federal courts (this power is also based in Article III, §1);
10. Power to declare war;
11. Power to raise and maintain armies;
12. Power to regulate and dispose of federal property;
13. Power to acquire private property for a public use, as long as just compensation is paid.
14. Power to pass regulations for the District of Columbia.

> **STUDY TIP:** Be careful about this last power. **Congress has no enumerated power to regulate for the general welfare of the country as a whole (it has no general police power), but it does have a specific power to pass police power regulations for the District of Columbia.** If Congress wants to regulate for the general welfare of the entire country, it usually does so under the Commerce Power.

1. NECESSARY AND PROPER CLAUSE. [§144]

Under Article I, §8, Clause 18, Congress has the power to pass laws to enable itself or any branch or officer of the federal government to carry out any constitutional power. Congress may, as a result, legislate for the executive and judicial branches, as well as for itself.

a. Must Be Used With Another Constitutional Provision. [§145]

The Necessary and Proper Clause cannot be used by itself as a source of power. It must be coupled with some other constitutional provision.

(1) When Congress passes laws regulating the conditions under which aliens may become citizens, it is acting pursuant to the Necessary and Proper Clause and its Article I power to establish a uniform rule of naturalization.

(2) When Congress passes a law making it a crime to threaten the President's life, the law is based on the Necessary and Proper Clause and Article II (which establishes the office of the Presidency).

(3) When Congress passes a law setting up a system of federal magistrates, the law is based on the Necessary and Proper Clause and Article III (which establishes the federal judiciary).

b. Congress May Choose Any Reasonable Means. [§146]

The Supreme Court has interpreted the Necessary and Proper Clause to mean that Congress may choose whatever means it deems convenient to carry out some power of government. *McCulloch v. Maryland*, 17 U.S. 316 (1819). Thus, "necessary" does not require that the only, or even least drastic, means to achieve a congressional goal be used.

2. COMMERCE POWER. [§147]

Under Article I, §8, Clause 3, Congress has the power "to regulate Commerce with foreign Nations, and among the several States, and with the Indian Tribes." Law school courses focus on Congress' ability to regulate commerce among the several states.

a. Two Main Issues That Arise in the Commerce Clause Area. [§148]

(1) What Is the Scope Or Reach Of The Commerce Power? [§149]

What people or activities fall within the definition of "interstate commerce," and are thus regulable by Congress under that power? If a person or activity is not in interstate commerce, Congress may not regulate that person or activity under its Commerce Clause power.

(2) Does A Congressional Act Unduly Abridge States' Rights? [§150]

Even if the regulated person or activity is in interstate commerce, Congress may not regulate so as to contravene essential attributes of state sovereignty. (See §166 for a discussion of attributes of state sovereignty)

(These issues are specific examples of the "Two Ways To Invalidate A Statute," referred to above at Part V, A., 2.)

b. Scope of the Commerce Power. [§151]

Today, most persons and activities are within the reach of the commerce power of Congress. Thus, it is extremely difficult to invalidate a federal Commerce Clause law on the basis that the law regulates someone or something that is outside the scope of interstate commerce. Prior to 1937, the Court did rule that certain activities were not in interstate commerce, and as a result could not be reached by Congress under its commerce power. From 1937 to 1995, virtually everything was within the scope of the commerce power and thus regulable by Congress. In 1995, the Court once again ruled that the Constitution does place limits on the ability of Congress to reach local activities under the Commerce Clause.

(1) Pre-1937 Examples of Local Activities That Were Not Within the Commerce Power. [§152]

(a) Manufacturing. [§153]

The Court held that Congress' Commerce Power was not broad enough to reach the manufacture of refined sugar within a state. Thus, the Sherman Antitrust Act could not be used to break up a 98% monopoly of sugar refineries. *U.S. v. E.C. Knight Co.* , 156 U.S. 1 (1895).

(b) Child Labor. [§154]

The Court held that the Congress could not impose standards for the employment of children within the various states. Again, the idea was that production of goods, even by children, is a purely local matter, the regulation of which is solely reserved to the states under the Tenth Amendment. *Hammer v. Dagenhart*, 247 U.S. 251 (1918).

(c) Wage and Hour Restrictions. [§155]

The Court held that Congress could not require certain bituminous coal producers to comply with federal minimum-wage and maximum-hour requirements. The mining of coal was a purely local activity that fell outside the reach of the Commerce Power. *Carter v. Carter Coal Co.*, 298 U.S. 238 (1936).

(2) Post-1937 Expansion of the Commerce Power: The Switch in Time That Saved Nine? [§156]

Up through 1936, the Supreme Court consistently invalidated congressional legislation designed to help pull the country out of the Depression. President Roosevelt, frustrated by the Court's rulings, proposed his famous Court Packing Plan in February 1937. Under this plan, the President would be given authority by Congress to appoint one new Justice for each Justice who was 70 years old, and had served as a judge for at least ten years. The Plan would have set the maximum member of Justices at fifteen, a number that would have been reached because there were six Justices over the age of 70 at the time of the proposal by President Roosevelt. Shortly after the proposed Court Packing Plan, the Court began to use a broader Commerce Clause analysis which gave much greater power to Congress to regulate activities or people within the states.

(3) Judicial Justifications For an Expanded Commerce Power. [§157]

(a) Close and Substantial Effect on Commerce. [§158]

Congress can, under the Commerce Power, reach intrastate activities if those activities have a close and substantial effect on interstate commerce. Thus, Congress could restrict the ability of a steel company to discharge employees because of union activity. The Commerce Clause was held to be a sufficient basis for the National Labor Relations Act which Congress passed to deal with labor-management issues. *NLRB v. Jones & Laughlin Steel Corp.*, 301 U.S. 1 (1937).

(b) Aggregation Theory. [§159]

Congress can, under the Commerce Power, reach an intrastate activity which, by itself, has a minimal impact on interstate commerce, if that activity, taken together with all other examples of that activity, has a substantial impact on interstate commerce. In *Wickard v. Filburn*, 317 U.S. 111 (1942), the Court upheld, as applied to a small farmer, a federal law limiting the amount of wheat that could be grown by one person. Even though Filburn's activity, by itself, had a negligible impact on commerce, Congress could regulate him because, in the aggregate, Filburn's activity, together with that of other farmers across the country, had a substantial impact on interstate commerce.

(c) Congressional Finding of Effect on Commerce. [§160]

The Court will defer to a congressional finding that a regulated activity or person affects interstate commerce if there is any rational basis for such a finding. If Congress meets this de minimis standard, the only remaining question for the Court is whether the means chosen is rationally related to achieving the legitimate congressional goal. *Hodel v. Virginia Surface Mining and Reclamation Association*, 452 U.S. 264 (1981).

(4) Examples of the Modern Scope of the Commerce Power. [§161]

(a) Crime. [§162]

National Organization for Women (NOW) v. Scheidler, 114 S.Ct. 798 (1994). NOW asserted that a coalition of anti-abortion groups called the Pro-Life Action Network (PLAN) conspired to shut down abortion clinics through a pattern of racketeering activity, in violation of the Racketeer Influenced and Corrupt Organizations (RICO) chapter of the Organized Crime Control Act of 1970. The lower court dismissed the action on the basis that RICO required that the racketeer have an economic or profit motive. The Court ruled that RICO does not require proof that a racketeering enterprise be motivated by an economic purpose. As a result, abortion clinics need not show any economic motive to assert a claim under RICO.

(b) Civil Rights. [§163]

The Court upheld the ability of Congress to pass Title II of the Civil Rights Act of 1964 which forbade discrimination by race or color in hotels, motels, or restaurants that are in interstate commerce. The Court upheld the application of Title II to Ollie's Barbecue, a small restaurant in Birmingham, Alabama, on the theory that the discrimination by Ollie's Barbecue was representative of many other discriminations across the country, and was therefore within the reach of Congress' Commerce Power. *Katzenbach v. McClung*, 379 U.S. 294 (1964).

(5) The Commerce Power Does Not Allow Congress to Regulate Purely Local Activities. [§164]

Congress may not use the Commerce Clause as a justification to criminalize local activity when that activity does not, even when aggregated with similar activity across the country, have a substantial effect on interstate commerce. In *U.S. v. Lopez*, 115 S.Ct. 1624 (1995), the Court invalidated a federal criminal law that prohibited the possession of a firearm within 1,000 feet of a school. The Court, 5-4, reasoned that gun possession in a school zone is not an economic activity that, even when considered along with similar activity nationwide, has a substantial impact on interstate commerce. In addition, the Court ruled the federal law invalid because it did not provide for any case-by-case determination that a particular act of gun possession had a direct relationship with interstate commerce.

c. COMMERCE POWER AND FEDERALISM. [§165]

When Congress, acting under its Commerce Power, passes a law which interferes with some attribute of state sovereignty, a state may assert the Tenth Amendment as a defense against that congressional action.

(1) Tenth Amendment. [§166]

Under the Tenth Amendment, "[t]he powers not delegated to the United States by the Constitution, nor prohibited by it to the States, are reserved to the States respectively, or to the people." **The Court has interpreted the Tenth Amendment to mean that there are certain aspects of sovereignty that a state must have to function as a state and to occupy its proper place in a federal system.** Judicial interpretation of the Tenth Amendment has changed over time, but today the Court focuses on whether a federal law impairs a state's ability to structure itself (determine which forms and procedures to use) or to provide services to its citizens (police, fire, schools). The Tenth Amendment serves as a source of power for the states (also referred to as a state's police power), as well as a defense asserted by a state against congressional action (a federal law impairs the ability of a state to provide adequate police services).

(2) Major Cases in the Development of the Commerce Power and the Tenth Amendment. [§167]

In a case where Congress regulates under the Commerce Clause, be very careful about who is regulated. Is Congress regulating just states, or is it regulating both states and private entities (such as a minimum-wage law that applies to all employers)? If Congress is regulating both states and private entities, the only protection states have from congressional impingement on states' rights is their participation in the national political process. The Court defers to congressional decisions as reflecting the will of the States. If Congress regulates just states, the Court will determine if the federal law unduly interferes with an essential attribute of state sovereignty, such as the delivery of police services.

(a) *Maryland v. Wirtz*, 392 U.S. 183 (1968). [§168]

The Court upheld the application of the Fair Labor Standards Act minimum-wage and maximum-hour provisions to state schools and hospitals. The Court reasoned that the law did not contravene the Tenth Amendment because states were simply held to the same standards as private employers.

(b) *National League of Cities v. Usery*, 426 U.S. 833 (1976). [§169]

The Court, by a 5-4 vote, overruled *Maryland v. Wirtz*. The Court ruled that, while the general subject matter of wages and hours is within the scope of the Commerce Power, Congress may not regulate the wages and hours set by a state as an employer because the federal law operated to directly displace the States' freedom to structure integral operations in areas of traditional governmental functions. The Court reasoned that the added obligations of the federal wage and hour provisions deprived a state of the power to deliver essential police services to its citizens.

(c) *Garcia v. San Antonio Metropolitan Transit* Authority, 469 U.S. 528 (1985). [§170]

The Court overruled *National League of Cities v. Usery*, and adopted a new Commerce Clause analysis for cases in which Congress regulated both private and governmental actors. The Court said that it would not assert the Tenth Amendment on behalf of the states as a defense against congressional action. In other words, the Court rejected the balancing approach of earlier cases. In its place the Court said that states were protected by their participation in the national political process. If a state has Senators and Representatives who participate in the national political process, the Court will presume that the state's interests are protected against undue congressional interference. If the legislative process works properly, the Court will not involve itself in changing the result of any given congressional vote. Under *Garcia*, the Court is extremely deferential to any congressional action which regulates both states and private entities. *Garcia* is the current analysis for cases in which Congress, acting within the scope of the commerce power, regulates both private and governmental actors.

(d) *New York v. U.S.*, 112 S.Ct. 2408 (1992). [§171]

The Court invalidated part of a congressional Commerce Clause law which required certain states to take title to all low-level radioactive waste generated in the state, take possession of the waste, and be liable in damages suffered by the owner or generator of the waste. The Court, by a 6-3 vote, distinguished this case from *Wirtz, National League of Cities*, and *Garcia* on the basis that those cases involved generally applicable laws (both states and private entities were regulated by the laws in those cases), whereas this law regulated only state governments. The Court said that the federal law commandeered state legislative processes by directly forcing them to enact and enforce a federal regulatory program. The Court said that the law overstepped the boundary between federal and state authority, regardless of whether one concludes that the law is outside the scope of the Commerce Power, or infringes on some aspect of state sovereignty. In other words, the Court refused to say which method of analysis it was using: eliminating the Commerce Clause as the constitutional provision justifying the law; or asserting that the Tenth Amendment right of the state to set its legislative agenda had been unduly abridged by the federal law.

(e) *Printz v. U.S.*, ___ S.Ct. ___ (1997). [§171.1]

The Court, by a 5-4 vote, invalidated a provision of the Brady Handgun Violence Prevention Act (the Act) that required the chief law enforcement officer of each local jurisdiction in the country to conduct background checks on prospective handgun buyers and to perform other ministerial tasks related to the purchase of handguns. The Court ruled that, similar to *New York v. U.S.*, (previous case), Congress' commandeering of state executive officers violated the system of dual sovereignty mandated by the structure of the Constitution. Compelling state officers to execute federal laws, especially without the states' consent, violates longstanding, constitutional practice and contravenes the Court's prior holdings, which make clear that Congress may not compel states to enact or administer a federal regulatory program. The Act also contravenes principles of separation-of-powers in that it transfers the President's power to execute federal laws to local law-enforcement officers throughout the country.

(3) Present State of the Law When Congress Regulates Under the Commerce Power. [§172]

If you see a federal law based on the Commerce Clause, determine who is regulated. If both private and governmental actors are subject to the law, *Garcia* applies, and the only protection a state receives is from its participation in the national legislative process. If only a state is regulated, and Congress is effectively commandeering a state legislature or a state executive officer, the federal law will be invalid because Congress cannot force state officials to perform federal functions. This kind of law violates the principle of "dual sovereignty," under which states must be free to structure themselves and their essential activities in accordance with the wishes of the state electorate.

3. TAXING POWER. [§173]

Article I, Section 8 gives Congress the power to lay and collect taxes, imposts, and excises, but requires that all duties, imposts, and excises be uniform throughout the United States. This uniformity limit pertains to geographical uniformity, requiring uniform application (no discrimination) among the several states. The uniformity requirement is not violated if a tax is not uniform in relation to individual persons.

a. TWO WAYS A TAX CAN BE VALID. [§174]

A taxing measure passed by Congress can be valid in one of two ways: as a revenue-raising measure, or as a means to achieve a valid regulatory goal of Congress.

(1) Tax as Revenue-Raiser. [§175]

As long as the purpose of a taxing measure is to raise revenue, it will be upheld, even if the amount of the tax is oppressive or even destructive. *Bailey v. Drexel Furniture Co.*, 259 U.S. 20 (1922).

(2) Tax as a Means to Achieve a Valid Regulatory Goal of Congress. [§176]

A taxing measure will also be valid if it is a means to achieve a valid regulatory goal of Congress. If Congress can regulate something under its commerce power, it may tax that activity as a means to achieve its permissible regulatory purpose. The theory is that if Congress may regulate or even prohibit an activity under its commerce power, it certainly may employ the less intrusive means of taxing that activity. Because of the broad scope of the modern commerce power (See §, above), it is not surprising that, since the late 1930's, the Court has upheld every federal tax attacked as a regulation.

b. CONSTITUTIONAL LIMITATIONS ON THE TAXING POWER. [§177]

Even though virtually every tax would be upheld today, you should be aware that a federal tax measure may be overturned if it contravenes other constitutional protections.

(1) Fifth Amendment Privilege Against Self-Incrimination. [§178]

A federal tax may be invalid if, as one of its ancillary reporting provisions, it requires a taxpayer to file a return which reveals illegal sources of income, thereby forcing the taxpayer to incriminate himself or herself in violation of the privilege against self-incrimination. *Marchetti v. U.S.*, 390 U.S. 39 (1968).

(2) Tenth Amendment. [§179]

Since the 1930's, the Court has not invalidated a federal tax solely because of its impact on the operations of state government. However, two cases, one of which came down shortly after the Commerce Clause case of *National League of Cities v. Usery*, 426 U.S. 833 (1976), (see §169) and the other of which came down shortly after the Commerce Clause case of *Garcia v. San Antonio Metropolitan Transit Authority*, 469 U.S. 528 (1985), (see §170), are worth noting for the analysis used by some members of the Court.

In *Massachusetts v. U.S.*, 435 U.S. 444 (1978), the Court upheld a federal registration tax on all civil aircraft, including police aircraft, used by the State of Massachusetts. Justice Brennan, writing for four members of the Court, voted to uphold the tax, but said that two issues raised by a tax imposed on an instrumentality of a state are whether the tax unduly impairs a state's ability to deliver traditional governmental services, and whether the sovereignty of the state-regulatee is protected by the state's participation in the national political process. The crux of the second issue is whether the Senators and Representatives of the allegedly aggrieved state had an opportunity, as part of the national legislative process, to protect the interests of the state through lobbying and voting.

In *South Carolina v. Baker*, 485 U.S. 505 (1988), the Court upheld a federal law which removed the federal income tax exemption for interest earned on certain state and local bonds, unless the bonds were registered in the owner's name. South Carolina had argued that the federal law was invalid because it, in effect, commandeered the state legislative process by forcing states to pass laws authorizing a certain form of bond registration. Relying on *Garcia* (See §170), the Court upheld the law on the basis that South Carolina participated in the national political process and thus had no Tenth Amendment challenge to the federal law.

4. SPENDING POWER. [§180]

Under the Spending Power, Congress has the power to spend "for the general welfare." Remember that Congress does not have any explicit constitutional power to **regulate** for the general welfare (even though it may do so under the Commerce Power). In other words, Congress has no general police power similar to that of the states. Remember that Congress does have a constitutionally-based police power over the District of Columbia. **The issue of what is "for the general welfare" belongs to Congress, and the Court will uphold a spending measure if there is any rational basis to support Congress' conclusion that the law will advance the general welfare.**

a. REGULATION THROUGH THE SPENDING POWER. [§181]

When Congress imposes conditions on the receipt of federal money, the Court will uphold the spending measure so long as the recipient is free to reject the federal money and exercise his or her rights (in the case of an individual) or powers (in the case of the state). There are three issues to look for when analyzing a congressional spending measure to see if it is constitutional:

(1) Is the Law Voluntary? [§182]

If the law leaves the recipient with a theoretical choice to accept or reject the federal "strings" accompanying the grant, the law will be upheld. The last time the Court invalidated a spending measure on the basis that it was coercive rather than voluntary was in 1936. In *United States v. Butler*, 297 U.S. 1 (1936), the Court struck down a federal law under which the government contracted with farmers to limit the number of acres of specified crops they planted. The Court ruled that the regulation was not voluntary because, due to the Depression, the farmers had no choice except to agree to the terms offered by the government.

(2) Is the Condition on the Receipt of Money Related to the General Purpose of the Federal Grant? [§183]

Although the Court has never invalidated a law on the basis that a condition on the receipt of federal funds was unrelated to the general purpose of the federal expenditure, it has raised the possibility that conditions on federal grants may be invalid if unrelated to the federal purpose in passing the spending measure. *South Dakota v. Dole*, 483 U.S. 203 (1987). For example, this issue would arise if Congress conditioned the receipt of federal highway funds on a state's willingness to pass a restrictive abortion law.

(3) Are There Any Other Constitutional Provisions Which Would Limit Congress' Ability to Impose a Condition on the Receipt of Money? [§184]

Other provisions of the Constitution may serve as possible limitations on the Spending Power.

(a) Tenth Amendment. [§185]

Since the *Butler* case in 1936 (see §182), the Court has not invalidated any spending measure on the basis that it violates the Tenth Amendment rights of states.

(b) Individual Rights. [§186]

Congress may not spend money in a way that violates the constitutional rights of individuals.

(i) Establishment Clause. [§187]

Congress may not spend money so as to establish religion in contravention of the First Amendment. (See §919, below).

(ii) Equal Protection. [§188]

Congress may not spend in a way that violates the equal protection principle of the Due Process Clause of the Fifth Amendment. In *Califano v. Goldfarb*, 430 U.S. 199 (1977), the Court struck down a provision of the Social Security Act which granted benefits to widows but not widowers, thus discriminating on the basis of gender.

(iii) Other Constitutional Rights. [§189]

Congress may not grant or withhold federal funds on any conditions it chooses. The conditions themselves must be constitutionally valid. For example, Congress could not validly condition housing assistance money to states on the adoption of a state policy restricting public housing solely to white people, or to Christians, or to married couples. The condition itself would violate individual rights to equal protection, religion, and privacy.

5. WAR POWER. [§190]

Under Article I, Section 8 of the Constitution, Congress has the power to declare war, raise armies and navies, and provide for the national defense. When used together with the Necessary and Proper Clause, Congress may exercise this power in peacetime as well as in wartime. Not only may Congress declare war, it may also prepare for future wars, wage war once it has begun, and deal with the social and economic consequences of past wars.

Woods v. Cloyd W. Miller Co., 333 U.S. 138 (1948). The Court upheld the continuation of federal rent control after the end of World War II. The Court said that the war power does not necessarily end with the cessation of hostilities; Congress must be able to remedy conditions created by the mobilization of persons and materials for war. As long as the effects of war continue to be felt in society and are reasonably traceable to the war, Congress may use the war power to alleviate problems which flowed from the hostilities.

6. FOREIGN AFFAIRS POWERS. [§191]

Congress and the President have very broad powers in the area of foreign affairs. As an element of its intrinsic sovereignty, the United States has the power to deal with foreign nations, even if the congressional or presidential action is not specifically authorized by a provision of the Constitution.

a. CONGRESS MAY DELEGATE TO THE PRESIDENT THE POWER TO ACT IN FOREIGN AFFAIRS. [§192]

As part of the government's power to deal in foreign affairs, Congress may vest discretion in the President to implement congressional policy on foreign affairs. Such a delegation need not be based in a specific constitutional provision; it is justified under Congress' intrinsic powers to deal in foreign affairs.

U.S. v. Curtiss-Wright Export Corp. 299 U.S. 304 (1936). The Court upheld the power of Congress to pass a Joint Resolution authorizing the President to place an embargo on the sale of arms to countries involved in armed conflict in South America. The President issued a proclamation imposing such an embargo. The Court rejected the argument that the Joint Resolution was an unconstitutional delegation of power to the President, emphasizing that the federal government's powers to deal in foreign affairs do not depend on specific affirmative grants from the constitution; they are necessary elements of a country's sovereignty.

b. TREATIES AND EXECUTIVE AGREEMENTS. [§193]

(1) Treaties. [§194]

Under Article II, Section 2, Clause 2, the President has the power to enter into treaties with other countries. A treaty must be ratified by two-thirds of the Senate. There are two kinds of treaties: self-executing, and non-self-executing. Self- executing treaties do not need implementing legislation; they contain all the details of the agreement between the countries and have the force of law as soon as they are ratified by the Senate. Non-self-executing treaties need to be implemented by legislation passed by Congress. They do not have the force of law until the implementing legislation is passed.

(2) Executive Agreements. [§195]

An executive agreement is an agreement between the President and the chief executive of another country. Senate ratification of executive agreements is unnecessary. Executive agreements are not mentioned in the Constitution, but have become an accepted practice, reflecting the President's intrinsic powers in the area of foreign affairs (irrespective of any enumerated powers, the President, as the head of the Executive branch of the federal government, has the power to deal in foreign affairs).

c. RELATIONSHIPS AMONG TREATIES, EXECUTIVE AGREEMENTS, FEDERAL STATUTES, AND STATE LAWS. [§196]

Sum & Substance QUICK REVIEW of Constitutional Law

(1) Under the Supremacy Clause of Article VI, Treaties and Executive Agreements Always Take Precedence Over Conflicting State Laws. [§197]

An individual state cannot have the power to contravene a federal enactment in the area of foreign affairs.

(2) Operative Treaties Are on a Parity With Federal Statutes. [§198]

An operative treaty is a self-executing treaty (no legislation required), or a non-self-executing treaty plus its implementing legislation. **If there is a conflict between an operative treaty and a federal statute, the most recent enactment wins.** The result is that a treaty may supersede a prior federal law, or a federal law may supersede a prior treaty.

(3) An Operative Treaty or a Federal Statute Take Precedence Over a Conflicting Executive Agreement. [§199]

Treaties and statutes are enacted by specific constitutional procedures, requiring the participation of Congress and the President. These enactments trump an executive agreement entered into by the President with no congressional participation.

(4) A Treaty May be a Source of Legislative Power. [§200]

The ability of Congress to pass a law to implement a treaty constitutes an independent source of congressional power, over and above any enumerated powers the Constitution gives to Congress. The Court has treated Congress' power to pass laws to implement treaties as necessary and proper to the effectuation of the President's treaty power.

Missouri v. Holland, 252 U.S. 416 (1920). The Court upheld the federal Migratory Bird Treaty Act, implementing a treaty between the United States and Canada which regulated the taking of migratory birds. The Court ruled that a treaty may confer on Congress the power to legislate in an area over which it otherwise has no power; Congress may pass legislation necessary and proper for the implementation of a treaty. The Court also ruled that the Tenth Amendment is not a limitation on the treaty power of Congress.

(5) A Treaty or Executive Agreement Cannot Violate the Constitutional Rights of Individuals. [§201]

The Constitution is the supreme law of the land, and its protection of individual rights cannot be contravened by a treaty or executive agreement.

Reid v. Covert, 354 U.S. 1 (1957). The Court ruled that court-martial jurisdiction over civilian dependents of American soldiers abroad cannot be justified by an international executive agreement giving the armed forces jurisdiction to try such civilians for crimes. A treaty or executive agreement cannot authorize the violation of constitutional rights, such as the rights to an indictment and trial by jury, guaranteed by Article III and the Fifth Amendment.

7. PROPERTY POWER. [§202]

Under Article IV, Section 3, Clause 2, Congress has the power to dispose of and make all necessary rules and regulations respecting any property belonging to the United States. Pursuant to this provision, Congress may exercise almost unlimited power over federally owned lands and other property, including the power to control the occupancy and use of such lands, impose restrictions against trespass or injury to the land, and forbid exploitation of the natural resources of the land. Congress also has power to sell, lease, give away, or otherwise dispose of surplus government property upon whatever terms and conditions it chooses to impose.

a. CONGRESS MAY REGULATE WILD ANIMALS ON FEDERAL PROPERTY. [§203]

Congress may regulate wild animals on federal land, and can, under its Necessary and Proper Power, regulate them if they wander off federal land.

Kleppe v. New Mexico 426 U.S. 529 (1976). The Court upheld a federal statute which prohibited the shooting or capture of wild horses roaming free on federal lands located within the boundaries of one state. Any conflicting state statutes (permitting destruction of such animals to protect private ranchers) are invalid under the Supremacy Clause.

b. CONGRESS HAS THE POWER TO PASS LAWS TO GOVERN THE TERRITORIES OF THE UNITED STATES. [§204]

The Property Power provides the basis for Congress to govern territories of the United States, such as Guam, American Samoa, or the Virgin Islands. *Hooven & Allison Co. v. Evatt*, 324 U.S. 652 (1945).

8. POWER TO REGULATE IMMIGRATION AND NATURALIZATION. [§205]

Article I, Section 8, Clause 4 gives Congress the power to establish a uniform, national rule of naturalization. This is an exclusive power of Congress, and one that can be exercised on whatever terms Congress sets. Under this power, Congress may determine the process by which a person gains or loses citizenship, and the criteria under which those decisions are made. Congress also has a plenary, exclusive power to regulate immigration, including the power to determine the status and conditions of aliens in the country (such as the criteria under which aliens may enter and remain in the country). Congress also has the power to set the terms and conditions for deportation. (The issue of classifications based on alienage is treated in §590.)

a. IMMIGRATION LAWS RECEIVE RATIONALITY REVIEW. [§206]

The Court consistently defers to congressional action regarding the terms and conditions of immigration. Under rational basis review, the Court only requires that a law be rationally related to achieving a legitimate government interest. (See §federal laws.) Under this standard, it is extremely unlikely that a court will invalidate a law.

Fiallo v. Bell, 430 U.S. 787 (1977). The Court upheld a federal statute which excluded illegitimate children from certain immigration preferences if their, fathers were non- residents of the United States. Illegitimate children whose mothers were non-residents of the United States qualified for the preferences. (For instance, while all American citizens are entitled to bring in their alien children without regard to a statutory numerical quota, fathers (but not mothers) are denied this privilege with regard to their illegitimate children). The Court used a rational basis level of review, in deference to the sensitive political concerns relating to immigration.

b. CONGRESS' POWER OVER IMMIGRATION MAY TRUMP FIRST AMENDMENT RIGHTS. [§207]

Congress' power to regulate immigration is a compelling government interest which may justify an abridgement of individual rights.

Kleindienst v. Mandel, 408 U.S. 753 (1972). The Court upheld a provision of the Immigration and Nationality Act of 1952 making foreign Communists ineligible to receive visas for travel in the United States. The Act was applied to exclude a Belgian scholar who had been invited to lecture at American universities. The free speech concerns were outweighed by the power of Congress to exclude aliens on any grounds related to national policy.

c. LOSS OF CITIZENSHIP. [§208]

Congress may impose some conditions on the retention of citizenship, but may not involuntarily revoke a person's citizenship.

(1) A Citizen Must Voluntarily and Intentionally Relinquish Citizenship. [§209]

The government must prove a voluntary relinquishment of citizenship.

Vance v. Terrazas, 444, U.S. 252 (1980). The Court ruled that a citizen of the United States cannot lose that citizenship unless the government can prove, by a preponderance of the evidence, that the person voluntarily engaged in some action for which he or she could be expatriated, and that the person intended to give up U.S. citizenship when he or she took that action. Terrazas, who was a citizen of both the United States and Mexico at birth, took an oath of allegiance to Mexico and expressly renounced his United States citizenship. The Court ruled that the government must prove that Terrazas had a specific intent to renounce his citizenship.

(2) Congress May Not Involuntarily Revoke Citizenship. [§210]

Congress may not override the requirement that a person must voluntarily relinquish citizenship.

In *Afroyim v. Rusk*, 387 U.S. 253 (1967), Afroyim, who was a naturalized American citizen, went to Israel and voluntarily voted in an election for the Israeli legislature. The Court invalidated a federal statute which revoked Afroyim's U.S. citizenship as a penalty for voting in the foreign political election. Such an act did not evidence an intent to voluntarily relinquish citizenship.

(3) Congress May Impose Some Conditions on Retention of Citizenship. [§211]

Congress' power over naturalization is broad enough to justify the imposition of some conditions on the grant of citizenship to persons who were not born in the United States or eventually naturalized in the United States.

Rogers v. Bellei, 401 U.S. 815 (1971). The Court upheld a federal statute under which persons born abroad, who acquired citizenship by having a parent who was a U.S. citizen, would lose their citizenship if they did not return to the United States and reside here for five years continuously between the ages of 14 and 28.

REVIEW PROBLEMS — NATIONAL LEGISLATIVE POWER: SOURCES OF AND LIMITATIONS ON CONGRESSIONAL POWER

PROBLEM 1. Congress passes a new crime bill by which it imposes certain reporting requirements on state and local police agencies. One provision requires state police officers to fill out a detailed set of forms and notify the nearest U.S. Attorney's Office whenever someone is arrested with an automatic weapon. The purpose of the law is to keep track of these weapons, and to coordinate the federal government's response to the crime problem. Discuss the ability of Congress to pass this law, and a state's constitutional arguments against it.

> **Answer:** The issue of crime clearly has a close and substantial effect on interstate commerce, so Congress may reach this activity under the Commerce Clause and the Necessary and Proper Clause. The state will claim that the law violates its Tenth Amendment power to decide how to utilize its police officers. The state would also argue that its citizens would receive less police protection because of the federal requirement that the local police spend their time performing federally- mandated tasks. This case is like *New York v. U.S.* in that only state and local governments are regulated. It is different from New York v. U. S. in that the federal law does not commandeer the state legislature, but rather imposes requirements on local police officers. In *Printz v. U.S.* (see §171.1), the Court invalidated a law such as this one, asserting that Congress' commandeering of state executive officers (local police) violated the system of dual sovereignty required by the Constitution.

PROBLEM 2. As part of a treaty with the country of Freedonia, the United States has agreed that the citizens of each country, regardless of which country they are living in, shall receive only those constitutional protections to which they are entitled under the Constitution of their native country. As a result, Freedonians living in the United States are not entitled to protection against unreasonable searches and seizures, or compelled self-incrimination. Is this provision constitutional?

> **Answer:** No. The Constitution is the supreme law of the land, and a treaty may not violate its provisions. Constitutional protections of individual rights cannot be abridged by a treaty or executive agreement. (See §201.)

PROBLEM 3. As part of an "Energy Conservation Act," Congress provides that states will be entitled to federal money if they agree to pass legislation ensuring that three-time felons receive life in prison with no parole. Is this condition on the receipt of money constitutional?

> **Answer:** Maybe, but maybe not. (That's another way of saying that you better discuss both sides of the issue.) The general rule is that any condition on the receipt of federal money is constitutional. However, in *South Dakota v. Dole* [§183], the Court said that it might violate the Constitution for Congress to impose a condition on the receipt of money that is unrelated to the purpose of the federal grant. In this case, life imprisonment for three-time felons does not appear to fall within the purposes of a federal energy conservation law, so the argument is that this particular condition on the receipt of this federal money is unconstitutional.

PROBLEM 4. Congress passes a law which provides housing and education benefits for soldiers who participated in the Gulf War. What constitutional provision(s) would Congress cite to support such action?

Answer: Congress may pass such a law under its War Power coupled with the Necessary and Proper Clause. The War Power gives Congress the power to prepare for war, wage war, and deal with the after effects of war. (See §190.)

           Sum & Substance QUICK REVIEW of Constitutional Law

VII. SEPARATION OF POWERS: RELATIONSHIPS BETWEEN AND AMONG BRANCHES OF THE FEDERAL

A. OVERVIEW OF SEPARATION OF POWERS. [§212]

The doctrine of separation of powers involves the relationships between and among the branches of the federal government. The first three Articles of the Constitution set forth the powers of the respective branches: Article I deals with the powers of Congress; Article II deals with the powers of the President and the Executive Branch; and Article III deals with the powers of the Judiciary. You should read these Articles to get some sense of the powers of each branch of the federal government and how the Articles work together to create our basic constitutional structure. In a separation of powers case, one branch of the federal government has impinged on the power of another branch. In such a case, you must consider the constitutional basis for the action taken by the branch of government that has acted, as well as the constitutional basis for the argument the affected branch uses to challenge the law. For example, what if Congress were to pass a law authorizing the appointment of a special prosecutor to investigate alleged executive wrongdoing, and the law prohibited the President from firing the special prosecutor? Assume that the President challenges the part of the law prohibiting the President from removing the special prosecutor from office. The President's contention is that the Constitution prohibits Congress from imposing any restrictions on the President's power to remove an executive official such as a special prosecutor. The first step in analyzing the constitutionality of the restrictions on the President's removal power would be to see what constitutional provisions justified the law; the Necessary in addition to Proper Clause and Article II provide the answer (Congress has the power to pass laws for the executive branch). Second, you must ask what is the constitutional basis for the President's challenge to this law. The Article II basis is that the law unduly interferes with the power of the President to remove executive branch officials (allegedly an essential part of the President's power as head of the executive branch). For each step, the essence of the analysis is to tie the argument to some enumerated or implied power of each branch of government involved in the dispute.

As a general matter, you should follow these steps in any separation of powers analysis:

1. Determine which branch of the federal government is acting and which branch is being affected by the law. Who is doing what to whom?

2. Determine whether the challenge to the law is based on a specific provision of the Constitution which sets forth required rules or procedures. If such a provision exists, apply the rules given in the Constitution. For instance, under Article I, §7, before a bill may become law, it must be presented to the President for signature. If the House and the Senate passed a resolution which was supposed to operate as law, but was never presented to the President for signature, the argument against the law would be that it violated the specific requirement of presentment in Article 1, §7.

3. If no specific constitutional provision applies, a balancing approach is called for. On the side of the acting government, you must identify the constitutional power asserted as a basis for the action taken. On the side of the branch of government affected by the law, you must identify the essential attribute or power of that branch that is adversely affected, and determine whether the intrusion effected by the law is too great. By way of example, if Congress imposed restrictions on the President's power to fire an executive branch official, there is no specific constitutional prohibition of such action. To determine whether such a restriction violated separation of powers principles, the Court would ask whether the Congressional restrictions unduly interfered with the President's power as the head of the executive branch.

1. ENUMERATED POWERS OF THE BRANCHES OF THE FEDERAL GOVERNMENT. [§213]

Articles I, II, and III of the Constitution set forth certain specific powers of each of the branches of the federal government; these are the enumerated powers of Congress, the President, and the Judiciary respectively.

2. IMPLIED POWERS OF THE BRANCHES OF THE FEDERAL GOVERNMENT. [§214]

In addition to those powers specifically listed in the Constitution, the Court recognizes certain unenumerated (or implied) powers of each of the branches. These unenumerated powers are necessary to carry out the enumerated powers. For instance, Congress' enumerated powers to tax, spend, and coin money give rise to an unenumerated power to charter a national bank. The President's enumerated power as head of the executive branch gives rise to the unenumerated power to hire and fire executive branch officials (subject to certain exceptions, discussed at §§227, 230). The Court's enumerated power to hear cases involving constitutional rights gives rise to the unenumerated power to create procedural rules to protect those rights (such as the exclusionary rule, under which evidence obtained in violation of the Constitution is not admissible into evidence).

B. EXECUTIVE AND LEGISLATIVE POWERS. [§215]

The President's main enumerated powers are to execute the laws, act as Commander-in-Chief, enter into treaties, appoint officers of the federal government, veto congressional acts presented for the President's signature, and grant pardons for federal offenses. In addition, the President has implied powers, especially in the area of foreign affairs. The main congressional powers are set forth in Article I, §8, and are discussed at §143. Remember that Congress, under the Necessary and Proper Clause, Article 1, §8, cl. 18, has the power to make laws not only for itself, but for the President and the courts.

1. THE SPECIFIC POWERS OF THE PRESIDENT. [§216]

a. The President is vested with the executive power; specifically, the power to take care that the laws of the country are faithfully executed. Under Article II, all executive power is vested is the President.

b. The President is Commander-in-Chief of the armed forces.

c. The President has the power to make treaties, with the advice and consent of the Senate.

d. The President has the power, with the advice and consent of the Senate, to appoint ambassadors, ministers, consuls, and Justices of the Supreme Court. However, Congress may vest the appointment of inferior officers in the President alone, courts of law, or heads of departments.

e. The President has the power to veto congressional enactments. Congress may override a presidential veto by a two- thirds vote of those present, if the number present in each House constitutes a quorum.

f. The President has the power to grant pardons or reprieves for federal offenses, except in cases of impeachment. Remember that the President has no power to pardon someone who has violated state law. Such an attempt would raise Tenth Amendment problems of the President interfering with a state's sovereignty.

2. PRESIDENTIAL ACTION AFFECTING THE POWERS OF CONGRESS. [§217]

Generally, the President may not take action unless it is within one of the powers granted to the President by the Constitution. This rule does not apply as stringently when the President acts in the area of foreign affairs. As the representative of the United States, the President's actions in foreign affairs need not be based in a specific Article II power; they may be justified by the President's intrinsic power to represent and protect the sovereign interests of the country.

a. The President Does Not Have the Power to Seize Private Property. [§218]

Under the Fifth Amendment, it is Congress that has the power to take private property for public use, as long as just compensation is paid to the property owner. The President does not have any constitutional power to seize private property, nor to compensate the property owner for the seizure (again, it is Congress is the branch of the federal government authorized to spend money).

In *Youngstown Sheet & Tube v. Sawyer*, 343 U.S. 579 (1952), the Court reviewed President Truman's order to his Secretary of Commerce, Sawyer, to seize and operate most of the country's steel mills in order to avert a strike in the industry. President Truman argued that a steel strike would jeopardize the safety and effectiveness of troops engaged in the Korean police action. The Court invalidated the President's action as not being justified by either the President's power as Commander-in-Chief, or by his power to take care that the laws be faithfully executed. The Commander-in-Chief power was too attenuated a basis for the seizure of private property, and there was no law that the President was executing when he ordered the steel mills to be seized. Since Congress is the only branch of the federal government that may take and pay for private property (see §412, below), the President was violating separation of powers by performing what was essentially a congressional function.

Justice Jackson wrote an important concurrence in this case, in which he described his vision of how a court should analyze presidential action that arguably crosses the line into congressional powers. The three scenarios he posits are:

(1) When the President acts pursuant to an express or implied authorization from Congress, presidential power is at its maximum;

(2) When the President acts in the absence of either a congressional grant or denial of authority, the President's action is in a "twilight zone" of concurrent presidential and congressional authority, and the result of the case may depend more on the imperatives of events, rather than abstract theories of law;

(3) When the President acts contrary to the express or implied will of Congress, presidential power is at its minimum.

> **STUDY TIP:** Be aware of how the role of a reviewing court would change as we go through Justice Jackson's three fact patterns. If the President's power is at its maximum, the Court will be very deferential to presidential action. If the President's power is at its minimum, the Court will scrutinize the presidential action very carefully. If the presidential action falls within the "twilight zone" of concurrent presidential and congressional authority, the Court will have to balance the competing interests of the President and Congress. Should the role of the court change as a function of presidential and congressional agreement or disagreement?
> A conservative Justice is likely to say no: the Constitution delineates the spheres of power of the respective branches of the federal government, and Congress and the President may not, by agreement, alter that structure. A liberal Justice is likely to adjust the role of the Court depending on the agreement or disagreement of the other branches: if Congress and the President concur on a course of action, the Court should defer to the combined will of the political branches.

b. Congress May Explicitly or Implicitly Authorize Presidential Action. [§219]

Congress may, by statute or resolution, authorize the President to take certain action. Even without specific authorization, congressional acquiescence to presidential action may create an inference of congressional authorization.

In *Dames & Moore v. Regan*, 453 U.S. 654 (1981), the Court upheld Executive Orders implementing an Executive Agreement between the United States and Iran. The Executive Orders terminated all litigation between each government and nationals of the other country, set up a Claims Tribunal to settle any claims that might exist, nullified prejudgment attachments against Iran's assets, and ordered transfer to Iran of all its assets held in U.S. banks. Specifically, the Court ruled that the President's actions nullifying attachments and ordering the transfer of assets were authorized by a specific congressional statute. The President's suspension of claims was not authorized by statute, but was implicitly authorized by a congressional history of acquiescence to presidential claims settlements.

3. CONGRESSIONAL ACTION AFFECTING THE POWERS OF THE PRESIDENT. [§220]

Congress may not take any action which unduly interferes with an enumerated or unenumerated power of the President. Generally, the

Court determines which power of the President is being abridged, whether that power is central to the functioning of the Presidency, and whether Congress has unduly invaded presidential prerogatives.

a. Legislative Vetoes. [§221]

Under the Constitution, it is for Congress to pass laws, and for the executive branch to implement them. It has become an accepted practice, however, for Congress to delegate to executive branch agencies or officials the power to promulgate regulations which have the force of law. Congress must provide specific standards for the executive official to follow, and must not retain control over the execution of the laws by the executive branch official. **A legislative veto exists when Congress purports to give power to an executive agency or official, but keeps for itself the power to invalidate the ensuing executive action.** In other words, a congressional delegation to the executive branch must be clean, with no strings attached.

(1) Delegation of Power to the Executive Branch. [§222]

As a general matter, Congress may delegate to the President, other officers in the executive branch, or an independent regulatory commission, the power to promulgate rules and regulations to implement congressional goals. A delegation of power will be valid if:

(a) Congress has not attempted to give away some nondelegable power (declare war, consent to the appointment of a Justice);

(b) Congress has stated the objective of the law; and

(c) Congress has provided specific standards for the executive branch official or independent commission to follow. *Yakus v. U.S.*, 321 U.S. 414 (1944).

The Court has upheld every congressional delegation since 1935.

(2) A Legislative Veto May Invalidate an Otherwise Valid Delegation. [§223]

Whenever Congress passes a law, or takes action that is the equivalent of passing a law, it must meet both the bicameralism and presentment requirements of Article I, section 7. Bicameralism means that both the House and the Senate must pass the bill. Presentment means that the bill must be presented to the President for signature. For presentment purposes, it does not matter if the President does nothing or vetoes the bill; all that matters is that the President has been given an opportunity to sign it. For purposes of legislative veto analysis, the Court considers to be a "law" any bill that has gone through the normal legislative process, or any congressional action that has the effect of altering the legal rights, duties, and relations of persons.

(a) In *INS v. Chadha*, 462 U.S. 919 (1983), [§224] the Court invalidated a provision of the Immigration and Nationality Act of 1952 which authorized the Attorney General to suspend deportation of an alien under certain circumstances, but allowed either house of Congress to override the Attorney General's suspension and force the alien to be deported. The Court said that the House resolution requiring the deportation of Chadha was an exercise of legislative power (tantamount to a law) because it changed Chadha's legal rights and relations. This legislative action was therefore subject to the bicameralism and presentment requirements of the Constitution, both of which it failed. The House acted without its resolution being submitted to the Senate (no bicameralism) or to the President for signature (no presentment). If the law had not provided that either house could override the Attorney General's decision, the delegation to the executive branch would have been constitutional. The veto provision, however, allowed Congress to retain control of the ultimate outcome even after it attempted the delegation to the executive branch.

(b) *Metropolitan Washington Airports Authority v.* Citizens for the Abatement of Aircraft Noise, Inc., 501 U.S. 252 (1991). [§225]

The Court relied in large part on legislative veto analysis to invalidate a federal law under which Virginia and the District of Columbia agreed to transfer authority over two local airports to the Airports Authority, which was subject to the control of a review board made up entirely of members of Congress. The effect of the law was to give Congress, through its representatives, control (veto power) over the decisions of the Airport Authority. If Congress wanted to delegate power to the Authority, it had to do it cleanly, without retaining control.

(c) *WAR POWERS RESOLUTION.* [§226]

Under the War Powers Resolution, passed by Congress on November 7, 1973, Congress attempted to ensure that it would have an important role in the commitment of American troops to hostilities in foreign countries. An obvious response to the American experience in Vietnam, Section 5 (c) of the War Powers Resolution provides that ". . . at any time that United States Armed Forces are engaged in hostilities outside the territory of the United States, . . . without a declaration of war or specific statutory authorization, such forces shall be removed by the President if the Congress so directs by concurrent resolution." Under this law, bicameralism is present (there must be a concurrent resolution), but there is no presentment. This is a legislative veto under *Chadha* because the specific constitutional requirement of presentment is not met.

b. Appointment Power of the President. [§227]

Under Article II, the President nominates, with the advice and consent of the Senate, all principal officers of the United States, including ambassadors and members of the Judiciary. The President must also nominate, with Senate consent, all inferior officers, unless Congress has vested the appointment of specific inferior officers in the President alone, courts of law, or heads of departments.

(1) *Buckley v. Valeo*, 424 U.S. 1 (1976). [§228]

The Court invalidated a section of the Federal Election Campaign Act which provided for appointment of the members of the Federal Election Commission. Under the law, two commissioners were appointed by the President pro tem of the Senate, two by the Speaker of the House, and two by the President. This scheme violated the Appointments Clause of Article II because Congress vested the appointment of four of the six commissioners in the wrong persons. Under the Appointments Clause, Congress may vest the appointment of **inferior** officers in the President alone, a court of law, or a head of a department. The Speaker of the House and the President pro tem of the Senate are not on the list; therefore, the appointments they made were invalid, at least in terms of the enforcement powers of the Federal Election Commission. The four commissioners who were appointed by the wrong persons may still perform investigative and informative functions (simple legislative tasks) but may not perform any executive, enforcement functions.

(2) *Weiss v. U.S.*, 114 S.Ct. 752 (1994). [§229]

The Court ruled that the appointment process of military judges complies with the requirements of the Appointments Clause. Two marines were court-martialed and convicted for various violations of the Uniform Code of Military Justice. They appealed, in part on the basis that military judges lack the authority to convict because the manner in which they are appointed violates the Constitution. The Court said that all the military judges in this case were commissioned officers, and that all commissioned officers are appointed by the President with the advice and consent of the Senate. Their subsequent assignment to the position of military judge is not an appointment to a new position (it is simply an assignment of a military officer to another job within the armed forces), therefore the requirements of the Appointments Clause are irrelevant when a commissioned officer is assigned to the position of military judge.

(3) *Edmond v. U.S.*, 117 S.Ct. 1573 (1997). [§229.1]

The Court upheld the appointment of civilian judges of the Coast Guard Court of Criminal Appeals by the Secretary of Transportation. Congress had authorized such appointment, and the Court determined that the judges were "inferior" officers, and thus Congress could vest their appointment of the Secretary of Transportation. The Court articulated a test to determine whether an officer is inferior — "inferior officers' are officers whose work is directed and supervised at some level by others who were appointment by presidential nomination with the advice and consent of the Senate."

c. Congressional Restrictions on the President's Power to Remove Executive Branch Officers. [§230]

There is no specific constitutional provision which gives the President the power to remove executive branch officials. However, as a necessary incident of the office (an implied power), the President must be able to make personnel decisions within the executive branch, including removing some executive officers. A problem arises when Congress attempts to impose restrictions on the President's power to remove executive branch officials. While the Constitution has no explicit provision giving Congress the power to limit the President's removal power, Congress arguably possesses such a power under the Necessary and Proper Clause (see §144, above) and Article II of the Constitution. Combining these clauses, Congress has power to legislate for the executive branch, presumably including the power to impose restrictions on the President's removal power.

(1) Analysis of Congressional Restrictions on the President's Power to Remove an Executive Branch Officer. [§231]

The Court will determine if the restrictions on removal imposed by Congress unduly interfere with an essential attribute or power of the Presidency. Under this approach, the Court must identify which power of the President is being abridged, and whether Congress has interfered too greatly with that power. A minority view on the Court (see Justice Scalia's opinion in *Morrison v. Olson* at §236) is that Article II gives all executive power to the President, and **any** diminution of that power by Congress violates the Constitution. Justice Scalia does not believe it appropriate for the Court to decide "how much is too much" when it comes to congressional abridgment of the President's power to remove an executive branch officer.

(2) Evolution of Case Law Dealing With Congress Restricting the President's Removal Power. [§232]

When Congress imposes restrictions on the President's power to remove an executive branch official, the Court focuses on the functions performed by that official, and whether the President must have unfettered power to remove that person from office. Supreme Court analysis in removal cases has evolved from a categorical approach (focusing exclusively on the nature of the person whom the President is trying to remove), to a balancing approach which looks at whether the removal restrictions impermissibly interfere with presidential power. The Court determines which attribute of presidential power is affected by the removal restriction, and whether the restriction unduly interferes with that presidential power.

(a) Early Case Law. [§233]

The President Has Almost Unlimited Power to Remove Officials Who Perform Purely Executive Functions.

In *Myers v. U.S.*, 272 U.S. 52 (1926), the Court broadly ruled that the President had the power to remove executive branch officials. The Court struck down a statute that allowed the removal of first-class postmasters only if the President had the consent of the Senate.

(b) Rise of the Administrative State. [§234]

Congress May Restrict the President's Power to Remove Officials Who Perform Quasi-Legislative or Quasi-Judicial Functions.

Humphrey's Executor v. U.S., 295 U.S. 602 (1935). This case came down in the post-Depression era when administrative agencies were starting to proliferate. The Court ruled that the President had unrestricted power to remove an official who performed purely executive functions, but Congress could impose restrictions on the President's power to remove officials who perform quasi-legislative or quasi-judicial functions. The theory was that the administrative agency officials were to be independent from presidential influence, and therefore could not be subject to removal at will by the President. *Humphrey's Executor* still reflected a categorical approach under which the scope of the power of the President to remove an executive official was a function of the nature of the position held by that employee.

(c) Modern Case Law. [§235]

The Court Asks Whether Removal Restrictions Imposed by Congress Unduly Interfere With An Essential Attribute of the Presidency.

(i) In *Morrison v. Olson*, 487 U.S. 471 (1988), [§236] the Court upheld the Ethics in Government Act of 1978. Under this law, Congress created a Special Division of the Court of Appeals which could, under certain circumstances, appoint a special prosecutor to investigate alleged wrongdoing in the executive branch. Congress also limited the President's power to fire the special prosecutor. *Morrison* deals with issues of removal restrictions, the Appointments Clause, and a general separation of power analysis. Each of these issues in *Morrison* will be discussed separately.

Removal. Removal restrictions imposed by Congress will be valid unless they unduly interfere with an essential attribute of the Presidency. The law in *Morrison* provided for the appointment of a special prosecutor (or independent counsel) to investigate and, if indicated, prosecute wrongdoing by certain executive branch officials. Obviously, Congress thought it unwise to allow the President free rein to fire an independent counsel who was investigating high-level executive officials. As a result, Congress said that the Attorney General could only remove the independent counsel for "good cause," as defined in the statute. This restriction on the Attorney General also restricts the President, who constitutionally has the power to control the Justice Department. The Court, 7-1, upheld the removal restrictions. Chief Justice Rehnquist reasoned that the imposition of a "good cause" standard for removal of the special prosecutor did not unduly trammel on executive authority. While the majority in *Morrison* used a balancing analysis to determine the constitutionality of the removal restrictions, Justice Scalia, in dissent, said that the Constitution had already decided this issue by giving all executive power to the President. He argued that the Court should not be deciding when a congressional intrusion into presidential power is excessive; any intrusion is too much.

Appointments. Under the Ethics in Government Act, the independent counsel is appointed by a Special Division of the Court of Appeals of the District of Columbia. This court is made up of three Court of Appeals judges or Supreme Court Justices, to be appointed by the Chief Justice of the United States for two- year terms. The appointment of the independent counsel by the Special Division of the Court of Appeals was upheld as consistent with the Appointments Clause of Article II. The Court in *Morrison* determined that the independent counsel was an inferior officer, due primarily to the nature and scope of her charge and her jurisdiction, and that Congress legitimately vested the appointment of this inferior officer in a court of law — the Special Division of the Court of Appeals.

General Separation of Powers Analysis. The Court in *Morrison* also held that the Ethics in Government Act, as a whole did not violate the separation of powers doctrine because it in no way unduly interfered with the functions of the executive branch. Congress did not attempt to increase its own powers at the expense of the President, and there was no judicial usurpation of presidential power because the Special Division's role was basically limited to appointing the independent counsel.

(ii) In *Bowsher v. Synar*, 478 U.S. 714 (1986), [§237] the Court reviewed a federal law designed to balance the budget and eliminate the federal deficit by 1991. Under the law, the Comptroller General of the United States was to receive reports from selected government officials and then give the President his recommendations on where to cut expenditures to help balance the budget. The Court declared that the Comptroller General was performing an executive function by engaging in the budget-cutting process. The issue in *Bowsher* was whether Congress could delegate executive functions to a government officer (the Comptroller General) who is removable by Congress. **Congress may not have removal power over an executive official, whether a person is an executive official by status (under the President on the organizational chart) or by function (given executive functions by statute).** The only way that Congress may remove an executive officer is by impeachment. Thus, the delegation by Congress to the Comptroller General in *Bowsher* was unconstitutional. The court also characterized Congress' power to remove the Comptroller General as a legislative veto. The power to remove is the power to control; Congress may not delegate executive functions to someone whom it can fire.

4. EXECUTIVE PRIVILEGE. [§238]

Executive privilege means that a President has a presumptive right to refuse to disclose materials, documents, or communications that are generated during that President's tenure in office. It is a presumptive privilege (the burden is on the party seeking disclosure to justify the production of the materials) which may be overridden by a sufficiently weighty reason for disclosure. The privilege is based on the need of the President to be able to conduct the affairs of office free from excessive public scrutiny. Any analysis of an executive privilege question must include the following steps:

a. Someone, such as a litigant in a criminal or civil trial, subpoenas a President to testify or turn over documents, tapes, or other materials;

b. The President opposes production, and asserts executive privilege as a bar to turning over the requested items;

c. The judge decides whether the requested material is relevant evidence in the proceeding for which it is requested. If irrelevant, the President need not disclose it;

d. If the material is relevant, the district court, in an **in camera** proceeding, balances the need for disclosure against the President's reasons for keeping the material secret; and

e. The district court will decide whether the material requested will be disclosed.

> **STUDY TIP: Be as specific as possible about the precise reason for the assertion of executive privilege and about the need for disclosure. As these interests change, the ultimate balance will change.** For instance, it is a relatively weak argument for the President to assert a general, undifferentiated need for secrecy (forced disclosure would impair the ability of the President to communicate with subordinates). It is much better for the President to assert that forced disclosure of documents would endanger some specific, compelling government interest, such as foreign affairs (a President would be able to successfully assert executive privilege to block a subpoena requesting sensitive military documents during wartime). The reason for disclosure will vary with the nature of the proceeding in which disclosure is sought. For instance, presidential documents may be subpoenaed in a criminal case to protect the fundamental rights of the defendants, or they may be requested by the Senate Judiciary Committee during a judicial confirmation hearing to help the Senate carry out its advise and consent function in the appointment of judges.

(1) In *U.S. v. Nixon*, **418 U.S. 683 (1974),** [§239] the Court unanimously upheld a subpoena duces tecum issued in a criminal trial of seven of President Nixon's political associates which directed President Nixon to turn over certain tapes and materials which were

generated during his Presidency and which pertained to the Watergate burglary. The Court held that a presumptive executive privilege existed as a function of the separation-of-powers doctrine. The Court reasoned that the checks and balances inherent in our constitutional structure required some degree of secrecy regarding presidential communications. On balance, the Court ruled that President Nixon's generalized claim of privilege (no national security or foreign affairs argument was advanced) was outweighed by the fundamental due process rights of the parties in a criminal prosecution.

(2) *Nixon v. Administrator of General Services*, 433 U.S. 425 (1977). [§240]

On the day he was pardoned, President Nixon and the Administrator of General Services (GSA) entered into an agreement which provided rules of access to President Nixon's presidential materials. Neither President Nixon nor GSA could have access to the materials without the other's consent, and President Nixon could withdraw or order the destruction of any materials after a certain number of years. In response to this agreement, Congress passed the Presidential Recordings and Materials Preservation Act, which provided new guidelines for review and release of these materials. Under the statute, GSA had control over President Nixon's materials, and was to formulate regulations to ensure public access to them. President Nixon objected, in part on the basis that executive privilege protected his materials from forced disclosure in the manner prescribed by Congress. The Court upheld the law on its face, but ruled that a former President is able to assert executive privilege for any materials generated during his or her time in office. President Nixon argued that non-disclosure was necessary to protect the President's ability to receive candid advice from aides and advisors. The Court ruled that the interest asserted by President Nixon was outweighed by Congress's interest in preserving the materials for historical and archival purposes, restoring public confidence in our political processes, and the importance of the materials for pending or future civil or criminal litigation.

5. EXECUTIVE IMMUNITY. [§241]

Executive immunity means that the President is immune from liability for damages in a civil suit for any official act performed while the President is in office. As with executive privilege, there is no constitutional provision conferring such immunity, but the Court has recognized it as a necessary incident of the powers of the President.

a. Absolute Immunity for the President. [§242]

The Court has ruled that a President has absolute immunity from civil damages liability for his or her official acts, as long as the President was acting within the outer perimeter of the duties of the office. As long as the President was arguably performing the duties of the office, the President is protected by absolute immunity.

In *Nixon v. Fitzgerald*, 457 U.S. 731 (1982), the Court affirmed a summary dismissal of a lawsuit against President Nixon by a former employee of the Department of the Air Force whose job was terminated after he testified before Congress about cost overruns on an airplane. The Court refused to subject the President to potential liability on every employment decision which could be traced back to the President as head of the executive branch.

b No Temporary Immunity from Civil Damages Litigation for Events that Occurred Before the President Took Office. [§242.1]

Separation-of-powers principles do not require federal courts to stay all civil damages litigation against a sitting President until he leaves office. The Constitution does not require temporary immunity from a civil damages lawsuit during a President's term in office.

In *Clinton v. Jones*, 117 S.Ct. 1636 (1997), the Court refused to stay a civil lawsuit against President Clinton for actions that allegedly occurred before he became President. Paula Corbin Jones sued President Clinton under federal and state law, alleging that, while he was Governor of Arkansas, Mr. Clinton made "abhorrent" sexual advances toward her, and that her rejection of those advances had adverse consequences on her government employment. The Court, ruling that the Constitution does not require that a lawsuit for civil damages against a sitting president be deferred until the President leaves office, rejected the President's argument that defending such a lawsuit would necessarily interfere too greatly with the President's ability to carry out the duties of the office.

c. Qualified Immunity for Presidential Aides and Advisors. [§243]

Executive branch officials other than the President have qualified immunity from civil damages liability. To determine whether qualified immunity applies, ask whether a reasonable person in an official capacity knew or should have known that his or her actions were violating clearly established constitutional rights. If the U.S. Attorney General were to authorize what was clearly an illegal wiretap of a political enemy, the Attorney General would be subject to a suit for civil damages because the Attorney General knew or should have known that such action violated the Fourth Amendment rights of the person subject to the wiretap.

Harlow v. Fitzgerald, 457 U.S. 800 (1982). In this companion case to *Nixon v. Fitzgerald* (above at §242), the Court set forth the general rule of qualified immunity for presidential aides or advisors — an executive branch official other than the President will be immune from civil damages liability unless the official, judged by a reasonableness standard, knew or should have known that he or she was violating clearly established constitutional rights. **However, the Court said that if a presidential aide were entrusted with discretionary authority in a highly sensitive national security or foreign affairs position, that aide might be entitled to absolute immunity to protect the performance of functions vital to our national interest.** Absolute immunity for presidential aides would require a fact-specific finding of the importance of the job performed by the aide, and would clearly be an exception to the general rule of qualified immunity.

6. LEGISLATIVE IMMUNITY. [§244]

Under the Speech or Debate Clause, Article 1, section 6, clause 1, Senators and Representatives are immune from civil or criminal suit

for any words or conduct that are an integral part of the legislative process.

a. *U.S. v. Brewster*, 408 U.S. 501 (1972). [§245]

The Court ruled that the Speech or Debate Clause does not protect a Senator from criminal prosecution if the prosecution can reasonably be deemed to be based on words or conduct that were not an essential part of the legislative process. The Speech or Debate Clause did not protect a Senator from prosecution for solicitation and acceptance of bribes in exchange for favorable votes on future legislation.

b. *Gravel v. U.S.*, 408 U.S. 606 (1972). [§246]

Senator Gravel was protected by the Speech or Debate Clause when he read into the Congressional Record a stolen "Top Secret- Sensitive" copy of the Pentagon Papers (a history of American decisionmaking in Vietnam). However, private republication of the Pentagon Papers in the Beacon Press was not protected under the Speech or Debate Clause because republication was not essential to the deliberations of the Senate. The Court in *Gravel* also ruled that a legislative aide or assistant is entitled to the same immunity as his or her boss under the Speech or Debate Clause.

c. *Hutchinson v. Proxmire*, 443 U.S. 111 (1979). [§247]

Senator Proxmire used to give a "Golden Fleece Award" to publicize what he considered wasteful government spending. Giving the award on the floor of the Senate was protected activity, but republication through a press release, newsletters, a television show, and phone calls to government agencies was not protected under the Speech or Debate Clause.

C. CONGRESSIONAL ACTION AFFECTING THE JUDICIARY. [§248]

Whenever Congress takes an action that affects the judiciary, ask whether the law is unduly interfering with an essential attribute of the judiciary or undermining the integrity of the judicial branch. The main attribute of the federal judiciary is to hear cases which fall within the Article III jurisdiction of federal courts — cases involving a federal question, or cases in which there is diversity of citizenship between the parties.

1. Congress' Ability to Determine the Scope of Federal Judicial Power. [§249]

Under Article III, there must be a Supreme Court. Its original jurisdiction, which is set by the Constitution, includes all cases affecting Ambassadors, other public Ministers and Consuls, and those in which a State shall be a party. The Supreme Court has appellate jurisdiction in all other cases (as long as a federal question or diversity of citizenship is present) with such exceptions and regulations as Congress shall make. Under Article III, and Article I, section 8, clause 9, Congress has the power to establish lower federal courts.

a. Jurisdiction Stripping. [§250]

With the exception of the constitutionally-mandated original jurisdiction of the Supreme Court, Congress has the power to set the original jurisdiction of federal district courts, and the appellate jurisdiction of the U.S. Courts of Appeals and the Supreme Court. There is a question whether there are any constitutional limits on Congress' ability to set the appellate jurisdiction of the Supreme Court or the jurisdiction of lower federal courts. This issue may arise if Congress attempts to excise certain kinds of cases from a court's jurisdiction. What if Congress said, for instance, that the Supreme Court does not have appellate jurisdiction to review lower federal court decisions involving the constitutionality of a federal school prayer law? This kind of "jurisdiction- stripping" case present a specific kind of constitutional balance. On one side of the scale is the explicit constitutional power of Congress to determine the appellate jurisdiction of the Supreme Court (or the jurisdiction of lower federal courts). On the other side is an implied separation-of-powers concept and two individual rights arguments. Take the law mentioned above, eliminating Supreme Court appellate jurisdiction to review school prayer cases coming from lower federal courts. Congress would argue that it has an unlimited Article III power to make exceptions to the appellate jurisdiction of the Supreme Court. To attack the law, you would argue that the jurisdiction-stripping statute violates separation of powers because it removes the Supreme Court from the system of checks and balances. With no ultimate Court review of such a law, we go from a three-branch system of government to a two-branch system (or even one branch if Congress overrides a presidential veto to pass the school prayer law). The next argument would be that a litigant has a procedural due process right to a federal judicial forum, and that the jurisdiction-stripping statute deprives the litigant of the right to have the Supreme Court hear the case. The last argument is that the jurisdiction-stripping statute effectively deprives the litigant of the substantive right involved in the case — here the First Amendment right to be free from the establishment of religion.

Ex Parte McCardle, 74 U.S. 506 (1869). During the post-Civil War Reconstruction era, Congress passed a statute giving federal circuit courts the power to hear petitions for writs of habeas corpus from persons who thought they were imprisoned in violation of federal law. Under the jurisdiction- granting statute in *McCardle*, if a petition were denied by a federal circuit court, appeal could be taken to the Supreme Court. McCardle, imprisoned by the military government of Mississippi, sought a petition for habeas corpus from a federal circuit court, and the court denied his request. He appealed to the Supreme Court, which accepted his case and held oral arguments. After oral arguments, but before the case was decided, Congress withdrew appellate jurisdiction from the Supreme Court in this kind of case. The Court dismissed McCardle's case for want of jurisdiction. Be careful not to read *McCardle* too broadly. McCardle could still file his petition for habeas corpus directly with the Supreme Court and possibly get Supreme Court review. There has never been a Supreme Court decision dealing with, let along upholding, complete withdrawal by Congress of the Court's ability to hear a particular kind of case. All *McCardle* stands for is that Congress, under its power to make exceptions to the appellate jurisdiction of the Supreme Court, was able to withdraw one avenue of appeal to the Supreme Court.

b. Developing Sentencing Guidelines. [§251]

It does not violate the Constitution for federal judges to sit on a commission which develops sentencing guidelines for federal courts.

In *Mistretta v. U.S.*, 488 U.S. 361 (1989), the Court upheld the Sentence Reform Act of 1984 which created the U.S. Sentencing Commission as an independent commission and placed it in the judicial branch of the federal government. The commission was made up of seven voting members appointed by the President (no Appointments Clause problem — see §227, above), three of whom were to be federal judges. The Court asked two questions: Did Congress give the commission powers that are more appropriately performed by other branches of the federal government and; does the inclusion of judges on the commission and its placement in the judicial branch undermine the integrity of the judiciary? The Court answered both questions "NO". On the first, the Court said that judges are the ones who sentence criminals every day, so they are uniquely able to contribute to a sentencing commission's deliberations. Secondly, the integrity of the judiciary was not affected because the power of the judiciary was not expanded (it was in fact reduced by limiting a judge's discretion in the sentencing process), and it has become accepted practice to ask judges to engage in rulemaking.

REVIEW PROBLEMS — SEPARATION OF POWERS: RELATIONSHIPS BETWEEN BRANCHES OF THE FEDERAL GOVERNMENT

PROBLEM 1. As part of an executive agreement with the country of Someko, the President of the United States has agreed to return certain Somekon prisoners who are in jail in the State of Oz (a state of the United States) for having violated numerous state laws. The President issues pardons for all the prisoners, and demands their release. Does the Constitution give the President the power to take this action with regard to the prisoners?

> **Answer:** No. The Constitution only gives the President the power to pardon federal offenses. There is no presidential power to pardon someone who has violated state law. (See §216 for review.)

PROBLEM 2. The legislature of the State of Oz has delegated to state administrative agencies the power to promulgate rules for the operation of those agencies. Before the rules go into effect, they must be approved by a joint committee composed of three members of the State Senate and three members of the State House of Representatives. Is this system constitutional? Assume that all rules of United States constitutional law apply in Oz.

> **Answer:** No. This is a legislative veto. The joint committee has a veto power over the decisions of the administrative agencies. This would violate presentment because the action of the joint committee is not presented to the Governor for approval. It would also probably violate bicameralism because, even though there are members of both houses on the commission, the Constitution contemplates the participation of the full House and the full Senate in any lawmaking. (See §221 for review.)

PROBLEM 3. President Jefferson Hope is sued for firing state employees based on their race while he was the governor of the State of Oz. The plaintiffs seek monetary damages under appropriate federal statutes. The alleged discrimination occurred before the President took office. In his defense, the President asserts executive immunity. Will the President prevail?

> **Answer:** Perhaps. In *Jones v. Clinton*, 869 F.Supp. 690 (E.D. Arkansas 1994), a federal district court ruled that a sitting President was entitled to temporary immunity from immediate trial for actions occurring before the President took office. The court ruled that the discovery and deposition process could proceed as to all persons, including the President, but that the President should not be subject to the demands of trial while still in office. A federal appeals court later ruled that a sitting President is not immune <u>from civil suit</u> alleging actionable behavior that happened before he became President. *Jones v. Clinton*, 72 F.3d 1354 (1996). (See §§241-242 for review.)

PROBLEM 4. Congress has given the Secretary of State the power to appoint ambassadors and deputy ambassadors to foreign countries. Pursuant to this power, Jane Jones, the Secretary of State, appointed Helen Hale to be ambassador to the Ukraine, and appointed Bob Brown to be deputy ambassador. Are these appointments constitutional?

> **Answer:** No, and Yes. Under the Appointments Clause, principal officers must be nominated by the President and confirmed by the Senate. Helen is a principal officer, so she cannot be appointed by the Secretary of State. Bob, on the other hand, is an inferior

officer whose appointment can be vested in the head of a department, such as the Secretary of State. (See §227 for review.)

VIII. STATE POWER TO REGULATE COMMERCE: CONSTITUTIONAL LIMITATIONS

A. INTRODUCTION. [§252]

The Tenth Amendment states that, "[t]he powers not delegated to the United States by the Constitution, nor prohibited by it to the States, are reserved to the States respectively, or to the people." The Court has interpreted the Tenth Amendment to be the basis of a state's "police power" — the state's ability to regulate for the health, safety, welfare, and morals of its citizens. **A law passed pursuant to a state's police power is presumptively valid, but may run into problems if it interferes with the flow of interstate commerce or treats out-of-staters differently from the way it treats instaters.** For instance, a state law which prohibits the instate disposal of toxic waste that was generated out of state obviously interferes with interstate commerce, and is probably invalid. A state law which restricts the ability to practice law to state residents interferes with the right of persons to travel from state to state to pursue an occupation.

If you see a state law which interferes with interstate commerce or treats out-of-staters worse than it treats instaters, you should consider the following analyses as possible methods of finding the law unconstitutional.

1. Dormant Commerce Clause

2. Privileges and Immunities Clause of Article IV (not the Fourteenth Amendment)

3. Equal Protection Clause.

B. DORMANT COMMERCE CLAUSE — NEGATIVE IMPLICATIONS OF THE COMMERCE CLAUSE. [§253]

The Commerce Clause serves not only as a source of power for congressional action (see §147, above), but also serves as a limitation on state action that impedes the free flow of commerce. **The dormant commerce clause doctrine (the Commerce Clause is "dormant" because Congress has not acted under it) applies when a state, in the absence of any preempting federal action, passes a law which interferes with interstate commerce. (Interstate commerce is any interstate transaction involving access to, sale, or purchase of any good, service, or natural resource).** In the absence of congressional action, the Court applies the Commerce Clause as a limitation on state action. Keep in mind that Congress, as the ultimate holder of the commerce power, may "overrule" a Court decision interpreting the Commerce Clause as a limiter of state action. There are two ways that a state may interfere with the free flow of commerce: discriminate against interstate commerce, and burden interstate commerce.

1. STATE DISCRIMINATION AGAINST INTERSTATE COMMERCE. [§254]

To use the discrimination analysis, you must be able to show that the state law, by purpose or effect, treats out-of-staters differently from instaters. The main rationale for the rule against a state discriminating against out-of-staters is to prohibit local economic protectionism and the economic balkanization of the country through retaliatory laws passed by the various states. For instance, if the Court upheld a state law prohibiting the importation of solid waste into the state, other states might pass the same kind of law, with the cumulative result being the destruction of the interstate market in waste disposal.

a. Analysis of a State Law That Discriminates Against Out-of-Staters. [§255]

(1) Identify the Discrimination. [§256]

You must show that the law, by purpose or effect (facially or as applied), classifies along state lines — that instaters are treated better than out-of-staters. The discrimination may take the form of a disadvantage imposed on out-of-staters (denial of access to an instate market), or a benefit given to instaters (exemption of an instate business from an otherwise generally applicable tax).

(2) Identify the Reason for the Discrimination. [§257]

You have two choices: local economic protectionism; or some valid police power reason such as health or safety. **Discrimination against interstate commerce for the purpose of favoring local business or investment interests is per se invalid.** It is not a legitimate state interest for a state to try to secure an economic advantage for local business interests. If the discrimination is justified by a valid police power interest unrelated to economic protectionism, and there are no other means to achieve that interest, the law may be valid.

b. Aspects of Discrimination Analysis Under the Dormant Commerce Clause. [§258]

(1) Strict Scrutiny of Facially Discriminatory Laws. [§259]

Facial discrimination against out-of-staters invokes judicial strict scrutiny. Under strict scrutiny, a state must show that it has a compelling reason for its discrimination against out-of-staters, and that the discrimination effected by the state law is narrowly tailored to achieving the state's goal.

(a) *Hughes v. Oklahoma*, 441 U.S. 322 (1979). [§260]

The Court invalidated an Oklahoma ordinance that banned the exportation for sale outside the state of minnows that were procured within the waters of Oklahoma. The Court said that such facial discrimination invokes the strictest scrutiny of any purported legitimate purpose and of the absence of nondiscriminatory alternatives.

(b) *Maine v. Taylor*, 477 U.S. 131 (1986). [§261]

The Court upheld a law that discriminated on its face against out-of-staters. Maine prohibited the transfer into Maine of live baitfish from out of state. The Court upheld the ban even though it would benefit Maine's baitfish industry. The Court was persuaded by Maine's argument that its unique population of wild fish would be threatened by parasites that might be brought in with out-of-state fish, and that there was no less discriminatory means to protect against the importation of the parasites.

(c) *Oregon Waste Systems, Inc. v. Dept. of Environmental Quality of Oregon*, 114 S.Ct. 1345 (1994). [§262]

The court invalidated an Oregon law that imposed a $2.50 per ton surcharge on the disposal of solid waste generated in other states, but only an $0.85 per ton fee on solid waste generated within the state. The Court said that Oregon's restrictions failed to pass the "strictest scrutiny" indicated by the facial discrimination against out-of-staters.

(2) Requirement that the Discrimination be Between Similarly Situated Entities. [§262.1]

To be a violation of the Dormant Commerce Clause, the alleged discrimination must be between similarly situated entities. Two companies are not similarly situated if they provide different products and serve different markets, and would continue to do so even if the supposedly discriminatory burden were removed.

In General Motors Corporation v. Tracy, 117 S.Ct. 811 (1997), the Court upheld an Ohio law that imposed a sales and use tax on purchases of natural gas, but provided an exemption from the tax for purchases from local distribution companies (LDCs). General Motors Corporation (GMC), which purchased its natural gas from an independent marketer, argued that the tax exemption violated the Dormant Commerce Clause because while all the LDCs were in-state, most of the independent marketers were out-of-state. The Court observed that a history of state regulation of the natural gas industry had resulted in a distinction between natural gas sold to individual consumers "bundled" with various protections, and "unbundled" gas sold to larger corporate consumers. This had the effect of creating two separate products and markets for natural gas, to the point that the enterprises should not be considered 'similarly situated' for purposes of a claim of facial discrimination under the Commerce Clause. Although the LDCs also participated in the "unbundled" natural gas market, the Court accorded controlling significance to the individual consumer market in which the LDCs alone operated. Since the purpose of Dormant Commerce Clause jurisprudence is to protect a national market from state-granted preferences to its own residents, "in the absence of actual or prospective competition between the supposedly favored and disfavored entities in a single market there can be no local preference . . . to which the dormant Commerce Clause may apply."

(3) Risk of Multiple Burdens. [§263]

If a state law creates a risk of multiple burdens, it may be unconstitutional. Ask what would happen if other states had the same kind of law. **The cumulative impact of a number of states each passing a law which prohibited out-of-staters from doing business instate would severely hurt the interstate market.** The question under the multiple burdens doctrine is "What if everybody did it?" If the answer is that everybody doing it would severely impair interstate commerce, the law is invalid.

Baldwin v. Seelig, 294 U.S. 511 (1935). The Court invalidated a New York law that prohibited the sale in New York of milk bought outside New York below a price set by New York law. This law created too

OUTLINE

great a risk of multiple burdens. If other states passed the same kind of law, the national market would be fragmented.

(4) Reciprocity Requirements. [§264]

Reciprocity requirements violate the dormant interstate commerce clause because they create too great a risk of multiple burdens on interstate commerce. For dormant commerce clause purposes, a reciprocity requirement is a law which allows residents of State B to do business in State A only if State B grants the same privilege to residents of State A. If such a law were upheld, the result would be the balkanization of the national market.

(a) *Great A. & P. Tea Co. v. Cottrell*, 424 U.S. 366 (1976). [§265]

The Court invalidated a reciprocity requirement under which Mississippi said that milk from another state could be sold in Mississippi only if Mississippi milk could be sold in the other state.

(b) *Sporhase v. Nebraska*, 458 U.S. 941 (1982). [§266]

The Court invalidated a Nebraska reciprocity requirement that denied a permit to withdraw and transport Nebraska water for use in another state unless the other state granted reciprocal rights to transfer its water into Nebraska.

(5) Requiring Business to be Performed Instate. [§267]

A state cannot require business to be performed instate if that business could be performed more efficiently out of state.

Pike v. Bruce Church, 397 U.S. 137 (1970). The Court invalidated an Arizona law requiring that growers of Arizona cantaloupes pack them in Arizona. The court noted that it would view with particular suspicion state statutes that required business operations to be performed instate that could more efficiently be performed out of state. The Court said that this kind of law is virtually **per se** illegal, even if it has a legitimate purpose.

(6) Discrimination by Political Subdivision of a State; Less Drastic Means. [§268]

It is discrimination against interstate commerce for a political subdivision of a state (such as a city or a county) to exclude out-of-staters from doing business within their boundaries. If a city or county discriminates against people who reside outside the city or county boundaries, that will count as a discrimination against out-of-staters even though some instaters are also excluded from doing business inside the city or county.

Dean Milk v. Madison, 340 U.S. 349 (1951). The Court invalidated a Madison, Wisconsin ordinance that prohibited the sale of any milk in Madison that was not pasteurized within five miles of the town square. The Court ruled that this law discriminated against interstate commerce even though some people within Wisconsin (those outside the five-mile limit) were also disadvantaged. The Court also ruled that the law was unconstitutional because Madison had less drastic means available to achieve its goal of ensuring healthy milk.

(7) Subsidy for Instate Economic Interests. [§269]

A state may not set up a system under which it subsidizes instate economic interests at the expense of out-of-state economic interests.

West Lynn Creamery v. Healy, 114 U.S. 2205 (1994). The Court invalidated a Massachusetts pricing order which imposed an assessment on all fluid milk sold by dealers to Massachusetts retailers. Most of the milk is produced out of state, but the entire assessment is paid into a fund to be distributed to Massachusetts dairy farmers. The Court ruled that the law discriminated against interstate commerce because it benefited the local dairy industry at the expense of out-of-state interests. The disbursements from the fund amounted to a subsidy of instate dairy interests.

(8) Protecting Privacy Rights of Residents. [§270]

A municipality may protect the privacy rights of its citizens, even if interstate commerce is indirectly affected by the regulation.

Breard v. Alexandria, 341 U.S. 622 (1951). The Court upheld a local ordinance which prohibited door-to-door solicitation, even though the ordinance may have had the effect of discriminating against interstate commerce. The Court upheld the ordinance because its purpose was to protect the privacy rights of homeowners, not to provide an economic advantage to local businesses.

(9) Waste Disposal Cases. [§271]

There are five waste disposal cases which illustrate the non-discrimination principles of dormant commerce clauses analysis.

(10) No Distinction Between Nonprofit and For-profit Enterprises. [§271.1]

For purposes of Commerce Clause analysis, the Court will not treat nonprofit and for-profit enterprises differently. Discrimination against interstate commerce in a nonprofit area violates the Commerce Clause.

In *Camps Newfound/Owatonna Inc. v. Harrison*, 117 S.Ct. 1590 (1997), the Court struck down a Maine property tax that exempted property owned by charitable organizations, unless the organization operated primarily for the benefit of nonresidents. A church camp, 95% of whose campers were from outside the state, challenged the tax law. The Court held that the camp was engaged in commerce because it both purchased and provided goods and services, and the tax law was facially discriminatory against interstate commerce. The Court refused to treat nonprofit organizations any differently for purposes of Dormant Commerce Clause analysis, concluding that there is no reason why the nonprofit character of an enterprise should exclude it from either affirmative or negative Commerce Clause analysis.

(a) Banning the Importation of Solid Waste. [§272]

A state may not prohibit the importation of waste into the state.

Philadelphia v. New Jersey, 437 U.S. 617 (1978). The Court invalidated a New Jersey law which prohibited the importation into

New Jersey of any solid or liquid waste which originated or was collected outside New Jersey. New Jersey attempted to use health and environmental concerns in support of the law. **The Court said that if simple economic protectionism is effected by the law, a virtual *per se* rule of invalidity applies.** It also said that whatever the purpose of the law, a state may not choose a means which discriminates against articles coming from out of state unless there is some reason other than their place of origin to treat them differently. **The Court also reiterated the rule that a state may not give its residents a preferred right of access over out-of-staters to natural resources located within the state's borders.** A big factor in the Court's decision was the issue of multiple burdens. **If the Court upheld this law, it would be an invitation for every state to pass a law prohibiting the importation of solid, hazardous, or nuclear waste, thereby destroying the interstate market for the sale and processing of these items.**

(b) Extra Fee on Out-of-State Waste. [§273]

A state may not charge out-of-staters an extra fee for dumping waste.

Chemical Waste Management v. Hunt, 504 U.S. 334 (1992). The Court invalidated an Alabama law which imposed an extra fee of $72 per ton on the disposal of hazardous waste from out of state when the waste was disposed of in privately-owned landfills in Alabama. The Court said that even if the law were aimed at health, safety, or environmental concerns of Alabama, it could not employ a means which facially discriminated against the interstate market. Less drastic means were available, such as a per-mile tax on all vehicles transporting hazardous waste in the state.

(c) County Approval for Dumping Waste From Outside the County. [§274]

A ban by a county on out-of-county waste violates the dormant commerce clause. If a city or county bans the importation of goods or materials from outside the city or county, the Court will consider the law to be discriminatory against interstate commerce.

Fort Gratiot Sanitary Landfill, Inc. v. Michigan Dept. of Natural Resources, 504 U.S. 353 (1992). The Court invalidated a state law which prohibited private landfill owners from accepting any solid waste that originated outside the county where the landfill was located, unless the county specifically approved such importation. The Court relied on *Dean Milk v. Madison* (see §262), to conclude that such a ban by a county discriminates against interstate commerce even though some in-staters may also be hurt by their inability to transfer waste into a particular county.

(d) Higher Fee for Dumping Out-of-State Waste. [§275]

A higher fee for out-of-state dumpers of waste fails strict scrutiny.

Oregon Waste Systems, Inc. v. Dept. of Environmental Quality of Oregon, 114 S.Ct. 1345 (1994). The court invalidated an Oregon law that imposed a $2.50 per ton surcharge on the disposal of solid waste generated in other states, but only an $0.85 per ton fee on solid waste generated within the state. The Court said that Oregon's restrictions failed to pass the "strictest scrutiny" indicated by the facial discrimination against out-of-staters. The Court said that even if landfill space could be considered a natural resource, a state may not accord its own citizens a preferred right of access over consumers in other states to natural resources located within the state's borders.

(e) Requiring Waste to be Processed Locally. [§276]

A town cannot require waste to be processed locally when it could be processed more cheaply elsewhere.

Carbone v. Town of Clarkstown, New York, 114 S.Ct. 1677 (1994). The Court invalidated a local ordinance which authorized a private contractor to build, within town limits, a solid waste transfer station for the purpose of separating recyclable from non-recyclable waste. To finance the operation, the town guaranteed a minimum waste flow to the transfer station. The operator of the station was authorized to charge a "tipping fee," which was higher than the cost of disposing of unsorted waste in the private market. To meet the waste flow guarantee, the town passed an ordinance requiring all nonhazardous solid waste within the town limits to be disposed of at the transfer station. Carbone received solid waste at his own sorting station and separated it into recyclable and non-recyclable items. Carbone was then required to take the sorted materials to the transfer station and pay the tipping fee, even though the trash had already been sorted. Carbone was also prohibited from shipping its sorted trash directly; it had to go through the transfer station. The court ruled that the town ordinance discriminated against interstate commerce, and that the article of commerce here was not so much the trash itself as the service of processing and disposing of it. The Court said that the town had less drastic means available to achieve its goals, such as uniform safety regulations.

2. STATE LAWS THAT ONLY BURDEN INTERSTATE COMMERCE. [§277]

A state law affecting commerce that treats instaters and out-of-staters the same will be considered merely a burden on interstate commerce and will be analyzed under a balancing test. The fact that instaters are subject to the same burdens as out-of-staters makes it less likely that the law will violate the central commerce clause principle that there should be one national market, not a number of regional or state markets. **A nondiscriminatory state law that interferes with interstate commerce is constitutional if it is supported by a legitimate state interest and only incidentally affects interstate commerce, unless the burden on interstate trade is clearly excessive in relation to the local benefits.** *Pike v. Bruce Church*, 397 U.S. 137 (1970).

a. Steps to Follow In Determining the Constitutionality of a State Law That Burdens Interstate Commerce. [§278]

(1) Make sure there is no discrimination, by purpose or effect, against out-of-staters. Instaters and out-of-staters are subject to the same burdens and regulations.

(2) Identify the local interest advanced by the law. Economic protectionism is never a valid state interest, so the state should assert some police power goal such as health or safety.

(3) See if the law only incidentally affects interstate commerce. The primary purpose and effect of the law must be to advance the state's police power interest.

(4) Balance the adverse impact on interstate commerce against the extent to which the state's goals are advanced by the law.

(5) See if there are any less drastic means by which the state could achieve its goals.

(6) See if the law, if upheld, would create too great a risk of multiple burdens.

b. Issues to Look For When Applying Dormant Commerce Clause Analysis to a State Law That Burdens Interstate Commerce. [§279]

(1) Determine Whether the Subject Matter Regulated Is Local Or National In Nature. [§280]

In conducting a Dormant Commerce Clause balance, consider the nature of the subject matter regulated. If the subject matter is national in scope, thus requiring uniform regulation, a state law will be harder to uphold. For example, what if Chicago passed its own laws and regulations for air-traffic controllers. This is the kind of subject matter that had better be regulated in one, uniform way by the federal government. However, if a state or city is regulating something local in nature, the Court will be more disposed to uphold the law.

(a) *Cooley v. Board of Wardens*, 53 U.S. 299 (1851). [§281]

The Court upheld a Pennsylvania law that required ships using the local harbor to take on a local pilot. The Court focused on the nature of the subject matter regulated, concluding that the specific needs of local harbors required diverse, local regulations rather than a uniform, national scheme of regulation.

(b) *Southern Pacific v. Arizona*, 325 U.S. 761 (1945). [§282]

The Court invalidated an Arizona law that limited the length of trains in the state to seventy freight cars. The Court said that the Arizona law imposed too great a burden on an aspect of interstate commerce that is national in scope (interstate rail transportation), and thus required uniformity of regulation.

(c) *Kassel v. Consolidated Freightways Corp.*, 450 U.S. 662 (1981). [§283]

The Court invalidated an Iowa law that prohibited 65-foot double trailers from operating in the state. The Court alluded to the strong presumption in favor of state highway regulations, but said that Iowa failed to present any persuasive evidence that 65- foot double trailers are any more dangerous than 55-foot single trailers.

(2) Determine Whether the Law Creates a Risk of Multiple Burdens. [§284]

If a state law creates the potential for conflicting laws to be enacted by other states, that may be enough to invalidate the law under the Dormant Commerce Clause.

Bibb v. Navajo Freight Lines, 359 U.S. 520 (1959). The Court invalidated an Illinois law requiring that special mudguards be welded onto all trucks operating within the state. This law caused long delays for trucks entering Illinois from other states. State highway safety regulations carry a strong presumption of validity, but the Illinois law imposed too great a burden on interstate commerce. There were less drastic means by which Illinois could have achieved its safety goals, and the law created too great a risk of multiple burdens.

If the Illinois law were upheld, any number of other states could pass laws requiring their own kind of contoured mudguards, thereby causing a multiplicity of burdens on interstate commerce.

(3) Determine Whether a Price Affirmation Law Has Extraterritorial Effects. [§285]

A state may not pass a law which effectively sets prices in other states.

Healy v. Beer Institute, 491 U.S. 324 (1989). The Court invalidated a Connecticut law that required out-of-state shippers of beer to affirm that the prices they would charge Connecticut wholesalers were no higher at the time of affirmation than the prices charged in the four states bordering Connecticut. The Court focused on the extraterritorial effect of the law, asserting that a state may not pass a law which has the practical effect of setting a price scale for use in other states. The Court also cited the multiple-burdens problem, asking what would happen if a number of other states passed this kind of law.

(4) Determine Whether the State Law Causes Business to Shift From One Out-of-Stater to Another. [§286]

It is not unconstitutional for a state law to cause some interstate business to shift from one interstate supplier to another, as long as the total flow of goods in interstate commerce is not diminished.

Exxon Corp. v. Maryland, 437 U.S. 117 (1978). The Court upheld a Maryland law that prohibited petroleum producers (such as Exxon) from operating retail gas stations in the state. The purpose was to avoid the situation in which, during a gas shortage, big producers would supply their own retail stations and shut out independent gas station owners. **There was no discrimination against the interstate market because all petroleum sold in the state would continue to come from out of state.** There is no impermissible burden on interstate commerce where a state law causes some business to shift from one interstate supplier to another.

(5) Determine Whether the State Law Simply Prefers One Kind of Container Over Another. [§287]

It is not unconstitutional for a state to distinguish between kinds of containers, even though there may be an incidental effect on out-of-state suppliers.

Minnesota v. Clover Leaf Creamery, 449 U.S. 456 (1981). The Court upheld a Minnesota law that banned nonreturnable milk containers made of plastic, but allowed other nonreturnable milk containers, such as those made of pulpwood. Since the law differentiated between the type of container rather than instate versus out-of-state producers, the Court found no discrimination against interstate commerce. The State's environmental and ecological arguments outweighed any burden on interstate commerce.

3. MARKET PARTICIPANT EXCEPTION TO DORMANT COMMERCE CLAUSE ANALYSIS. [§288]

A state is a market regulator when it acts in its sovereign capacity to regulate what other parties can do within their contractual relationships. It is a market participant when it is a party to a contract and makes business decisions for itself. When a state acts as a market participant, rather than a market regulator, it may discriminate against out-of-staters for any reason, including local economic advantage, and be immune from a Dormant Commerce Clause analysis. In such cases, a state may limit its sales to instate buyers or limit its purchases to instate sellers.

> **STUDY TIP:** The "market participant exception" only frees a state from a Dormant Commerce Clause analysis. It does **not** immunize a discriminating state from an Article IV Privileges and Immunities Clause of analysis, or from an Equal Protection analysis. Under an Article IV Privileges and Immunities Clause argument, a state cannot deny to out-of-staters certain basic rights which it grants to its own citizens, unless it has an important reason for the discrimination. Under an Equal Protections argument, a state cannot treat out-of-staters worse than instaters, unless it has a legitimate reason for doing do.

a. Examples of "Market Participant" Cases. [§289]

The Court has upheld the ability of a state to prefer local economic interests over those of out-of-staters.

(1) State-Owned Auto Salvage Business. [§290]

A state may discriminate against out-of-staters in the operation of a state-owned auto salvage business.

Hughes v. Alexandria Scrap, 426 U.S. 794 (1976). The Court upheld a Maryland law that was designed to rid the state of old, inoperable automobiles. Under the law, a person who owned an old automobile could transfer it to a scrap processor who could claim a bounty from the state for the destruction of the automobile. Under a 1974 amendment to the law, a processor had to submit title documentation to the state to claim the bounty. The title documentation requirements were more lenient for instate processors than they were for out-of-state processors. The Court upheld the different requirements because the state had entered the auto salvage market, and could discriminate against out-of- staters if it chose to do so.

(2) State-Owned Cement Company. [§291]

A state may discriminate against out-of-staters in the sale of cement by a state-owned cement company.

Reeves v. Stake, 447 U.S. 429 (1980). The Court upheld a South Dakota policy of preferring in-state buyers of cement produced at a state-owned cement plant. As a result of a cement shortage, South Dakota built and operated a cement plant. For almost 60 years, South Dakota sold cement to both in-state and out-of-state buyers. In 1978, in the midst of a cement shortage, South Dakota decided to sell cement to instaters first with out-of-staters getting what was left after in-state demand was met. The Court ruled that because South Dakota was a market participant its preference for instaters was not subject to a Dormant Commerce Clause challenge.

(3) State as Party to Construction Contracts. [§292]

A city may discriminate against non-residents of the city in the awarding of city-funded construction contracts.

White v. Massachusetts Council, 460 U.S. 204 (1983). The Court upheld an executive order of the Mayor of Boston requiring that all construction projects funded by the city be performed by a work force made up of at least 50% Boston residents. For the Court's treatment of such a program under the Privileges and Immunities Clause of Article IV, see *United Building and Construction Trades Council v. Camden*, 465 U.S. 208 (1984), below, at §302.

b. Limits of the Market Participant Doctrine. [§293]

A state will be treated as a market participant as long as it is making purchase or sales decisions in relation to a contract to which it is a party. As soon as it tries to control the terms of a contract to which it is not a party, it is acting as a market regulator and the Dormant Commerce Clause will restrict its actions.

South-Central Timber Development Co. v. Wunnicke, 467 U.S. 82 (1984). A plurality of the Court found that Alaska was not acting as a market participant when it sold state-owned timber to buyers, but required as part of the contract that the timber be processed in the state of Alaska before it could be shipped out of state. According to the plurality, the problem was that Alaska was trying to control a market transaction that occurred subsequent to the initial sale of timber by the state.

C. THE PRIVILEGES AND IMMUNITIES CLAUSE OF ARTICLE IV. [§294]

As a general rule, the Privileges and Immunities Clause of Article IV (not the Privileges or Immunities Clause of the Fourteenth Amendment) prohibits a state from denying to out-of-staters privileges that it grants to its own citizens. This clause only protects individuals, not corporations, and applies only when a state is discriminating against out-of-staters in relation to the exercise of a basic or fundamental right. For Article IV Privileges and Immunities purposes, the basic rights protected are the right to pursue an occupation, the right to own or dispose of property within the state, the right of access to state courts, and the right to come into the state to exercise a fundamental right.

1. STANDARD OF REVIEW IN PRIVILEGES AND IMMUNITIES CLAUSE OF ARTICLE IV CASES. [§295]

To justify a discrimination against out-of-staters and to withstand an Article IV Privilege and Immunities attack, a state must show that it has a substantial reason for treating out-of- staters differently from its own citizens, and that the discrimination is substantially related to achieving the state's goals.

2. APPLICATION OF ARTICLE IV PRIVILEGES AND IMMUNITIES CLAUSE ANALYSIS. [§296]

a. Durational Residency Requirements for Voting. [§297]

A one-year residency requirement for voting is unconstitutional.

Dunn v. Blumstein, 405 U.S. 330 (1972). The Court said that, under the Privilege and Immunities Clause of Article IV, it is permissible for a state to require that voters be bona fide residents of the state. However, the Court, under the Equal Protection clause, invalidated a Tennessee voter registration requirement that voters live in the state for one year, and in the county for three months.

b. State Statute Limiting Abortions to State Residents. [§298]

A state may not prohibit out-of-state women from coming instate to have an abortion.

Doe v. Bolton, 410 U.S. 179 (1973). The Court invalidated a Georgia statute which prohibited an abortion from being performed in the state unless the patient requesting the abortion certified in writing, under oath, that she was a legal resident of the state of Georgia. The Court ruled that a state cannot limit the medical care available within its borders to its own residents.

c. Elective Office Limited to Residents. [§299]

A state may limit the right to hold elective office to state residents.

Kanapaux v. Ellisor, 419 U.S. 891 (1974). The Court upheld a South Carolina law which restricted to state residents the right to hold elective office in the state.

d. Higher License Fees for Out-of-Staters. [§300]

Higher commercial license fees for out-of-staters are constitutionally suspect. Such fees run afoul of the central purpose of the Article IV Privileges and Immunities Clause, which is to outlaw classifications based on non-citizenship of a state unless the non-citizens constitute a particular evil at which the statute is directed.

Toomer v. Witsell, 334 U.S. 385 (1948). The Court invalidated a South Carolina law which charged out-of-staters $2500 for a commercial shrimp license while charging instaters only $250. This law also created a risk of multiple burdens if other states imposed the same kind of requirement.

e. Hiring Preferences for Instaters. [§301]

A state may not require private employers to give a hiring preference to state residents.

Hicklin v. Orbeck, 437 U.S. 518 (1978). The Court invalidated an Alaska law that required private employers in a number of oil and gas operations to give a hiring preference to Alaska residents over out-of-staters.

f. Construction Set-Asides for Local Residents. [§302]

A city ordinance requiring that a certain number of jobs on city funded construction projects be set aside for city residents is subject to attack under the Privileges and Immunities Clause of Article IV.

United Building and Construction Trades Council v. Camden, 465 U.S. 208 (1984). The Court held that the Privileges and Immunities Clause of Article IV is available as a challenge to a municipal ordinance that set aside a certain percentage of jobs on city-funded construction projects for city residents. The Court rejected arguments that the clause does not apply when a city (as opposed to a state) prefers its own residents. The Court remanded the case to state court for a determination as to whether there was a substantial reason for the City of Camden to reserve a percentage of city jobs for city residents.

g. Excluding Out-of-Staters from the Practice of Law. [§303]

A state may not exclude non-residents from the practice of law within the state.

The Court has consistently invalidated requirements that a lawyer be a resident of the state (or of the Virgin Islands) before being admitted to practice in the state. Practicing law is a basic right, and the exclusions did not meet the test of being substantially related to a substantial state objective. *New Hampshire v. Piper*, 470 U.S. 274 (1985) (A resident of Vermont took and passed the New Hampshire bar examination, but was not allowed to be sworn in as a lawyer until she established a residence in New Hampshire); *Supreme Court of Virginia v. Friedman*, 487 U.S. 59 (1988) (An attorney who resided in Maryland was not allowed admission to the Virginia bar "on motion" — that is, without having to take the Virginia bar examination — even though Maryland allowed Virginia attorneys to become members of the Maryland bar on that basis); *Barnard v. Thorstenn*, 489 U.S. 546 (1989) (To be admitted to the bar of the District Court of the Virgin Islands, an attorney had to demonstrate that he or she had resided in the Virgin Islands for at least one year and intended to continue to reside and practice in the Virgin Islands if admitted to practice).

3. ARTICLE IV PRIVILEGES AND IMMUNITIES CLAUSE DOES NOT APPLY TO NON-BASIC RIGHTS. [§304]

The protections of the clause only apply when a basic right is abridged (see §294). If one of the basic rights is not affected, an out-of-stater will not be able to assert the Article IV Privileges and Immunities Clause as a challenge against the discriminatory state law.

Baldwin v. Fish and Game Commission of Montana, 436 U.S. 371 (1978). The Court held that the Privileges and Immunities Clause of Article IV did not apply to a Montana law that charged out-of-staters a higher fee than instaters for a private, non-commercial hunting license. This case, unlike *Toomer* (see §300 above), did not involve state discrimination in relation to the basic right of pursuing an occupation.

D. CONGRESSIONAL POWER TO AUTHORIZE STATE DISCRIMINATION AGAINST INTERSTATE COMMERCE. [§305]

If Congress authorizes a state to impose a discriminatory tax on out-of-state entities, such a tax will be immune from a Dormant Commerce Clause challenge, but will be invalid under the Equal Protection Clause if the only reason for the law is local economic protectionism. Since Congress is the ultimate holder of the commerce power, it may give to states the power to discriminate against out-of-state commerce. However, Congress does not have a power to violate the Equal Protection principle of the Constitution, so it may not give such a power to the states.

> **STUDY TIP:** If you see Congress passing a law which gives states the power to impose discriminatory taxes on out-of-staters, be careful about the specific constitutional challenge to the state tax. If it is only that the state tax violates the Dormant Commerce Clause, the tax is valid. If the challenge is that the state tax violates the Equal Protection Clause, the tax is unconstitutional if the state is simply promoting domestic business by discriminating against nonresident competitors.

(1) *Prudential Insurance Co. v. Benjamin*, 328 U.S. 408 (1946). [§306]

The Court upheld, against a Dormant Commerce Clause challenge, a South Carolina law that taxed out-of-state insurance companies at a higher rate than instate insurance companies. Congress had authorized this tax under the McCarran Act.

(2) *Metropolitan Life Insurance Co. v. Ward*, 470 U.S. 869 (1985). [§307]

The Court, relying on the Equal Protection Clause, invalidated an Alabama law that taxed out-of-state insurance companies at a higher rate than instate insurance companies.

E. STATE POWER TO TAX INTERSTATE COMMERCE. [§308]

In general, states have a presumptive power to tax interstate business operating within the state. To deny states that power would force them to provide services to out-of-state businesses without being able to recoup any of the costs of providing those services. **The main limitations on a state's power to tax interstate commerce come from the Dormant Commerce Clause, the Due Process Clause, and the Equal Protection Clause.** Under the Dormant Commerce Clause, the principle is that interstate businesses should pay their fair share for services received from the state. The Court is concerned about whether the tax passes an unfair share of the tax burden onto interstate commerce, or unduly burdens interstate commerce. Under the Due Process Clause, the main concern is the fundamental fairness of the state tax; are an individual's connections with a state substantial enough to justify the state tax? Under Equal Protection Clause, the question is whether the state has a legitimate reason for discriminatory taxation of out-of-staters, and whether it has chosen rational means to achieve its goal. Remember that it is not a legitimate government interest to prefer local economic interests for purely protectionist reasons.

1. DORMANT COMMERCE CLAUSE LIMITATIONS ON A STATE'S POWER TO TAX INTERSTATE COMMERCE. [§309]

The Court has adopted a four-part test by which to analyze a state tax that is challenged under the Dormant Commerce Clause. This test comes from *Complete Auto Transit, Inc. v. Brady*, 430 U.S. 274 (1977), in which the Court upheld Mississippi's tax on the privilege of doing business within the state. The Court looked to the practical effect of the tax, rather than its label, to see if it violated the Commerce Clause. **Under the four-part test, a state tax will survive a Commerce Clause challenge if the tax: 1) is applied to an activity with a substantial nexus to the taxing state; 2) is fairly apportioned; 3) does not discriminate against interstate commerce; and 4) is fairly related to the services provided by the state.**

a. Cases illustrating each of the elements of the four-part test of *Complete Auto Transit*. [§310]

(1) Substantial Nexus. [§311]

The activity taxed must have a substantial nexus to the taxing state.

Wisconsin v. J.C. Penney Co., 311 U.S. 435 (1940). The Court upheld, against a Due Process challenge, a Wisconsin tax on corporations chartered out of state, but doing business instate. The test for Due Process purposes is whether the taxing power exerted by the state bears fiscal relation to protection, opportunities, and benefits given by the state; has the state given anything for which it can ask something in return.

(2) Fair Apportionment. [§312]

A state tax which is not apportioned to the amount of business a company does in the state violates the Dormant Commerce Clause.

Western Live Stock v. Bureau of Revenue, 303 U.S. 250 (1938). The Court discussed the issue of multiple (or cumulative) tax burdens being placed on interstate commerce if there were no apportionment requirement. Not only would the multiple taxes (by each state in which an entity does business) impose an unfair burden on the taxed corporation, it would discriminate against interstate commerce by virtue of local commerce being free from any cumulative tax burden.

(a) A State's Choice of Apportionment Scheme Will be Upheld if at all Rational. [§313]

The Court uses rational basis scrutiny to evaluate a state's choice of an apportionment scheme. It is difficult for a state apportionment scheme to fail this test.

(b) Single-Factor Apportionment Scheme Valid. [§314]

It is constitutional for a state to use a single-factor apportionment scheme which compares instate sales to total gross sales.

Moorman Manufacturing Co. v. Bair, 437 U.S. 267 (1978). The Court upheld an Iowa tax which used a single-factor apportionment formula which compared Iowa sales to total gross sales. The tax had been applied to an Illinios manufacturer. The Court said that the Due Process Clause imposes two restrictions on a state's ability to tax the income of an interstate business: there must be some minimal connection between the activities taxed and the taxing state, and the income attributed to the state for tax purposes must be rationally related to values connected with the taxing state.

(c) Two Factors to Determine if Apportionment Scheme is Valid. [§315]

It is constitutional for a state to use a two-factor apportionment scheme which looks at whether the apportionment formula is internally and externally consistent.

Container Corporation v. Franchise Tax Board, 463 U.S. 159 (1983). The Court upheld California's tax apportionment scheme. The Court looks at two factors to see if an apportionment formula is constitutional: 1) Is it internally consistent — that is, if the same formula were applied by every jurisdiction, would it result in no more than 100% of the business' income being taxed; and 2) Is it externally consistent — that is, does the apportionment formula reflect a reasonable sense of how income is generated? The taxpayer has the burden of proving that the apportionment formula is unconstitutional because there is no rational relationship between the income attributed to the state, and the intrastate value of the enterprise taxed.

(d) Multiple Burdens and Apportionment Schemes. [§316]

An apportionment scheme will be constitutional if it does not expose foreign corporations to impermissible multiple tax burdens.

Barclay's Bank PLC v. Franchise Tax Board of California, 114 S.Ct. 2268 (1994). The Court upheld California's "worldwide combined reporting" method of calculating the corporate franchise tax owed by unitary multinational corporations. This is the same method of taxation approved in *Container Corporation* (see previous case supra), only here it is applied to foreign corporations or domestic corporations with foreign parents. The Court found that this tax met the four-part test of *Complete Auto Transit*, and that it does not expose foreign multinational corporations to constitutionally impermissible multiple tax burdens.

(3) Non-Discrimination Against Interstate Commerce. [§317]

The purpose of a discriminatory tax cannot be local economic advantage. A tax which applies equally to all products, regardless of their destination, is constitutional.

(a) *Boston Stock Exchange v. State Tax Commission*, 429 U.S. 318 (1977). [§318]

The Court invalidated a New York law which reduced the tax liability on the sale of corporate shares or stock certificates if they were sold in the state of New York rather than out of state. This tax was an unconstitutional discrimination against interstate commerce because the higher tax burden on out-of- staters was for the purpose of securing an economic advantage for instate stock transactions and the New York Stock Exchange.

(b) *Commonwealth Edison v. Montana*, 101 S.Ct. 2946 (1981). [§319]

The Court upheld a Montana severance tax on coal. The rate of the tax varied, but could not exceed 30% of the contract price. The tax was challenged as discriminatory against interstate commerce because 90% of Montana coal was shipped to other states. The Court said that all coal, regardless of destination, was taxed at the same rate, so there was no impermissible discrimination against out-of-staters.

(4) Relation to Services Provided. [§320]

A state tax on an interstate business must be fairly related to services provided by state.

General Motors v. Washington, 377 U.S. 436 (1964). The Court, in upholding Washington's tax on doing business in the state, shed some light on the requirement that a tax must be fairly related to the services provided by the state: The question is whether the state has exerted its power in proper proportion to the taxpayer's activities within the state, and to the taxpayer's consequent enjoyment of the opportunities and protections of the state.

b. Dormant Commerce Clause as a Limitation on State Sales Taxes. [§321]

A State Sales Tax on Every Interstate Bus Ticket Sold Instate Does Not Violate the Commerce Clause.

Oklahoma Tax Commission v. Jefferson Lines Inc., 115 S.Ct. 1331 (1995). The Court upheld an Oklahoma sales tax on bus tickets sold in Oklahoma for interstate travel. The Court applied the four-part test of *Complete Auto Transit*, and determined that the state sales tax met the requirements of the Commerce Clause: it is applied to an activity with a substantial nexus to the taxing state; it is fairly apportioned; it does not discriminate against interstate commerce; and it is fairly related to services provided by the taxing state.

2. DUE PROCESS LIMITATIONS ON A STATE'S POWER TO TAX INTERSTATE COMMERCE. [§322]

A state law which taxes an interstate business operating within the state will withstand a Due Process challenge only if there are "minimum contacts" between the entity taxed and the taxing state, and there is a rational relationship between the income attributed to the taxing state and the intrastate values of the enterprise taxed. See *Wisconsin v. J.C. Penney Co.*, supra at 311.

a. *Braniff Airways, Inc. v. Nebraska State Board of Equalization and Assessment*, 347 U.S. 590 (1954). [§323]

The Court upheld Nebraska's ad valorem tax on the equipment of Braniff, even though the airline made only eighteen stops a day in the state. The Court said that Braniff had established a taxable situs for due process purposes through its habitual use of the property in the state. The test is whether the tax in practical operation has relation to opportunities, benefits, or protection conferred by the taxing state.

> **NOTE:** The Due Process "minimum contacts" test differs from the Dormant Commerce Clause "substantial nexus" test. In *Quill Corp. v. North Dakota*, 112 S.Ct. 1904 (1992), the Court made it clear that the nexus requirements of the Due Process and Commerce Clauses are not identical. The Due Process "minimum contacts" test focuses on an individual and the fundamental fairness of the tax. The Commerce Clause "substantial nexus" test looks at the structural concerns of the interstate market. A corporation may have "minimum contacts" with a taxing state for Due Process purposes, but lack the "substantial nexus" required by the Commerce Clause.

3. EQUAL PROTECTION LIMITATIONS ON A STATE'S POWER TO TAX INTERSTATE COMMERCE. [§324]

A state may not impose a higher tax on out-of-staters than on instaters if the only reason is to prefer local business interests. If a state law is passed for the sole reason of securing a local economic advantage, that law fails rational basis scrutiny under Equal Protection analysis.

Metropolitan Life Insurance Co. v. Ward, 470 U.S. 869 (1985). The Court invalidated, on Equal Protection grounds, a state tax on out-of-state insurance companies that was higher than the tax on instate companies. This tax was designed solely for economic protectionism, and failed rationality review.

4. CONSTITUTIONAL LIMITATIONS ON A STATE'S POWER TO TAX IMPORTS OR EXPORTS. [§325]

Article 1, section 10, clause 2 of the Constitution prohibits a state from laying "any Imposts or Duties on Imports or Exports . . . ." Once goods have arrived at their destination for sale or distribution in a state, they are no longer in foreign commerce, and are outside the restrictions of the Import-Export Clause.

Michelin Tire Corp. v. Wages, 423 U.S. 276 (1976). The Court upheld Georgia's nondiscriminatory, general ad valorem property tax as applied to imported tires that were stored in a warehouse ready for sale or distribution. The Court said that this kind of tax, applied to goods that were no longer in transit, was not prohibited by the Import-Export Clause.

5. STATE-IMPOSED COMPENSATING USE TAXES ARE CONSTITUTIONAL DESPITE THEIR IMPACT ON INTERSTATE COMMERCE. [§326]

A state may impose a compensating use tax, up to the amount of the state sales tax, on goods purchased out of state (where there is no sales tax, or one lower than that of the state imposing the use tax), and brought into the state for use. A compensating use tax puts instate sellers (who must charge the sales tax) on the same footing with out-of-state sellers (who do not have to charge a sales tax). A use tax is invalid if it discriminates against interstate commerce. It will be discriminatory if the use tax imposed on out-of-state goods is higher than the sales tax imposed on instate goods; that would discourage a buyer from going to another state to buy a product.

Sum & Substance QUICK REVIEW of Constitutional Law

For example, the amount of a use tax in State A cannot exceed the sales tax in State A minus the sales tax in State B. If State A has a sales tax of 4%, and State B has no sales tax, the use tax in State A may go up to 4%. If State A has a sales tax of 4%, and State B has a sales tax of 2%, State A's use tax may go as high as 2%.

a. *Henneford v. Silas Mason*, 300 U.S. 577 (1937). [§327]

The Court upheld a use tax imposed on construction equipment purchased out of state. The Court reasoned that this tax was not a tax on interstate commerce, but on the use of the product after it had become situated in the state.

b. *Associated Industries of Missouri v. Lohman*, 114 S.Ct. 1815 (1994). [§328]

The state of Missouri imposed an "additional use tax" on goods purchased outside the State and stored, used, or consumed within the state. The tax was supposed to compensate local jurisdictions for lost sales tax revenue. However, local sales tax rates vary from county to county and in many jurisdictions the use tax exceeded the sales tax. The tax scheme was challenged on the ground that it violated the Commerce Clause. The Court held that the use tax discriminates against interstate commerce in those jurisdictions where the use tax exceeds the sales tax. The compensatory tax doctrine saves the use tax in the jurisdictions where the use tax does not exceed the sales tax. Therefore, the tax scheme is not altogether invalid. It is only invalid in those jurisdictions where the additional use tax imposes a greater burden on interstate commerce than the local sales tax imposes on local, intrastate commerce.

OUTLINE

REVIEW PROBLEMS — STATE POWER TO REGULATE COMMERCE: CONSTITU- TIONAL LIMITATIONS

PROBLEM 1. The legislature of the State of Oz (a state of the United States) passes a law which prohibits darkened glass from being used on the windows, windshields, or rear windows of automobiles being driven within the state. The purpose of the law is to allow police officers to see what the occupants of cars are doing. Bob is from the State of Id, which allows darkened glass on cars. Bob is arrested while driving through Oz. Discuss the Dormant Commerce Clause issues that Bob would raise in challenging the Oz statute.

> **Answer:** This law is similar to the one invalidated in *Bibb v. Navajo Freight Lines*, at §284. The law treats all automobiles the same, wherever they come from, so there is no discrimination against interstate commerce. However, this law would be unconstitutional because of the great burden it imposes on commerce: cars from certain states are, in effect, prohibited from entering the State of Oz. See §277 for further review.

PROBLEM 2. The legislature of the State of Oz is concerned about the growing scarcity of landfill space within the state, the financial well-being of instate garbage haulers, and the safety and health of its citizens. The State, under its power of eminent domain, acquires all the existing landfill space within the state. It then accepts for disposal only garbage generated within the State of Oz. Jane's Disposal Services, Inc., an out-of-state disposal company, challenges this law as violating its rights under the Dormant Commerce Clause, the Privileges and Immunities Clause of Article IV, and the Equal Protection Clause. Discuss each of these arguments.

> **Answer:** Ordinarily, such blatant discrimination against out-of-staters would violate the Dormant Commerce Clause. However, based on these facts, the State of Oz has entered the market of waste disposal, so the market participant exception exempts the State of Oz from any Dormant Commerce Clause analysis. It may discriminate against out-of-staters for whatever reason, and not be subject to any Commerce Clause constraints. Jane's Disposal Services, Inc., as a corporation, is not protected by the Privileges and Immunities Clause of Article IV, so it cannot assert the argument that the State of Oz is denying it the basic right to pursue an occupation within the state. Under Equal Protection analysis, rational basis review is applied, and the discrimination will be upheld if rationally related to a legitimate government interest. Preferring local economic interests is not a legitimate government concern, so Oz's only chance of having the law upheld is if a court accepts its safety or health arguments. See §§252, 253, for further review.

IX. FEDERAL PREEMPTION OF STATE LAWS.

A. INTRODUCTION.
[§329]

Under the Supremacy Clause of Article 6, the U.S. Constitution, federal laws, and treaties take precedence over contrary state constitutional provisions, statutes, or common law. Federal preemption of contrary state laws is grounded in the basic constitutional structure of a national government composed of various states, with each of the states being sovereign within its own boundaries. When any branch of the federal government acts it is deriving its power from the Constitution, which is the supreme law of the land. From the standpoint of constitutional federalism, it would make no sense for one state, through its laws, to be able to frustrate the operation of federal law; the result of such a system would be to vest each state with a veto power over federal action.

1. A Preemption Question Exists When Both Congress and a State Have Regulated the Same Activity. [§330]

A preemption issue arises when Congress, acting under one of its constitutional powers, regulates a certain activity and a state, acting under its Tenth Amendment police power, regulates the same activity. For preemption analysis to apply, both laws must be valid. For instance, assume that Congress and a state each passed a law regulating the construction of nuclear power plants. The first step would be to see if both laws are constitutional — that is, Congress' law as an exercise of its commerce power, and the state's law as an exercise of its police power. If both are valid, there is a preemption question — does the state law conflict or interfere with the operation of the federal law? If the answer is yes, the state law is invalid under preemption principles. If the federal law is invalid, it is out of the analysis (there is no preemption issue), and the only remaining question is whether the state law violates some implicit constitutional limitation such as the dormant commerce clause (see §253 above).

A preemption analysis has two steps:

a. Make sure that the federal and state laws are valid; and

b. See if the state law interferes with the operation of federal law.

2. Preemption May Occur in Three Ways. [§331]

a. Conflict between federal and state laws — federal law wins. A conflict may occur when it is not possible to comply with both laws, or when compliance with the state law would frustrate the purpose of the federal law.

b. Congress expressly says it intends to occupy an entire area of regulable activity — federal law wins, even if there is no conflict between the federal and state laws.

c. Congress has regulated an area so pervasively that a court may reasonably infer that Congress intended to occupy the entire field of regulable activity.

Each of these types of preemption is illustrated below.

B. CONFLICTING LAWS. [§332]

This kind of preemption involves two distinct kinds of cases: in one, it is physically impossible to comply with both laws; in the other, it is possible to comply with both, but compliance with the state law frustrates the purpose of the federal law. The second category usually involves a state law which imposes more stringent restrictions on a person or activity than does the applicable federal law.

1. *Southland Corp. v. Keating,* 465 U.S. 1 (1984). [§333]

The Court invalidated, on preemption grounds, a California law that required certain contractual disputes to be adjudicated in court rather than sent to arbitration. The state law conflicted with a federal law which prohibited states from requiring adjudication when contracting parties had agreed to arbitration.

2. *Hines v. Davidowitz,* 312 U.S. 52 (1941). [§334]

The Court invalidated, on preemption grounds, a Pennsylvania law requiring aliens to register yearly, and to carry an identification card to be shown to certain specified government officials. This state law frustrated the purposes and objectives of the federal law which required aliens to register once, and did not require the carrying of an identification card.

C. EXPRESS STATEMENT OF CONGRESS' INTENT TO PREEMPT. [§335]

If Congress says that it intends to occupy an entire field of regulation, state regulation in the area is prohibited, regardless of whether the state law conflicts with the federal law.

Aloha Airlines, Inc. v. Director of Taxation, 807 F.Supp. 1501 (1983). The Court invalidated, on preemption grounds, a state tax on the annual gross income of airlines operating within the state. The Court relied on a federal statute which expressly preempted any such gross receipts tax.

> **STUDY TIP: [§336]** When analyzing a preemption question, be careful about which specific field has been preempted by Congress. In *Pacific Gas & Electric Co. v. State Energy Resources Conservation & Development Commission*, 461 U.S. 190 (1983), the Court found no preemption of a California law that prohibited the construction of nuclear power plants until the state was satisfied that a particular project satisfied its concerns of cost and consumer need. Congress had preempted the narrow field of safety in nuclear-power production, but the state law operated in a specific area that Congress had not touched.

D. PERVASIVE REGULATION BY CONGRESS. [§337]

If Congress regulates an area very comprehensively, a court may draw the inference that Congress intended to occupy that area.

Burbank v. Lockheed Air Terminal, Inc., 411 U.S. 624 (1973). The Court invalidated, on preemption grounds, a city curfew on aircraft flights from the local airport. Despite a legitimate local interest, noise control, pervasive federal regulation of aircraft traffic led the Court to conclude that Congress had intended to preempt the field of airport regulation.

> **EXAMPLE: [§338]** *Pennsylvania v. Nelson*, 350 U.S. 497 (1956). The Court invalidated, on preemption grounds, Pennsylvania's Sedition Act. Extensive federal regulation of the area of anti-communist laws led the Court to consider the field preempted.

REVIEW PROBLEM — FEDERAL PREEMPTION OF STATE LAWS

PROBLEM: Congress passes a law which sets the standards of maturity that kiwi fruit must meet before it is shipped in interstate commerce. The State of Oz has a law which sets different standards for kiwi maturity before the fruit can be sold in the state. Is the Oz law constitutional?

Answer: No. The Oz law is preempted by the federal law setting minimum standards for the interstate shipment of kiwi fruit. While it may be possible to comply with both the federal and state laws, the state law certainly frustrates the purpose of the federal law, which is to balance the needs of the growers, the consumers, and the interstate market. You should think about the danger to interstate commerce that would flow from numerous state laws setting standards different from those of the federal government. See §332 for further review.

OUTLINE

X. STATE ACTION REQUIREMENT FOR THE APPLICATION OF CERTAIN CONSTITUTIONAL PROTECTIONS

A. INTRODUCTION. [§339]

Most of the provisions of the Constitution which protect individual rights limit government actors, but are irrelevant when a private actor abridges someone's rights. The Bill of Rights limits the federal government, and the Fourteenth and Fifteenth Amendments limit state governments. (The Thirteenth Amendment prohibits all slavery whether engaged in by a government or by a private actor.) **The "state action" requirement (actually "government action," since it applies to the federal government also) becomes an issue when a private actor harms someone in such a way that a constitutional issue would arise if the harm were inflicted by a government actor, and when there is some reason to impute government action to the private individual who caused the harm.** To be able to assert that a private actor violated his or her constitutional rights, a plaintiff must be able to argue that the private party's actions are sufficiently imbued with state action to make the Constitution applicable. In other words, when is there enough of a connection between the private actor and a government so that the Court will treat the private actor as if he or she is the equivalent of a government actor?

B. GENERAL ANALYSIS OF STATE ACTION QUESTIONS. [§340]

There are three main factors the Court considers when deciding whether to impute state action to a private party, thus making constitutional limitations applicable to the actions of the private party:

1. To what extent does the private actor rely on governmental assistance and benefits;

2. Whether the actor is performing a traditional governmental function that has been engaged in exclusively by government;

3. Whether the injury caused is aggravated in a unique way by government intervention.

> **STUDY TIP:** Be aware that these categories will overlap in many of the cases. For instance, the Court has found state action when an attorney in a civil case exercises a peremptory challenge based on race. (See §356). In such case, the Court has said that state action could be imputed to the attorney because jury selection is a traditional, exclusive government function, and because the state court was significantly involved in racial discrimination by enforcing the peremptory challenge.

C. RELIANCE ON GOVERNMENTAL ASSISTANCE AND BENEFITS. [§341]

This is pretty much a "kitchen-sink" kind of analysis. **The plaintiff argues every possible connection between the private actor and the state, and the Court looks at the totality of circumstances to see if there is enough of a connection between the private actor and a government to apply constitutional protections.** Be aware of the number and kinds of relationships between the private actor and the government. The Court today is not very willing to impute state action to private actors.

1. Symbiotic Relationship Between Government and Private Actor. [§342]

Numerous relationships between a private actor and a government may be enough to impute state action to the private actor.

Burton v. Wilmington Parking Authority, 365 U.S. 715 (1961). The Court found state action on the part of a private restaurant owner who refused to serve members of racial minorities. The Court looked at all the connections between the state and the restaurant and found the Fourteenth Amendment applicable. The restaurant was located in a state-owned parking authority, and was leased from the authority. The Court focused on the interdependence between the restaurant and the parking authority, including the fact that the restaurant would share the parking authority's tax exemption in relation to any improvements done to the restaurant.

2. Government Involvement in a Racially Discriminatory Bequest. [§343]

There is state action if government officials act as trustees of a racially discriminatory private will. State action may also be present if there are enough connections between a city and land devised for use as a whites-only park.

Evans v. Newton, 382 U.S. 296 (1966). The Court found state action when Senator A.O. Bacon devised land to Macon, Georgia for use as a whites-only park. The Court had previously ruled that it was state action for government officials to act as trustees of a racially discriminatory private will. In *Evans*, the Court also found state action after private trustees had been substituted for the original public trustees. The park had long been an integral part of the city's activities, had been granted a tax exemption, and had been maintained by the city. The Court also alluded to the municipal nature of the services provided by such a park.

3. State Constitutional Authorization of Racial Discrimination. [§344]

State action existed when a private party, relying on a state constitutional provision (since repealed), refused to rent an apartment because of the race of the lessee.

Reitman v. Mulkey, 387 U.S. 369 (1967). The Court found state action in a private party's refusal to rent an apartment to someone because of the applicant's race. A provision of the California constitution authorized racial discrimination in the sale or rental of property. The right to discriminate based on race was a part of the basic charter of the state, and, as such, implicated the state in any refusal to sell or rent because of race. (This provision of the California Constitution was repealed in 1974.)

4. Liquor License. [§345]

A state granting a liquor license to a private bar or club does not make the bar or club a state actor.

Moose Lodge v. Irvis, 407 U.S. 163 (1972). The Court found no state action simply because a state grants a liquor license to an establishment. Irvis was refused service at a local Moose Lodge because of his race. He asserted state action by virtue of the lodge's liquor license.

5. Relationships Between a State and a Private School. [§346]

Extensive funding, heavy regulation, and large student referral by the state are not enough to confer state action on a private school.

Rendell-Baker v. Kohn, 457 U.S. 830 (1982). The Court found no state action on the part of a private school that allegedly discharged some teachers without affording them procedural due process. The Court rejected the teachers' claim under 42 U.S.C. §1983 that their free speech rights were violated because they were fired allegedly for supporting student grievances against the school. There was no state action despite nearly all the students being referred to the school by government agencies (such as the Drug Rehabilitation Division of the Massachusetts Department of Mental Health), the school being heavily regulated by the state, and public funds accounting for 90-99% of the school's operating budget.

6. State Help in Executing an Attachment. [§347]

Active participation by state officials in executing a prejudgment attachment will constitute state action.

In *Lugar v. Edmonson Oil Co.*, 457 U.S. 922 (1982), an oil company which supplied oil to the operator of a truck stop was not paid. The oil company sued on the debt in state court and, pursuant to state law, sought prejudgment attachment of certain of the debtor's property. The Court found state action because the state statute authorized a court clerk and the sheriff to authorize and execute a prejudgment attachment of a debtor's property. The active participation of these state officials distinguishes this case from *Flagg Bros. v. Brooks* (see §359 below).

7. United States Olympic Committee is Not a State Actor. [§348]

There was no government action by virtue of Congress giving the United States Olympic Committee the power to control the use of the word "Olympic."

San Francisco Arts & Athletics, Inc. v. U.S. Olympic Committee, 483 U.S. 522 (1987). The Court found no government action on the part of the U.S. Olympic Commitee (USOC), despite the fact that Congress explicitly gave the USOC power to allow or prohibit the use of the word "Olympic" by other groups. The organizers of the "Gay Olympic Games" sued, asserting that the USOC violated their equal protection rights under the Due Process Clause of the Fifth Amendment. The Court ruled that there were insufficient connections between Congress and the USOC to impute state action.

8. National Collegiate Athletic Association is Not a State Actor. [§349]

The NCAA is not a government actor; it is a voluntary organization made up of both private and public institutions.

NCAA v. Tarkanian, 488 U.S. 179 (1988). The Court found no state action on the part of the National Collegiate Athletic Association (NCAA) when the University of Nevada, Las Vegas (UNLV) suspended its basketball coach (Jerry Tarkanian) under threat by the NCAA to impose sanctions on UNLV if it did not take action against Tarkanian. Tarkanian sued the university and the NCAA, alleging a violation of due process. The Court ruled that the NCAA, being a private association composed of both private and public universities, was not a state actor.

The Court will find state action when a private party is performing a function that has traditionally been performed by government. In recent years the Court has insisted that the function be one that has been exclusively performed by government. The result has been a reluctance by the Court to find state action under this theory.

1. Elections. [§351]

Any pre-primary or primary election that feeds into a general election will be considered state action.

a. In *Smith v. Allwright*, **321 U.S. 649 (1944), [§352]** Lonnie Smith, a black resident of Harris County, Texas, sued officials of the Democratic Party of Texas who refused to allow him to vote in a primary election of the Democratic Party. The Court found state action on the part of the Democratic Party when it excluded Smith and other blacks from voting in the primary election. State delegation to a political party to set the qualifications for primary elections is a delegation of a state function which implicates the state in the party's actions. The Court decided *Smith* on the basis of the Fifteenth Amendment, which prohibits a state from abridging the right to vote on account of the race of the voter.

b. In *Terry v. Adams*, **345 U.S. 461 (1953), [§353]** the Court found state action on the part of the Texas Jaybird Democratic Association when it excluded blacks from its pre-primary elections. *Terry* was a class action brought by black citizens challenging the actions of a self-governing voluntary political association which held its own primary elections which, in effect, determined who would run as candidates in the official primary election of the Texas Democratic Party. The Jaybird Democratic Association did not allow blacks to vote or run in their pre-primary elections. The rule seems to be that any party or association activity that feeds into a general election will be deemed state action.

2. Company Town. [§354]

If a company town performs the traditional functions of a municipality, it will be treated as a state actor.

In *Marsh v. Alabama*, 326 U.S. 501 (1946), Grace Marsh, a Jehovah's Witness, was distributing literature on the premises of a company-owned town contrary to the wishes of the town's management. She was asked to stop, she refused, and was arrested by a Deputy Sheriff who had been hired to serve as the town's policeman. She was convicted of trespass under a state statute making it a crime to remain on the premises of another after having been asked to leave. The Court found state action, reasoning that the town was the functional equivalent of a municipality, so the First Amendment would apply there as it would in any town.

3. Privately-Owned Shopping Center. [§355]

No state action is involved when the owner of a privately-owned shopping center excludes speakers from the shopping center.

In *Hudgens v. NLRB*, 424 U.S. 507 (1976), union members began to picket their employer's store in a shopping center, but left when told they would be arrested for trespassing. The picketers asserted a First Amendment right to picket in the shopping center which they claimed was the functional equivalent of a municipal shopping district. The Court found no state action when the owner of the privately-owned shopping center excluded the picketers from the shopping center premises. The relatively limited nature of the place distinguishes this case from the company-town case of *Marsh v. Alabama* (previous case). However, a state may, by its constitution, give speakers access to privately-owned shopping centers. *Pruneyard Shopping Center v. Robins*, 447 U.S. 74 (1980).

4. Peremptory Challenges to Jurors. [§356]

The use of peremptory challenges, in a criminal or civil case, involves state action.

In *Edmonson v. Leesville Concrete Co.* , 500 U.S. 614 (1991), Edmonson sued Leesville Concrete in federal district court, alleging that Leesville's negligence had caused him personal injury. Leesville used two of its three peremptory challenges to exclude black jurors. Edmonson, who is black, asserted that the racial exclusion of jurors violated his equal protections rights under the Fifth Amendment Due Process Clause. The Court found state action on the basis of Leesville's attorney using peremptory challenges to exclude jurors because of their race. Selecting a jury is a quintessential, exclusive governmental function, and when the court confers on a private party the power to determine who gets on a jury, the private attorney's actions will be limited by the Constitution. The Court also said that state action was present because the state court, by enforcing the peremptory challenges, significantly involved itself in invidious racial discrimination.

5. Public Defenders. [§357]

Public defenders are not considered state actors, even though they are paid by the state.

In *Polk County v. Dodson*, 454 U.S. 312 (1981), Richard Dodson, who was convicted of robbery in state court, filed a 42 U.S.C. §1983 claim against his public defender, alleging ineffective assistance of counsel. The Court found that there is no state action on the part of a public defender when he or she is acting in the adversarial role of appointed counsel.

6. State-Granted Monopolies. [§358]

A public utility, even if granted monopoly status by a state, is not a state actor.

In *Jackson v. Metropolitan Edison Co.*, 419 U.S. 345 (1974), Catherine Jackson filed a 42 U.S.C. §1983 action against Metropolitan Edison, claiming violation of her due process rights. The Court found no state action when the heavily regulated electric company discontinued Jackson's service without providing her with notice, a hearing, and an opportunity to pay her bills. The Court said even if the company had been granted a monopoly by the state, that fact would not be dispositive of the state action issues. The Court ruled that supplying electricity was not traditionally the exclusive prerogative of the state, so no state action could be imputed to the electric company.

7. Statutory Warehouseman's Lien. [§359]

No state action exists when a state authorizes an owner of a warehouse to sell the belongings of someone who did not pay his or her bill.

Flagg Bros., Inc. v. Brooks, 436 U.S. 149 (1978). The Court found no state action when a state statute authorized the owner of a warehouse to sell the belongings of someone who had not paid her storage bill. Shirley Brooks sued under 42 U.S.C. §1983, alleging an unconstitutional deprivation of property when the owner of a warehouse threatened to sell her property pursuant to the statutory authorization. The Court emphasized that the activity sought to be characterized as state action must be an exclusive governmental function, and that this self-help remedy was simply one means among many to resolve this kind of dispute.

E. STATE-COURT INTERVENTION WHICH AIDS PRIVATE DISCRIMINATION. [§360]

The Court has used this kind of state action analysis exclusively where a white homeowner breaches a restrictive covenant with other white homeowners not to sell a house to a black buyer. In these cases, the Court has found state action whether the plaintiff seeks injunctive relief (enforcement of the restrictive covenant), or attempts to recover money damages from the breaching party.

1. STATE-COURT INJUNCTION. [§361]

The Court has found sufficient state action. In the case where the plaintiff seeks an injunction forcing the white seller to comply with the terms of the restrictive covenant, the white homeowner has sold his or her house to a black buyer, and the buyer will move in unless the state court enforces the restrictive covenant. In other words, the state-court injunction will directly cause the discrimination against the black buyer to take place. The Court has found state action in such a case.

Shelley v. Kraemer, 334 U.S. 1 (1948). The Court found state action when a state court issued an order enforcing a restrictive covenant in which white homeowners agreed not to sell property to black buyers. State action was present by virtue of the state-court judge ordering the white seller to comply with the terms of the restrictive covenant; in effect, the decree of the state court directly prevented the black buyer from moving into the house.

2. STATE-COURT AWARD OF MONEY DAMAGES. [§362]

In the second case, where the plaintiff seeks money damages from the white homeowner who breached the restrictive covenant, the Court found state action because a state-court award of money damages against the white seller would be tantamount to imposing a penalty against the white seller for refusing to discriminate on racial grounds in the sale of a house.

Barrows v. Jackson, 346 U.S. 249 (1953). The Court found state action in a state-court suit for monetary damages for breach of a racially restrictive covenant. While this suit would not have resulted in judicially enforced discrimination (as in *Shelley v. Kraemer*), the practical effect of an award of money damages would be that the state would be enforcing a penalty against a seller who chose not to discriminate against a buyer because of race.

F. NO STATE ACTION WHEN INJURIES ARE INFLICTED BY PRIVATE PARTIES. [§363]

A State's failure to protect an individual from violence by a private party does not constitute a violation of the Due Process Clause. The government has no obligation to protect a person from harm by another person. There will be state action, however, if a person is injured while under the custody or control of the state.

DeShaney v. Winnebago Dept. of Social Services, 489 U.S. 189 (1989). The Court found no state action when a state social worker investigated allegations of child abuse, found some corroborating evidence, but left the little boy in his home where he was severely beaten by his father. The boy suffered brain damage and, as a result of the beatings, became profoundly retarded. The Court rejected the argument that the social worker's failure to act deprived the boy of due process. A state's failure to protect a person from private violence does not involve state action unless the state takes a person into custody and holds that person there involuntarily.

G. A CORPORATION THAT IS CREATED AND CONTROLLED BY THE GOVERNMENT IS SUBJECT TO CONSTITUTIONAL

A corporation is a government actor when it is created by a special congressional statute which establishes detailed goals for the corporation, sets forth is structure and powers, and gives the President the power to appoint a majority of its board of directors.

Lebron v. National Railroad Passenger Corp., 115 S.Ct. 961 (1995). Lebron, a creator of billboard displays that comment on public issues, sued the National Railroad Passenger Corporation (Amtrak), claiming that Amtrak violated his First Amendment rights by rejecting a billboard display he designed because of the political nature of the billboard's message (criticizing the Coors beer company for supporting the Nicaraguan Contras and other right-wing causes). The Court held that Amtrak is a government actor, despite the fact that the congressional statute creating Amtrak provided that Amtrak was not an agency of the U.S. Government. The Court noted that Amtrak was created by a special authorizing statute, the statute set forth the structure and powers of Amtrak, and the President had the power to appoint a majority of Amtrak's board of directors.

PROBLEM 1. Pat Jones filed a civil lawsuit against Christine Smith, alleging that Christine engaged in gender discrimination by refusing to promote Pat because he is a man. During jury selection, the attorney for Christine uses all her peremptory challenges to exclude male jurors. Pat claims that the use of peremptory challenges to exclude male jurors violates the Fourteenth Amendment's prohibition against gender discrimination. Is there sufficient state action for Pat to have an equal protection argument?

> **Answer:** Yes. The Court has ruled that picking a jury is an exclusive, traditional sovereign function, and that state action exists whenever an attorney, in a civil or criminal case, exercises peremptory challenges. See §356.

PROBLEM 2. The Lizard Lounge, which is a bar owned by the Mayor of Id, has a liquor license issued by the State of Oz. The Mayor has instructed the doorkeepers (a politically correct term for bouncers) to admit to the bar only those persons who voted for the Mayor in the last election. Jane and Bob, vocal political opponents of the Mayor, are refused admission because they voted against him in the last election. They want to file a civil rights lawsuit against the Mayor, arguing that his policy violated their rights to free speech and political association. Do they have a case?

> **Answer:** No. The mere granting of a liquor license does not turn the bar owner into a state actor. For Jane and Bob to have any chance of proceeding with their lawsuit, they would have to show a number of significant relationships between the government and the Lizard Lounge, such as a lease agreement, maintenance and protection by the city, and location within a city-owned building. (See *Burton v. Wilmington Parking Authority* §342.)

PROBLEM 3. The State of Oz, through its Racing Commission, grants franchises to operate off-track betting (OTB) establishments, where a person may go to place a bet on horse races occurring all over the state. Betty's Betting Parlor, which has a state-granted franchise, restricts access to U.S. citizens. Bob, a citizen of Canada, sues, claiming that Betty is violating his equal protection rights. Does Bob have a case?

> **Answer:** Probably not. In *Jackson v. Metropolitan Edison Co.*, the Court said that even if a state had granted a monopoly to a utility company, that alone would not constitute state action. Presumably, the granting of a franchise by the state would not be state action either. See §358 for further review.

XI. CONGRESSIONAL ENFORCEMENT OF CIVIL RIGHTS

A. INTRODUCTION TO CIVIL RIGHTS LEGISLATION. [§365]

Following the Civil War, the Constitution was amended three times in an attempt to eliminate not only slavery as an institution, but also the vestiges of slavery (disabilities imposed because of a person's race or color). The Civil War Amendments provide, in pertinent part:

Thirteenth Amendment (1865): Section 1."Neither slavery nor involuntary servitude . . . shall exist within the United States. . . ."

Section 2."Congress shall have power to enforce this article by appropriate legislation." (Note: There is no state action requirement in the Thirteenth Amendment.)

Fourteenth Amendment (1868): Section 1.". . . No State shall have or enforce any law which shall abridge the privileges or immunities of citizens of the United States; nor shall any State deprive any person of life, liberty, or property, without due process of law; nor deny to any person within its jurisdiction the equal protection of the laws."

Section 5."The Congress shall have power to enforce, by appropriate legislation, the provisions of this article."

Fifteenth Amendment (1870): Section 1."The right of citizens of the United States to vote shall not be denied or abridged by the United States or by any state on account of race, color, or previous condition of servitude."

Section 2."The Congress shall have power to enforce this article by appropriate legislation."

1. GUARANTEE OF INDIVIDUAL RIGHTS. [§366]

The first section of each of the Civil War Amendments provides a guarantee that states (and under the Thirteenth Amendment, private parties as well) will not abridge the individual rights of persons covered by the Amendments. In other words, each amendment creates a right that is assertable against a state (or private party with the Thirteenth Amendment) if the state abridges the specific activity protected by the amendments. An individual may use section 1 of any of these amendments as the basis of a constitutional claim against a state.

2. CONGRESSIONAL ENFORCEMENT OF RIGHTS GUARANTEED BY THE CIVIL WAR AMENDMENTS. [§367]

The enabling clauses of the Civil War Amendments (section 2 of the Thirteenth and Fifteenth Amendments, and section 5 of the Fourteenth Amendment) give Congress the power to pass laws effectuating the guarantees of these amendments. Under the enabling clauses, Congress is able to pass legislation which directly limits the ability of states to engage in activity which might abridge the rights protected under the amendments. In other words, Congress may create statutory causes of action against states that violate the rights protected by the amendments. Congress has passed various statutes under these enabling clauses. The most important are:

— 42 U.S.C. §1981 (1866) "Equal rights under the law. All persons . . . shall have the same right in every State . . . to make and enforce contracts, to sue, be parties, give evidence, and to the full equal benefit of all laws and proceedings for the security of persons and property as is enjoyed by white citizens. . . ."

— 42 U.S.C. §1982 (1866) "Property rights of citizens. All citizens of the United States shall have the same right, in every State . . . , as is enjoyed by white citizens thereof to inherit, purchase, lease, sell, hold and convey real or personal property."

— 42 U.S.C. §1983 (1871) "Civil action for deprivation of rights. Every person who, under color [of state law], subjects . . . any citizen of the United States or other persons within the jurisdiction thereof to the deprivation of any rights, privileges or immunities secured by the Constitution and laws, shall be liable to the person injured in an action of law, suit in equity or other proper proceeding. . . ."

— 42 U.S.C. §1985 (1871) "Conspiracy to interfere with civil rights . . . . If two or more persons in any State . . . conspire . . . for the purpose of depriving, either directly or indirectly, any person or class of persons of the equal protection of the laws, or of equal privileges and immunities under the laws; . . . the party so injured or deprived may have an action for the recovery of damages, . . . against any one or more of the conspirators."

B. CONGRESSIONAL IMPLEMENTATION OF THE CIVIL WAR AMENDMENTS. [§368]

When Congress enacts legislation under an enabling clause of one of the Civil War Amendments, it is protecting the substantive rights guaranteed by the specific amendment. For example, if Congress, acting under the enabling clause of the Thirteenth Amendment, prohibits private schools from excluding students based on their race, it is necessarily saying that such racial exclusion is a badge or incident of slavery which Congress may prohibit under its constitutional power to enforce the guarantees of the Thirteenth Amendment. The Court has given Congress great leeway to legislate under the enabling clauses of the Civil War Amendments. For instance, the Court has ruled that Congress, acting under section 5 of the Fourteenth Amendment, may prohibit literacy tests as a prerequisite for voting, even though the Court has never ruled that literacy tests are unconstitutional under section 1 of the Fourteenth Amendment. In this chapter, we deal with congressional interpretation of the guarantees of the Civil War Amendments. In subsequent chapters, we deal with the Court's interpretation of the substantive guarantees of those amendments.

1. Congressional Regulation of Private Actions Under the Thirteenth Amendment. [§369]

The Thirteenth Amendment does not require state action; all slavery is prohibited, whether engaged in by private or governmental entities.

a. Congress May Prohibit Private Racial Discrimination in the Sale or Lease of Property. [§370]

Refusal to sell or lease property based on race is a badge of slavery, and is actionable under 42 U.S.C. §1982.

Jones v. Alfred H. Mayer Co., 392 U.S. 409 (1968). The Court upheld the constitutionality of 42 U.S.C. §1982. A black couple was not allowed to purchase a home because of their race. All the defendants were private parties, and no state action was involved. The Court relied on the

Thirteenth Amendment as the basis for §1982's prohibition of racial discrimination in private actions regarding the sale of property. The Court held that refusal to sell or lease property based on someone's race is a badge or incident of slavery under the Thirteenth Amendment and, as such, is an activity that Congress has the authority to prevent.

b. Congress May Prohibit Private Racial Discrimination in Contractual Relationships. [§371]

Racial discrimination in private contracts is actionable under 42 U.S.C. §1981.

Runyon v. McCrary, 427 U.S. 160 (1976). The Court ruled that 42 U.S.C. §1981 prohibits private, commercially operated, non-sectarian schools from excluding qualified children solely because of their race. The statute prohibits racial discrimination in the making and enforcement of private contracts, including the general offer by the school to attract qualified students. The Court said it was not considering the question of a religious school practicing racial discrimination for religious reasons; this was simply a private contractual situation.

c. Congress May Prohibit Private Racial Discrimination in Commercial Relationships. [§372]

Racial discrimination by private employers is actionable under 42 U.S.C. §1981.

McDonald v. Santa Fe Trial Transportation Co., 427 U.S. 273 (1976). The Court ruled that 42 U.S.C. §1981 prohibits private employers from discriminating on the basis of race. Two white employees who were fired for theft sued on the basis that a black employee who had done the same thing was not fired. The Court ruled that whites, as well as blacks, have a cause of action under §1981.

d. Congress May Prohibit Private Racially-Motivated Conspiracies Depriving Someone of Civil Rights. [§373]

Private Race-based Conspiracies to Deprive Someone of Civil Rights are Actionable under 42 U.S.C. §1985.

In *Griffin v. Breckenridge*, 403 U.S. 88 (1971), the white defendants, acting under a mistaken belief that the black plaintiffs were workers for a civil rights organization, stopped the plaintiffs' car on a public highway in Mississippi and assaulted them. The Court ruled that 42 U.S.C. §1985 provides a cause of action for private conspiracies to deprive a person of the right to interstate travel, so long as the plaintiff can show some racial or class-based motivation for the interference with the right. The Court based its ruling on both the Thirteenth Amendment and Congress' power to protect the exercise of the right to interstate travel, which is guaranteed against both private and governmental intrusion.

e. Congress May Not Regulate Absent Racial Motivation. [§374]

Private conspiracies must be racially motivated to be actionable under 42 U.S.C. §1985.

In *United Brotherhood of Carpenters v. Scott*, 463 U.S. 825 (1983), a group of men protesting a construction company's practice of hiring nonunion workers assaulted two of the company's employees and destroyed some construction equipment. The group consisted of several truckloads of local union members who were part of a protest meeting two days prior to the assault, and who had planned the assault on the nonunion workers. The Court ruled that 42 U.S.C. §1985 does not protect against a private conspiracy to infringe free speech rights, as long as there was no racial motivation for the conspiracy. The Court distinguished *Griffin* (previous case) as a case involving Thirteenth Amendment rights, plus the right to travel — neither requiring state action for abridgement to occur. First Amendment rights, on the other hand, are only protected from state action.

2. Congressional Enforcement of the Fourteenth Amendment. [§375]

Under section 1 of the Fourteenth Amendment, a state may not deprive a person of equal protection of the laws, or of life, liberty, or property without due process of law. Section 1 of the amendment does not apply to the actions of private parties. Accordingly, Congress may regulate only state action when it legislates under section 5 of the Fourteenth Amendment.

a. Generally, Congress May Only Prohibit State Deprivations of Individual Rights. [§376]

When legislating under section 5 of the Fourteenth Amendment, Congress is limited to remedying state action.

Civil Rights Cases, 109 U.S. 3 (1883). The Court ruled that §5 of the Fourteenth Amendment did not give Congress the power to pass the Civil Rights Act of 1875, which prohibited racial discrimination in places of public accommodation. The Court held that the Fourteenth Amendment deals only with state action; invasion of individual rights by private persons is not within the scope of the amendment, and therefore Congress may not reach such activity under §5.

b. Congress May Prohibit Deprivations of Civil Rights Engaged in Jointly By Private and State Actors. [§378]

Joint action by private and governmental actors meets the state action requirement of the Fourteenth Amendment.

U.S. v. Price, 383 U.S. 787 (1966). Under 18 U.S.C. §§241 and 242, it is a crime to conspire to deprive a person of his or her civil rights. In *Price*, several indictments alleged that three police officers and fifteen private citizens murdered three civil rights workers, thereby depriving them of their due process rights. The Court ruled that indictments could be brought against the private parties because a private person is deemed to be "acting under color of state law" for purposes of civil rights statutes if he or she is jointly engaged with state officials in the prohibited activity.

c. Congress May Criminalize a Private Conspiracy to Deprive a Person of the Right to Interstate Travel. [§379]

The right to interstate travel is a fundamental right of national citizenship which Congress may protect from even private interference.

In *U.S. v. Guest*, 383 U.S. 745 (1966), the defendants were indicted under a federal civil rights law (42 U.S.C. §241) for conspiring to interfere with a black citizen's right to travel freely to and from the State of Georgia. The Court held that the indictment was proper, because the right to interstate travel is fundamental, and Congress may criminalize even private conspiracies engaged in with the specific intent to deprive a person of that right.

d. Congress May Prohibit Literacy Tests for Voting. [§380]

A person may not be denied the right to vote because of an inability to read or write the English language.

Katzenbach v. Morgan, 384 U.S. 641 (1966). The Court upheld a provision of the Voting Rights Act of 1965 which provided that no person who has completed the sixth grade in a Puerto Rican school in which instruction was in a language other than English shall be denied the ability to vote in any election because of an inability to read or write English. The federal law nullified New York literacy tests for voting. The Court held that Congress, acting under §5 of the Fourteenth Amendment, may prohibit literacy tests as a prerequisite for voting, even though the Court has not ruled them to be unconstitutional.

e. Congress Does Not Have the Power to Set the Voting Age in State and Local Elections. [§381]

States have the power to set the qualifications for voters in state, county, and municipal elections.

Oregon v. Mitchell, 400 U.S. 112 (1970). Seven Justices, in a fragmented set of opinions, cut back on the *Morgan* (previous case) dictum that Congress has unlimited power to define substantive equal protection guarantees. The Justices invalidated a section of the 1970 amendments to the Voting Right Act which lowered the minimum voting age in state and local elections from 21 to 18 years of age. (The decision resulted in the passage of the Twenty-Sixth Amendment in 1971, accomplishing that result.) *Morgan* was distinguished as being limited to cases involving congressional protection of racial or ethnic minorities. In *Mitchell*, the Justices focused on the importance, from a state's rights perspective, of a state being able to determine the qualifications of its own voters for state, county, and municipal offices.

f. Congress Does Not Have the Power Under §5 of the Fourteenth Amendment to Define Substantive Rights. [§381.1]

Congress can only remedy violation of rights defined by the Court; it may not create substantive rights.

In *Boerne v. Flores*, ___ S.Ct. ___ (1997), the Court by a 6-3 vote, held that the Religious Freedom Restoration Act (RFRA) exceeded Congress' enforcement power under §5 of the Fourteenth Amendment. In *Boerne*, the Catholic Archbishop of San Antonio applied for a building permit to enlarge a church. The local zoning authorities denied the permit on the basis of a historic preservation ordinance which the zoning authorities said applied to the church. The Archbishop challenged the zoning ordinance, relying in part on RFRA, which would require the city to show a compelling reason for the permit denial and that it had chosen the least restrictive means to achieve the purposes of the historic preservation ordinance. RFRA applied to any branch of federal or state government, to all federal or state officials, and to all federal or state laws. §5 of the

Fourteenth Amendment gives Congress the power to enforce the equal protection and due process guarantee of the Fourteenth Amendment. The Court said that Congress does not have the power to define substantive rights under the Fourteenth Amendment; it only has the power to remedy violations of rights that have been defined by the Court under its power to interpret the Constitution. For Congress to define (not simply protect) substantive rights would violate separation-of-powers principles. The Court also said that RFRA, by defining substantive rights enforceable against states, violates the states' traditional prerogatives to regulate for the health and safety of its citizens.

3. Congressional Enforcement of the Fifteenth Amendment. [§382]

To enforce the Fifteenth Amendment's prohibition against discrimination in voting based on race, Congress passed the Voting Rights Act of 1965. The Act is directed at forcing governmental entities (such as cities or counties) to comply with congressional mandates requiring fairness in the voting process; it does not provide a private cause of action for a person who might be aggrieved by some governmental action that abridged his or her right to vote, such as a state literacy test.

a. Congressional Prohibition of Literacy Tests for Voting is Constitutional. [§383]

Congress may prohibit literacy tests as a means of eliminating racial discrimination in voting.

South Carolina v. Katzenbach, 383 U.S. 301 (1966). The Court upheld provisions of the Voting Rights Act of 1965 which prohibited states from using discriminatory literacy tests and other devices as a means of denying the right to vote on racial grounds. The main provision suspended the use of literacy tests (as a qualification for voting) for a period of five years from the last occurrence of substantial voting discrimination. This provision of the Act automatically applied to any state or political subdivision of a state which used a literacy test as a qualification for voting, and in which fewer than 50% of its voting-age residents were registered to vote on November 1, 1964. South Carolina challenged the act as exceeding congressional authority and encroaching on an area reserved to the states by the Constitution. The Court held that, even in light of the Tenth Amendment powers of the states, Congress may use any rational means to effectuate the prohibition of racial discrimination in voting as set forth in the Fifteenth Amendment.

b. Use of Racial Criteria in Drawing Voting Districts is Constitutional When Done to Comply With the Voting Rights Act. [§384]

A state may create or maintain a black-majority voting district to comply with federal law.

United Jewish Organizations v. Carey, 430 U.S. 144 (1977). A majority of the Justices (seven Justices agreed in the judgment, but there was no majority opinion) upheld, against Fourteenth and Fifteenth Amendment challenges, provisions of a New York state legislative apportionment statute which used racial criteria to change the size of nonwhite majorities in some districts. To attain a 65% nonwhite majority in one district, a

Hasidic Jewish community was split between two districts. A state may create or maintain black majorities in certain districts to ensure that its apportionment plan complies with the Voting Rights Act.

c. Congress May Ban Electoral Changes That Have a Discriminatory Effect, Even if There is No Intent to Discriminate. [§385]

Congress' remedial power under §2 of the Fifth Amendment is broad enough to allow it to prohibit even non-intentional racial discrimination that affects a person's right to vote.

Rome v. U.S., 446 U.S. 156 (1980). The Court upheld the Attorney General's refusal, under §5 of the Voting Rights Act, to approve certain electoral changes on the basis that the changes had a racially discriminatory effect. (The changes involved reducing the number of electoral wards in the city, changing the terms of government officials, and adopting ward- based residency requirements). The Court ruled that the Voting Rights Act ban on electoral changes with a discriminatory effect is constitutional, even if there is no showing that the governmental unit ever intended to discriminate. While §1 of the Fifteenth Amendment prohibits only intentional discrimination in voting, Congress may, under §2, prohibit any practice that has a nonintentional discriminatory effect.

PROBLEM 1. While driving down the street in the City of Id, Ben Jaines was stopped by two city police officers. The police asked Ben to get out of his car, and when Ben refused, the officers pulled him from the vehicle. While making racial slurs (Ben was not of the same race as the officers), the officers began to hit and kick Ben. Two young men came by, and, while not actually participating in the beating of Ben, stood by threateningly, and prevented Ben from escaping. The police officers and the two young men were indicted under federal laws making it a crime to conspire to deprive a person of his or her Fourteenth Amendment rights. Are the indictments of the two young men valid?

> **Answer:** Yes. If private parties are engaged in a joint endeavor with government officials to deprive someone of his or her civil rights, indictments may be brought against the private individuals. See §370 for further review.

PROBLEM 2. The Court has ruled that, as a general matter, literacy tests for voting do not violate the Fourteenth Amendment. May Congress, acting under its enforcement power from §5 of the Fourteenth Amendment, prohibit literacy tests as a prerequisite to voting in state elections?

> **Answer:** Yes. Congress may, under its §5 enforcement power, go beyond what the Court rules in terms of protecting individual rights. When a person sues under §1 of the Fourteenth Amendment, he or she is arguing that his or her individual rights have been violated. When Congress acts under §5, it is trying to remediate institutional problems by imposing requirements on entire political subdivisions. See §370 for further review.

PROBLEM 3. May Congress pass a law prohibiting racial discrimination in the sale or lease of real property? Discuss.

> **Answer:** Yes. Racial discrimination in the sale or lease of real property falls under the Thirteenth Amendment's prohibition of slavery. A refusal to sell or lease property is a badge or incident of slavery, and Congress may prohibit such activity under its enforcement power flowing from §2 of the Thirteenth Amendment. Remember that there is no state action requirement under the Thirteenth Amendment; slavery is prohibited, whether engaged in by private or governmental actors. See §370 for further review.

A. CONSTITUTIONAL STATUS OF LAWS THAT OPERATE RETROACTIVELY. [§386]

The Constitution has a number of provisions that prohibit the state and federal governments from passing laws that retroactively impair substantive rights. Fundamental fairness prohibits a government from imposing a civil or criminal penalty on someone who engaged in conduct which was not criminal or otherwise objectionable at the time it occurred. Retroactive laws also create notice problems; a person is entitled to know that certain activity is punishable before he or she has engaged in it. The three specific kinds of retroactive legislation studied in Constitutional Law classes are ex post facto laws, bills of attainder, and laws which impair the obligations of contracts.

B. EX POST FACTO LAWS. [§387]

An ex post facto law imposes criminal punishment for an act that was not a crime when it was done, or increases the punishment for a crime over and above the punishment prescribed at the time the crime was committed. There are two Ex Post Facto provisions in the Constitution. Article 1, §10 prohibits states from passing Ex Post Facto laws, and Article 1, §9 prohibits the federal government from doing so. For a law to be an ex post facto law, it must operate to the detriment of the defendant; any retroactive changes in the criminal law which do not hurt the defendant do not fall within the definition of an ex post facto law. As a general rule, these provisions limit only the power of legislatures to adopt new statutes; they do not limit the power of a court to overrule precedent and apply that ruling retroactively.

1. NON-VIOLATIONS. [§388]

The following laws do not violate the Ex Post Facto provisions of the Constitution.

a. Sentencing of Habitual Offenders. [§389]
Increased punishment for recidivists does not violate the prohibition against Ex Post Facto laws.

In *Gryger v. Burke*, 334 U.S. 728 (1948), the State of Pennsylvania imprisoned Francis Gryger for life as a habitual offender. One of the convictions on which his life sentence was based occurred before enactment of the Pennsylvania Habitual Criminal Act. The Court held that the Pennsylvania law did not violate the prohibition against Ex Post Facto laws because his sentence as a habitual offender is not to be viewed as additional punishment for earlier crimes; it is simply a stiffened penalty for the latest crime.

b. Deportation of Aliens. [§390]
Deportation of aliens has been held not to constitute punishment for purposes of the Ex Post Facto Clause.

In *Harisiades v. Shaughnessy*, 342 U.S. 580 (1952), the Court dealt with the question of whether the United States constitutionally may deport legally resident aliens because of membership in the Communist Party which ended before enactment of the federal law under which the aliens were deported. The Court held that the Ex Post Facto provisions of the Constitution only apply to penal laws which increase criminal punishment for previously lawful conduct. Deportation is a civil procedure which does not fall within the reach of the Ex Post Facto Clause.

c. Reducing a Sentence. Reducing the penalty for a crime does not violate the Ex Post Facto Clause because it does not hurt the defendant. [§391]

Rooney v. North Dakota, 196 U.S. 319 (1905). A legislature may retroactively reduce the penalty for a crime. This does not violate the Ex Post Facto law ban because the defendant is not hurt by the change in the law.

2. VIOLATIONS. [§392]

The following laws violate the Ex Post Facto Clause.

a. Reduction of "Good Time" A Prisoner May Earn. [§393]

Reducing the amount of "Good Time" a prisoner may earn violates the Ex Post Facto Clause because it adversely affects the prisoner's rights.

Weaver v. Graham, 450 U.S. 24 (1981). A state law, passed after a prisoner was convicted and sentenced, which reduced the amount of good time deductible from his sentence, was invalid as an Ex Post Facto law because it lengthened the amount of time the prisoner would be incarcerated.

b. Retroactive Cancellation of Early Release Credits. [§393.1]

Retroactively cancelling a prisoner's early release credits, regardless of the reason the credits were awarded, violates the Ex Post Facto Clause because it retroactively increases the prisoner's punishment.

In *Lynce v. Mathis*, 117 S.Ct. 891 (1997), the Court held that the retroactive application of a state law to cancel early release credits awarded to inmates convicted of murder and attempted murder violated the Ex Post Facto Clause. The fact that the credits were awarded solely because of concerns of prison overcrowding, and not for good behavior, was irrelevant to the Ex Post Facto inquiry. The law clearly operated retroactively, and also resulted in increased punishment (the petitioner had already been released from prison, so the law resulted in his rearrest and reincarceration).

c. Revising a Sentencing Statute. [§394]

Application of a revised sentencing statute to pre-revision crimes violates the Ex Post Facto Clause where the result is an increased sentence.

Miller v. Florida, 482 U.S. 423 (1987). Application of a state's revised sentencing statute to a defendant for crimes committed before the statute's revisions became effective violated the Ex Post Facto Clause. At the time the defendant committed the crime, the original statute provided a range of 3 1/2 to 4 1/2 years as a sentence. After the crime was committed, the statute was changed to provide for 5 1/2 to 7 years in prison.

d. Involuntary Civil Commitment of Dangerously Mentally Ill Persons. [§394.1]

Involuntary commitment of a mentally ill person has been held not to constitute punishment for purposes of the Ex Post Facto Clause. Such a commitment after a person has already served a prison sentence for a crime does not violate the Ex Post Facto Clause because it is not imposing additional punishment for the crime.

In Kansas v. Hendricks, ___ S.Ct. ___ (1997), the Court upheld Kansas' Sexually Violent Predator Act, which established procedures for the civil commitment of sexually violent offenders who suffer from a mental abnormality or personality disorder which makes the person likely to engage in the predatory acts of sexual violence. Leroy Hendricks, who was imprisoned for a sexual offense involving two 13-year-old boys and was diagnosed as a pedophile, was committed under the Act, after his release from prison. He argued that the Act was an Ex Post Facto law, since it retroactively increased the punishment for his crime. A 5-4 majority of the Court held that the Act did not establish criminal proceedings because its purpose was the protection of the public from harm, not punishment or deterrence, and was limited to persons who suffered from a volitional impairment rendering them dangerous beyond their control. Since restricting the freedom of the dangerously mentally ill is a legitimate nonpunitive governmental objective, and since the Act does not impose punishment, it does not violate the Ex Post Facto Clause.

C. BILLS OF ATTAINDER. [§395]

A Bill of Attainder is a legislative act imposing punishment on an individual or an easily identifiable group of individuals without the benefit of a judicial trial. A Bill of Attainder punishes on the basis of a past or unalterable trait, and is aimed at named individuals or a small class of individuals who engaged in some specific conduct. If the legislature defines the class of individuals based on their having engaged in specific conduct, the law will qualify as a Bill of Attainder. There are two Bill of Attainder clauses in the Constitution: Article 1, §10 limits states, and Article 1, §9 limits the federal government.

1. FACTORS TO DETERMINE IF A LAW IS A BILL OF ATTAINDER. [§396]

The Court has identified three questions to ask in deciding whether a law is a bill of attainder. If you can answer these questions in the affirmative, the law will likely be held invalid as a bill of attainder.

1. Does the law fall within the historical meaning of legislative punishment? The Court has included within this definition imprisonment, banishment, the punitive confiscation of property, and the legislative prohibition of individuals or groups from employment or vocational opportunities;

2. Can the law reasonably be said to further only punitive legislative purposes? The Court looks at the nature and severity of the burden imposed to see if the law is directed to punishment, or to the accomplishment of some nonpunitive goals; and

3. Does the legislative record reveal a legislative intent to punish? The Court looks to the legislative history, legislative record, and pattern of laws dealing with a specific subject to discern the motivation of the legislature

in passing the law (did they intend to punish?). *Selective Service System v. Minnesota Public Interest Research Group*, 468 U.S. 841 (1984).

2. LAWS THAT ARE BILLS OF ATTAINDER. [§397]

a. Forbidding Salary Payments. [§398]

A federal law that forbade salary payments to named federal employees has been held to violate the prohibition against Bills of Attainder.

In *U.S. v. Lovett*, 328 U.S. 303 (1946), the Court reviewed a federal law which, motivated by a congressional intent to purge the federal government of subversive employees, prohibited salary payments to three named federal employees. The Court invalidated this law as a bill of attainder, reasoning that the law operated as a perpetual exclusion from government employment, which qualified as punishment under the Ex Post Facto Clause.

b. Exclusion of Communists From Union Positions. [§399]

Prohibiting communists from being union officers violates the prohibition against Bills of Attainder.

U.S. v. Brown, 381 U.S. 437 (1965). The Court invalidated, as a bill of attainder, a federal law prohibiting anyone who had been a member of the Communist Party during the last five years from being a labor union officer. Under this law, a person would be punished based on past, unalterable characteristics.

3. LAWS THAT DO NOT CONSTITUTE BILLS OF ATTAINDER. [§400]

a. Disposition of Presidential Papers. [§401]

A federal law taking custody of presidential materials does not constitute a Bill of Attainder.

Nixon v. Administrator of General Services, 433 U.S. 425 (1977). The Court rejected a bill of attainder argument against a federal law which provided for the custody and disposition of the papers and materials of former President Nixon. The law was not a Bill of Attainder for two reasons: it did not inflict punishment on former President Nixon, and it was not aimed at him as an individual (although he was the only one affected by the law), but rather at him as a "legitimate class of one."

b. Denial of Education. [§402]

Denial of education grants for failure to register for the draft was held not to constitute a Bill of Attainder.

Selective Service System v. Minnesota Public Interest Research Group, 468 U.S. 841 (1984). The Court rejected a Bill of Attainder argument against a federal law which denied federal higher education money to male students who had not registered for the draft. The law was not a Bill of Attainder for two reasons: denial of educational benefits was not punitive, and the law did not unalterably hurt male students because they could register late and still receive benefits.

Sum & Substance QUICK REVIEW of Constitutional Law

D. CONTRACTS CLAUSE. [§403]

The Constitution prohibits a state from passing a law which impairs the obligations of existing contracts. The Contracts Clause has nothing to do with a state passing a law which affects someone's ability to contract in the future. The Contracts Clause, which is part of Article 1, §10, only limits states; if the federal government passes a law impairing the obligations of a contract, an attack on the law would be based on the Due Process Clause of the Fifth Amendment. The analysis under either clause would be the same, but a different constitutional provision would apply, depending on whether a state or the federal government acts.

1. CONTRACTS CLAUSE ANALYSIS. [§404]

Not all modifications of the obligations of existing contracts will violate the Contracts Clause. In Contracts Clause cases, the Court has balanced the constitutional prohibition of a state impairing the obligations of contracts against the exercise of the state's police power. In 1983, the Court summarized existing Contracts Clause law as follows: If either a state or the federal government passes a law which impairs the obligations of an existing contract, the Court uses a three-part test to determine the constitutionality of that law. The Court asks:

a. Has the law substantially impaired an obligation of an existing contract;

b. Does the government have a significant and legitimate reason for the impairment; and

c. Is the law based on reasonable conditions and is it appropriate to the public purpose underlying the law?

Energy Reserves Group v. Kansas Power & Light Co., 459 U.S. 400 (1983).

EXAMPLE: [§405] For instance, assume that a state passes a no-fault divorce law, replacing its old law which required a showing of some statutorily-defined reason for granting a divorce (cruelty, abandonment, adultery). To determine whether the no-fault divorce law would survive a Contracts Clause challenge, apply the three-part test from *Energy Reserves Group*. First, ask whether the new no-fault divorce law substantially impairs an obligation of existing marriage contracts. The party challenging the law would argue that the basis on which marriage contracts could be terminated is an important part of the contracts, and the passage of a no-fault divorce law substantially impairs that obligation. Second, discuss the state's

---

reasons for switching to a no-fault divorce system. The state would argue that no-fault is a more civil, less destructive method of terminating marriages than requiring a husband or wife to get on the witness stand and testify about the shortcomings of his or her spouse. Third, discuss whether the change in the state's divorce law is appropriate to achieving the state's purpose. If the state's interest is avoiding the effects of spouses testifying against each other, along with the unpleasant consequences of such testimony, adoption of a no-fault system seems appropriate, and the law would be held constitutional.

---

2. APPLICATION OF CONTRACTS CLAUSE ANALYSIS. [§406]

a. Mortgage Moratorium Law. [§407]

A state law imposing a temporary moratorium on mortgage foreclosures does not violate the Contracts Clause.

Home Building & Loan Association v. Blaisdell, 290 U.S. 398 (1934). The Court upheld, against a Contracts Clause challenge, a post-Depression mortgage moratorium law which postponed the exercise of the contractual right of banks to foreclose on home mortgages within the state. The underlying mortgage indebtedness was not affected by the law. Important factors were: the Depression created an emergency need for such a law; no special group was advantaged — society in general benefited; and the relief was appropriately tailored and limited to the duration of the emergency. While this case was decided prior to the codification of Contracts Clause law in *Energy Reserves Group* (see §403), the Court looked at precisely the same factors. The state law in *Blaisdell* substantially impaired an obligation of existing mortgage contracts — when a bank could foreclose on home mortgages for non-payment. However, ameliorating the effects of the Depression was certainly a significant state interest. Finally, the temporary postponement of the banks' right to foreclose was an appropriate response to a broad-based societal problem. After considering these factors, the Court held that the Minnesota law did not violate the Contracts Clause.

b. Altering a State's Own Obligation. [§408]

A state law altering the obligations of a contract to which the state is a party may violate the Contracts Clause.

U.S. Trust v. New Jersey, 431 U.S. 1 (1977). The Court invalidated a New Jersey statute which impaired the obligations of earlier contractual obligations of New York and New Jersey with Port Authority bondholders. New York and New Jersey had statutorily-based commitments to Port Authority bondholders not to use certain revenues for any railroad facility that was not self-supporting. The states passed statutes repealing the existing commitments to the bondholders, thereby enabling the Port Authority to use those revenues for previously prohibited purposes. The Court balanced the prohibitive language of the Contracts Clause against the collective police powers of the two states, but emphasized that complete deference to a legislature's decision to change contractual obligations was not appropriate when the state's self-interest may be advanced by the change in contract terms. The Court held that the New Jersey statute violated the Contracts Clause.

c. Adding Obligations to a Contract. [§409]

A state law adding obligations to a contract is subject to contracts clause analysis.

Allied Structural Steel Co. v. Spannaus, 438 U.S. 234 (1978). The Court invalidated a Minnesota law which imposed additional pension obligations on a company, over and above what it had agreed to in labor negotiations. The state law required the company to pay full pensions to employees who had worked ten years or more for the company, even though the labor-management agreement set varying, and usually longer, periods for company contribution to a pension plan. The Court focused on the severe impact on the company (clearly a substantial impairment of a contractual obligation), the company's reliance on the original plan, and the very narrow focus of the law (unlike the broad societal interest in *Blaisdell*, above). The fact that specific companies were singled out to bear the cost of protecting the economic interest of retiring workers led the Court to conclude that the means chosen by the state to deal with the problem of retirees having no pension benefits were not appropriately tailored to ameliorating any broad-based societal problem. As a result, the Minnesota law was held violative of the Contracts Clause.

d. Limiting Prices. [§410]

A state law limiting price increases which a natural gas supplier could charge a public utility under a price-escalator clause of a pre-existing contract does not violate the Contracts Clause.

In *Energy Reserves Group, Inc. v. Kansas Power & Light Co.*, 459 U.S. 400 (1983), the Court upheld a state law which prohibited the price that a supplier of natural gas could charge to a public utility from rising to a level set by a previous contract between the supplier and the utility. The Court reasoned that the state had a substantial reason for the law: protecting consumers of natural gas from increases in the cost of natural gas caused by federal deregulation of the industry. The Court held that the state law did not violate the Contracts Clause.

> **STUDY TIP:** Usually, a Contracts Clause challenge is raised when a state impairs the obligations of a contract between two private parties. Be careful about a state impairing the obligations of a contract between itself and a private party. The danger in such a case is that the state may be changing the terms of the contract to benefit itself rather than to address some broad-based societal problem. If a state changes the obligations of its own contract, the same three-part test applies, but a court will apply it more stringently to protect against a state advancing its own interests by trying to get out from under unfavorable contract obligations.

REVIEW PROBLEMS — RETROACTIVE LEGISLATION

PROBLEM 1: Randy Rowdy was arrested on June 1, 1994, for violation of a state criminal law making it a misdemeanor to sell under 50 grams of cocaine. If convicted under this statute, Randy could get a prison term of two to five years. On August 30, 1994, the state legislature made the sale of over 25 grams of cocaine a felony, punishable by a prison term of fifteen to twenty-five years. After Randy's conviction for selling 40 grams of cocaine, the state trial judge applied the new felony sentencing guidelines, and gave Randy fifteen years in prison. Is the sentence constitutional?

> **Answer:** No. It is in violation of the constitutional prohibition against ex post facto laws for a sentencing statute to be applied to a crime that was committed before the statute went into effect.

PROBLEM 2: Assume that the United States is involved in a very long, costly, and deadly war with the county of Freedonia. As a result, many people are protesting the war, some by joining radical, subversive groups whose purpose is to overthrow the U.S. government by force or violence. In response, Congress passes a law which prohibits any person who has ever been a member of a subversive group from joining the armed forces of the United States. This law also precludes these persons from ever being eligible for student loans which are available for ex-members of the military. Fred Frag had been a member of a subversive group, but saw the error of his ways and quit. He tries to enlist in the Air Force, but is refused because of his past membership in the subversive group. Does Fred have a bill of attainder argument?

> **Answer:** Yes. This law is designed to punish someone for past, unalterable traits. To have the law upheld, Congress would have to show that the law furthers some nonpunitive purpose, and that Congress did not intend to punish former members of subversive groups. See §§395-397 for further review.

PROBLEM 3. The legislature of the State of Oz is concerned about the widespread use of automatic weapons in the state. To combat the problem, the State passes a law which prohibits the sale of certain weapons in the state. Gunther's Guns, a very successful gun shop, has a contract with Barb's Ballistics, Inc., to purchase three hundred automatic weapons over the next two years. Under the new state law, any future sales or purchases of automatic weapons would be illegal. Does Gunther have an argument that the Oz law violates his rights under the Contracts Clause?

> **Answer:** Yes. A state has impaired the obligations of an existing contract, so Gunther does have an argument. This law substantially impairs the obligations of his contract by prohibiting any sale of these weapons. The question then is whether the state has a significant reason for the law (reducing crime) and whether the means are appropriately tailored to achieving that goal. Obviously, the state has a significant interest in reducing crime, so the analysis devolves to the appropriateness of the means chosen by the state. This law imposes a great burden on gun dealers who have existing contracts to purchase certain weapons, and might, on balance, violate the Contracts Clause. See §§403-405 for further review.

A. INTRODUCTION. [§411]

The Fifth Amendment provides that the federal government may take private property for a public use only if just compensation is paid to the property owner. This protection against governmental appropriation of private property has been incorporated through the Due Process Clause of the Fourteenth Amendment to apply to the states.

1. THE TAKINGS CLAUSE IS NOT AN INDEPENDENT SOURCE OF LEGISLATIVE POWER. [§412]

The Takings Clause is not an independent source of power. It must be exercised in conjunction with some other enumerated power of Congress, or in conjunction with the Tenth Amendment police power if a state is taking property. For instance, if Congress takes private property so that it may build a post office, that congressional action is based in part on Congress' postal power, coupled with its power under the Takings Clause.

2. KEY CONCEPTS IN TAKINGS CLAUSE ANALYSIS. [§413]

a. Eminent Domain. [§414]

Eminent domain is an inherent power of the federal government and of the states. **The power of eminent domain is the power of a government to force the owner of real or personal property to transfer that property to the government.**

b. Taking of Private Property. [§415]

In a classic "taking" case, the government expressly exercises its power of eminent domain and offers compensation for the property taken. The questions then arise whether the taking is for a "public use," and whether the compensation offer is fair.

c. Public Use. [§416]

Under the Takings Clause, private property may only be taken for a public use. **A public use is any use that advances a legitimate power of the government and accrues to the benefit of the general public.** The Court will virtually always accept the government's contention that a taking is for a public use.

In most Constitutional Law classes, two issues predominate in Takings Clause discussions: what is a "public use"; and when does a government regulation (which is not compensable) so severely diminish a property owner's use of the property that the regulation should be treated as a taking (which is compensable)?

B. "PUBLIC USE" REQUIREMENT. [§417]

When a legislature exercises its power of eminent domain, it must be for a public use. In public use cases, the issue is not whether there has been a taking — there has. The issue is why the government condemned the property. **If a legislature says a taking is for a public use, a court will almost always agree, even if the condemned property is transferred to another private party.**

1. ELIMINATING URBAN BLIGHT. [§418]

Condemnation of private property in an effort to eliminate urban blight will be considered a public use.

Berman v. Parker, 348 U.S. 26 (1954). The Court found that a public use existed when Congress authorized a federal agency to condemn property in the Washington, D.C. area for the purpose of eliminating urban blight. (Most of the condemned property was substandard housing and rundown commercial establishments). The Court upheld the "public use" aspect of the taking even though the condemned property at issue, a department store, did not itself pose any problem of blight. The Court recognized that Congress' plan required the development of a large part of the Washington, D.C. area, rather than proceeding by a piecemeal approach. When a legislature declares that a taking is for a public use, the court's review role is extremely narrow; if the taking arguably advances the public use asserted by the legislature, the taking will meet the public use requirement.

2. DISPERSING LAND OWNERSHIP. [§419]

A transfer of private property from one party to another in an effort to reduce the concentration of land ownership will be considered a public use.

Hawaii Housing Authority v. Midkiff, 467 U.S. 229 (1984). The Court found a public use when Hawaii, in an effort to break up an extremely high concentration of land ownership, used the power of eminent domain to transfer land from a small group of wealthy private owners to their former tenants. The Court found that the State had a legitimate interest in reducing the perceived economic and social evils of concentrated land ownership.

3. TRANSFER OF PROPERTY FROM ONE PRIVATE OWNER TO ANOTHER. [§420]

A condemnation may be for a public use even though the property is transferred from one private party to another.

Poletown Neighborhood Development Council v. City of Detroit, 304 N.W. 2d 455 (1981). The Michigan Supreme Court found a public use when the city of Detroit condemned an entire neighborhood and then transferred the land to General Motors to build an auto plant. The Court reasoned that what is good for General Motors is good for Detroit.

C. WHEN SHOULD A REGULATION BE TREATED AS A TAKING? [§421]

In a typical taking case, a government takes someone's property and offers compensation in return. The burden of the taking does not fall on the public in general, nor does the benefit of the compensation accrue to the general public. However, when a government imposes a regulation (such as a zoning law) applicable to all residents or activities within its jurisdiction, no compensation is paid to those regulated. There is no specific taking of property (just a limitation on the use of property in general), so no particularized offer of compensation is made. A problem arises when the general regulation so severely affects the use of someone's property or diminishes its value that the property owner claims the regulation is tantamount to a taking, and should be compensated.

1. PHYSICAL OCCUPATION OR INVASION OF PROPERTY WILL BE CONSIDERED A TAKING. [§422]

A general regulation that effects a physical occupation or invasion of property will be considered a taking.

a. Permanent Physical Occupation of Property Will Be a Taking. [§423]

Government authorization to a private party to occupy someone else's property will be treated as a taking.

Loretto v. Teleprompter Manhattan CATV Corp., 458 U.S. 419 (1982). The Court found a taking when New York City authorized a cable TV company to permanently affix their cables to the walls and roofs of certain privately-owned apartment buildings. The Court emphasized that a permanent physical occupation of property has invariably been found to be a taking.

b. Physical Invasion of Property Will Be a Taking. [§424]

Government action that effectively takes an easement of a private party's airspace will be treated as a taking.

U.S. v. Causby, 328 U.S. 256 (1946). The Court found a taking when army planes flew over Causby's chicken farm, making the chickens too nervous to lay eggs. The government had taken an easement of air space, for which it was required to pay compensation.

2. DENIAL OF ALL ECONOMICALLY BENEFICIAL USE OF THE PROPERTY CONSTITUTES A TAKING. [§425]

Government action that deprives a property owner of all economically viable use of his or her property will be treated as a taking.

a. Laws Requiring Coal to Be Left in Place. [§426]

A law prohibiting a coal company from mining coal on its property will be treated as a taking if the coal company is deprived of all economically viable use of its property.

(1) *Pennsylvania Coal Co. v. Mahon*, 260 U.S. 393 (1922). [§427]

The Court found a taking when a Pennsylvania statute prohibited coal-mining companies from mining coal on its land if the mining would cause a subsidence of the surface. The coal company had sold the surface rights, but had expressly reserved the right to remove all the coal under the surface. The statute effectively destroyed the mining rights reserved under the contract, and thereby effected a compensable taking. Compare with the next case.

(2) *Keystone Bituminous Coal Association v. DeBenedictis*, 480 U.S. 470 (1987). [§428]

The Court found no taking in a challenge to Pennsylvania's Subsidence Act that prohibited mining of coal so as to cause subsidence of buildings. As applied, the law required 50% of coal under protected structures to be kept in place. Distinguishing this case from *Mahon*, above, the Court said that this Pennsylvania statute advanced important public interests (safety and water supplies), and did not deprive the coal company of all economically viable use of its land since the law affected less than 2% of its coal.

b. Restrictions on Building Imposed by Landmarks Preservation Law. [§429]

Application of a Landmarks Preservation Law will not be treated as a taking if the law applies to many buildings and the owner still has an economically viable use for the property.

Penn Central Transportation Co. v. New York City, 438 U.S. 104 (1978). The Court found no taking as a result of New York's Landmarks Preservation Law being applied to prevent construction of a skyscraper office building in the airspace above Grand Central Terminal. The law applied to a large number of buildings, was designed to benefit the public generally, and did not unduly impair the owner's economically viable use of the property.

c. Zoning Ordinance Limiting Number of Houses on Parcel of Land. [§430]

No taking is effected by a zoning ordinance limiting the number of houses an owner can put on a parcel of land.

Agins v. City of Tiburon, 454 U.S. 1098 (1980). The Court found no taking by the application of a zoning ordinance which limited the number of houses which the owner could put on a parcel of property. This ordinance did not prevent all economically viable use of the land, and, on balance, it was justified by the city's interest in promoting orderly land development.

d. Rent-Control and Limitations on Terminating a Tenancy. [§431]

No taking was effected by a combination of city laws which controlled rent and limited the grounds on which a mobile home owner could terminate a tenancy.

Yee v. City of Escondido, 112 S.Ct. 1522 (1992). The Court found no taking, rejecting the argument that the combination of two laws effected a physical occupation under *Loretto*, §423 above. Escondido had two laws that regulated mobile home parks: one was a rent-control ordinance, the other a limitation on the grounds on which the owner of a mobile-home park could terminate a mobile home owner's tenancy. Facially, these ordinances did not result in any physical invasion of the park owner's property.

e. Law Prohibiting Building Houses on Seashore Lots. [§432]

The Court has remanded a case in which a state law prohibiting building any occupiable dwelling on seashore lots was challenged as effectuating a taking.

Lucas v. South Carolina Coastal Council, 112 S.Ct. 2886 (1992). The Court remanded to state court this case challenging a state law which barred building any occupiable dwellings on seashore lots. The law was applied to two lots which were zoned for single-family dwellings and purchased two years before the law went into effect. The Court held that a State could avoid paying compensation where a regulation deprives a landowner of all economically viable use of his land only if it could show that the landowner's proposed use could have been enjoined as a private or public nuisance. It then remanded for consideration of whether principles of nuisance and property law prohibited the landowner from using the land as he intended. On remand, the South Carolina Supreme Court held that the State could not prohibit the landowner from constructing habitable dwellings on his land, and that the landowner had suffered a compensable temporary taking during the period in which he was enjoined from doing so.

f. Laws Requiring Destruction of Cedar Trees. [§433]

No taking was effected by a state law requiring the destruction of cedar trees located near apple orchards; the public benefited so greatly that no compensation was required.

Miller v. Schoene, 276 U.S. 272 (1928). The Court found no taking by a state law requiring destruction of red cedar trees within a stated distance of apple orchards. On balance, the destruction of one class of property to save another was of such great value to the public as not to be a compensable taking.

3. CONDITIONS OF THE GRANTING OF BUILDING PERMITS. [§434]

The Court has ruled that a government imposing conditions on the granting of building permits effects a taking.

a. Granting an Easement as a Condition of Receiving a Building Permit. [§435]

Requiring the granting of a public easement as a condition of granting a building permit is a taking.

Nollan v. California Coastal Commission, 483 U.S. 825 (1987). The Court found a taking when the Commission refused to issue a building permit for beachfront property unless the landowners granted a public easement across their property to the ocean. The permit condition severely diminished the landowners' use of their property, and did not substantially advance the government interest of enhancing the ability of the public to view the ocean.

b. Unconstitutional Conditions Attached to the Granting of a Building Permit. [§436]

A government may not condition the granting of a building permit on the property owner's dedication of part of her property for public uses.

Dolan v. Tigard, 114 S.Ct. 2309 (1994). The Court found a taking when a local planning commission conditioned the approval of Dolan's application to expand her store and parking lot upon the dedication of a portion of her land for a public greenway to minimize possible flooding, and a pedestrian/bike path to relieve traffic congestion. Dolan's request for variances from the condition was denied. The Court relied on the doctrine of "unconstitutional conditions," under which a government may not extract private property in exchange for a discretionary benefit that the government might confer. The Court found an "essential nexus" between each permit condition and the legitimate state interest stated in each condition by the commission. However, the inquiry then turned to whether the permit conditions bear "rough proportionality" to the projected impact of the proposed development (Dolan's expansion). The government must make some individualized determination that the land sought to be extracted is related in nature and in extent to the proposed development's impact. The commission failed to show that either condition was reasonably related to the public benefits that would purportedly flow from imposing those conditions on Dolan's application.

4. TEMPORARY TAKINGS ARE COMPENSABLE FOR THE PERIOD WHEN USE OF THE PROPERTY WAS DEPRIVED. [§437]

Temporary takings of property are compensable on the same theory as are permanent takings — the property owner is deprived of all economically viable use of the property, even though temporarily.

First English Evangelical Lutheran Church v. County of Los Angeles, 482 U.S. 304 (1987). The Court found a compensable temporary taking during the period when an interim flood-control ordinance deprived a church of all economically viable use of its property. The ordinance temporarily prohibited the reconstruction of church buildings that had been destroyed by a flood.

D. "JUST COMPENSATION" EQUALS FAIR MARKET VALUE AT THE TIME OF THE TAKING. [§438]

The general rule is that a government must pay the property owner the fair market value of the property at the time of the taking. The Court, taking a very pragmatic view of this concept, has focused on what a willing buyer would pay in cash to a willing seller. This issue rarely comes up in law school discussions, but is very important in real-world cases involving takings of property.

REVIEW PROBLEMS — THE TAKINGS CLAUSE

PROBLEM 1. The City of Id wanted to develop its waterfront area. The Planning Commission approved a plan for a private developer to build a marina, as well as a very large shopping mall on the waterfront. To accomplish this goal, the City had to acquire property on and near the waterfront. Exercising its power of eminent domain, the City condemned three entire blocks of residences, then sold the land to a private development company. Joe Jones, one of the former homeowners, brought suit to block the sale. He claims that transferring property from one private owner to another is not taking land "for a public use." Will Joe win on this argument?

> **Answer:** No. Courts consistently hold that if a legislature says a taking is in the public interest, the taking will be for a public use. This includes taking property from one private owner and transferring it to another. See §420 for further review.

PROBLEM 2. Edna Eggers owned some beautiful beachfront property which she wanted to develop. She applied to the City Planning Commission for a building permit, and was told that she could have the permit only if she would allow part of her property to be used as a walkway to allow the public to have access to the beach. Edna sues, challenging the condition on the granting of the building permit. Will she win?

> **Answer:** Yes. The government may not condition the granting of a permit on a landowner's giving up private property. If the government wants a walkway, it must use its power of eminent domain, and pay Edna the fair market value of the land it has taken. See §436 for further review.

PROBLEM 3. Over the course of a few months, there were a number of sightings of strange objects in the sky over the City of Id. Many people were convinced that UFOs were visiting the city. One night, one of the objects crashed in an area on the outskirts of town. The City of Id and the State of Oz began investigations. As part of their investigations, the City of Id passed an emergency ordinance prohibiting all activity, including building, on the suspected crash site. Beulah Bodine owned the property, and was about to start construction of a major amusement park. Beulah was not able to use her property for the nine months it took to complete the investigations. At that point, the City repealed its ordinance, and Beulah began building. Beulah sues to recover compensation for the time period when she could not use her property. Does she have a case?

> **Answer:** Yes. Temporary takings are compensable as long as they meet the requirement of depriving the owner of all economically viable use of the land for a certain period of time. See §437 for further review.

XIV. PROCEDURAL DUE PROCESS

A. INTRODUCTION. [§439]

The Fifth Amendment prohibits the federal government from depriving a person of life, liberty, or property without due process of law. The Fourteenth Amendment imposes the same limitation on states. **The due process clauses are intended to ensure that a government uses a fair procedure when it singles out an individual for a deprivation of life, liberty, or property.** Procedural due process analysis deals with the **manner** in which a government acts; its purpose is to prevent the government from arbitrarily depriving a person of life, liberty, or property. This chapter will deal only with deprivations of liberty or property; deprivation of life will be dealt with in Chapter XX: Cruel and Unusual Punishment.

1. Main Requirements of a Procedural Due Process Analysis. [§440]

The three main requirements of procedural due process are an impartial decisionmaker, notice, and a hearing. Decisionmakers must not have prejudged an issue before them, or have a monetary interest in the outcome of a case. Notice must be reasonably calculated, under all the circumstances, to apprise parties of the nature of the charge or action against them. Depending on the importance of the interest being affected and the competing government interests, a person's right to respond may take the form of either a pre-deprivation or post-deprivation hearing. Consider these factors as you go through the cases in this section.

2. Three-Prong Balancing Analysis. [§441]

Once you have identified the liberty or property interest that has been allegedly abridged, you must determine how much procedural protection is required. To answer that question, the Court looks at the following three factors:

a. The private interest affected by the government action;

b. The risk of erroneous deprivation of that interest through the procedure presently in place; and

c. The government interest, including the added fiscal and administrative burdens that the new procedure would entail. *Mathews v. Eldridge*, 424 U.S. 319 (1976).

B. GOVERNMENT ACTION REQUIREMENT. [§442]

Procedural due process guarantees apply only to government action. There is no procedural due process issue if a private person or institution is depriving someone of liberty or property. For a discussion of how to make a "state action" argument, see Chapter X.

C. INTENTIONAL DEPRIVATION. [§443]

Procedural due process analysis applies only to an intentional deprivation of liberty or property. A negligent deprivation of liberty or property does not give rise to a procedural due process argument. *Daniels v. Williams*, 474 U.S. 327 (1986). The Court rejected a 42 U.S.C. §1983 action by an inmate who sued a jail officer for injuries suffered when the inmate slipped and fell on a pillow negligently left on a stairway by the jail officer. The Due Process Clause is not implicated by a state official's negligent act causing unintended loss of or injury to life, liberty, or property.

D. DEPRIVATION OF LIBERTY OR PROPERTY. [§444]

For procedural due process analysis to apply, a government must be intentionally depriving a person of a liberty or property interest which is cognizable by a court. If the interest is not a judicially recognized liberty or property interest, no procedural due process argument is available.

1. LIBERTY INTERESTS. [§445]

Procedural due process protects individuals when they are arrested or incarcerated. (Those issues are outside the scope of this outline.) Procedural due process also applies in a number of civil contexts where freedom of movement or the exercise of a fundamental right is curtailed.

a. Commitment to Mental Institutions. [§446]

Involuntary commitment to a mental institution involves a cognizable liberty interest.

(1) Adults. [§447]

Although the Court has not been specific about which procedures are required, an adult must be given fair due process protection prior to involuntary commitment to a mental institution, including a pre-commitment adversary hearing, *O'Connor v. Donaldson*, 422 U.S. 563 (1975).

The standard of proof for involuntary civil commitment of an adult is clear and convincing evidence that the person meets the statutory commitment requirements. *Addington v. Texas*, 441 U.S. 418 (1979). [§448]

(2) Children. [§449]

No pre-commitment adversary hearing is required when a parent or the state commits a child to a mental institution against his or her will. However, a child is entitled to a finding by a "neutral fact-finder" that the commitment meets all statutory requirements. *Parham v. J.R.*, 442 U.S. 584 (1979).

(3) Inmates. [§450]

An inmate has a liberty interest in not being transferred from prison to a mental institution for treatment. The Court ruled that an inmate is entitled to notice, a hearing, and appointment of counsel before such a transfer. *Vitek v. Jones*, 436 U.S. 407 or 445 U.S. 480 (1980).

b. Parolees' Interests. [§451]

A parolee has a liberty interest involved when a state revokes parole. A parolee has a liberty interest in pursuing a normal life after release from prison. If a state chooses to revoke parole, the individual is entitled to notice of the reason for revocation and a hearing to determine whether parole restrictions have been violated. *Morrissey v. Brewer*, 408 U.S. 471 (1972). The same rule applies to revocation of probation. *Gagnon v. Scarpelli*, 411 U.S. 778 (1973).

c. Prisoners' Interests. [§452]

A prisoner has no liberty interest in not being transferred from one prison to another, or in not being placed in administrative segregation

(1) Prison Transfers. [§453]

A prisoner has no liberty interest in not being transferred from prison to prison, so no notice or hearing is required before such a transfer. *Olim v. Wakinekona*, 461 U.S. 238 (1983).

(2) Prison Segregation. [§454]

A prisoner has no constitutionally-based liberty interest in not being placed in administrative segregation. However, if state statutes and regulations prescribe certain procedures for placing someone in administrative segregation, a prisoner does have a statutorily-based liberty interest in remaining in the general prison population. *Hewitt v. Helms*, 459 U.S. 460 (1983).

d. Liberty Interests of Children. [§455]

Corporal punishment in public schools does involve a liberty interest of the child. Disciplinary corporal punishment in public schools does involve a liberty interest, but there is no procedural due process right to notice or a hearing prior to imposing the punishment. Post-punishment judicial remedies for excessive punishment are sufficient to protect a child's liberty interests. *Ingraham v. Wright*, 430 U.S. 651 (1977).

e. Termination of Parental Rights. [§456]

A liberty interest is involved when a state acts to terminate parental rights.

(1) Appointment of Counsel. [§457]

The Constitution does not require a state to appoint counsel for every indigent parent facing termination of parental rights. A parent does not have a sufficiently important liberty interest in the parent-child relationship to automatically require the appointment of counsel for every indigent parent whose parental rights are to be terminated. *Lassiter v. Dept. of Social Services*, 452 U.S. 18 (1981).

(2) Evidence of Unfitness to Parent. [§458]

A State must show clear and convincing evidence of unfitness to parent before it may terminate parental rights. A state may not terminate parental rights, thereby extinguishing a parent's liberty interest in his or her child, unless it shows by clear and convincing evidence that a parent is unfit. *Santosky v. Kramer*, 455 U.S. 745 (1982).

(3) Trial Transcripts. [§458.1]

An indigent person who wants to appeal a court order terminating his or her parental rights is entitled to a free trial transcript. A state may not deny an appeal of a termination order simply on the basis that the person cannot afford the record preparation fees. *M.L.B. v. S.L.J.*, 117 S.Ct. 555 (1997) (see §532.1).

f. Reputation. [§459]

Injury to reputation alone is not a liberty interest protected under procedural due process. However, if injury to reputation is linked to some other interest, such as pursuing employment, there may be a liberty interest involved. The Court rejected a due process argument by a plaintiff whose reputation was allegedly injured by police circulation to merchants of a flyer designating plaintiff an "active shoplifter." Since damage to his reputation was not tied to any other interest such as employment, there was no protectable liberty interest. *Paul v. Davis*, 424 U.S. 693 (1976).

2. PROPERTY INTERESTS. [§460]

Procedural due process guarantees apply when the government intentionally deprives an individual of real or personal property. The applicability of procedural due process analysis becomes an issue when a government deprives a person of some non-traditional form of property, such as welfare or disability payments. **The general rule is that government benefits will be considered property for procedural due process purposes if the recipient is "entitled" to receive the benefit. An entitlement (as opposed to a mere expectation) exists when, under the law granting the benefit, the recipient is entitled to receive the benefit as long as specified conditions of eligibility are met.**

a. Government Employment. [§461]

Government employment will not be a property interest if the employee can be fired at will (for no reason); it will be a property interest if the employee can only be fired "for cause" (such as a tenured teacher). A property interest in government employment may arise from express contractual language, or from the facts and circumstances surrounding a particular employment relationship (such as an oral promise by the boss to continue an employee's employment).

(1) Tenure Rights Qualify As a Property Interest. [§462]

No express or implied tenure rights in a teaching position at a public university means no property interest.

Board of Regents v. Roth, 408 U.S. 564 (1972). The Court found that a state university professor had no property interest in his teaching job. The professor had been hired for one year, and there were no express or implied tenure rights granted to him. He had no entitlement to his job, simply a unilateral expectation of continued employment. Since he had no property interest in his job, he was not entitled to a hearing, or even a formal statement of the reasons why he was not retained.

(2) Implied Tenure Rights May Qualify As a Property Interest. [§463]

Policies and practices of a school may create an entitlement to a job.

Perry v. Sindermann, 408 U.S. 593 (1972). The Court ruled that a state college teacher with ten years experience who had been let go without a hearing must have a chance to prove that he had an entitlement to continued employment based on the policies and practices of the institution which allegedly created an implied tenure system.

(3) Tenured Employee Entitled to Pretermination Hearing. [§463.1]

A tenured govenment employee is entitled to a limited pretermination hearing.

Cleveland Board of Education v. Loudermill, 470 U.S. 532 (1985). The Court held that an employee terminable only for cause was entitled to procedural due process protections prior to termination. This requires some form of a pretermination hearing, coupled with post-termination administrative procedures for review. The pretermination hearing need only be designed to determine "whether there are reasonable grounds to believe that the charges against the employee are true and support the proposed action." This satisfies the essential requirements of due process, namely, notice and an opportunity to be heard.

(4) Suspension of Tenured Employee Without Pay. [§463.2]

A tenured employee in a position of public trust and visibility who is charged with a felony is not entitled to a hearing prior to suspension without pay. A prompt post-suspension hearing will suffice.

Gilbert v. Homar, 117 S.Ct. 1807 (1997). The Court assumed, but did not explicitly hold, that the suspension without pay of a tenured employee infringed a protected property interest, but held that in circumstances involving an employee in a position of public trust and visibility who is charged with a felony, the employee is not entitled to a pre-suspension hearing. A police officer at a state university was suspended without pay after being charged with a felony drug offense, without a pre-suspension hearing. Prior decisions indicate that a tenured employee is entitled to a pretermination hearing to provide a check against erroneous deprivations by assuring that there are reasonable grounds for dismissal. In this case, however, because the fact that the employee was charged with a felony eliminated the risk of the suspension being an erroneous deprivation, due process would be satisfied by a prompt post-suspension hearing.

b. Government Benefits. [§464]

When a government seeks to terminate a benefit which it has conferred, the court will look to the importance of that benefit to the recipient; the question is whether the recipient's interest in avoiding the loss outweighs the government's interest in terminating the benefit without providing notice or a hearing.

(1) Welfare Recipients. [§465]

Welfare recipients are entitled to a pre-termination hearing.

Goldberg v. Kelly, 397 U.S. 254 (1970). The Court ruled that welfare recipients are entitled to an evidentiary hearing prior to termination of their benefits. Welfare benefits are needed for the purposes of subsistence, so the Court refused to allow a summary termination of benefits pending resolution of a recipient's eligibility.

(2) Disability Benefits Recipients. [§466]
Disability benefit recipients are not entitled to a pre-termination hearing.

Mathews v. Eldridge, 424 U.S. 319 (1976). The Court ruled that there is no right to a hearing prior to the termination of disability benefits. The Court said that receipt of disability payments is simply not as crucial as receipt of subsistence welfare payments.

c. Public School Education. [§467]
A public school student has a property interest in his or her education which may not be taken away without due process protections. Be sure to distinguish between a disciplinary suspension, as opposed to an academic dismissal; the Court uses a different rule in each of these cases.

(1) Disciplinary Suspension. [§468]
No formal hearing is required before a student receives a temporary disciplinary suspension.

Goss v. Lopez, 419 U.S. 565 (1975). The Court ruled that, as a general matter, before a student is given a temporary disciplinary suspension (ten days or less) from public school, he or she must be given notice (oral or written) of the reasons for the suspension, and at least an informal opportunity to respond to the charges. A full-blown adversary hearing is not required.

(2) Academic Dismissal. [§469]
No hearing is required before a student is dismissed for academic reasons.

Board of Curators v. Horowitz, 429 U.S. 912 (1978). The Court ruled that a medical student was not entitled to any sort of hearing or opportunity to respond before an academic dismissal. In this case, the school used a long, extensive evaluation process which the Court deemed adequate to protect the student's interests.

d. Judicial Review of Punitive Damages Award. [§470]
Limiting judicial review of the amount of a punitive damages award may violate procedural due process guarantees.

Honda Motor Co. v. Oberg, 144 S.Ct. 2331 (1994). The Court invalidated an Oregon law barring judicial review of the amount of a jury's punitive damages award unless the court affirmatively finds that there is no evidence to support the verdict. Such a rule violates procedural due process protections because it abrogates a traditional common-law safeguard against arbitrary deprivations of property, without providing any adequate substitute.

REVIEW PROBLEMS — PROCEDURAL DUE PROCESS

PROBLEM 1. Timmy Toon was a second-grader at Id Elementary School, a public school within the State of Oz. One day, while Timmy's class was returning from a field trip on the school bus, Timmy was so tired that he fell asleep in the back of the bus. Dana Dancer, Timmy's teacher, herded forty second- graders off the bus, did a quick search of the seats, and left Timmy on the bus. Dana never did see Timmy in the back seat. A very frantic Timmy was rescued three hours later. Timmy's parents file a 42 U.S.C. §1983 suit against Dana, claiming a deprivation of Timmy's liberty without due process of law. Do they have a case?

> **Answer:** No. There was no intentional deprivation of Timmy's rights. Procedural due process rules apply only to intentional deprivations, and this certainly sounds like mere negligence on the part of Timmy's teacher. See §443 for further review.

PROBLEM 2. Sam Soathe was a welfare recipient in the State of Oz. Sam was not the easiest person in the world to get along with, and he argued constantly with his caseworker at the state welfare office. After one of these sessions, the caseworker decided that Sam no longer met the eligibility requirements, and terminated his benefits. Sam sues, claiming a procedural due process violation. Does he have a case?

> **Answer:** Yes. A welfare recipient is entitled to an evidentiary hearing prior to the termination of benefits. See §§464-465 for further review.

PROBLEM 3. The State of Oz has a law which provides that parental rights may be terminated if the State is able to show by a preponderance of the evidence that a person is an unfit parent. Does this law comport with procedural due process requirements?

> **Answer:** No. A state may not terminate parental rights unless it can show by clear and convincing evidence that a person is an unfit parent. See §§458 for further review.

PROBLEM 4. Arleena Addams was an assistant professor at a very prestigious state law school. She had a one-year contract with no express tenure rights or right of renewal of the contract. Halfway through her contract, she mentioned to the Dean of the law school that she would certainly like to buy a house and establish some roots in the community. The Dean said, "Go ahead. We will have needs in your teaching areas for at least three years." Acting on this statement, Arleena bought a house. At the end of her year-long contract, she was let go by the law school. Arleena sues, claiming a deprivation of a property interest. Does she have a case?

> **Answer:** Yes. A property interest may arise not only from contractual language, but also from facts and circumstances which give rise to an implied promise to continue the employment relationship. The Dean's comments were tantamount to an oral promise to retain Arleena beyond her one-year contract. See §461 for further review.

XV. SUBSTANTIVE DUE PROCESS AND FUNDAMENTAL RIGHTS

A. INTRODUCTION.
[§471]

The Constitution protects an individual from government action which abridges fundamental personal rights. If a state or the federal government takes action which adversely affects a person's individual rights and that person challenges the law, the challenge must be based on a specific provision of the Constitution. The Due Process Clauses of the Fifth and Fourteenth Amendments provide potential bases for challenging government action which arguably impinges on individual rights. Under substantive due process analysis, a court is asked to determine the constitutionality of a law which abridges the rights of a class of persons (for example, a state law which prohibits any pregnant woman from having an abortion). Under procedural due process analysis (see §439), a court is asked to determine the constitutionality of the procedures used when a government deprives an individual of life, liberty, or property (for example, a state law which terminates a specific person's welfare benefits without any pre-termination hearing).

Under substantive due process analysis, the Court reviews the substance of legislation to see if it unduly interferes with an individual's rights or interests that are protected by the Due Process Clauses of the Constitution. The Court protects certain individual rights (such as the right to marry, the right to procreate, or the right to refuse medical treatment) from government abridgement because those rights are aspects of liberty protected by the Due Process Clauses of the Constitution. If the federal government acts, the Fifth Amendment Due Process Clause is the appropriate provision for a plaintiff to use; if a state acts, the Fourteenth Amendment Due Process Clause is the appropriate provision. Once you identify the right or interest being abridged, you must argue that it is an aspect of liberty under the appropriate due process clause; then you must determine if it is simply a low-level liberty interest (relatively unimportant) or a fundamental right (very important). A right will be deemed fundamental if it is essential to an Anglo-American system of jurisprudence, or implicit in the concept of ordered liberty. (See §475). **The importance of the right being abridged sets the level of scrutiny that a court will use to review the law. The more important the right, the higher the level of scrutiny.** Setting the level of scrutiny also determines who has the burden of proof - the plaintiff or the government. **At rationality review, the plaintiff always has the burden of proving that the law is irrational. At strict scrutiny, once the plaintiff has made a prima facie showing that a fundamental right has been abridged, the burden shifts to the government to show that it has a compelling reason for the law, and that the government has used narrowly tailored means to achieve its goal (means that are directed specifically at the source of the evil the government is trying to prevent).** For instance, a state could not deny a marriage license to a person (thus depriving him of the fundamental rights to marry) based on his failure to pay child support for his children; there are less drastic means available to achieve the state's goal of ensuring payment of child support obligations (such as initiating a lawsuit to collect the back payments). The Court will balance the abridgement of the right asserted against the proferred government justification for the law.

In addition to the Due Process Clause, the Fourteenth Amendment contains the Privileges or Immunities Clause, which precludes any state from making or enforcing any law which shall abridge privileges or immunities flowing from the federal government. This clause is to be distinguished from the Privileges and Immunities Clause of Article IV (see §294 above), which prohibits a state from discriminating against out- of-staters in relation to state-granted rights or privileges. The Court has interpreted the Fourteenth Amendment Privileges or Immunities Clause so that it is a virtual nullity in terms of providing an effective challenge to a state law.

Slaughterhouse Cases 83 U.S. 36 (1873). The Court upheld a state law which granted a monopoly to a certain slaughterhouse to engage in the livestock business in the city of New Orleans. In rejecting an argument based on the Privileges or Immunities Clause of the Fourteenth Amendment, the Court held that the clause did not incorporate any of the protections of the Bill of Rights, but rather protected only those rights which flow from the relationship between a United States citizen and the federal government. The rights which theoretically are protected under the clause are: the right to petition the government for redress of grievances, the right to petition for a writ of habeas corpus, the right to use the navigable waters of the United States, the right to come to the seat of government to transact business, rights secured by treaties with foreign countries, and the rights secured by the Thirteenth and Fifteenth Amendments and by other provisions of the Fourteenth Amendment. However, remember that only once in the history of the Court has it used the clause to invalidate a state law, and that case was overruled five years later (See *Colgate v. Harvey*, 296 U.S. 404 (1935), overruled in *Madden v. Kentucky*, 309 U.S. 83 (1940).

B. SUMMARY OF
STEPS IN A
SUBSTANTIVE
DUE
PROCESS
ANALYSIS. [§473]

1. Identify which government is acting, federal or state. This step is important because if a state is acting, the Fourteenth Amendment Due Process Clause applies, whereas if the federal government is acting, the Fifth Amendment Due Process Clause applies.

2. Describe in layperson's terms the interest that has been abridged. For instance, if a state imposes a two-year training requirement for drivers of large trucks, a person challenging that law will argue that his or her interest in pursuing an occupation has been abridged.

3. Place the abridged interest in the Constitution (assert that it is an aspect of liberty under the appropriate due process clause). Driving a truck (or, pursuing an occupation) is an aspect of liberty under the Fourteenth Amendment Due Process Clause (if a state has passed the law), or the Fifth Amendment Due Process Clause (if the federal government has passed the law).

4. Ascribe constitutional weight to the interest abridged - is it a low-level liberty interest or a fundamental right? You must look to Supreme Court cases to determine whether the Court has accorded a specific interest the status of a fundamental right.

5. Set the appropriate level of scrutiny. Remember that, under substantive due process, a law abridging a non-fundamental right receives only rational-basis review, whereas a law abridging a fundamental right receives strict scrutiny.

6. Balance the abridgment of the individual right against the proferred government interest. Be as specific as possible when articulating the right abridged and the specific government interest underlying the law.

C. LEVELS OF SCRUTINY UNDER SUBSTANTIVE DUE PROCESS. [§474]

RATIONAL BASIS REVIEW

NATURE OF RIGHT ABRIDGED	ENDS	MEANS	BURDEN OF PROOF
Low-Level Liberty Interest	Legitimate Government Interest (within an enumerated power of Congress or 10th Amendment Police Power of a state.)	Rationally Related (arguably advances the goal sought)	Stays with plaintiff.

STRICT SCRUTINY

NATURE OF RIGHT ABRIDGED	ENDS	MEANS	BURDEN OF PROOF
Fundamental Right	Compelling Government Interest (very important government goal)	Narrowly Tailored (directly and narrowly addresses the problem - not overbroad)	Shifts to the government after the plaintiff has shown an abridgement of the fundamental right.

D. SUBSTANTIVE DUE PROCESS REVIEW OF ECONOMIC LEGISLATION. [§475]

From 1897 to 1934, the Court used the doctrine of substantive due process to strike down state laws which abridged the liberty to contract. **From 1934 to the present, the Court has upheld virtually all state laws which regulate economic matters. For substantive due process purposes, the right to contract and the right to pursue employment are low-level liberty interests, the abridgment of which receives only rationality review (the Court asks whether a legitimate government interest is being advanced by the law, and whether the means chosen can rationally be said to advance that interest).**

1. Early Substantive Due Process Cases Dealing With Economic Interests. [§476]

Until 1934, the Court considered the right to contract to be an important aspect of liberty.

Allegeyer v. Louisiana, 165 U.S. 578 (1897). [§477]

The Court invalidated, on substantive due process grounds, a Louisiana law which precluded unapproved insurance companies from issuing policies on property located within the state. The Court relied on the liberty interests of pursuing an occupation and freely entering into contracts.

Lochner v. New York, 198 U.S. 45 (1905). [§478]

The Court invalidated a New York law that limited the number of hours a person could work in a bakery to no more than 60 per week or 10 per day. The liberty provision of the due process clause of the Fourteenth

Amendment protects the ability to contract and to purchase or sell labor. The Court rejected the state's health argument that the law was needed to protect the health of bakery employees. The Court's ruling obviously promoted a laissez faire theory of employment, at the expense of the state's power to regulate for the common good.

2. The Modern Hands-Off Approach to Cases Dealing with Economic Interests. [§479]

Beginning in 1934, the Court began to reject the right to contract as a limitation on government power.

Nebbia v. New York, 291 U.S. 502 (1934). [§480]

The Court upheld a New York law that regulated milk prices. Contract rights, while part of the liberty protected by the due process clause, are not absolute, and may be abridged when the state regulates in the common interest. Such a law will be upheld if it is not arbitrary or capricious, and has a reasonable relation to a proper legislative purpose.

West Coast Hotel Co. v. Parrish, 300 U.S. 379 (1937). [§481]

The Court upheld a Washington state law setting a minimum wage for women. The Court accepted the state's police power argument of protecting female workers, and rejected the plaintiff's argument that the law unduly abridged the liberty interest in freely entering into a contract.

U.S. v. Carolene Products Co., 304 U.S. 144 (1938). [§482]

The Court upheld a federal law that prohibited the shipment of "filled milk" in interstate commerce ("filled milk" refers to milk or cream to which fat or oil has been added). The Court said it should uphold the law if any state of facts existed, or could have been presumed to exist, which would support the law. Any arguably rational basis for the law would be enough to uphold it.

Day-Brite Lighting v. Missouri, 342 U.S. 421 (1952). [§483]

The Court upheld a law that required employers to give employees paid time off to vote. The Court refused to sit as a "super-legislature" that would second-guess the state; debatable economic or social issues should be left to state legislatures.

Williamson v. Lee Optical, 348 U.S. 483 (1955). [§484]

The Court upheld an Oklahoma law which prohibited optometrists from fitting eyeglass lenses without a prescription from an ophthalmologist. The Court said it would uphold a law if the legislature thought an evil existed and the law was a rational way to correct it.

Ferguson v. Skrupa, 372 U.S. 726 (1963). [§485]

The Court upheld a Kansas law prohibiting anyone but lawyers from engaging in the business of debt adjusting ("debt adjusting" was defined by the statute as the practice of a debtor hiring a debt adjuster who, for a fee, would distribute among certain specified creditors money that was paid periodically by the debtor). The Court said that courts should not substitute their social and economic beliefs for those of a state legislature.

Duke Power Co. v. Carolina Environmental Study Group, Inc., 438 U.S. 59 (1978). [§486]

The Court upheld a federal law setting a cap on monetary damages recoverable in nuclear power plant accidents. The Court said it would defer to the congressional judgment unless it was arbitrary or irrational. It also said that in economic cases, laws come to the Court with a presumption of constitutionality, and the burden is on the one attacking the law to prove that the legislature acted irrationally.

E. SUBSTANTIVE DUE PROCESS REVIEW OF SOCIAL LEGISLATION. [§487]

Not all liberty interests are fundamental; some may be abridged upon a showing of rationality by the state. The Court uses low-level rationality review when a law is challenged as violating some non-fundamental social interest. The following are cases in which the Court determined the right at issue to be merely a low-level liberty interest.

1. Choice of Hairstyle. [§488]

A police officer's right to choose his or her hairstyle is a low-level liberty interest.

Kelley v. Johnson, 425 U.S. 238 (1976). The Court upheld a police department regulation regulating the length and style of hair of police officers. The Court said that even if a liberty interest were implicated by the regulation, there is no fundamental or basic right of police officers to wear their hair any way they want. The plaintiffs were not able to show that the regulation was without a rational basis.

2. Registration of Prescription Drug Users. [§489]

Prescription drug users do not have a right to prevent their names from being placed on a state computer list. This is another low-level liberty interest.

Whalen v. Roe, 429 U.S. 589 (1977). The Court upheld a New York law that required the names of prescription-drug users to be sent to a central computer for record-keeping purposes. The Court found no fundamental privacy interest implicated here, so rationality review applied. The legislature could rationally have concluded that the law would aid in deterring and catching people who were abusing prescription drugs.

F. SUBSTANTIVE DUE PROCESS REVIEW OF FUNDAMENTAL RIGHTS. [§490]

Whenever a government regulation abridges a fundamental right, the Court will use strict scrutiny to review the law; the state will have to show a compelling interest and narrowly tailored means to justify the law. The fundamental right may be enumerated (such as certain provisions of the Bill of Rights which have been applied to the states), or unenumerated (such as the right to privacy). A right will be deemed fundamental if it is "essential to an Anglo-American system of jurisprudence," or "implicit in the concept of ordered liberty." (See §471.)

1. TWO TYPES OF FUNDAMENTAL RIGHTS - ENUMERATED OR UNENUMERATED. [§491]

Fundamental rights may be enumerated or unenumerated. **Enumerated fundamental rights are those provisions of the Bill of Rights which are so important that they are applied against the states as well as against the federal government.** The Court has selectively incorporated certain

Bill of Rights provisions by declaring them to be aspects of liberty under the Due Process Clause of the Fourteenth Amendment. Unenumerated fundamental rights are rights which are not listed in the Constitution, but have been deemed by the Court to be so important as to be protected by the Constitution against government intrusion (such as the right to privacy).

a. The Bill of Rights provisions that have been incorporated are:

(1) All First Amendment rights: Speech, both religion clauses, press, to peaceably assemble, and to petition the government for the redress of grievances;

(2) The Fourth Amendment prohibition against unreasonable searches and seizures;

(3) All provisions of the Fifth Amendment, except the requirement that all criminal prosecutions be started only on a grand jury indictment;

(4) All Sixth Amendment rights;

(5) All Eighth Amendment rights.

b. Unenumerated fundamental rights are:

(1) The right to privacy;

(2) The right to interstate travel;

(3) The right to vote; and

(4) The right of political association.

2. ALTERNATIVE TO SUBSTANTIVE DUE PROCESS: FUNDAMENTAL RIGHTS STRAND OF EQUAL PROTECTION. [§492]

When a legislature passes a law that abridges a fundamental right, a court may apply one of two methods of analysis: substantive due process, or the fundamental rights strand of equal protection. In both, the level of judicial scrutiny rises from rationality review to strict scrutiny because a fundamental right is abridged. **A substantive due process analysis is called for when a legislature passes a mandatory law (a requirement or a prohibition) which affects all persons within the relevant population (such as a state law prohibiting abortions to all women). A fundamental rights strand of equal protection analysis is called for when the legislature sets up a classification system which deprives only a certain group of persons of a fundamental right (a poll tax classifies along wealth lines, and deprives poor people of the right to vote).** Usually, there is nothing about the classification itself that raises the level of scrutiny (there is no suspect class being disadvantaged), but the fact that the classification system operates to deprive a class of persons of a fundamental right raises the scrutiny. Courts are not always clear about which analysis they are using, but one thing is certain - whichever label is applied to the analysis, the Court applies strict scrutiny because a fundamental right is being abridged.

As you go through the following cases, be aware of whether the state law applies to all persons who possess the trait the government is trying to regulate. If the law affects all persons within the relevant population, then substantive due process analysis will apply. For example, if a state wanted to cleanse the gene pool by sterilizing all felons who committed crimes involving moral turpitude, that law would be analyzed under substantive due process. If the law affects only a certain group of persons within the relevant population, then the fundamental rights strand of equal protection analysis is called for. If the state sterilized only some morally corrupt felons, but not others, that law would be analyzed under the fundamental rights strand of equal protection (equal protection principles are applied because the government has set up classifications within a category of persons, all of whom have a trait relevant to the purpose of the law).

3. SPECIFIC FUNDAMENTAL RIGHTS. [§493]

The following cases illustrate the development of fundamental rights in the areas of procreational and family autonomy, interstate travel, voting, and political association.

a. Right to Direct the Educational Upbringing of Your Children. [§494]

The Court has said that there is a fundamental right of parents to decide where and how to educate their children.

(1) Choice of School. [§495]

Parents Have a Right to Determine Which Schools Their Children Will Attend.

Meyer v. Nebraska, **262 U.S. 390 (1923). [§496]** The Court invalidated a state law which prohibited the teaching of any foreign language (other than the "dead" ones) in any elementary school. The Court relied on the unenumerated rights to marry, establish a home, and bring up children.

Pierce v. Society of Sisters, **268 U.S. 510 (1925). [§497]** The Court invalidated a state law which required all students to attend public, rather than private or religious, schools. The Court referred to the right of parents and guardians to direct the upbringing and education of children under their control.

(2) No Right to a Public School Education. [§498]

There is no right to a public school education. State methods of funding public education receive rational basis review. As long as every student in the state receives a minimally adequate education, the Court will uphold the funding scheme. It does not make the funding system unconstitutional for some school districts to be funded at higher levels than others.

San Antonio Independent School District v. **Rodriguez, 411 U.S. 1 (1973). [§499]** The Court upheld a Texas system of financing public schools under which per-pupil funding varied from $356 to $594 per student. The Court applied rationality review, asserting that there is no fundamental right to a public school education, and that a state's funding scheme is constitutional if it provides an adequate minimum educational offering in every school in the state.

Plyler v. Doe, **457 U.S. 202 (1982). [§500]** The Court invalidated, under equal protection analysis, a Texas statute that denied free public education to the children of illegal aliens. Applying heightened scrutiny (but not strict), the Court appeared to treat public school education as more important than a mere government benefit. The critical factor was that a state, by law, completely excluded a class of children from its public schools.

Kadrmas v. Dickinson Public Schools, 487 U.S. 450 (1988). [§501] The Court upheld, under rationality review, state and local laws which resulted in some school districts charging a fee for bus transportation to public schools. The Court restricted *Plyler* (previous case) to its facts, and emphasized that since there is no fundamental right to a public school education, rationality review is appropriate. Even though poor students could not afford the bus ride to school, the Court found the fee requirement rationally related to the legitimate government interest of saving money for other school district operations.

b. Right to Privacy. [§502]

There is no right to privacy enumerated in the Constitution. **The Court has offered different doctrinal bases for the existence of such a right (see, *Griswold v. Connecticut*, §506), but today it is accepted that the right to privacy is an aspect of liberty protected by the due process clauses.**

(1) Abortion and Reproductive Freedom. [§503]

The Court has extended constitutional protection to such activities as marriage, contraception, and abortion. In each of these areas, the Court has ruled that there is a constitutional right of privacy which presumptively protects the ability of a person or persons to engage in certain activity. A state must have a compelling reason to restrict or prohibit the exercise of one of these rights. The following cases trace the Court's development of the right of privacy in the areas of marriage and procreational autonomy.

(a) Right to Marriage and Procreation. [§504]

The Court has recognized marriage and procreation as fundamental rights that are protected by the Due Process Clauses of the Constitution.

Skinner v. Oklahoma, 316 U.S. 535 (1942). The Court invalidated, under equal protection, an Oklahoma law that authorized the sterilization of repeat felons whose crimes involved moral turpitude. The law was designed to cleanse the gene pool of the offspring of recidivist felons. Under the law, however, white-collar crooks were exempted from the sterilization requirement. The Court used strict scrutiny because the law deprived certain persons of the fundamental rights of marriage and procreation. This case involves a non-suspect classification (one set of recidivist felons versus another) that in turn abridged fundamental rights. If the legislature had said that all recidivist morally turpitudinous felons were to be sterilized, this would be a substantive due process case.

(b) Right to Marry. [§505]

The Court has held that the right to marry is an aspect of liberty protected by the Due Process Clauses of the Constitution.

Zablocki v. Redhail, 434 U.S. 374 (1978). The Court invalidated, under equal protection, a Wisconsin law that refused to grant a marriage license to anyone who had minor children whom he or she was obligated to support, unless there was proof of payment of the child-support obligations. The classification effected by the law significantly interfered with the exercise of the fundamental right to marry.

(c) Right of Married Couples to Receive Information About Contraceptives. [§506]

The Court has recognized the right of privacy as encompassing the right of married couples to receive information about contraceptives.

Griswold v. Connecticut, 381 U.S. 479 (1965). The Court invalidated a state law which made it a crime to give advice or information about contraceptives to married couples. The Court said that the law violated a fundamental right to marital privacy. Justice Douglas said the right to marital privacy came from penumbras, formed by emanations from the First, Third, Fourth, Fifth, and Ninth Amendments (enumerated rights have certain corollary rights which flow from them). Justice Douglas did not place the right to marital privacy in the liberty provision of the due process clause, but that is where the Court places it today.

(d) Right of Unmarried Persons to Receive Contraceptives. [§507]

The Court has held that unmarried persons, as well as married couples, have a constitutional right to access to contraceptives.

Eisenstadt v. Baird, 405 U.S. 438 (1972). The Court invalidated, under equal protection, a Massachusetts law criminalizing the distribution of contraceptives to unmarried persons. This law violated the rights of single persons, under the Equal Protection Clause, to be treated the same as married persons in terms of access to contraceptives. In effect, the Court recognized a fundamental right of unmarried adults to have access to contraceptives.

(e) Right of Minors to Purchase Non-Prescription Contraceptives. [§508]

The Court has held that minors have a privacy right to obtain non-prescription contraceptives.

Carey v. Population Services International, 431 U.S. 678 (1977). The Court invalidated a New York law which, in part, prohibited the sale of non-prescription contraceptives to persons under the age of 16. A plurality said that a state law inhibiting the privacy rights of minors would be valid only if it advanced some significant (not compelling) state interest. A ban on contraceptives to minors would not serve the state interest of deterring underage sex.

(f) Abortion Rights. [§509]

The Court has held that a woman has a fundamental right to decide whether or not to terminate her pregnancy.

OUTLINE

Roe v. Wade, 410 U.S. 113 (1973). The Court invalidated state laws criminalizing abortion, except in a case where the woman's life was in danger. The Court, 7-2, ruled that a pregnant woman has a fundamental right to decide whether or not to terminate her pregnancy. The Court recognized two state interests, each of which becomes compelling at a different point during pregnancy. A state's interest in maternal health or life becomes compelling at the end of the first trimester, providing a basis for regulation during the second and third trimester. A state's interest in potential human life becomes compelling at viability (24-28 weeks) and provides a basis for a state restricting or prohibiting abortion during the third trimester. The Court also held that a fetus is not a person entitled to protection under the Fourteenth Amendment.

(i) Spousal Consent Laws Invalid. [§510]

The Court has held that states may not require a woman to obtain the consent of her spouse before she may have an abortion.

Planned Parenthood v. Danforth, 428 U.S. 52 (1976). The Court invalidated a state law requiring spousal consent for an abortion, and requiring parental consent for an unmarried woman under the age of 18 to get an abortion. A husband cannot be given a veto power over his wife's decision to terminate a pregnancy; as between spouses, the woman's interest always prevails.

(ii) Judicial Bypass Procedure When a Minor Wants an Abortion. [§511]

The Court has held that parental consent laws are invalid unless accompanied by a judicial bypass procedure.

Bellotti v. Baird, 443 U.S. 622 (1979). The Court invalidated a Massachusetts law which required the consent of both parents before a minor could have an abortion. A plurality set forth rules for a judicial bypass to allow a minor to get an abortion without her parents' notice or consent. If a state requires parental consent (one or both), it must also provide a confidential alternative procedure (usually a court hearing, but not necessarily) at which a judge makes one of two decisions. If the minor is competent to make the abortion decision, she decides. If she is not competent, due to age or mental status, the judge decides what is in her best interest.

(iii) Government Funding of Abortion. [§512]

The Court has held that a woman's right to decide whether or not to terminate her pregnancy is not violated by a state law which refuses to fund welfare abortions.

Maher v. Roe, 432 U.S. 464 (1977) and *Harris v. McRae*, 448 U.S. 297 (1980). The Court held that neither a state nor the federal government has a duty to pay for abortions for indigent women, even if the government pays the expenses of childbirth for indigent women. The Court said that the government, through its refusal to subsidize welfare abortions, was placing no obstacle in the path of an indigent woman who wanted an abortion - her poverty was the obstacle. These cases are not true substantive due process cases because there was no government action mandatorily prohibiting abortions by indigent women. In other words, she still had a choice to exercise her right to terminate her pregnancy. The plaintiffs in these cases argued that non-funding of welfare abortions effectively prohibited women from exercising their right to terminate their pregnancies.

(iv) Use of Public Facilities or Employees to Perform Abortions. [§513]

The Court has held that states may prohibit the use of public facilities or employees to perform abortions.

Webster v. Reproductive Health Services, 492 U.S. 490 (1989). The Court ruled on a number of provisions of a Missouri law regulating abortion. The Court refused to rule on the preamble of the law which declared that human life begins at conception. It said that no one had been injured by the language of the preamble, so it created no ripe case or controversy. The Court upheld provisions of the law prohibiting the use of public employees or public facilities to perform an abortion unless necessary to save the life of the mother. Use of public employees or facilities was considered a form of subsidy which the state had no duty to provide. The Court also upheld a provision of the law which required physicians to perform certain tests on a fetus of any woman who wants an abortion, and is at twenty or more weeks of pregnancy (the earliest point of viability was at twenty-four weeks). The Court upheld this second-trimester law designed to protect the state's interest in potential human life because of a possible four-week margin of error in estimating gestational age.

(v) Two-Parent Notification; 48-Hour Wait for a Minor Seeking an Abortion. [§514]

The Court has upheld state laws requiring a minor to notify both parents as long as an appropriate judicial bypass was available. Also, states may require a minor to wait 48 hours after notifying one parent before she can have an abortion.

Hodgson v. Minnesota, 497 U.S. 417 (1990). The Court invalidated a state law which required two-parent notification (not consent) coupled with a 48-hour wait before a minor could get an abortion. The two-parent notification requirement, without any bypass provided, was held to be counterproductive to the state's goal of promoting family harmony when there was a non- communicative, dysfunctional family, and superfluous when there was a well-functioning family. The Court upheld the two-parent notification requirement with bypass, and upheld a 48-hour wait for a minor after she notified one parent of her intent to have an abortion.

(vi) Federally-Funded Family Planning Clinics; Conditions on Receipt of Federal Money. [§515]

The Court has held that Congress may properly withhold federal funds from family planning clinics that mention abortion as a method of family planning.

Rust v. Sullivan, 111 S.Ct. 1759 (1991). The Court upheld a federal law which prohibited federally-funded family planning clinics from mentioning abortion as a method of family planning. The Court treated this as a subsidy case, and reasoned that the clinics had a choice - they could refuse the federal money and discuss abortion as a method of family planning, or accept the federal money and comply with the conditions on the receipt of the money. Since this was a federal (not state) law, the liberty interest asserted was based in the Fifth Amendment Due Process Clause.

(vii) "Undue Burden" Analysis in Abortion Cases. [§516]

Justice O'Connor has adopted an "undue burden" analysis in abortion cases. Post-viability, a state may restrict or prohibit abortion. Pre-viability, a state may not pass a law which, by purpose or effect, imposes an undue burden on a woman's decision to terminate her pregnancy.

Planned Parenthood of Southeastern Pennsylvania v. Casey, 112 S.Ct. 2791 (1992). In *Casey*, the Court reviewed five provisions of a Pennsylvania law regulating abortion. The Court upheld an informed consent requirement for adult women, a requirement that an adult woman wait twenty-four hours after receiving certain information before she can have an abortion, a requirement that a minor get the informed consent of one of her parents before she has an abortion (a judicial bypass was provided if the minor does not want to or cannot get the consent of a parent), and certain reporting requirements. The Court struck down a spousal notification requirement.

Although the Court retained the central holding of *Roe*, that a woman has a fundamental right to decide whether to terminate her pregnancy, seven Justices rejected the trimester framework of *Roe*. Four Justices (Rehnquist, White Scalia, and Thomas) voted to overrule *Roe* completely. Two Justices (Blackmun and Stevens) voted to retain all of *Roe*. Three Justices (O'Connor, Kennedy, and Souter) voted to throw out the trimester framework, but retain the central right to decide. Justice O'Connor, writing the operative opinion in *Casey*, split pregnancy into two parts: pre- viability and post-viability. Post-viability, a state may seriously restrict, even prohibit, abortion. Pre-viability, a state may impose relatively nonintrusive requirements, but may not place an "undue burden" on the woman's decision to abort. An undue burden exists when a state law has the purpose or effect of placing a substantial obstacle in the path of a woman who wants to abort a non-viable fetus. Criminalizing abortion would be an undue burden as would spousal consent, or the spousal notice law struck down in *Casey*. Some informed consent laws, and a twenty-four hour waiting period for an adult woman would not be undue burdens. Many of the restrictions received by the Court in pre-*Casey* cases will have to be revisited to see how they fare under the undue burden standard of *Casey*.

(2) No Right to Adult, Consensual Homosexual Activity. [§517]

The Court refused to extend the fundamental right of privacy to protect the ability of consenting adults to engage in homosexual activity.

Bowers v. Hardwick, 478 U.S. 186 (1986). The Court upheld the application of a Georgia criminal sodomy statute to consenting adults who engaged in homosexual activity. The Court rejected the argument that the constitutional right of privacy was broad enough to protect this activity, and also rejected the claim that this activity was protected because it took place in the home. The Court was unwilling to travel down the road of saying that otherwise illegal activity is constitutionally protected if it takes place in the home.

(3) Liberty Interest in Refusing Unwanted Medical Treatment. [§518]

A majority of the Court has recognized a low-level liberty interest in refusing medical treatment; so far, this has not been deemed to be a fundamental right.

Cruzan v. Director, Missouri Department of Health, 497 U.S. 261 (1990). The Court upheld a Missouri statute that required proof by clear and convincing evidence that an incompetent person would have wanted to discontinue lifesaving food and water from being artificially administered. Nancy Cruzan had been in a persistent vegetative state for seven years when her parents sued to have the tubes removed. A majority of the Court found that there was a liberty interest in refusing unwanted medical treatment, but only four Justices deemed the interest fundamental.

(4) No Fundamental Right to Physician-Assisted Suicide. [§518.1]

The Due Process Clause of the Fourteenth Amendment does not create or protect a fundamental liberty interest in assisted suicide.

Washington v. Glucksberg, ___ S.Ct. ___ (1997). The Court unanimously upheld a State of Washington law which criminalizes assisting a person to commit suicide. The plaintiffs (including three seriously ill patients and four doctors) asserted a Due Process Clause liberty interest of a mentally competent, terminally ill adult to commit physician-assisted suicide. Relying heavily on history and legal tradition (mainly Anglo-American common law), the Court concluded that there exists no fundamental liberty interest in committing physician-assisted suicide. As part of its substantive due process analysis, the Court required a "careful description" of the asserted liberty interest. Rejecting broader characterizations of the asserted liberty interest (i.e., the "right to die," or the "liberty to shape death") the Court concluded that the proper tradition to consult was that concerning physician-assisted suicide. After concluding that no such fundamental liberty interest existed, the Court found that Washington's asserted state interests, including preserving human life and avoiding a possible slide toward voluntary and involuntary euthanasia, easily met the rational-basis test of being legitimate government interests.

OUTLINE

(5) No Equal Protection Violation When A State Allows a Patient to Refuse Lifesaving Medical Treatment But Prohibits Physician-Assisted Suicide. [§518.2]

Under the Equal Protection Clause, there is a rational distinction between a patient refusing unwanted lifesaving medical treatment, and a patient receiving assistance in committing suicide.

Vacco v. Quill, ___ S.Ct. ___ (1997). The Court unanimously ruled that New York does not violate the Equal Protection Clause by allowing competent adults to refuse unwanted lifesaving medical treatment, but prohibiting assisted suicide. The Court said that since a prohibition on assisted suicide does not abridge any fundamental right (See *Glucksberg,* prior case), or discriminate against any suspect or quasi-suspect class, rational basis scrutiny is called for under equal protection analysis. Disagreeing with the Second Circuit Court of Appeals, the Court saw a clear distinction between refusing unwanted medical treatment (thus letting nature take its course), and taking affirmative steps to bring about death (by allowing a doctor to prescribe life-ending medication). The Court recognized a number of state interests that justified its ban on assisted suicide, among them preserving life, avoiding a possible slide towards euthanasia, and maintaining the physician's role as healer.

(6) Family Living Arrangements. [§519]

Family living arrangements are protected as an aspect of liberty, but the Court has not clearly elevated this activity to fundamental right status.

Belle Terre v. Boraas, 416 U.S. 1 (1974). [§520] The Court upheld, under rationality review, a village zoning ordinance which limited land use to one-family dwellings. Plaintiffs were six unrelated college students who were prohibited from living together. The Court treated this as a law which affected only low-level social interests, and was therefore valid under rational basis review.

Moore v. East Cleveland, 431 U.S. 494 (1977). [§521] The Court invalidated a zoning ordinance which prohibited Grandma from living with her two grandsons, who were cousins, but would have allowed the living arrangement if the grandsons were brothers. While not crystal clear on the level of scrutiny it used, the Court said it would "examine carefully" any zoning law which affected freedom of personal choice in matters of family life.

c. Right to Interstate Travel. [§522]

The Court has recognized a fundamental right to interstate travel, but has not been clear about its constitutional basis.

(1) *Shapiro v. Thompson,* 394 U.S. 618 (1969). [§522.1]

The Court invalidated, under equal protection, state statutes which denied welfare payments to indigents who had lived in the state less than a year. The classification system set up by these statutes unduly deterred or punished the fundamental right to interstate travel, and was thus invalid as not being narrowly tailored to achieve any compelling government interest.

(2) *Starns v. Malkerson*, 401 U.S. 985 (1971). [§522.2]

The Court summarily affirmed the decision of the District Court, which held that a one-year waiting period to establish resident status for in-state tuition purposes at a state university did not violate equal protection. Since higher education, although valuable, is not a basic necessity of life, and the waiting period did not have the purpose of deterring people from moving into the state, the District Court held that the waiting period did not infringe on the exercise of the right to interstate travel. Without the infringement of a fundamental right, the classification received only rational basis scrutiny, and was upheld.

(3) *Memorial Hospital v. Maricopa County*, 415 U.S. 250 (1974). [§522.3]

The Court struck down, under equal protection, an Arizona statute that required a one-year residency as a condition to an indigent receiving nonemergency medical care at the county's expense. Although wealth is a nonsuspect class, the Court held that strict scrutiny applied because the classification operated to deter or penalize the exercise of the fundamental right to interstate travel. The Court stated that not all waiting periods or residency requirements would be held to violate the right to interstate travel, and suggested that the determinative inquiry is whether the benefit being withheld constitutes a "basic necessity of life." Thus, waiting periods that operate to withhold welfare benefits or medical care will be subject to strict scrutiny, but the Court has declined to strike down ones that only affect whether a person receives lower, in-state tuition (prior case).

d. Right to Vote. [§523]

While the right to vote is not enumerated in the Constitution, the Court considers it a fundamental right. Notice how the following cases use the Equal Protection Clause to invalidate restrictions on voting.

(1) Unequal Numbers of People in Voting Districts. [§524]

The Court has held that if electoral districts within a state have greatly varying numbers of voters in them, the right to vote of persons in the more populous districts will be diluted.

Reynolds v. Sims, 377 U.S. 533 (1964). The Court invalidated, under equal protection, a number of state laws which set up electoral districts with greatly varying numbers of people in them. The disparity in numbers among districts meant that some persons' votes were worth more than others. The Court said that the right to vote is a fundamental matter in a democratic society, and is preservative of other basic civil and political rights.

(2) Poll Tax. [§525]

The Court has held that a state-imposed poll tax as a prerequisite to voting is unconstitutional.

Harper v. Virginia State Board of Elections, 383 U.S. 663 (1966). The Court invalidated, under equal protection, a poll tax imposed as a prerequisite to voting. While the wealth classification by itself did nothing to raise the level of scrutiny, the Court based its analysis on the fundamental right to vote, which is preservative of all other rights.

(3) Voting Limited to Certain Parties. [§526]

The Court has held that states may not pass laws that limit the right to vote in school district elections to property owners or parents with children in the local public schools.

Kramer v. Union Free School District, 395 U.S. 621 (1969). The Court invalidated, under equal protection, a state law that restricted voting in school district elections to property owners or parents who had children in the local public schools. The Court used strict scrutiny to invalidate the law.

(4) Durational Residency Requirements for Voting. [§527]

The Court has held that certain durational residency requirements for voting violate equal protection.

Dunn v. Blumstein, 405 U.S. 330 (1972). The Court invalidated, under equal protection, a state requirement that a person have resided in the state for one year and in the county for three months before being eligible to vote. The Tennessee law curtailed the fundamental interest in voting.

e. Right to Political Association. [§528]

While the Constitution does not enumerate such a right, the Court has deemed it fundamental because it is essential to our system of government. If a state law imposes a severe burden on the right of political association, the state must show that the law is narrowly tailored to achieve a compelling state interest. If the state law does not impose a severe burden on the right of political association, the state must show that its regulatory interests are sufficiently weighty to justify the abridgement of the right.

(1) Restricting Access to the Ballot. [§529]

The Court has held that states may not preclude access to the ballot without a showing of a compelling government interest and means that are narrowly tailored.

Williams v. Rhodes, 393 U.S. 23 (1968). The Court invalidated, under equal protection, a number of Ohio laws which made it virtually impossible for a new political party to be placed on the ballot. The laws violated the right to vote, and the right of political association, and were not narrowly tailored to achieve any compelling governmental interest.

(2) Filing Fee to Become a Candidate. [§530]

The Court has invalidated, as an abridgement of the right of political association, filing fees that unduly burdened a minority party's or an indigent candidate's right to get on the ballot.

Lubin v. Parish, 415 U.S. 709 (1974). The Court invalidated, under equal protection, a California law requiring payment of a filing fee of 2% of the salary of the office sought. The filing fee kept indigents off the ballot in some cases. A filing fee to become a candidate cannot unduly burden a minority party's or an indigent candidate's right of political association.

(3) Banning a Person From Being the Candidate of More Than One Party. [§530.1]

State laws that prohibit candidates from being nominated for the same office by more than one party do not unconstitutionally abridge the right to political association of a party unable to nominate another party's candidate.

Timmons v. Twin Cities Area New Party, 117 S.Ct. 1364 (1997). The Court upheld Minnesota "anti-fusion" statutes which prohibit a person from appearing on the ballot as the candidate of more than one party. Reaffirming the existence of a fundamental right of political association, the Court adopted a sliding-scale analysis to analyze the infringement of the right. State laws imposing severe burdens on the right of political association must be narrowly tailored to achieve a compelling state interest. Lesser burdens receive a lower level of review, and a state's important regulatory interests will usually justify reasonable, non- discriminatory restrictions. The Minnesota laws in *Timmons* were justified by the state's interest in ballot integrity and political stability.

f. Right of Access to Courts. [§531]

Be aware of how the importance of the right sought to be protected in court determines whether the Court is willing to protect access to the courts. For example, the Court has ruled that a state court must waive court costs for an indigent who wants to file a divorce action, but a federal court does not have to waive court fees for an indigent who wants to file for bankruptcy. The inference is that the right to dissolve a marriage is more important than the right to go bankrupt.

(1) Trial Transcripts. [§532]

The Court has held that an indigent defendant who wants to appeal his or her conviction is entitled to a free trial transcript.

Griffin v. Illinois, 351 U.S. 12 (1956). The Court ruled that a state must give a free trial transcript (or its equivalent) to an indigent criminal defendant who wants to appeal his or her conviction. Both equal protection and due process principles dictate that protecting an appellant's fundamental rights to a fair trial cannot depend on the amount of money the appellant has.

(2) Trial Transcript for Appeal of an Order Terminating Parental Rights. [§532.1]

An indigent person who wants to appeal a court order terminating his or her parental rights is entitled to a free trial transcript.

In *M.L.B. v. S.L.J.*, 117 S.Ct. 555 (1997), the Court held that a mother whose parental rights were terminated by a court order may not be denied an appeal simply on the basis that she cannot afford the record preparation fees. Although fee requirements normally receive rational basis scrutiny, the Court held that since this case involved state intrusions into fundamental family relationships, both equal protection and due process principles required a closer scrutiny. This case is similar to a fundamental rights strand of equal protection analysis, but the Court is careful to not explicitly analyze the case in that manner. Those cases typically involve a law that, through a nonsuspect classification, interferes with the exercise of a fundamental right, but here the fee requirements interfere with the exercise of the right to appeal, which is not a fundamental right in civil cases. But because of the relationship between the right to appeal and the protection of the underlying right of a parent to rear her child, the Court employed heightened scrutiny. The Court declared that since termination orders are "unique" in their severity of state intrusion, this holding does not extend to appeals by indigent persons from other civil cases, including those involving other domestic relations matters.

(3) Appointed Counsel for First Appeal of a Conviction. [§533]

The Court has held that a state must appoint counsel for an indigent defendant pursuing his or her first appeal of a conviction.

Douglas v. California, 368 U.S. 815 (1963). The Court ruled that a state must appoint counsel for an indigent pursuing his or her first appeal, as of right. Again, principles of equal protection and due process dictated this result.

(4) Waiver of Court Fees to Get a Divorce. [§534]

The Court has held that a state must waive court fees for an indigent seeking a divorce.

Boddie v. Connecticut, 401 U.S. 371 (1971). The Court invalidated the application of a state's court fees and costs to an indigent seeking to go to court to get a divorce. Since this was the only forum in which a divorce could be obtained, a state could not use a system which excluded poor people from that forum. Does *Boddie* mean that there is a fundamental right to divorce?

(5) No Waiver of Court Fees to go Bankrupt. [§535]

The Court has held that a federal bankruptcy court does not have to waive the filing fee for an indigent who wants to declare bankruptcy.

U.S. v. Kras, 409 U.S. 434 (1973). The Court ruled that federal fees imposed as a condition of filing for bankruptcy did not violate the due process or equal protection principles of the Fifth Amendment. Going bankrupt is not a fundamental right, but only a low-level economic interest which may be abridged by a showing of rationality.

REVIEW PROBLEMS — SUBSTANTIVE DUE PROCESS AND FUNDAMENTAL RIGHTS

PROBLEM 1.: The State of Oz has stringent regulations regarding safety equipment on boats using its waterways. To enhance water safety in general, Oz has set up roving patrol boats to make sure that boaters using the navigable waters of the United States also comply with the Oz safety requirements. Bill Boater, while using his boat on U.S. waters, was stopped by the Oz patrol boat and had his boat inspected by Oz officials. Bill sues to stop this practice, claiming that his rights under the Privileges or Immunities Clause of the Fourteenth Amendment have been violated. Does Bill have a case?

> **Answer:** Maybe. In the *Slaughterhouse Cases*, the Court said that the right to use the navigable waters of the United States is within the protection of the Privileges or Immunities Clause of the Fourteenth Amendment. However, that clause has been interpreted in such a way as to be of virtually no value in challenging a state law. See §472 for further review.

PROBLEM 2. The State of Oz passed a law which requires that all abortions be performed in full-service hospitals with neo-natal intensive care units (a neo-natal intensive care unit provides specialized care for newborn infants). Jane Roe has just found out she is pregnant, and wants an abortion. She is in her seventh week of pregnancy. Is this law constitutional?

> **Answer:** No. This law would be an undue burden on a woman's right to an abortion prior to viability. At seven weeks of pregnancy, there is no chance that the fetus will survive, so the requirement of a neo-natal intensive care unit is irrational, and would clearly impose an undue burden on a woman who wants a pre-viability abortion. See §§509; 516 for further review.

PROBLEM 3. The State of Oz passed a law prohibiting home schooling; all children must attend state-approved public, private, or religious schools. Tina and Tom want to educate their children at home. What constitutional argument might they make to challenge this law?

> **ANSWER:** Tina and Tom would want to argue that there is an unenumerated right of parents to direct the educational upbringing of their children. The Court has, in the past, struck down state laws which imposed too great a burden on this right. For example, remember that in *Pierce v. Society of Sisters*, 268 U.S. 510 (1925), the Court invalidated a state law which required all students to attend public, rather than private or religious, schools. See §§494-497 for further review.

PROBLEM 4. The City of Id School District has a regulation prohibiting the possession of condoms on school property. The school authorities claim that students having condoms in school contributes to sexual activity among the students. Stan Studly, a senior at Id High School, files a lawsuit challenging this policy. Does he have an argument?

> **Answer:** Yes, the Court has said that minors do have a privacy interest in acquiring and possessing non-prescription contraceptives. However, this right may be abridged if the government has a significant (not compelling) reason for its action. Unfortunately, the Court has never indicated what sort of government interest would indeed be significant

OUTLINE

enough to justify such an abridgment. The argument that it would deter sexual activity by minors has been expressly rejected. See §508 for further review.

PROBLEM 5. The State of Oz is having troubles with school financing. Millage requests are consistently rejected by the voters (millages are special property-based taxes commonly used to fund public schools). Part of the problem is that Oz has a very large retirement community, and many of the older folks do not want to spend money on educating someone else's kids. As a result, Oz passes a law that restricts voting in school district elections to property owners or parents who have children in Oz public schools. Is this law constitutional?

> **Answer:** No. The Court has ruled that there is a fundamental right to vote, and that this sort of classification violates the voting rights of the excluded classes of people. See §526 for further review.

XVI. EQUAL PROTECTION

A. INTRODUCTION.
[§536]

Under equal protection analysis, the Court reviews legislation to see if a government is intentionally discriminating against a class of people entitled to special constitutional protection. Remember that there is only one Equal Protection Clause: it is in the Fourteenth Amendment, and only pertains to states and political subdivisions of states. If the federal government discriminates, the plaintiff's argument is based in the Due Process Clause of the Fifth Amendment; this is because the Court has said that there is an equal protection component of the Due Process Clause of the Fifth Amendment (See *Bolling v. Sharpe*, 347 U.S. 497 (1954)). Under equal protection analysis, individuals who are similarly situated must be treated substantially the same under the law. Under equal protection analysis, it is the classification that is the focus of scrutiny, whereas under substantive due process, the focus is on the individual right being abridged.

When doing an equal protection analysis, see if the government is classifying retrospectively or prospectively; is it trying to punish, or is it trying to prevent? If a government is trying to punish someone for acts already done, it may base the classification system on relevant facts (all drunk drivers who committed accidents will be thrown in jail — this is a very tight classification because it is based on proven facts). If a government is trying to prevent undesirable future conduct, it must guess who is going to engage in the conduct. For instance, if a state wants to prevent drunk driving, it may decide to set its drinking age at 21, based on the assumption that people over 21 years old are generally more responsible than those under 21. This classification is underinclusive (does not reach enough people) because there are irresponsible people over the age of 21. It is overinclusive (reaches too many people) because there are people under 21 who are responsible. Under equal protection analysis, when a government is trying to prevent certain conduct from happening in the future, the Court will scrutinize how well the government guessed at which people will engage in the undesirable conduct.

Under equal protection analysis, the Court determines which class of persons has been disadvantaged by a law (for instance, a law may disadvantage women by excluding them from certain employment opportunities). The Court then decides whether the disadvantaged class is "suspect" (race, ethnicity, or sometimes alienage), "quasi-suspect" (gender or illegitimacy), or "non- suspect" (age, wealth, mental status, sexual orientation, socio- economic, or sometimes alienage).

If a government intentionally disadvantages a "suspect" class, strict scrutiny applies; if a government intentionally disadvantages a "quasi-suspect" class, intermediate scrutiny applies; and if a government intentionally disadvantages a "non- suspect" class, rational basis review applies.

Historically, the reason for the Court applying strict scrutiny to laws that classified on the basis of race or ethnicity was that members of racial minority groups were politically powerless in the sense that they could not vote and, hence, could not protect themselves by participating in the democratic process. To compensate for this inability of certain groups to protect themselves through the ballot box, the Court looked very carefully at (applied strict scrutiny to) laws which discriminated on the basis of race.

Suspect Classes	Quasi-Suspect Classes	Non-Suspect Classes
Race	Gender	Age
Ethnicity	Illegitimacy	Wealth
Alienage (sometimes)		Mental Status
		Sexual Orientation
		Socio-Economic
		Alienage (sometimes)

To make a prima facie equal protection argument, a plaintiff must show disparate impact and intent. To demonstrate, "disparate impact," the plaintiff must prove that the law disproportionately burdens a particular group. (In attacking a state law that gives veterans a lifetime preference on civil service exams, a female plaintiff showed that women were disproportionately burdened by the law because 98% of the beneficiaries of the veterans' preference law were men.) "Intent" means that the government intended to discriminate against a class **because of** a specific trait such as race or gender. The plaintiff may prove intent by demonstrating that a statute facially discriminates against a group of people, or that enough circumstances exist so that a reasonable inference of intent exists. For instance, a plaintiff may show governmental intent to discriminate by looking at legislative history, departure from normal procedures in enacting a law, or the degree or foreseeability of the disparate impact of the law. A law may be facially discriminatory (the classification is obvious from the language of the law), or discriminatory as applied (the law is facially neutral, but is applied so as to intentionally disadvantage a certain class of persons).

B. LEVELS OF SCRUTINY. [§537]

Under equal protection analysis, how suspect the class is determines the level of scrutiny (and who has the burden of proof).

1. RATIONAL BASIS REVIEW. [§538]

If a government is intentionally discriminating against a non-suspect class, rational basis review is used by a court. At rationality review, the plaintiff has the burden of proof all the way through the case: the plaintiff must show that there is no legitimate reason for the law, or that the means (the classification system) are not rationally related to the goal sought.

SUSPECTNESS OF CLASS DIS-ADVANTAGED	ENDS	MEANS	BURDEN OF PROOF
Non-Suspect	Legitimate Government Interest (within an enumerated power of Congress or 10th Amendment Police Power of a state.)	Rationally Related (may be very under- or over- inclusive)	Stays with plaintiff.

2. INTERMEDIATE SCRUTINY. [§539]

If a government is intentionally discriminating against a quasi-suspect class, intermediate scrutiny is used by a court. At intermediate scrutiny, the burden of proof shifts to the government once the plaintiff shows that a quasi-suspect class has been disadvantaged.

SUSPECTNESS OF CLASS DIS-ADVANTAGED	ENDS	MEANS	BURDEN OF PROOF
Quasi-Suspect	Significant or Important	Substantially Related (not very under - or over inclusive)	Shifts to the government after plaintiff has shown an intentional discrimination against one of the appropriate classes

3. STRICT SCRUTINY. [§540]

If a government is intentionally discriminating against a suspect class, strict scrutiny is used by a court. At strict scrutiny, the burden of proof shifts to the government once the plaintiff shows that a suspect class has been disadvantaged.

SUSPECTNESS OF CLASS DIS-ADVANTAGED	ENDS	MEANS	BURDEN OF PROOF
Suspect	Compelling government interest (very important government goal)	Narrowly Tailored Tailored (very little under- or over-inclusiveness)	Shifts to the government after plaintiff has shown an intentional discrimination against an appropriate class

C. INTENT REQUIRED TO MAKE AN EQUAL PROTECTION ARGUMENT. [§541]

The Constitution prohibits only intentional discrimination (See *Washington v. Davis*, 426 U.S. 229 (1976)). To make out a prima facie equal protection argument, a plaintiff must show both disparate impact and intent. Intent to discriminate may be evident in the language of the statute (facial discrimination), or it may be inferred from the circumstances surrounding the passage or application of a facially neutral statute (as applied discrimination).

1. EXAMPLES OF CASES DEALING WITH THE INTENT REQUIREMENT. [§542]

a. Unequal Application. [§543]
The Court has held that intent may be shown by the manner in which a facially neutral law is applied.

Yick Wo v. Hopkins, 118 U.S. 356 (1886). The Court invalidated a San Francisco ordinance prohibiting laundries from operating in wooden buildings unless a board of supervisors granted an exemption. All non-Chinese applicants got exemptions, and no Chinese applicants got them. Even though the ordinance was neutral on its face, it was applied "with an evil eye and an unequal hand," and was based solely on hostility toward Yick Wo's race and nationality.

b. Statistical Evidence. [§544]
Statistical evidence alone is not enough to show intent.

Washington v. Davis, 426 U.S. 229 (1976). The Court upheld the validity of a test used to screen applicants for jobs as police officers in the District of Columbia, even though the test had a racially disproportionate impact. The statistical evidence alone was not enough to make out a prima facie case of an equal protection argument; intent was also needed, and could not be inferred from language of the test itself, or from its application.

c. Factors. [§545]
The Court has identified several factors to consider when trying to prove intent. Each factor is applied to determine whether there is a constitutionally neutral reason for a law (other than mere racial or sexual discrimination, for instance). The factors include the statistical impact of the law on a particular group, the legislative history of the law, departure from normal procedures in passing the law, and any other evidence that would indicate a purely racial or sexual purpose underlying the law.

Arlington Heights v. Metropolitan Housing Development Corp., 429 U.S. 252 (1977). The Court rejected an equal protection challenge to a village zoning ordinance which had the effect of prohibiting racially integrated low-income housing. No racially discriminatory intent was shown. The Court said that a plaintiff need not show that racial animus was the sole motivation behind a law, just that a discriminatory purpose was **a** motivating factor behind the government action. **There are a number of things to consider when trying to prove intent: the statistical impact of the law on a particular group; a pattern or effect of the law unexplainable on grounds other than race; the legislative or actual history of the government action; or a departure from normal procedural sequence.** While none of these alone may be dispositive of intent, a court will consider the totality of circumstances in deciding the intent question.

d. Degree and Foreseeability of Disparate Impact. [§546]
The Court has held that the degree of the disparate impact, along with its foreseeability, are relevant to proving intent; that is, if the disparate impact is unusually severe and was easily foreseen by the legislators who passed the law, a court may consider those factors when determining whether intentional discrimination exists.

Personnel Administrator v. Feeney, 442 U.S. 256 (1979). The Court upheld a Massachusetts law giving a lifetime preference on civil service exams to veterans, even though 98% of the beneficiaries of the law were men. While rejecting the gender-based equal protection challenge, the Court said that degree of disparate impact, as well as its foreseeability are relevant factors in determining intent.

2. INTENT IN JURY SELECTION CASES. [§547]

In jury selection cases involving both grand and petit juries, the Court has almost gotten to the point of accepting a racially discriminatory effect alone as establishing a prima facie case of an equal protection violation. **The rule in jury selection cases is that once a litigant shows substantial underrepresentation of a certain racial (or gender) group, he or she** has made a prima facie case of showing discriminatory purpose, and the burden of proof shifts to the government.

a. Disproportionate Representation. [§548]

Disproportionate representation of racial or ethnic groups on juries is sufficient to make a prima facie case of discriminatory purpose.

Castaneda v. Partida, 430 U.S. 482 (1977). The Court held that a defendant had made out a prima facie case of discrimination against Mexican-Americans in the composition of the grand jury that indicted him. The equal protection argument was based on the disparity between the numbers of Spanish- surnamed persons in the county and those on the grand jury. Once the defendant shows such a disparity, the burden shifts to the government to justify it on some neutral basis.

b. Peremptory Challenges. [§549]

A defendant in a criminal case may make a prima facie case of discriminatory purpose by showing the use of peremptory challenges to exclude racial or ethnic groups from the jury.

Batson v. Kentucky, 476 U.S. 79 (1986). The Court held that a defendant in a criminal case may make out a prima facie equal protection case by showing that a prosecutor used peremptory challenges to exclude jurors because of their race. The defendant must show that he or she is a member of a cognizable racial group, and that the prosecutor has used peremptory challenges to exclude members of the defendant's race. The exclusion of members of a certain racial group, coupled with any other relevant circumstances (such as the prosecutor's questions during voir dire), may create an inference of intent to discriminate based on race. (The Court has extended this analysis to civil cases, and to the use of peremptory challenges based on gender. *Edmonson v. Leesville Concrete Co.* , 111 S.Ct. 2077 (1991); *J.E.B. v. Alabama ex rel T.B.*, 114 S.Ct. 1419 (1994).)

3. INTENT IN RACIAL GERRYMANDERING CASES. [§550]

The shape and size of voting districts may be relevant to showing intent. For example, an oddly-shaped voting district that contains predominantly white voters may indicate intentional discrimination.

a. Shape of Voting Districts. [§551]

A plaintiff may prove intent by showing a drastic change in the geographical shape of a voting district.

Gomillion v. Lightfoot, 364 U.S. 339 (1960). The Court found intent to discriminate and allowed a cause of action based on an alleged violation of the Fifteenth Amendment (prohibiting racial discrimination in relation to voting). An Alabama law changed the shape of Tuskegee from a square to a 28- sided figure, allegedly removing from the city all but four or five black voters, and leaving all the white voters in the city. This bizarre redistricting seemed to reflect nothing but racial discrimination.

b. Strangely Shaped Voting Districts. [§552]

The strange shape of a particular district is relevant to proving intentional discrimination.

Shaw v. Reno, 113 S.Ct. 2816 (1993). The Court concluded that the plaintiffs had stated a claim on which relief could be granted under the Equal Protection Clause. The case involved an alleged racial gerrymander, in which a North Carolina congressional district snaked 160 miles through ten counties, and was, for much of its length, not much wider than the interstate highway it followed. The purpose of the districting plan was to increase black voting strength and create a majority-black district. A plaintiff challenging such a plan may make an equal protection claim by alleging that the law, though facially race-neutral, rationally cannot be understood as anything but an attempt to segregate voters based on race. The Court remanded the case to district court for consideration of whether the North Carolina redistricting plan violated the Equal Protection Clause.

Shaw v. Hunt ___ S.Ct. ___ (1996). This case is a continuation of *Shaw v. Reno* (previous case). In *Reno*, the Court remanded the case to district court for further consideration of whether the North Carolina redistricting plan classified voters by race and whether that classification survived strict scrutiny. The district court held that the plan was constitutional, but the Supreme Court ruled that the plan violated the Equal Protection Clause because it was not narrowly tailored to achieve the state's proffered compelling interests of ameliorating past racial discrimination or complying with provisions of the federal Voting Rights Act.

c. Race as the Predominant Factor in Drawing District Lines. [§553]

There is no threshold requirement of showing a bizarre district shape to make an equal protection argument. All the plaintiff must show is that race was the predominant factor underlying the drawing of the district lines.

Miller v. Johnson, 115 S.Ct. 2475 (1995). The Court held that a party challenging a state's legislative redistricting plan is not confined in his or her proof to evidence regarding a district's shape, nor must the plaintiff make a threshold showing that the challenged district has a bizarre shape (See *Shaw v. Reno*, §552). **The primary element of an equal protection challenge to a state redistricting plan is that race was the predominant factor underlying the state's drawing the voting district lines.** The Court invalidated a Georgia congressional redistricting plan because it found that race was the predominant factor underlying the state's drawing the voting district lines. Specifically, the Court found that Georgia drew the district lines according to race in order to create a third majority-black district to comply with preclearance demands of the Justice Department. The Court found that the majority-black population centers were all at the periphery of the district which covered over 6,700 square miles and split eight counties and five municipalities while extending from Atlanta to the Atlantic.

Bush v. Vera, ___ S.Ct. ___ (1996). The Court ruled that three bizarrely shaped Texas congressional districts failed strict scrutiny analysis under the Equal Protection Clause because the state reapportionment plan was not narrowly tailored to achieving the state's proffered compelling interests of remedying past racial discrimination or complying with provisions of the federal Voting Rights Act. Justice O'Connor, writing for herself, Chief Justice Rehnquist, and Justice Kennedy, asserted that strict scrutiny of congressional redistricting plans is required when a plaintiff shows that race was the predominant factor motivating the legislative and redistricting decision. Justice Thomas, writing for himself and Justice Scalia, asserted that strict scrutiny is required when a plaintiff shows that race was **a** factor in the creation of a majority-minority voting district.

D. REVIEW OF LAWS THAT DISCRIMINATE ON THE BASIS OF RACE OR ETHNICITY. [§554]

Any racial classification will receive strict scrutiny from a reviewing court. State or federal laws that invidiously discriminate on the basis of race (those that reinforce race- based stereotypes) receive strict scrutiny. State or federal race-based affirmative action laws also receive strict scrutiny. Affirmative action laws are those that discriminate against a particular racial or ethnic group to compensate for a prior discrimination against another racial or ethnic group.

1. SEPARATE BUT EQUAL. [§555]

From 1896 to 1954, the Court upheld the "separate but equal" doctrine, under which a law separating the races was constitutional if it provided equal facilities or benefits for each race. The Court simply ignored the blatant racial discrimination intrinsic in the very act of separation.

> **STUDY QUESTION:** Is there a constitutional difference between imposed segregation and requested segregation? It would clearly violate equal protection if a state university prohibited black and white students from living in the same dormitory. Is it any different if black students, for reasons of racial pride and cultural integrity, request and receive separate living quarters (or a student union)? Does the reason for the segregation change its constitutional status?

a. "Separate But Equal" Constitutional. [§556]

The Court, in 1896, upheld a state law requiring separate railroad accommodations for blacks and whites.

Plessy v. Ferguson, 163 U.S. 537 (1896). The Court upheld a Louisiana law requiring that railway companies provide "equal but separate accommodations for the white and colored races." Plessy, who asserted that he was seven-eighths Caucasian and one-eighth African blood, was arrested for refusing to leave a whites-only passenger car. The Court rejected the argument that the law imposed a badge of inferiority on blacks, asserting that if any feelings of inferiority flowed from the application of the law, it was "solely because the colored race chooses to put that construction upon it."

b. "Separate But Equal" Unconstitutional. [§557]

The Court, in 1954, ruled that separate educational facilities are inherently unequal and therefore unconstitutional.

Brown v. Board of Education I, 347 U.S. 483 (1954). The Court ruled that separate educational facilities for children in public schools are inherently unequal. The Court said that such segregation violates the equal protection clause even if the physical facilities and other tangible benefits may be equal. While public school education is not a fundamental right, it is preservative of other basic interests such as the right to participate in the processes of government. Enforced separation of the races not only reinforces a sense of inferiority on the part of black school children, but severely affects their motivation to learn.

c. Integration of Segregated Schools. [§558]

The Court has held that court-ordered integration is an appropriate remedy for segregated schools.

Brown v. Board of Education II, 349 U.S. 294 (1955). The Court remanded the cases it decided in *Brown I*, with directions for the lower courts to take such actions as necessary to integrate the public schools with all deliberate speed.

d. Equal Protection As Applied to the Federal Government. [§559]

The Court has held that equal protection guarantees bind the federal government through the Due Process Clause of the Fifth Amendment.

Bolling v. Sharpe, 349 U.S. 294 (1954). On the same day as *Brown I*, the Court ruled unconstitutional public school segregation in the District of Columbia schools. Since Congress (not a state) passes laws for the District of Columbia (Article 1, section 8, clause 17), the Fourteenth Amendment was not applicable to the case. The Court ruled that separate-but- equal schools violated the Due Process Clause of the Fifth Amendment, which has an implicit equal protection guarantee within it.

2. POST-*BROWN* REMEDIES FOR SCHOOL SEGREGATION. [§560]

After the *Brown* cases, school desegregation became a widespread and controversial topic across the country. **When deliberate (intentional) segregation of schools was found, courts would order remedial steps to be taken.** Intentional segregation would be found if a school district was operating a dual school system (primarily one-race schools), and was under a statutory mandate to segregate at the time of *Brown I*. If there was no statutory mandate as of 1954, a plaintiff would have to make the normal showing of intent under equal protection analysis. **Once a school district is found to have intentionally created a dual school system, the remedial powers of district courts are very broad, including ordering busing, reassignment of teachers and students, and altering of attendance zones.**

> **STUDY TIP:** Whenever you see a school desegregation question, determine whether there was a law or policy on the books in 1954 that required segregated schools. If so, the Court will impute segregative intent to a school district presently operating a system of one-race schools (a dual school system). If no statute or policy required segregation in 1954, a plaintiff will have to prove intent by looking at the actions of the school board.

a. Post-*Brown* Cases Involving School Desegregation. [§561]

The Court dealt with strong resistance by some school districts to the mandate of *Brown*. In those cases, the Court made it clear that state officials could not use the fear of public hostility or violence as an excuse to maintain segregated schools. In other cases, the Court had to evaluate school districts' attempts to comply with *Brown*, along with the power of federal courts to require local school districts to comply with the mandate to desegregate local schools.

(1) Attempted Nullification of *Brown* by State Officials. [§562]

The Court rejected an attempt by state officials to nullify *Brown* by preventing black students from attending public high schools.

Cooper v. Aaron, 358 U.S. 1 (1958). The Court unanimously reaffirmed *Brown* in the face of massive resistance from the Governor and legislature of Arkansas. After school authorities set up a desegregation plan, Governor Faubus sent troops to stop black students from entering previously all- white Central High School. Faubus was enjoined from further interference by a federal district court, and federal troops were sent to Arkansas to protect the rights of the black high school students. The Court refused to delay the integration of Little Rock schools, despite the argument that the intense publicity and hostility engendered by the desegregation plan would detract from the educational process. The Court said that *Brown* could not be nullified, directly or indirectly, by the actions of state officials.

(2) County-Run Private White Schools. [§563]

A county may not operate private white schools in an attempt to avoid integration.

Griffin v. County School Board, 375 U.S. 391 (1964). The Court, saying that the time for deliberate speed had run out, invalidated the action of a county closing its public schools to avoid complying with a desegregation order. Private white schools were set up and supported by state and local grants. A state may not allow one county to close its public schools for the sole purpose of racial discrimination, and then subsidize allegedly "private" schools for whites.

(3) Freedom-of-Choice Plans. [§564]

States may not enact so-called "freedom of choice" plans in an attempt to avoid integration. "Freedom of choice" plans purport to allow students to choose where they will attend school. The problem with such a plan as an integrative remedy is that virtually none of the white students chose to attend schools with high minority enrollment.

Green v. County School Board, 391 U.S. 430 (1968). The Court invalidated a "freedom-of-choice" plan which did virtually nothing to integrate public schools which had been segregated by law as of *Brown I*. The Court said that school boards operating state-compelled dual school systems as of 1954 had an affirmative duty to integrate their schools. In effect, the Court said that the law requiring segregated schools in 1954 created the intent necessary for an equal protection argument. Once that is present, all that need be shown is disparate impact, in the form of a dual school system.

(4) Presuming Intent Throughout a School District. [§565]

Where a court finds segregative intent on the part of a school board in relation to a large part of a school district, a court will presume that the intent to discriminate exists throughout the entire district.

Keyes v. School District, 413 U.S. 189 (1973). The Court, for the first time, dealt with an equal protection challenge to school board action when there had never been a law requiring segregated schools. The Court held that a finding of segregative intent by the school board in relation to a meaningful portion of a school district (an attendance zone within the district) creates a presumption that the intentionally segregative actions of the school board were responsible for segregated schools in the rest of the district. The school board would then have the burden of showing that segregation in the other schools was not a result of its actions.

(5) Dual School System. [§566]

The failure of a school board to eliminate its dual school system has been found to support an Equal Protection claim.

Columbus Board of Education v. Penick, 443 U.S. 449 (1979). The Court upheld a system-wide desegregation remedy. Even though there was no state law mandating segregation, the lower court found that the Columbus schools were officially segregated by race in 1954. This, plus the fact that the board knowingly continued to fail to take steps to eliminate its dual school system, allowed the plaintiffs to show both dual school system and intent, thereby making out a prima facie equal protection argument.

b. Post-*Brown* Cases Dealing With the Remedial Power of Federal Courts. [§567]

Federal courts have extremely broad equitable powers to remedy unconstitutional school segregation by ordering busing, redrawing district lines, or assigning teachers or students based on race. An interesting question is when should a court end its supervision of a local school board's activities? For the answer, see the *Dowell* 570 and *Freeman* 571 cases, later in this subsection.

(1) Remedial Powers. [§568]

Federal courts have broad remedial powers to remedy segregation.

Swann v. Charlotte-Mecklenburg Board of Education, 402 U.S. 1 (1971). The Court set guidelines for the exercise of equitable jurisdiction by lower courts in desegregation cases. Once a right and a violation have been shown, the scope of a district court's power to remedy past wrongs is broad. The Court listed the following guidelines: a court may consider the racial composition of the students in a school district as a starting point for crafting an equitable remedy (there is, however, no constitutional right to any certain degree of racial balance within the school system); a small number of one-race schools does not necessarily mean that the school district is segregated by law; alteration of the boundaries of school districts or attendance zones is permissible, even if administratively awkward or inconvenient; and busing may be used to desegregate, as long as it does not detract from the educational process by requiring inordinately long bus rides.

(2) Cross-District Busing. [§569]

Cross-district busing may be an appropriate remedy where segregation in one school district produces a segregative effect in another.

Milliken v. Bradley, 418 U.S. 717 (1974). The district court in *Milliken* ordered cross-district busing between Detroit and 53 suburban school districts. While the Court invalidated this particular busing order, it said that cross- district busing would be a permissible remedy if there had been a constitutional violation in one district that produces a significant segregative effect in another. The general principle is that the scope of the remedy must be proportionate to the scope of the proven constitutional violation; whichever school districts are proven to be co-discriminators may be included within a busing order.

(3) Termination of Federal Court Supervision. [§570]

A desegregation decree should be dissolved if the school board has complied with the decree in good faith and the vestiges of past discrimination have been eliminated to the extent practicable.

Oklahoma City Board of Education v. Dowell, 498 U.S. 237 (1991). The Court dealt with the question of when a remedial court order should be dissolved. The Oklahoma City Board of Education had been under a court order to integrate its schools, which it did, in part through a busing plan. The Board wanted to adopt what was basically a neighborhood school system, but the result was that about half the schools became one-race schools because of housing patterns. The Court said that the desegregation decree should be dissolved if the school board has complied in good faith, and the vestiges of past discrimination have been eliminated to the extent practicable. Justice Marshall, in dissent, said that a court order imposing a desegregation plan should not end so long as conditions likely to inflict the stigmatic injury persist, and there are feasible methods of eliminating such conditions (there always are - just leave the desegregation decree in effect).

(4) School Board Compliance With Discrete Requirements of a Court Decree. [§571]

Federal courts need not retain control over every aspect of school administration where the school board has shown it has complied with some specific requirements of the court decree.

Freeman v. Pitts, 503 U.S. 467 (1992). The Court said that when a court is deciding whether to end a court-ordered desegregation plan, it may withdraw judicial supervision of discrete categories of activity in which the school district has achieved compliance; it need not retain control over every aspect of school administration until full compliance is achieved. Three factors to consider when deciding to terminate a desegregation plan are: whether there has been full compliance with the decree; whether retention of judicial control is necessary or practicable to achieve compliance with the decree; and whether the school district has demonstrated a good-faith commitment to complying with the decree.

(5) Court-Ordered Salary Increases and Funding of Remedial Education Programs. [§572]

Federal courts may not fashion interdistrict remedies that exceed the scope of an intradistrict violation.

Missouri v. Jenkins, 115 S.Ct. 2038 (1995). The Court, reaffirming the three-part test of *Freeman v. Pitts* (previous case), ruled that a federal district court exceeded its remedial authority when it required Missouri to fund salary increases for virtually all instructional and noninstructional staff within the Kansas City School District, and to continue to fund remedial "quality education" programs. The district court has found an intradistrict violation in that student achievement levels in the Kansas City School District were still at or below national norms at many grade levels. The order requiring salary increases, which was designed to improve the "desegregative attractiveness" of the Kansas City schools (to attract white suburban students to the Kansas City School District), was an interdistrict remedy beyond the scope of the intradistrict violation in the case. Furthermore, the order requiring continued funding of "quality education" programs was based on an erroneous assumption by the district court; whether or not Kansas City students are at or below national norms of student achievement is not the test for determining whether a previously segregated school district has achieved unitary status — the three-part test of *Freeman v. Pitts* is the appropriate standard. Under *Freeman*, a court should ask the following: whether the school district has fully complied with the desegregation decree; whether continued judicial control is necessary or practicable to achieve compliance with the decree; and whether the school district has demonstrated a good-faith commitment to complying with the decree.

(6) Termination of Federal Court Supervision. [§573]

A state has not met its burden of proving that the prior segregative system has been dismantled if it perpetuates policies that continue to have segregative effects.

U.S. v. Fordice, 112 S.Ct. 2727 (1992). The Court dealt with the question of whether Mississippi had taken appropriate steps to dismantle a public university system in which some schools were almost exclusively white and some were almost exclusively black. The Court remanded for review in light of the following standard: If the State perpetuates policies and practices traceable to its prior system that continue to have segregative effects, and such policies are without sound educational justification and can be practicably eliminated, the State has not met its burden of proving that it has dismantled its prior system.

3. AFFIRMATIVE ACTION. [§574]

An affirmative action program is a government program which gives a preference to members of specified racial or ethnic groups. These programs are most common in the areas of education and employment. Affirmative action programs are compensatory; they are

designed to make up for past discrimination against members of the racial or ethnic groups favored by the affirmative action program. For an affirmative action program to be constitutional, it must be a remedy for a past violation. Also, the scope of the affirmative action plan must be proportionate to the scope of the violation. Past discrimination by society as a whole (engaged in by both governmental and private actors) does not count as a violation which will justify a state or federal affirmative action program based on race. To justify such a program, there must be some basis in evidence indicating that the government (or some specific agency of government) contributed in some discernible way to a prior system or scheme of racial discrimination. For instance, if a state (or the federal government) wanted to implement a voluntary affirmative action program based on race, the state must show that it contributed (at least as a passive participant) to a previous racially discriminatory system or scheme. The Court does not force a state to admit an intentional act or pattern of past racial discrimination (that would subject the state to civil rights lawsuits), it simply requires the state to assert that it had been a passive, negligent, or inadvertent contributor to past racial discrimination. This kind of admission qualifies as a past wrong which will justify a remedial race-based affirmative action program. **Race-based affirmative action programs, whether they are imposed by a state or the federal government, receive strict scrutiny by a reviewing court: the government has the burden of showing that the affirmative action program is narrowly tailored to achieve a compelling government interest.**

a. State Race-Based Affirmative Action Plans. [§575]

State race-based affirmative action programs receive strict scrutiny: The government must show a compelling reason for the program, and the means must be narrowly tailored to achieve that goal. Societal discrimination does not count as a violation that would justify a state race-based affirmative action plan. To have a voluntary affirmative action plan based on race, a state must show at least that it was a passive participant in some prior discrimination against a racial group. For instance, a state spending millions of dollars in the construction industry contributed to the systematic discrimination against racial groups in the industry.

(1) Race-Based Exclusions. [§576]

The Court has held that exclusion from a program based solely on race is illegal, even if the purpose of the exclusion is to increase the number of racial minority members who participate in the program.

Regents of the University of California v. Bakke, 438 U.S. 265 (1978). The Court, in a divided vote, issued two rulings: The University of California at Davis Medical School violated the federal statutory rights of Allan Bakke, a white applicant to medical school who was denied access to 16 (out of 100) spots set aside for minority applicants; and race may be considered as one of many factors in a university admissions program. In addition to his claim that his Fourteenth Amendment rights were violated by the set-aside program, Bakke also alleged that the Davis program violated his rights under Title VI of the Civil Rights Act of 1964, which prohibits racial discrimination in any program receiving federal funds. Justice Powell, along with Chief Justice Burger and Justices Stewart, Stevens, and Rehnquist ruled in favor of Bakke's Title VI claim. Justice Powell also said (alone) that Bakke's Fourteenth Amendment rights were violated. Justice Powell, joined by Justices Brennan, White, Marshall, and Blackmun, ruled that race may be considered as one factor in an admissions program. Justice Powell made the following constitutional points: strict scrutiny is the appropriate level of review in race-based affirmative action cases; societal discrimination does not count as a violation justifying an affirmative action plan; and, while attainment of a diverse student body may be a compelling government interest, exclusion of applicants from a certain number of spots, based on their race alone, is not a narrowly-tailored means because it is not related to any prior discrimination by the medical school (in fact, the medical school was found to have a clean record in terms of past racial discrimination). Justice Brennan argued that past societal discrimination does count as a violation that would justify an affirmative action program, that intermediate scrutiny is the appropriate level of review, and that whites, as a group, do not suffer the same kind of stigma as blacks when their respective groups are discriminated against. Justice Stevens, relying solely on Bakke's statutory argument, concluded that Title VI prohibited the exclusion of any individual from a federally funded program based on race.

(2) Race As One Factor In A Law School Admissions Process. [§577]
A federal Court of Appeals has held that, contrary to *Bakke* (previous case), a state law school may not even consider race as one factor in a law school admissions process.

Hopwood v. Texas, 78 F.3d 932 (1996), (cert. den., July 1, 1996). The Fifth Circuit Court of Appeals struck down a race-based affirmative action program used by the University of Texas School of Law (UT). UT's admissions process gave substantial racial preferences to African-Americans and Mexican- Americans, to the detriment of whites and non-preferred minorities. The Fifth Circuit, totally discrediting Justice Powell's opinion in *Bakke*, ruled that race can never be considered as a factor in a law school admissions program. The court also rejected UT's proffered justifications for its program: obtaining a diverse student body, and remedying the present effects at the law school of past discrimination in the entire Texas educational system (including primary and secondary schools and Texas colleges and universities).

(3) Proportional Representation By Race in the Work Force. [§578]
Layoffs are an impermissible means to achieve equal representation in the work force.

Wygant v. Jackson Board of Education, 476 U.S. 267 (1986). The Court invalidated a plan of the Jackson, Michigan school board under which white teachers with more seniority would be laid off before minority teachers who were retained to keep a certain percentage of minority teachers in the classroom. There was no majority opinion of the Court, but five Justices agreed that layoffs of innocent white teachers was an unconstitutional means to achieve even permissible goals. Five Justices also rejected societal discrimination as the violation which would justify an affirmative action plan, and rejected the school board's "role model" argument, under which a certain percentage of minority teachers must be maintained as role models for minority students.

(4) Standard of Review. [§579]

When reviewing a state-based affirmative action program, courts will apply strict scrutiny. In addition, states may not use societal discrimination as a basis for enacting an affirmative action program.

Richmond v. J.A. Croson Co., 488 U.S. 469 (1989). The Court invalidated a Richmond, Virginia set-aside program under which 30% of city construction money was earmarked for Minority Business Enterprises. A majority of the Court agreed that a state race-based affirmative action program should receive strict scrutiny, and that societal discrimination would not justify such a program. If a state or city wants to set up a voluntary affirmative action program, it must show that it was at least a "passive participant" in a system of racial discrimination. The idea is to have the state or city admit to some complicity in past racial discrimination so that there is something more specific than societal discrimination to justify the voluntary affirmative action plan.

b. Federal Race-Based Affirmative Action Plans. [§580]

Federal race-based affirmative action programs receive strict scrutiny: The government must show a compelling reason for the program, and the means must be narrowly tailored to achieve that goal. After *Adarand v. Pena* (see §584), the rules for federal affirmative action programs based on race are the same as the rules for state affirmative action programs based on race.

(1) Pre-*Adarand* Federal Race-Based Affirmative Action Cases. [§581]

Prior to the *Adarand* case (see, §584), federal race-based affirmative action programs received intermediate scrutiny from the courts.

(a) Federal Minority Business Set-Asides. [§582]

Pre-*Adarand*, the Court upheld a federal set-aside for minority business enterprises.

Fullilove v. Klutznick, 448 U.S. 448 (1980). The Court upheld a federal set-aside of public works money for Minority Business Enterprises. There was no majority opinion of the Court, but Chief Justice Burger, writing for three Justices, did say that in a remedial context, Congress must have some leeway in crafting the means to achieve its goals. Justice Marshall, for three Justices, clearly advocated an intermediate level of scrutiny. Justice Stewart, for two Justices, said that race should never be the criterion used to allocate government benefits.

(b) Broadcast Licenses. [§583]

Pre-*Adarand*, the Court upheld the use of racial preferences in granting broadcast licenses.

Metro Broadcasting v. FCC, 497 U.S. 547 (1990). The Court upheld an FCC policy which granted a racial preference to applicants for broadcast licenses, and for the sale and transfer of certain licenses. A majority of the Court, through Justice Brennan, said that intermediate scrutiny is the appropriate standard of review for a congressional race-based affirmative action program. The Court also said that Congress may enact such programs even if they are not "remedial" in the sense of compensating victims of past governmental or societal discrimination. In other words, Congress may set up an affirmative action plan even without any assertion of past societal discrimination. In this sense *Metro Broadcasting* is clearly the most liberal of the Court's affirmative action rulings in the race area.

(2) Federal Race-Based Affirmative Action Programs Receive Strict Scrutiny. [§584]

After the *Adarand* decision, federal race-based affirmative action programs receive strict scrutiny - the same standard the Court uses when reviewing state race-based affirmative action programs.

Adarand Construction Inc. v. Pena, 115 S.Ct. 2097 (1995). In *Adarand*, the Court reviewed a clause in a federal highway construction contract which provided bonuses for subcontracting with small businesses owned by socially and economically disadvantaged individuals. Under the federal law, certain racial and ethnic minorities are presumed to be socially and economically disadvantaged. The Court held that strict scrutiny applies to all race-based affirmative action programs, state or federal. To the extent that *Fullilove* (see §582) and *Metro Broadcasting* (see §583) are inconsistent with this holding, they are overruled. The Court ruled that societal discrimination will not justify a federal race-based affirmative action program, and that Congress (like a state under *Croson* (see §579) must make a specific showing of some participation in past racial discrimination if it wants to implement a race-based affirmative action program. The Court remanded the case for consideration under the strict scrutiny standard.

4. INTERRACIAL SEXUAL RELATIONS. [§585]

A number of states, at one time or another, have had laws prohibiting sexual relations between blacks and whites (Alabama, in 1972, was the last state to repeal its anti-miscegenation law). These anti-miscegenation laws have consistently been struck down by the Court. In these cases, the state usually argued that there was not an equal protection problem because black people and white people were treated the same - neither could associate with the other. Be aware of the "separate but equal" aspect of this argument.

a. Interracial Sexual Relations. [§586]

The Court upheld an 1883 state law that prohibited interracial sexual relations.

Pace v. Alabama, 106 U.S. 583 (1883). The Court upheld an Alabama statute that prohibited adultery or fornication between a black person and a white person, and that imposed greater penalties on those persons than on sexual partners of the same race. The Court said that equal protection guarantees were not violated as long as the black and white participants in the offense were equally punished.

b. Overnight Visits. [§587]

A state may not pass a law that prohibits a biracial couple from staying together overnight.

McLaughlin v. Florida, 379 U.S. 184 (1964). The Court overruled *Pace v. Alabama* (previous case), and invalidated a Florida statute which made it a crime for a white person and a black person of opposite sexes, not married to each other, to habitually occupy the same room in the nighttime. The Court did not consider the racial classification in the law to be a rational means of achieving any legitimate state goal.

c. Interracial Marriage. [§588]

A state may not pass a law that prohibits interracial marriage.

Loving v. Virginia, 388 U.S. 1 (1967). The Court invalidated a Virginia law which criminalized marriage between a white and any non-white person. Any non-white racial classes could intermarry with no criminal sanctions. The Court thoroughly rejected the argument that equal protection guarantees were not violated because whites and blacks were treated equally - neither could marry the other. It recognized this law for what it was - a blatant attempt by the state to reinforce invidious stereotypes of racial inferiority (one of the asserted state interests underlying the law was to prevent "a mongrel breed of citizens"). Be aware that the law also abridged the fundamental right to marry.

d. Child Custody. [§589]

Child custody decisions may not be based solely on race.

Palmore v. Sidoti, 466 U.S. 429 (1984). The Court held violative of equal protection a state's denial of child custody to a white mother for the sole reason that her new husband was black. While race may not be the sole determining factor in a child custody decision, it may be considered along with other factors to determine who gets custody of a child.

E. REVIEW OF LAWS THAT DISCRIMINATE ON THE BASIS OF ALIENAGE. [§590]

An alien is a person who is not a citizen of the United States. Aliens are protected by the Equal Protection Clause of the Fourteenth Amendment, as well as the equal protection component of the Due Process Clause of the Fifth Amendment. Be careful about which government (federal or state) is discriminating against aliens. **A federal law discriminating against aliens will receive only rational basis review; the plaintiff must show that the law is not rationally related to a legitimate federal interest. When a state discriminates against aliens, strict scrutiny will apply, unless the state is excluding aliens from politically sensitive positions - then rational basis review will apply.** This "political function" exception applies when a state (or city) excludes aliens from elected positions, important non-elected positions (involving the formulation or implementation of public policy), or employment as public school teachers, police officers, or probation or parole officers.

Being a notary public is not within the political function exception, so a state exclusion of aliens from that position is subject to strict scrutiny.

1. FEDERAL LAWS THAT DISCRIMINATE AGAINST ALIENS. [§591]

Because of Congress' power to regulate immigration and naturalization, the Court is extremely deferential to federal laws regulating aliens: rationality review is the appropriate level of scrutiny.

a. Welfare Benefits. [§592]

Congress may impose restrictions on an alien's eligibility for welfare benefits.

Mathews v. Diaz, 426 U.S. 27 (1976). The Court upheld a federal law imposing restrictions on an alien's eligibility for Medicare benefits. The Court said that because alienage issues touch on our country's relations with foreign countries, the Court should be extremely deferential to any decision of Congress or the President dealing with aliens. The Court likened the Court's role in federal alienage cases to its role in political question cases.

b. Government Employment. [§593]

Congress may not bar resident aliens from civil service employment without a showing that the restrictions were based on a legitimate national interest.

Hampton v. Wong, 426 U.S. 88 (1976). The Court invalidated a federal regulation barring resident aliens from civil service employment. The Court said that when the federal government asserts a legitimate national interest as the basis for a law, the Court will apply only rational basis review. In this case, it was unclear whether the federal government acted to advance a national interest having to do with aliens or foreign relations, or whether it was simply regulating to enhance workplace efficiency.

2. STATE LAWS THAT DISCRIMINATE AGAINST ALIENS. [§594]

When a state discriminates against aliens, strict scrutiny applies unless the alien is being excluded from a politically sensitive position; then rationality review applies.

a. Government Employment in General. [§595]

A state cannot exclude aliens from all government employment.

Sugarman v. Dougall, 413 U.S. 634 (1973). The Court invalidated a New York law that excluded aliens from all employment subject to competitive tests. The Court applied the strict scrutiny standard, and said that New York's law was not narrowly drawn to achieve any compelling interest such as protecting the political process.

b. Practice of Law. [§596]

A state cannot exclude aliens from the practice of law.

In re Griffiths, 413 U.S. 717 (1973). The Court invalidated, under strict scrutiny, Connecticut's exclusion of resident aliens from the practice of law. The Court said that the practice of law was not so close to the core of the political process as to place lawyers within the political function exception.

c. Police Officers. [§597]
A state can exclude aliens from being police officers.

Foley v. Connelie, 435 U.S. 291 (1978). The Court upheld, under rational basis review, New York's exclusion of aliens from its police force. The Court reasoned that police perform discretionary functions which are essential to the carrying out of public policy and the laws of the state.

d. Public School Teachers. [§598]
A state can exclude aliens from positions as public school teachers.

Ambach v. Norwick, 441 U.S. 68 (1979). The Court upheld, under rational basis review, New York's exclusion of aliens from positions as public elementary or secondary teachers. The Court said that teachers are within the public function exception because they inculcate national ideals, and prepare students for the obligations of citizenship.

e. Probation Officers. [§599]
A state can exclude aliens from positions as probation officers.

Cabell v. Chavez-Salido, 454 U.S. 432 (1982). The Court upheld, under rational basis review, California's exclusion of aliens from positions as state probation officers. Probation officers, like police officers in general, perform functions that are central to the political functioning of the state - applying the criminal laws and public policy of California.

f. Notary Public. [§600]
A state cannot exclude an alien from a position as a notary public.

Bernal v. Fainter, 467 U.S. 216 (1984). The Court invalidated, under strict scrutiny, a Texas law that excluded aliens from positions as notaries public. Since this job was mainly clerical, and did not involve functions going to the heart of representative government, the political function exception did not apply, and strict scrutiny was called for.

> **STUDY TIP:** If you get an alienage question in which a state is discriminating against aliens, there is a good chance that the professor is asking about the political function exception. Be aware of the specific positions the Court has ruled on (teachers, police or probation officers, notaries public, and lawyers), as well as the principle that a state is usually free to exclude aliens from positions that go to the heart of representative government.

3. INTERPLAY BETWEEN PREEMPTION AND ALIENAGE ANALYSIS. [§601]

When a state law discriminating against aliens imposes requirements on aliens over and above those mandated by Congress, there may be a preemption problem in that the state law may be frustrating the purpose of the federal law. Be aware of this issue if you get a question that specifically mentions both a federal and a state law regulating aliens.

a. Instate Tuition. [§602]

A state cannot deny instate tuition to aliens domiciled in the state.

Toll v. Moreno, 441 U.S. 458 (1982). The Court invalidated, on supremacy grounds, a University of Maryland rule denying instate tuition to certain aliens, despite the fact that Congress had allowed these aliens to establish domicile in the state. This ancillary burden violated the Supremacy Clause because it imposed burdens on aliens over and above those imposed by Congress, thereby interfering with federal regulation of immigration.

b. Welfare Benefits. [§603]

A state cannot deny welfare benefits to resident aliens.

Graham v. Richardson, 403 U.S. 365 (1971). The Court invalidated, on supremacy grounds, state statutes which denied welfare benefits to resident aliens. The Court said that such laws conflict with overriding national policies in an area (the regulation of immigration) constitutionally entrusted to Congress.

F. REVIEW OF LAWS THAT DISCRIMINATE ON THE BASIS OF GENDER. [§604]

Federal or state laws that discriminate on the basis of gender receive intermediate scrutiny by the Court; government must show a significant or important reason for the classification, and means that are substantially related. The rules are the same whether females or males are disadvantaged. Under equal protection analysis, a government must treat equally those persons who are similarly situated in terms of the purpose of the law. In some cases, the Court has said that there are constitutionally relevant differences between women and men. For instance, if the purpose of the draft is to fill all positions in the military, men and women are similarly situated because both can hold military positions. However, if the purpose of the draft is to fill only combat positions, men and women are not similarly situated because (by federal law) only men can fill combat positions.

1. TRACING THE DEVELOPMENT OF GENDER ANALYSIS UNDER EQUAL PROTECTION. [§605]

The Court has gone from affording women virtually no constitutional protection (*Bradwell*, 606 below), to almost making gender a suspect classification (*Frontiero*, 608 below), to holding that gender is a quasi-suspect class, entitled to intermediate scrutiny review.

a. Women as Lawyers. [§606]

The Court upheld an early state law prohibiting women from being lawyers.

Bradwell v. Illinois, 83 U.S. 130 (1873). The Court upheld the power of the Illinois Supreme Court to deny women the opportunity to be lawyers. A concurring opinion said that the ". . . paramount destiny and mission of woman are to fulfill the noble and benign offices of wife and mother. This is the law of the Creator." While *Bradwell* has not been specifically overruled, such a law would clearly be unconstitutional today as lacking any legitimate reason for its existence.

b. Women as Estate Administrators. [§607]

A state cannot give an automatic preference to men as estate administrators.

Reed v. Reed, 404 U.S. 71 (1971). For the first time, the Court invalidated, on equal protection grounds, a state law discriminating on the basis of gender in the choice of estate administrators. The Court, not using any form of heightened scrutiny, said that the automatic preference for men over women was so arbitrary as to violate the Equal Protection Clause.

c. Spousal Dependency Allowances. [§608]

Federal law may not treat male and female members of the armed forces differently in relation to dependency allowances for spouses.

Frontiero v. Richardson, 411 U.S. 677 (1973). This case was the closest the Court has ever come to establishing gender as a suspect class. Justice Brennan, for four Justices, used strict scrutiny to invalidate a federal law which treated male and female members of the armed forces differently in terms of establishing dependency allowances for their spouses. A male soldier could automatically claim his wife as a dependent, even if she were rich. A female soldier, however, had to prove that her husband was dependent on her before she got the benefits. A majority of the Court agreed that this scheme violated the equal protection component of the Due Process Clause of the Fifth Amendment.

d. Drinking Age. [§609]

A state may not have different drinking ages for men and women.

Craig v. Boren, 429 U.S. 190 (1976). The Court, adopting the intermediate level of scrutiny, invalidated a law which discriminated against males by requiring them to be 21 years old to buy beer, when females could buy it at age 18. The idea underlying this prospective law (prospective because it attempted to prevent future misconduct rather than punish past misdeeds) was that 18-20 year-old males were likely to drink, drive, and cause accidents. However, only about 2% of that group actually engaged in the undesired behavior, making the law about 98% overinclusive - too much for intermediate scrutiny. At intermediate scrutiny, the means chosen by the government must be substantially related to achieving the goal of the law. The Court will not tolerate a high degree of overinclusiveness in cases of gender discrimination.

e. Peremptory Challenges. [§610]

Peremptory challenges based on gender may not be used to exclude potential jurors.

J.E.B. v. Alabama, 114 S.Ct. 1419 (1994). The State of Alabama used nine of its ten peremptory challenges to remove male jurors in a paternity and support trial against a putative father. The Court held that the Equal Protection Clause prohibits discrimination in jury selection on the basis of gender.

f. Nursing School. [§611]
Men cannot be prohibited from attending a state nursing school.

Mississippi University for Women v. Hogan, 458 U.S. 718 (1982). The Court invalidated a Mississippi statute which prohibited males from attending the Mississippi University for Women School of Nursing. The Court reaffirmed the intermediate level of review for gender cases, and said it made no difference that the plaintiff was male rather than female.

g. Military School. [§612]
Women cannot be prohibited from attending a state military school.

U.S. v. Virginia, ___ S.Ct. ___ (1996). The Court ruled that the Equal Protection Clause was violated by Virginia Military Institute (VMI), a state military college, excluding women from attending the school. The Court said that VMI would have to demonstrate an "exceedingly persuasive justification" for its male-only admissions policy, showing at least that the categorical exclusion of women from the student body was substantially related to an important governmental objective. The Court rejected Virginia's proposed remedy of creating a separate, all-female military training school in the state.

2. DISCRIMINATION BASED ON PREGNANCY IS NOT GENDER DISCRIMINATION UNDER THE EQUAL PROTECTION CLAUSE. [§613]

The Court has held that, under the Constitution, it is not gender discrimination for a state to discriminate on the basis of pregnancy. Pregnant persons are all female, but non-pregnant persons are both male and female. Therefore, the classification does not discriminate against all women, only pregnant women.

Geduldig v. Aiello, 417 U.S. 484 (1974). The Court upheld, against an equal protection gender-discrimination claim, California's exclusion of pregnancy and childbirth coverage from its disability insurance system. The Court said that, even though only women get pregnant, the law does not exclude anyone because of gender. The classes created by the law are pregnant persons versus non-pregnant persons. The first class is all female, but the second class is made up of both men and women, so there is no "clean" discrimination against women as a class. Since this case, Congress passed the Pregnancy Discrimination Act, which includes discrimination based on pregnancy within the definition of gender discrimination under Title VII.

3. REMEDIAL DISCRIMINATION IN FAVOR OF WOMEN. [§614]

Even under the intermediate level of scrutiny, the Court usually upholds laws which compensate women for past economic discrimination against them as a class. The Court is willing to accept societal discrimination against women as the justification for these "economic affirmative action plans."

a. State Property Tax Exemption for Widows. [§615]
The Court upheld a state law that provided property tax exemptions for widows but not widowers.

Kahn v. Shevin, 416 U.S. 351 (1974). The Court upheld a Florida property tax exemption for widows, but not widowers. Economically, women are in a worse position than men, and the tax exemption for widows simply recognizes and attempts to remedy that disparity. The Court said that "[w]hether from overt discrimination or from the socialization process of a male- dominated culture, the job market is inhospitable to the woman seeking any but the lowest paying jobs."

b. Higher Old-Age Benefits for Female Wage-Earners. [§616]

The Court upheld a federal law that provided higher old-age benefits to female wage-earners.

Califano v. Webster, 430 U.S. 313 (1977). The Court upheld a federal Social Security law which resulted in female wage-earners receiving higher monthly old-age benefits than male wage-earners. This law is valid as a means of redressing society's longstanding disparate treatment of women.

c. Alimony. [§617]

Females may not be exempted from paying alimony.

Orr v. Orr, 440 U.S. 268 (1979). The Court invalidated an Alabama law requiring husbands, but not wives, to pay alimony. The Court held that, on the facts, Alabama could not use gender as a substitute for need in determining who may receive alimony payments. Individualized hearings had already been provided for, and it would impose only minimally more of a burden on the state to make specific findings regarding the financial needs of particular spouses. Case-by-case determinations of who should receive alimony would be a more narrowly tailored means to achieve the state's goal of ensuring fairness in the payment and receipt of alimony.

4. IN SOME CASES, WOMEN AND MEN ARE NOT SIMILARLY SITUATED IN RELATION TO THE PURPOSE OF A LAW. [§618]

There may be constitutionally relevant differences between women and men in relation to the purpose of a law. The Court has held in a few cases that biological differences between the sexes may be the basis for a government treating men and women differently, as long as the government is not simply reinforcing gender stereotypes. These differences may make it permissible for a government to treat men and women differently.

a. Women as Prison Guards. [§619]

The Court upheld a state law that excluded women from **positions as guards in all-male prisons.**

Dothard v. Rawlinson, 433 U.S. 330 (1977). The Court upheld the exclusion of women from positions as guards in a male, maximum-security, unclassified prison. The Court said that a female guard's ability to maintain order could be adversely affected by the fact that she is a woman, irrespective of other physical traits such as height, weight, or strength. The Court found that women and men are not similarly situated in relation to the purpose of the law, which was to ensure safety and control in the prison.

b. Different Treatment of Males and Females Under a Statutory Rape Law. [§620]

Statutory rape laws that punish males for having sex with underage females, but do not punish the underage female, are permissible.

Michael M. v. Superior Court, 450 U.S. 4641 (1981). The Court upheld a California statutory rape law which punished males for having sex with underage females, but did not punish the underage female. Justice Rehnquist, for four Justices, said that the sexes were not similarly situated in relation to the purpose of this criminal law, which was deterrence. Justice Rehnquist said that only females can get pregnant, so only females have the natural deterrent of fear of pregnancy to keep them from engaging in underage consensual sex. Since males do not have this biological deterrent, the state may impose criminal penalties "to roughly 'equalize' the deterrents on the sexes."

c. Male-Only Registration for the Draft. [§621]

The federal government may require males only to register for the draft.

Rostker v. Goldberg, 453 U.S. 57 (1981). The Court upheld, against an equal protection gender challenge, the male- only registration for the military draft. Justice Rehnquist, for the Court, said that the gender discrimination was permissible because men and women are not similarly situated in relation to the purpose of the registration and the draft. According to Justice Rehnquist, men and women are not similarly situated because the purpose of the registration (and any potential draft) would be to fill combat positions, from which women were excluded by a pre-existing law. Justice Marshall, in dissent, said that the purpose of any potential draft would be to fill both combat and non-combat positions, so men and women are similarly situated, and the all-male registration violates the equal protection component of the Due Process Clause of the Fifth Amendment.

G. REVIEW OF LAWS THAT DISCRIMINATE ON THE BASIS OF ILLEGITIMACY. [§622] Whenever a government discriminates against illegitimate children, intermediate scrutiny applies - the government must show a significant or important reason for the law, and the means must be substantially related to achieving that goal. It is not a legitimate purpose for the government to try to punish illegitimate children for the actions of their parents, so do not accept any justification for a law that strikes you as punitive. From 1968 to 1988, the Court traveled an uneven path in illegitimacy cases, using some form of heightened scrutiny, but never articulating a clear standard. In 1988, in *Clark v. Jeter*, 486 U.S. 456 the Court unanimously adopted intermediate scrutiny as the standard in illegitimacy cases.

1. An Illegitimate Child Suing For His or Her Mother's Wrongful Death. [§623]

An illegitimate child cannot be prohibited from suing for his or her mother's wrongful death if a state allows a legitimate child to bring such an action.

Levy v. Louisiana, 391 U.S. 68 (1968). The Court invalidated a Louisiana wrongful death statute which precluded an illegitimate child, but not a legitimate child, from suing for the wrongful death of the mother. Birth status was irrelevant to any harm to the mother, and the law only advanced the illegitimate goal of punishing children for the actions of their parents. This law failed even rational basis review.

2. The Mother of an Illegitimate Child Suing For Her Child's Death. [§624]

A state cannot preclude the mother of an illegitimate child from suing for her child's death.

Glona v. American Guarantee & Liability Insurance Co., 391 U.S. 73 (1968). The Court invalidated a Louisiana law which precluded the mother of an illegitimate child from suing for her child's death. Finding no rational basis for the law, the Court rejected the argument that a woman would have a child out of wedlock just so she could be compensated for the child's death.

3. Intestacy. [§625]

A state may impose some restrictions on an illegitimate child's ability to inherit under intestacy laws.

Labine v. Vincent, 401 U.S. 532 (1971). The Court upheld a Louisiana law which precluded an illegitimate child from taking a father's property through intestate succession unless the father had legitimated the child. This case is something of an aberration in the development of the Court's illegitimacy cases.

4. Worker's Compensation Recovery. [§626]

A state may not preclude an illegitimate child from recovering under the state's Workers' Compensation laws.

Weber v. Aetna Casualty & Surety Co., 406 U.S. 164 (1972). The Court invalidated a Louisiana workers' compensation law which precluded recovery by dependent, unacknowledged illegitimate children, but allowed recovery by legitimate children and by acknowledged illegitimate children. While *Weber* did not overrule *Labine* (see previous case), it seriously undermined any precedential value it might have had.

5. Denial of Welfare Benefits. [§627]

Welfare benefits may not be denied to families with illegitimate children.

New Jersey Welfare Rights Organization v. Cahill, 411 U.S. 619 (1973). The Court invalidated a New Jersey law which disbursed benefits to poor families only if those families were composed of two married adults and one or more legitimate children. Married adults who had illegitimate children did not qualify for benefits. The Court reasoned that punishing the illegitimate child is an ineffectual way to deter adults from engaging in irresponsible sexual relationships.

6. Denying Illegitimate Children a Presumption of Dependency for Inheritance Purposes. [§628]

The federal government may deny illegitimate children a presumption of dependency for inheritance purposes.

Mathews v. Lucas, 427 U.S. 495 (1976). The Court upheld a federal law, challenged under the equal protection component of the Due Process Clause of the Fifth Amendment, which afforded a presumption of dependency to legitimate children and a certain class of illegitimate children (those whose parents had acknowledged paternity in writing) in terms of their ability to inherit from a deceased parent, while denying that presumption to all other classes of illegitimate children. The Court relied to a large extent on the fact that the statute allowed the class of excluded illegitimate children to prove their dependency and qualify for benefits.

7. Restrictions On Inheritance From An Intestate Father. [§629]

A state is limited in its ability to impose restrictions on an illegitimate child's ability to inherit from an intestate father.

Trimble v. Gordon, 430 U.S. 762 (1977). The Court invalidated an Illinois law that allowed children born out of wedlock to inherent by intestate succession only from their mothers, whereas children born in wedlock may inherit by intestate succession from both their mothers and fathers. The Court ruled that the statute went too far by requiring not only an acknowledgement by the father, but also the marriage of the parents, thereby excluding many illegitimate children whose rights could be protected by some less intrusive means that would still protect the state's interests.

8. Permissible Limitations On Inheritance From An Intestate Father. [§630]

A state may impose narrowly drawn restrictions on the ability of illegitimate children to inherit from intestate fathers.

Lalli v. Lalli, 439 U.S. 259 (1978). The Court upheld a New York law which precluded illegitimate children from inheriting from their fathers through intestate succession unless there was a court order during the father's life which established paternity. The plurality distinguished this case from *Trimble* (previous case) on the basis that the New York law did not require the marriage of the child's mother and father as a prerequisite to intestate inheritance.

9. Right to Veto An Illegitimate Child's Adoption. [§631]

It is impermissible for a state to give the mother, but not the father, of an illegitimate child the right to veto the child's adoption.

Caban v. Mohamed, 441 U.S. 380 (1979). The Court invalidated a New York law which gave the mother of an illegitimate child, but not the father, the right to veto the child's adoption. While this gender-based distinction makes sense when the child is an infant or when the father has never had any substantial relationship with the child, it is unconstitutional when the father has acknowledged paternity and established a substantial relationship with the child.

10. Father's Inability to Sue For the Wrongful Death of An Illegitimate Child. [§632]

A state may prohibit the father of an illegitimate child from suing for the child's wrongful death unless the father had legitimated the child.

Parham v. Hughes, 441 U.S. 347 (1979). The Court upheld a Georgia law which allowed the mother of an illegitimate child to sue for the child's wrongful death, but denied the father the right to sue unless he had legitimated the child. A plurality of the Court said that this law reflected the fact that mothers and fathers of illegitimate children are not similarly situated - everyone knows who the mother is, but it is not always clear who the father is.

11. Time Limit To Sue For Parental Support. [§633]

A state may not impose a one-year statute of limitations for an illegitimate child to sue for parental support.

Mills v. Habluetzel, 456 U.S. 91 (1982). The Court unanimously invalidated a Texas law requiring an illegitimate child to sue for parental support within the first year of the child's life, or be precluded from ever bringing a support action. There was no similar limitation placed on the ability of a legitimate child to sue for support.

12. Time Limit To Establish Paternity. [§634]

A state may not impose a two-year statute of limitations for an illegitimate child to establish paternity and receive support.

Pickett v. Brown, 462 U.S. 1 (1983). The Court unanimously invalidated a Tennessee law which set a two-year limit on an illegitimate child's right to sue to establish paternity and receive support. The Court ruled that the two-year limitation was not substantially related to the legitimate state interest of preventing fraudulent claims.

13. Different Statutes of Limitation For Legitimate and Illegitimate Children. [§635]

A state may not impose different statutes of limitations for legitimate and illegitimate children.

Clark v. Jeter, 486 U.S. 456 (1988). The Court unanimously invalidated a Pennsylvania law which allowed legitimate children to sue for parental support at any time, but required illegitimate children to bring support actions within six years of birth. Justice O'Connor, for the Court, said that both gender and illegitimacy classifications receive intermediate scrutiny, under which a statutory classification must be substantially related to an important government objective.

H. REVIEW OF LAWS THAT DISCRIMINATE ON THE BASIS OF AGE. [§636]

Laws that discriminate based on age receive rational basis scrutiny - the plaintiff must show that there is no legitimate reason for the law, or that the means are not rationally related to the asserted government interest.

1. Mandatory Retirement Age. [§637]

States may impose a mandatory retirement age for police officers.

a. *Massachusetts Board of Retirement v. Murgia*, 427 U.S. 307 (1976). [§638]

The Court upheld, under rational basis review, a state law requiring uniformed police officers to retire at age 50. It does not matter that some very healthy, fit police officers may be forced to retire by this bright-line rule. At rationality review, the law may be very overinclusive so long as it is not irrational.

b. *Gregory v. Ashcroft*, 501 U.S. 452 (1991). [§639]

The Court, using rational basis review, upheld a Missouri law which required judges to retire at age 70. Since no fundamental right was affected, there was nothing to raise the scrutiny from rationality review.

2. Different Retirement Ages for Different Workers. [§640]

Federal law may impose different mandatory retirement ages for different government jobs.

Vance v. Bradley, 440 U.S. 93 (1979). The Court upheld a federal law which required Foreign Service officers to retire at age 60, when most civil service employees were allowed to work until the age of 70. Congress implemented the lower retirement age for Foreign Service officers to ensure that those officers would be capable of facing the rigors of overseas duty. The Court applied rational basis scrutiny in upholding the law against the Fifth Amendment challenge.

> **STUDY TIP:** Age is a non-suspect class, and discrimination on that basis alone will do nothing to raise the level of judicial scrutiny. However, if an age classification is used to abridge a fundamental right, the scrutiny may go up because of the impact of the classification system on the right. For example, in *Carey v. Population Services International*, 431 U.S. 678 (1977), the Court used heightened scrutiny to invalidate a law prohibiting the sale of non-prescription contraceptives to minors under the age of 16. It was the right of privacy, not the age classification, which caused the Court to raise the level of review and invalidate the law.

I. REVIEW OF LAWS THAT DISCRIMINATE ON THE BASIS OF MENTAL STATUS. [§641]

Laws that discriminate against the mentally retarded or the mentally ill receive rational basis review - the plaintiff has the burden of showing that there is no legitimate reason for the law, or that the means are not rationally related to the asserted government interest.

1. Group Homes for the Mentally Retarded. [§642]

Laws that restrict the location of group homes for the mentally retarded may not be based on antipathy toward the mentally retarded.

City of Cleburne v. Cleburne Living Center, Inc., 473 U.S. 432 (1985). The Court invalidated, under rational basis review, a city's denial of a special use permit for the operation of a group home for the mentally retarded. The Court refused to afford the mentally retarded the status of a quasi-suspect or suspect class. The Court said that the mentally retarded are a very diverse class of people, and the lack of homogeneity within the class (mildly retarded to profoundly retarded) made this the kind of group of people best dealt with by a legislature. The Court was also unwilling to begin adding to the list of quasi- suspect or suspect classes. If the mentally retarded were given special protection by the Court, why not the mentally ill, the infirm, or the disabled? On the facts, the Court invalidated the law because its only real basis appeared to be antipathy toward the mentally retarded.

2. Different Treatment of the Mentally Ill and the Mentally Retarded. [§643]

State laws that distinguish beteen mentally ill and mentally retarded persons are permissible.

Heller v. Doe, 113 S.Ct. 2637 (1993). The Court, using rational basis review, upheld a Kentucky law which set different standards of proof for commitment of the mentally ill and the mentally retarded, and allowed guardians and family members to participate as parties in commitment proceedings for the mentally retarded, but not for the mentally ill. To commit a mentally ill person, the state had to show beyond a reasonable doubt that statutory criteria were met. To commit a mentally retarded person, the state only had to show by clear and convincing evidence that statutory criteria were met. The court said it was rational for Kentucky to distinguish between the two groups because mental retardation is a life-long condition that is easily diagnosed, whereas mental illness may not manifest itself consistently over time, and is more difficult to diagnose in many cases.

J. REVIEW OF LAWS THAT DISCRIMINATE ON THE BASIS OF SEXUAL ORIENTATION. [§644]

Laws that discriminate on the basis of sexual orientation receive rational basis review - the plaintiff must show that there is no legitimate reason for the law, or that the means are not rationally related to the asserted government interest. A voter-initiated state constitutional amendment prohibiting state or local governments from passing laws to protect persons of homosexual, lesbian, or bisexual orientation fails rational basis scrutiny under the Equal Protection Clause.

Romer v. Evans, 116 S.Ct. 1620 (1996). The Court invalidated a Colorado state constitutional amendment, passed by statewide referendum, which prohibited any unit of state or local government from taking any action which prohibited discrimination against or granted special protection to persons based on their homosexual, lesbian, or bisexual orientation or conduct. This amendment effectively repealed a number of municipal ordinances banning discrimination based on sexual orientation in housing, employment, education, public accommodations, and health and welfare services. The Court ruled that this amendment violated the Equal Protection Clause because it prohibited only a specific group of persons from using state and local electoral processes (short of a state constitutional amendment) to protect themselves from discrimination in a wide range of public and private transactions. The Court ruled that the amendment failed rational basis scrutiny because it identified persons by a single trait (sexual orientation), and then denied them the possibility of protection solely because they possessed that trait.

K. REVIEW OF LAWS THAT DISCRIMINATE ON THE BASIS OF SOCIAL OR ECONOMIC INTERESTS. [§645]

Laws that discriminate on the basis of social or economic interests receive rational basis review - the plaintiff must show that there is no legitimate reason for the law, or that the means are not rationally related to the asserted government interest. For instance, laws which discriminate between classes of people in relation to pursuing an occupation, receiving unemployment benefits, or receiving welfare payments will receive only rational basis review.

1. Selective Restrictions on Advertising. [§646]

The Court upheld an early state law that placed selective restrictions on advertising.

Railway Express Agency v. New York, 336 U.S. 106 (1949). The Court upheld, under rational basis review, a New York City traffic regulation which prohibited advertising for hire on vehicles on New York streets, but allowed the owner of a vehicle to advertise his or her own business on the vehicle. The Court accepted the city's argument that it was trying to enhance the safety of the streets, and set forth the rule that, at rationality review, a government may deal with a problem a bit at a time. The government may have concluded that truck owners who advertise their own goods pose less of a safety problem than those who advertise for hire. This case came down well before the Court gave First Amendment protection to commercial speech.

2. Selective Ban on Push-Cart Vendors. [§647]

The Court upheld a local ordinance that banned most, but not all, push-cart vendors.

New Orleans v. Dukes, 427 U.S. 297 (1976). The Court upheld, under rational basis review, a New Orleans ordinance banning push-cart vendors from the French Quarter, except those vendors who had worked there for eight or more years. Since there was no fundamental right abridged or suspect class disadvantaged, the Court upheld the law, saying that it is the job of the legislature, not the courts, to judge the wisdom of economic legislation.

3. Exclusion of Methadone Users from Government Employment. [§648]

Methadone users may be excluded from safety-sensitive as well as non-safety-sensitive government jobs.

New York City Transit Authority v. Beazer, 440 U.S. 568 (1979). The Court upheld, under rational basis review, a Transit Authority rule which excluded methadone users from any employment with the Authority. This ban included non-safety- sensitive jobs, and was upheld in the face of the statistical fact that 75% of those who have been on methadone for at least a year are free from illicit drug use. At rationality review, a law does not have to be narrowly tailored (or even substantially related to achieving the law's goal), and may be over-inclusive in that it disadvantages too many people.

4. Federal Retirement Law. [§649]

The Court upheld a federal retirement law that prevented certain employees from receiving "double-dip" retirement benefits.

United States Railroad Retirement Board v. Fritz, 449 U.S. 166 (1980). The Court upheld, under rational basis review, a federal law which prevented certain workers from receiving "double-dip" retirement benefits. Under the law, a person qualified for the windfall benefits only if he or she was active in the railroad business as of 1974. As a result, a person with 24 years of experience would not qualify for the windfall unless he or she worked for the railroad in 1974, whereas a person with 11 years of experience would qualify for the windfall if he or she worked with the railroad in 1974. The workers with more experience challenged the law under the equal protection component of the Due Process Clause of the Fifth Amendment. The Court found that Congress had not acted arbitrarily or irrationally, and said that it would uphold a law if there were any plausible reason for it, even though Congress may not have relied on the reason when passing the law.

5. Selective Welfare Payments. [§650]

Federal laws may place selective restrictions on who is eligible to receive welfare benefits.

Schweiker v. Wilson, 450 U.S. 221 (1981). The Court upheld, under rational basis review, a federal law which granted a welfare allowance to needy, aged, blind, and disabled persons only if the institutions in which they lived received Medicaid funds. The Court considered it rational for Congress to limit the allowances to those patients for whom Congress had already assumed most of the financial obligation, and leave it to the states to provide equivalent protection for those not covered by the federal program.

6. Tax Assessment Scheme for Real Property. [§651]

The Court struck down as irrational a state law that assessed real property at different rates.

Allegheny Pittsburgh Coal Co. v. County Commission of Webster County, 488 U.S. 336 (1989). The Court invalidated, under rational basis review, a real-property assessment system under which real property was reassessed for tax purposes when it was sold, but similar property that had not been transferred kept its old, much lower, tax rate. The state constitution guaranteed that all real property would be taxed at a uniform rate throughout the state, according to its market value. Given the state constitutional requirements, the Court found the assessment system to be arbitrary and irrational.

7. Limitations on Real Property Tax Rates and Increases. [§652]

The Court upheld a state law that resulted in different tax rates being imposed on different categories of real property.

Nordlinger v. Hahn, 112 S.Ct. 2326 (1992). The Court upheld, under rational basis review, California's Proposition 13, which imposed limits on real-property tax rates, and on the rate of yearly increases in real property assessments. Real property taxes are capped at 1% of a property's full cash value, figured at 1975-1976 tax rates, or at the appraised value of real property when purchased after the 1975 assessment. The problem here is that persons who had owned their homes a long time enjoy low tax rates, while newcomers are taxed on the current, much higher value of the property they recently brought. The Court said this assessment system was rationally related to California's legitimate interests in neighborhood stability and the protection of property owners' reliance interests.

L. IRREBUTTABLE PRESUMPTIONS USED TO DEPRIVE A PERSON OF A GOVERNMENTAL BENEFIT OR THE EXERCISE OF A RIGHT. [§653]

Under the irrebuttable presumption doctrine, a government sets up a conclusive presumption (no hearing provided) of disability or unfitness to perform a function or exercise a right. These bright-line rules disadvantage all persons within a class, and do not provide any mechanism for proving fitness or ability. The theoretical basis for the doctrine is not clear, but most commentators agree that it shares aspects of procedural due process and equal protection analyses. The cases present the procedural due process problem of not providing a hearing for those who are disadvantaged; they present the equal protection problem of classifying too broadly - too many people are disadvantaged by the classification effected by the law. This doctrine had its heyday in the mid-1970's, and is not used much by courts today.

1. Presumption that Unmarried Fathers are Unfit Parents. [§654]

States may not conclusively presume that all unmarried fathers are unfit parents.

Stanley v. Illinois, 405 U.S. 645 (1972). The Court invalidated an Illinois statute which conclusively presumed that all unmarried fathers are unfit parents. Upon the mother's death, the State, rather than the unmarried father, would get custody of a child. The Court said this classification was clearly overbroad in that it disadvantaged too many unmarried fathers (those who would be fit parents), and that the state must provide individualized hearings on the question of fitness.

2. Presumption that Certain College Students Are Not State Residents. [§655]

States may not conclusively presume that certain classes of college students are not state residents.

Vlandis v. Kline, 412 U.S. 441 (1973). The Court invalidated a Connecticut statute under which certain students were conclusively presumed to be out-of-staters, and thereby subject to a higher tuition regardless of their having established residency in the state. The Due Process Clause of the Fourteenth Amendment prohibited such an irrebuttable presumption, and required the state to give the student some sort of individualized opportunity to prove his or her residence.

3. Presumption of Ineligibility for Food Stamps. [§656]

Federal laws may not conclusively presume ineligibility for food stamps.

U.S. Department of Agriculture v. Murry, 413 U.S. 508 (1973). The Court invalidated a provision of the federal Food Stamp Act which provided that a household would not be eligible for food stamps if it included a person over 18 years of age who had been claimed as a tax dependent during the previous year by someone who was not a member of the household. The Court rejected this irrebuttable presumption, and said that the government must provide some kind of opportunity to show need.

4. Presumption that Pregnant Teachers Cannot Teach Beyond a Certain Time. [§657]

A state may not conclusively presume that a pregnant teacher is unable to teach beyond a certain time in her pregnancy.

Cleveland Board of Education v. LaFleur, 414 U.S. 632 (1974). The Court invalidated school board rules which required all pregnant teachers to take leave without pay for four or five months (depending on the school board) before the expected date of birth. The Court objected to the irrebuttable presumption of physical incompetency even when medical evidence would indicate that the pregnant teacher was fully able to continue teaching.

5. Presumption that Spouses of Stepchildren Do Not Qualify for Death Benefits. [§658]

A state may presume that spouses of stepchildren do not qualify for death benefits.

Weinberger v. Salfi, 422 U.S. 749 (1975). The Court upheld, against an irrebuttable presumption challenge, provisions of the Social Security Act which required a spouse or stepchild of a wage earner to have had their relationships to the wage earner for at least nine months before qualifying for death benefits. The Court distinguished the earlier irrebuttable presumption cases, saying that this one involved merely a noncontractual claim to receive funds from the public treasury, something which deserved no constitutional protection.

6. Presumption that Certain Workers are Disabled. [§659]

The Court upheld a federal law that provided for a presumption of total disability for coal miners with black-lung disease.

Usery v. Turner Elkhorn Mining Co., 428 U.S. 1 (1976). The Court upheld, against an irrebuttable presumption challenge, a provision of the Federal Coal Mine Health and Safety Act which said that if a coal miner can show by medical evidence that he or she has an advanced case of black-lung disease, the miner is irrebuttably presumed to be totally disabled. If the miner dies, it is irrebuttably presumed that the black-lung disease was the cause of death. The Court used rational basis review to uphold Congress' method of compensating coal miners who suffered from the disease.

7. Presumption that a Child Born to a Married Woman is a Child of Her Marriage. [§660]

A state may presume that a child born to a married woman is a child of her marriage.

Michael H. v. Gerald D., 491 U.S. 110 (1989). The Court upheld a California law which conclusively presumed that a child born to a married woman is a child of the marriage. Michael was, in all probability, the natural father of a child to whom he asserted parental rights. However, Gerald, not Michael, was the husband of the child's mother. Under California law, Gerald was conclusively presumed to be the child's father. In a plurality opinion, Justice Scalia rejected Michael's argument that the law created an unconstitutional irrebuttable presumption. Justice Scalia reasoned that since Michael had no fundamental parental interest simply because of genetic parenthood, the state's interest in protecting marital relationships was sufficient to override Michael's low-level liberty interest in seeing his child. Justice Brennan dissented, arguing that such a conclusive presumption has the fatal procedural flaw of not providing a hearing in which the adulterous father can offer proof of paternity.

REVIEW PROBLEMS — EQUAL PROTECTION

PROBLEM 1: Bob Green applied for a position as a state police officer with the State of Oz. He was rejected, following an interview with the personnel director. Bob is convinced that he was turned down because of his race. He files suit, claiming a violation of his equal protection rights under the Fourteenth Amendment. What does Bob need to prove to make out a prima facie case of an equal protection violation? Who has the burden of proof in this case?

> **Answer:** To make out a prima facie case of an equal protection violation, a plaintiff must show disparate impact and intent. Bob must show that members of his racial group have been disproportionately excluded from positions as state troopers. He must then show that the disparate treatment was intentional - the government was excluding people because of their race. Once Bob has shown disparate impact and intent, the burden shifts to the government to show a compelling reason for the discrimination, and narrowly tailored means. Remember that at rationality review, the burden of proof stays with the plaintiff, but at intermediate or strict scrutiny, it shifts to the government. See §§536, 540 for further review.

PROBLEM 2. The State of Oz has established an affirmative action program for its State Police Department (SPD). Concerned that racial minorities are not adequately represented in the ranks of command officers, the legislature has required that for every white officer promoted to a command position, an officer belonging to one of a listed number of racial or ethnic minorities also be promoted to a command position. Under this program, there are two promotion lists; one white and one non- white. Todd White, a white officer, was up for promotion to a command position, but was turned down. He claims that he was rejected because of his race. Todd's performance evaluations and test scores were higher than the non-white officer who received a promotion. Todd sues. Does he have a case?

> **Answer:** Yes. This is a state race-based affirmative action program, so strict scrutiny applies. The state must show a compelling interest and narrowly tailored means. With a state race-based affirmative action plan, societal discrimination does not count as the justification for the program. The State of Oz would have to show, at least, that it was a passive participant in some system or pattern of racial discrimination in the past. There is nothing in the facts to indicate that the State was implicated in any prior racial discrimination. If that is true, Todd cannot be excluded solely because of his race. See §§575, 579 for further review.

PROBLEM 3. The governor of the State of Oz has issued an order excluding aliens from serving on the governing boards of state colleges or universities. These are all appointed positions, and the governor has refused to consider applications or nominations from non-citizens of the United States. Harriet Howe was an alien, but applied for a position on the board of State University. Through a clerical mistake, her file was put in with those of citizens of the United States, and she got an interview with the governor. Upon learning of Harriet's alien status, the governor told her that she was not eligible for any such position. Harriet sues. Discuss her equal protection arguments.

> **Answer:** If a state discriminates against aliens, strict scrutiny applies, unless the alien is excluded from a position that deals with the formulation or implementation of public policy. If that is true, rational basis review applies. To answer this kind of question, you

must make a judgment call about the nature of the position from which aliens are excluded. If the governing boards of colleges and universities are engaged in important public policy decisions, then this position is within the political function exception and rationality review applies. If these positions are not all that important to the functioning of representative government, then strict scrutiny applies. See §§594-600 for further review.

PROBLEM 4: The City of Id owns and operates a very fancy country club, whose clientele is primarily male. To provide a pleasant atmosphere for its male members, the country club employs only females as servers in its dining room. Tom Penn applies for a job as a waiter and is rejected. He sues. Does Tom have a case?

Answer: Yes. Gender discrimination receives intermediate scrutiny. Tom will be able to show that he was intentionally discriminated against because he is a male. The city would then have to show a significant reason for the discrimination, and substantially related means. There is no significant reason for the gender discrimination here, so Tom would win. See §604 for further review.

XVII. FREEDOM OF SPEECH

A. OVERVIEW OF FREE SPEECH ANALYSIS. [§661]

The First Amendment says that Congress shall make no law abridging the freedom of speech. Freedom of speech is a fundamental right which applies to the states by way of the liberty provision of the Due Process Clause of the Fourteenth Amendment. For purposes of the First Amendment, speech includes oral, written, and symbolic communication. The first thing you must do in a free speech analysis is make sure that a court is willing to characterize certain activity as speech. While this is usually not a problem with oral or written communication (because words are used), it is an issue with symbolic speech (communication by conduct alone, without words). For instance, is flag burning speech? Nude dancing? Draft card burning? Cross burning? Blowing up a building to protest a war? Obviously, in some cases a court will not be willing to attach the label of "speech" (and thereby apply constitutional protections), even though on some level, something is communicated. (Yes, I took a gun and blew away that person, but it was simply an expression of my pent-up anger.) Remember that the First Amendment does not provide absolute protection for all speech. Speech may be regulated, or in some cases prohibited, if the government is able to show that a regulable, non-speech evil (such as a breach of the peace, or overthrow of the government) occurs at the same time as the speech activity or as a result of it. In general terms, free speech analysis is an inquiry about how convincingly the government has established a connection between the speech it is attempting to regulate and the evil which allegedly goes along with the speech. A court must resolve the question of whether the incidental restriction on speech is justified by the government's interest in preventing the non-speech evil.

1. PROCEDURAL ISSUES. [§662]

Once you are satisfied that speech is being regulated, check for certain procedural problems. The two procedural problems that arise most often are vagueness and overbreadth.

a. Vagueness. [§663]

A vague law provides no or insufficient standards for its enforcement. Two problems are presented by such a law: no notice to the person to whom the law may be applied; and too much discretion on the part of the government official applying the law.

b. Overbreadth. [§664]

A law is overbroad to the extent that it is capable of punishing protected speech. Remember that freedom of speech is a fundamental right, so the means of regulation must be narrowly tailored. An excellent example of an overbroad law occurred in *Board of Airport Commissioners v. Jews for Jesus, Inc.*, 482 U.S. 569 (1987), where the Court invalidated an airport authority regulation which prohibited all First Amendment activity in the airport terminal.

c. Licensing Systems for Movies or Books. [§665]

The Court has set forth rules for licensing systems for movies or books. Basically, the Court requires that if the government intends to deny a permit, it has the burden of going to court for a prompt judicial decision of the merits, and the government has the burden of justifying its refusal to grant the permit, (see §682).

2. IS THE GOVERNMENT PROHIBITING SPEECH OR MERELY CHANNELING IT? [§666]

See if the government is trying to prohibit the speech entirely, or just move it around (change the time, place, or manner of the speech). If the government is trying to prohibit the speech entirely, you will probably use one of the specific tests or analyses, such as clear and present danger, fighting words, obscenity, commercial speech, or defamation. If the government is just trying to move the speech around, you apply the rules for what are called "time, place, or manner restrictions." **To be valid, a time, place, or manner restriction must be: a) content-neutral (can't be regulating because the government disapproves of the speech); b) narrowly tailored to achieving a significant government interest; and c) leave open ample alternative channels of communication.**

B. DUE PROCESS CONCERNS THAT ARISE WITH LAWS THAT REGULATE SPEECH. [§667]

As alluded to earlier, remember that before you get to the merits of any speech analysis, you must consider whether the law raises issues of vagueness or overbreadth.

1. VAGUENESS. [§668]

Vagueness problems arise when a statute or regulation has no standards, or insufficient ones, to guide the government official applying the law. The absence of specific standards requires a person to guess whether he or she may be prosecuted under a certain statute, or will be granted a permit from a licensing board. The absence of notice to the person is compounded by the excessive discretion vested in the government. Without specific standards being provided, the police officer or the permit-giver gets to make up standards as he or she goes along.

a. Display of Red Flag. [§669]
It is unconstitutionally vague for a state to prohibit the public display of a red flag as a symbol of opposition to government.

Stromberg v. California, 283 U.S. 359 (1931). The Court invalidated, on vagueness grounds, a California statute which prohibited public use or display of a red flag "as a sign, symbol or emblem of opposition to organized government" (the legislature said that the use of red flags, especially by members of the Communist party, indicated opposition to organized government). While the opinion was phrased in terms of vagueness, the Court pointed out that this law was also potentially overbroad in that it could be used to punish constitutionally protected use of a red flag. The case is an early example of symbolic speech, where the communication happens without words, simply by some readily understandable conduct.

b. Attempts to Incite Insurrection. [§670]
It is unconstitutionally vague for a state to criminalize speech under a statute prohibiting attempts to incite insurrection when the statute does not include the occurrence or imminence of violence as an element of the offense.

Herndon v. Lowry, 301 U.S. 242 (1937). The Court invalidated, on vagueness grounds, an Alabama statute that made it a crime to attempt to incite insurrection, including persuading others to join in a combined resistance to the lawful authority of any state. The Court held that this statute did not provide a sufficiently ascertainable standard of guilt, and, as a result, could result in the punishment of much protected speech.

c. Treating a U.S. Flag Contemptuously. [§671]

It is unconstitutionally vague for a state to impose criminal penalties for treating contemptuously a United States flag.

Smith v. Goguen, 415 U.S. 566 (1974). The Court invalidated, on vagueness grounds, a statute which made it a crime to "treat contemptuously" a United States flag. The Court said that the statute provided no warning or notice to persons to whom it might be applied, and gave police, judges, and juries too much discretion to impose their personal preferences when applying the statute.

d. Being Required to Produce "Credible and Reliable" Identification. [§672]

It is unconstitutionally vague for a state to require a person to produce "credible and reliable" identification when requested to do so by a police officer.

Kolender v. Lawson, 461 U.S. 352 (1983). The Court invalidated, on vagueness grounds, a state law requiring persons on the street to present "credible and reliable" identification when asked by a police officer. The Court said this law, in its vagueness, gave too much discretion to the police for arbitrary and selective enforcement.

2. OVERBREADTH. [§673]

A statute is overbroad to the extent that it may be used to punish or restrict protected speech (speech that the government may not restrict under any of the First Amendment analyses). The Court has said that for a litigant to make a facial overbreadth challenge to a statute, he or she must show that the overbreadth of the statute is substantial in relation to the plainly legitimate applications of the law (in other words a facial challenge will be available only if the statute is capable of punishing a great deal of protected speech). While the vagueness and overbreadth analyses are separate and distinct inquiries, the two concepts frequently arise together. For instance, a vague statute (for example, anyone who wilfully annoys another person is guilty of a misdemeanor) is capable of being applied to protected speech because of the discretion it gives to the government official applying the law. As you read the following cases, be aware of the interplay between the vagueness and overbreadth doctrines.

a. Civil Service Employees Participating in Political Activities. [§674]

It is permissible for a state to restrict political activity by certain state employees.

Broadrick v. Oklahoma, 413 U.S. 601 (1973). The Court upheld, against a facial overbreadth challenge, an Oklahoma law restricting political activity by certain government civil service employees. The law

OUTLINE

prohibited them from taking part in political activity or campaigns. As part of their facial attack, plaintiffs challenged this law on the basis that it might be applied to speech activity which they had not engaged in (wearing buttons or displaying bumper stickers). The Court rejected their overbreadth challenge, saying that, especially when conduct and not merely speech is involved, the Court will entertain an overbreadth challenge only when the overbreadth is real and substantial in relation to the plainly legitimate sweep of the statute.

b. Use of the Word "Lust" to Define Obscenity. [§675]

It violates principles of overbreadth for a state to use the word "lust" in defining obscenity.

Brockett v. Spokane Arcades, Inc., 472 U.S. 491 (1985). The Court invalidated part of a state obscenity statute because it was overbroad in that it used the word "lust" in defining obscenity, a definition which would have allowed the punishment of constitutionally protected material. The Court said that the general rule on invalidation of a statute on overbreadth grounds is that a Court should, if possible, strike only the specific part of the statute that may have overbroad application, and leave the rest of the statute to be applied in a normal manner.

c. Congregating in Such a Manner as to Annoy Passersby. [§676]

It violates principles of vagueness and overbreadth for a city to criminalize merely congregating on a sidewalk in a manner annoying to passersby.

Coates v. Cincinnati, 412 U.S. 611 (1971). The Court invalidated, on vagueness and overbreadth grounds, an ordinance that made it a crime for three or more persons to assemble on a sidewalk and conduct themselves in a manner annoying to passersby. The Court said this statute was constitutionally defective because it provided no ascertainable standard of prohibited conduct, and because it could be used to punish protected exercises of the right to assembly.

C. PRIOR RESTRAINTS. [§677]

A prior restraint is any government action that stops speech before it can be communicated. A prior restraint is especially suspect because the government is prohibiting the speech based purely on speculation that it will cause some evil or societal harm that the government has a right to prevent. Constitutional law courses usually treat two kinds of prior restraints: 1) those imposed by an injunctive order of a court, and 2) those imposed by the application of a licensing system. Both kinds of prior restraints must be justified by an extremely important government interest. Other kinds of prior restraints that you should be aware of are informal prior restraints (government action short of passing a statute that prevents speech from being communicated), and contractually agreed on prior restraints.

1. INJUNCTIVE ORDERS IMPOSING PRIOR RESTRAINTS. [§678]

Court orders imposing prior restraints are presumed unconstitutional, and the government has a heavy burden of justifying such a restriction on speech. It would be possible to justify such an injunction if the government asserted some compelling reason of national security, military secrets, or the like.

a. Perpetual Injunction Against a Newspaper. [§679]

A court may not perpetually enjoin the publication in a newspaper of any malicious, scandalous, or defamatory material.

Near v. Minnesota, 283 U.S. 697 (1931). The Court invalidated, as a prior restraint, the application of an ordinance that authorized a court to perpetually enjoin the publication in a newspaper of any malicious, scandalous, or defamatory material. The Court said that prior restraints may be justified only in exceptional cases, such as to prevent obstruction of the nation's recruiting service, or to prevent the publication of the location of troops during wartime.

b. Publication of the Pentagon Papers. [§680]

The Court refused to enjoin the publication of the Pentagon Papers (pertaining to the Vietnam war) absent a compelling reason for the injunction.

New York Times Co. v. U.S., 403 U.S. 713 (1971) (The Pentagon Papers Case). The Court refused to enjoin newspapers from publishing a classified study of the history of U.S. decisionmaking in Vietnam. In a per curiam opinion, the Court said that any system of prior restraints comes to the Court with a heavy presumption against its constitutional validity, and that the government has a heavy burden of justifying the judicial enforcement of such a prior restraint.

c. Criminal Contempt Citation as a Prior Restraint. [§681]

The Court upheld criminal contempt citations of demonstrators who marched in violation of a court order.

Walker v. Birmingham, 388 U.S. 307 (1967). The Court upheld criminal contempt citations of demonstrators who had marched in violation of an injunctive order issued by an Alabama court. The order enjoined the demonstrators from marching without a permit issued pursuant to the local parade ordinance. The Court held that although the ordinance and the resulting order may have been unconstitutional prior restraints on speech, the demonstrators were not free simply to disregard the court order. They could have challenged the validity of the court order, but chose not to. In a later case, *Shuttlesworth v. Birmingham*, 373 U.S. 262 (1969), the Court reversed the convictions of another group of demonstrators who had been convicted of violating the ordinance that was the basis of the injunction in *Walker*. In that case, the Court was dealing with a violation of the ordinance itself, rather than a violation of an injunctive order. The Court found that the ordinance amounted to a prior restraint because it gave too much discretion to the permit-giver. The moral of the story is that the Court will not permit individuals to violate an injunctive order restricting speech, even though that order later turns out to be unconstitutional.

2. LICENSING SYSTEMS AS PRIOR RESTRAINTS: CASES INVOLVING REVIEW OF FILMS BEFORE EXHIBITION. [§682]

If properly drafted, a permit system for movies is constitutional. **For a movie-licensing system to pass constitutional muster, the government must have the burden of proving the work is obscene, must promptly go to court or issue the permit or license, and must ensure that there is a prompt, final judicial decision regarding the alleged obscenity of the work.**

a. Movie-Licensing Systems May Be Constitutional. [§683]

A film-licensing system may be constitutional if it meets specific constitutional standards.

Times Film Corp. v. Chicago, 365 U.S. 43 (1961). The Court rejected a facial challenge to the City of Chicago's film- licensing system under which a film must be submitted to the commissioner of police who must apply statutory standards to determine whether to grant or deny a permit. The applicant had a right to appeal a denial to the Mayor, whose decision was final. The Court upheld, in principle, the constitutionality of an appropriately drafted licensing system, and rejected the argument that the only way a government may fight obscenity is through a criminal prosecution after it has been disseminated.

b. Movie-Licensing Systems. [§684]

A movie-licensing system will be constitutional if the government has the burden of proving to a court that a certain movie is obscene.

Freedman v. Maryland, 380 U.S. 51 (1965). The Court set forth the procedure that must be followed for a local censorship board to revoke the license of a book or film distributor who is disseminating obscene material, or to impose a prior restraint on the dissemination of such material. The Court ruled that any system which requires the prior submission of a film or book to a censor must meet the following requirements: The government must meet the burden of proving that the work is obscene; the censor must issue the license promptly or go to court to enjoin the showing of the film or sale of the book; and there must be a prompt, final judicial decision, following an adversary hearing, to minimize the deterrent effect of a possibly erroneous denial of a license.

c. Permit Systems for Fundraisers. [§685]

A state may not impose a licensing scheme on professional fundraisers unless the scheme requires the state to issue the license or get a court order authorizing the denial of a license.

Riley v. National Federation of the Blind of North Carolina, Inc., 487 U.S. 781 (1988). The Court, using the *Freedman* standards (see previous case), invalidated a North Carolina law which required professional fundraisers to be licensed if they were going to solicit for charitable organizations. If the solicitor were a volunteer, or employed by the charity, he or she could solicit immediately upon submitting an application. This scheme violated *Freedman* because it did not require the government to promptly issue the license or go to court to get an order authorizing the denial of the license.

3. "INFORMAL" PRIOR RESTRAINTS. [§686]

Informal government action, short of passing a statute, may operate as a prior restraint. A state may not use its power to informally influence what books may be sold. For example, **it is unconstitutional for a state commission to threaten obscenity prosecutions against booksellers who sell books from a state- compiled list of objectionable books.**

Bantam Books v. Sullivan, 372 U.S. 58 (1963). The Court held unconstitutional the actions of the Rhode Island Commission to Encourage Morality in Youth, which included compiling a list of "objectionable" books and notifying distributors that the list would be given to local police departments. The Commission also informed the distributors that it had a duty, when appropriate, to urge the Attorney General's office to begin obscenity prosecutions against what it considered to be offending parties. The Court treated this scheme as an informal prior restraint, the purpose of which was to intimidate booksellers to stop selling the books on the list.

4. CONTRACTUALLY AGREED UPON PRIOR RESTRAINTS. [§687]

It is permissible for the CIA to require that its employees get agency approval before publishing a book about activities that occurred during their employment with the CIA.

Snepp v. U.S., 444 U.S. 507 (1980). The Court upheld the validity of an agreement between the Central Intelligence Agency and one of its employees under which he agreed not to publish any information he obtained during his employment with the CIA, unless he had the prior approval of the agency. Snepp published a book, without agency approval, about certain CIA activities in South Vietnam. The Court ruled that the government was entitled to a constructive trust on all profits Snepp might earn from the book. The Court said that the CIA, even without an agreement, could have imposed reasonable restrictions on the speech activity of employees to advance the government's compelling interests in the secrecy of information needed for national security, and in the appearance of confidentiality necessary for the functioning of an intelligence agency.

D. TIME, PLACE, OR MANNER RESTRICTIONS. [§688]

If the government is not completely prohibiting speech, but is just restricting its time, place, or manner, the Court uses the following four-part analysis:

1) Is the restriction **content-neutral**?

2) Is it directed at achieving a **significant government interest**?

3) Is it **narrowly tailored** to achieve that interest?

4) Does it leave open ample **alternative channels of communication**?

The rationale for restricting the speech is that the medium or method of communication creates certain secondary effects which the government has the power to regulate. For example, the government might want to regulate the location of adult movie theaters because of the effect they have on surrounding property values. **Remember that a government may never regulate speech just because it dislikes or disapproves of the speech; such a regulation would be content based, and would be invalid under a strict scrutiny analysis. (It is not a compelling, or even** legitimate, reason for a government to suppress speech because it does not approve of it.)

1. REQUIREMENTS FOR A VALID TIME, PLACE OR MANNER RESTRICTION. [§689]

For a time, place, or manner restriction to be constitutional, it must meet the following requirements. These analyses are discussed below.

a. The Restriction Must Be Content-Neutral. [§690]

A government may not restrict speech because of antipathy toward that speech. The Court casts this rule in terms of the requirement that a law be content-neutral if it is to be upheld as a valid time, place, or manner restriction. **The Court has treated laws as content-neutral under either of two analyses: the government does not even look at the content of the speech when it regulates; or the government looks at content, not to approve or disapprove of it, but to see if the content causes some "secondary effect" which the government has the power to regulate.**

(1) When the Government Does Not Even Consider Content. [§691]

An example of the first kind of content-neutrality, where the government does not even look at the content of the regulated speech, is *Ward v. Rock Against Racism*, 491 U.S. 781 (1989), in which the Court upheld a regulation of the City of New York requiring the use of sound systems provided by the city for concerts in Central Park. The regulation did not concern itself with the content of the music, just with its noise level. The City did not care whether it was Mozart or Metallica; it wanted to protect the peace and quiet of those who lived around Central Park.

(2) When the Government Considers Content to See if it Causes a Regulable "Secondary Effect." [§692]

The second kind of content-neutrality is illustrated by *Renton v. Playtime Theatres, Inc.*, 475 U.S. 41 (1986), in which the Court upheld a zoning ordinance which dispersed "adult movie theaters" throughout the city. Even though the government did look at the content of the movies to determine whether they fit the category of "adult entertainment," the Renton ordinance was directed at the secondary effects (crime rising and property values dropping) caused by a concentration of adult movie theaters in one section of the city. The Court treated this ordinance as content-neutral, and upheld it is a valid time, place, or manner restriction. The same kind of ordinance was upheld by the Court in *Young v. American Mini Theatres, Inc.*, 427 U.S. 50 (1976).

b. The Restriction Must Be Narrowly Tailored. [§693]

The regulation does not have to be the least drastic means of achieving the government's goal. **The Court has said that a regulation will be valid so long as the means are not substantially broader than necessary to achieve the government's goal; a court will not invalidate a law simply because it is able to conclude that the** government could have chosen some alternative means that might have been less restrictive of speech.

c. The Restriction Must Advance a Significant Government Interest. [§694]

The government does not need a compelling interest to support a time, place, or manner restriction. **A significant or important interest will suffice because the object of the law is not to suppress speech, but to deal with the non-speech secondary effect which the government has a right to prevent or restrict.**

d. The Restriction Must Leave Open Ample Alternative Channels of Communication. [§695]

Since the object of a time, place, or manner restriction is to move speech around, not to prohibit it, the government must leave available other ways for the speaker to communicate. If there are no ample alternative channels of communication, the regulation is tantamount to a prior restraint, and strict scrutiny applies.

2. TIME, PLACE, OR MANNER RESTRICTIONS IN A PUBLIC FORUM. [§696]

The time, place, manner rules developed in the public forum area. Public forum doctrine is treated more fully later in the book (see §810, below), but **the main idea is that certain public places (streets, sidewalks, parks, public amphitheaters) have been used for speech purposes for so long that the public has a right of access to them for speech purposes. Since there is a guaranteed right of access to these places, the government may not prohibit persons from speaking; it may only impose time, place, or manner restrictions.** In these public forum cases, remember that the government owns the property, and the place is used for some non-speech purpose (such as a post-office, a military base, state government buildings, parks, or even streets). **Time, place, or manner analysis in public forum cases is used to strike a balance between the speaker's right of access, and the government's ability to maintain the use of the place for its intended purpose.**

a. Prohibition of Loud Noise. [§697]

A city may prohibit sound trucks from operating above a certain decibel level.

Kovacs v. Cooper, 336 U.S. 77 (1940). The Court upheld a Trenton, New Jersey ordinance which prohibited any sound truck or loudspeaker which emitted loud and raucous noises. Justice Reed, for a plurality, said that the ordinance, as interpreted by state courts, permitted the use of electronic amplification devices, and was only directed at the loud and raucous manner of the broadcast.

b. Prohibition of Picketing Based on Its Content. [§698]

A city cannot selectively prohibit picketing based on the message on the picket signs.

Police Department of Chicago v. Mosley, 408 U.S. 92 (1972). The Court invalidated a Chicago ordinance prohibiting picketing within 150 feet of a school, with the exception of peaceful picketing of any school involved

OUTLINE

in a labor dispute. The Court said this ordinance was not content neutral, and therefore was not to be analyzed under time, place or manner rules.

c. Prohibition of Loud Noise Near a School. [§699]

A state can prohibit loud noise near a school building while the school is in session.

Grayned v. Rockford, 408 U.S. 104 (1972). The Court upheld an anti-noise ordinance which prohibited any person on property adjacent to a school building from making any noise which would disrupt the functioning of the school. Unlike *Mosley* (previous case), there were no exceptions for any specific kinds of speech. The Court treated this ordinance as simply a restriction on the manner of speech, irrespective of the content.

d. Prohibition of the Broadcast of Offensive Language During Daytime. [§700]

The federal government can prohibit an indecent radio broadcast during the daytime when children are likely to be in the audience.

FCC v. Pacifica Foundation, 438 U.S. 726 (1978). The Court upheld an action by the Federal Communications Commission to channel an indecent radio broadcast to times when children probably would not be in the audience. The FCC basically told the station not to play George Carlin's "Seven Dirty Words" monologue when children are likely to be listening to the radio. This is a permissible time regulation because the government was trying to prevent offending the sensibilities of children (which is a significant government interest), the means were narrowly tailored, and the monologue could still be disseminated to the public.

e. Picketing Outside the Supreme Court Building. [§701]

The federal government cannot prohibit picketing or demonstrating on public sidewalks outside the Supreme Court Building.

U.S. v. Grace, 461 U.S. 171 (1983). The Court invalidated a federal law which prohibited picketing or the carrying of flags or banners on the public sidewalks outside the Supreme Court building. The Court rejected the time, place, or manner argument, saying that this law operated as a total prohibition of a specific kind of speech.

f. Sleeping Overnight in a National Park. [§702]

The National Park Service can prohibit sleeping overnight in a national park, even if the sleeping constitutes symbolic speech.

Clark v. Community for Creative Non-Violence, 468 U.S. 288 (1984). The Court upheld the action of the National Park Service which refused permission for demonstrators to sleep overnight in a national park near the White House. The protesters wanted to dramatize the plight of the homeless. Assuming that symbolic speech was involved, the Court used time, place, manner analysis to uphold the restriction.

g. Focused Picketing Outside a Residence. [§703]

A town can prohibit focused picketing outside someone's house as long as the picketers are free to walk up and down the block to demonstrate.

Frisby v. Schultz, 487 U.S. 474 (1988). The Court upheld a town ordinance forbidding focused picketing in front of a person's residence. (Focused picketing is picketing in one place - here, outside someone's residence.) The Court said that this law met time, place, or manner requirements because it was passed to protect the privacy interests of residents, and left open the ability to walk up and down the street with picket signs as a means of protest.

h. Prohibition of Signs that Cast Foreign Embassies into Public Disrepute. [§704]

The District of Columbia cannot prohibit signs near embassies just because the signs might denigrate the foreign countries which operate the embassies.

Boos v. Barry, 485 U.S. 312 (1988). The Court invalidated a District of Columbia ordinance banning the display of any sign within 500 feet of a foreign embassy if the sign would tend to bring the foreign government into "public odium" or "public disrepute." The Court rejected the argument that the law was content neutral; it was directed at the emotive impact of the speech, something which is not a "secondary effect" for purposes of content neutrality.

i. Prohibition of Political Activity Near a Polling Place. [§705]

A state can prohibit political activity near a polling place on election day.

Burson v. Freeman, 112 S.Ct. 1846 (1992). With no majority supporting a particular rationale, the Court upheld a Tennessee law prohibiting the display or distribution of campaign material or the soliciting of votes within 100 feet of the entrance to a polling place. The Court did not apply time, place, or manner analysis because the restriction was found to be content-based. Four Justices said the law passed strict scrutiny analysis, and Justice Scalia upheld it on the basis that a polling place is not a traditional public forum, so reasonable restrictions are acceptable.

j. Prohibition of Residential Signs. [§706]

A city cannot prohibit all (or most) residential signs; such a ban forecloses an entire medium of communication.

Ladue v. Gilleo, 114 S.Ct. 2038 (1994). The Court invalidated a city ordinance which barred all residential signs, except those falling within one of ten exemptions. The city's asserted interest was to reduce visual blight. Gilleo had displayed on her front lawn a sign protesting the Persian Gulf war. Assuming that the law was content-neutral, the Court ruled that the ordinance was not a valid time, or place, or manner restriction because it did not leave open adequate alternative channels of communication. The ordinance virtually foreclosed an important medium of communication of political or religious messages.

k. Prohibition of the Distribution of Anonymous Literature. [§707]

A government cannot prohibit the distribution of anonymous literature.

(1) *Talley v. California*, 362 U.S. 60 (1960). [§708]

The Court invalidated a Los Angeles ordinance which prohibited the distribution of unsigned literature. In *Talley*, the ordinance was applied to the distribution of anonymous handbills urging people to boycott certain Los Angeles merchants who allegedly engaged in discriminatory employment practices. The Court rejected the argument that the ordinance was a sufficiently tailored means to identify those engaged in fraud, false advertising and libel.

(2) *McIntyre v. Ohio Elections Commission*, 115 S.Ct. 1511 (1995). [§709]

The Court invalidated an Ohio statute prohibiting the distribution of anonymous campaign literature designed to promote election or defeat of candidates, to promote adoption or defeat of any issue, or to influence voters in elections. The Court treated the Ohio statute as a content-based restriction on core political speech, and concluded that it was not justified by Ohio's asserted interests in preventing fraudulent and libelous statements and in providing the electorate with relevant information about political campaigns.

l. Limitations on Charitable Solicitation in Federal Offices. [§710]

The President may, by executive order, limit access to federal offices for purposes of soliciting funds for charity.

Cornelius v. NAACP Legal Defense and Educational Fund, Inc., 473 U.S 788 (1985). The Court upheld an executive order limiting participation in a charitable solicitation drive in federal places of employment to non-profit charitable groups which provided certain health or welfare services. The Court reasoned that the charitable solicitation project was a non- public forum, and that restricting access to federal offices for purposes of charitable solicitation was a reasonable means of ensuring the efficient functioning of the workplace.

3. TIME, PLACE, OR MANNER RESTRICTIONS IMPOSED THROUGH AN INJUNCTION, RATHER THAN A GENERALLY APPLICABLE ORDINANCE. [§711]

The Court has said that a time, place, or manner restriction imposed by an injunctive order is to be subject to more stringent review than one effected by a general ordinance. Because the injunction is directed at an actual or threatened violation of a legislative or judicial decree (as opposed to an ordinance, which is directed at an entire class of potential violators), it carries greater risks of censorship and discrimination. **The test for a content-neutral injunction is whether it burdens no more speech than is necessary to serve a significant government interest.**

a. Injunctive Orders Prohibiting Demonstrations for a Certain Period of Time. [§712]

The Court invalidated an ex parte order restraining a white supremacist group from holding any rally for ten days in the county, if the rally would disturb or endanger the citizens of the county.

Carroll v. President and Commissioners of Princess Anne, 393 U.S. 175 (1968). The Court invalidated an ex parte order, granted with no notice to or communication with a white supremacist group, prohibiting the group from holding any demonstration or rally within the county for ten days if the rally would disturb or endanger the citizens of the county. The Court said that any such order must be precisely tailored to the facts of the case, and must be couched in the narrowest terms that will accomplish the pin-pointed objective permitted by the essential needs of public order.

b. Restrictions on Expressive Activity Around Abortion Clinics and Residences of Clinic Staff. [§713]

The Court has upheld certain restrictions on expressive activity near abortion clinics, but has invalidated others as burdening more speech than necessary to achieve the government's interests.

(1) *Madsen v. Women's Health Center, Inc.*, 114 S.Ct. 2516 (1994). The Court reviewed an injunction issued by a Florida state court which prohibited anti-abortion protesters from demonstrating in certain places and in various ways outside a health clinic that performs abortions. **The Court said that the injunction must burden no more speech than is necessary to serve the significant government interests of protecting a pregnant woman's freedom to seek lawful medical or counseling services, ensuring public safety, and protecting property and privacy rights.** The Court upheld a 36-foot buffer zone around the clinic entrances and driveway. It also upheld noise restrictions which were in effect during surgery and recovery periods at the clinic.

The Court struck down, as overinclusive, the following restrictions in the injunction: a 36-foot buffer zone around private property to the north and west of the clinic; a 300-foot "no-approach zone" around the clinic, in which anti-abortion protesters were barred from approaching clinic patients; and a 300-foot buffer zone around the residences of clinic staff, in which there can be no picketing or demonstrating. The Court also invalidated a blanket ban on images that were observable to patients inside the clinic (such as posters with pictures of aborted fetuses).

(2) *Schenck v. Pro-Coice Network of Western New York*, 117 S.Ct. 855 (1997). The Court reviewed an injunction issued by a New York state court that imposed "fixed" and "floating" buffer zones around abortion clinics and women who wanted to enter the clinics. The Court reaffirmed *Madsen* (prior case), saying that a time, place and manner restriction imposed by injunctive order (rather than by statute) must burden no more speech than necessary to serve a significant government interest. Applying that test, the Court upheld 15-foot "fixed" buffer zones which prohibited demonstrating around abortion clinic doorways, parking lot entrances and driveways. The Court also upheld an order that allowed two "sidewalk counselors" inside the "fixed" buffer zone (to try to dissuade a woman from having an abortion), but required the counselors to "cease and desist" their counseling if requested to do so by the woman to whom they were talking. The Court struck down that part of the injunctive order that created 15-foot "floating" buffer zones around persons or vehicles entering or leaving the abortion clinics. These buffer zones prevented speakers from talking to someone from a normal conversational distance or from leafletting on a public street. In its analysis, the Court used the same government interests it relied on in *Madsen*: ensuring public safety and order, promoting the free flow of traffic on streets and sidewalks, protecting property rights, and protecting a woman's right to seek pregnancy-related medical services.

E. CONTENT-BASED RESTRICTIONS ON SPEECH. [§714]

There are certain times when the government looks at the content of speech to determine whether and how to regulate the speech. Be aware of the evil that the government is trying to prevent or punish. Identification of the evil will take you into the appropriate analysis, and will answer the question of which test to use to answer an exam question.

> **STUDY TIP: When you get a free speech question, and are trying to figure out which test to use, focus on the evil the government is trying to prevent. Once you identify the evil, it will take you directly into the appropriate analysis.** For instance, if the government is concerned about consumers being defrauded by certain types of advertising, it's a commercial speech case; if the government is trying to prohibit sexually-oriented speech because it lowers the moral tone in the community, or causes anti-social sexual behavior, it's an obscenity case. Be aware of this issue as we go through the different sections and cases.

1. CLEAR AND PRESENT DANGER ANALYSIS. [§715]

Under clear and present danger analysis, the government tries to punish a speaker for inciting a listener to engage in illegal activity. This is a case-by-case determination which looks at all the circumstances surrounding the speech (intent of the speaker, nature of the speech, identity of the speaker, composition of the audience, political or military climate) to see if there is a high enough probability that the speaker would have incited or did incite a listener or listeners to break the law. **The modern test, from the *Brandenburg* case (see §725), asks whether the speaker's advocacy of illegal action is directed to inciting or producing imminent lawless action and is likely to incite or produce such action by the audience.**

a. In General. [§716]

The purpose of the clear and present danger test is to determine when the government may punish a speaker for causing his or her audience to engage in illegal acts. In some cases, a legislature may be able to establish that some regulable evil always happens when certain speech is engaged in (burning one's draft card always impairs the functioning of the Selective Service system). When a legislature cannot categorically establish that a regulable evil always happens when certain speech occurs, the clear and present danger is used to connect the regulable evil and the speech, thus enabling the government to restrict speech as a by-product of regulating the non-speech evil.

b. Development of the Clear and Present Danger Doctrine. [§717]

The clear and present danger test began as a tool of statutory construction in 1919. The Court used the test to allow the punishment of speech under a federal Espionage Act. **By 1969, in** *Brandenburg v. Ohio* **(see §725), the test had become constitutionalized in the sense that the First Amendment now prohibits the punishment of speech unless it creates a clear and present danger of some evil that the government has a right to prevent.**

(1) Genesis of the Clear and Present Danger Doctrine. [§718]

The clear and present danger doctrine began in 1919 when the Court used it to affirm convictions under the 1917 Espionage Act.

Schenck v. U.S., 249 U.S. 47 (1919). The Court affirmed convictions for violations of the 1917 Espionage Act, which made it a crime to attempt to cause insubordination in the armed forces or obstruct recruiting. The defendants mailed literature to men eligible for the draft, arguing that the draft violated the Thirteenth Amendment prohibition of slavery. Justice Holmes said that the question is whether words are used in such circumstances and are of such a nature as to create a clear and present danger of an evil that Congress has the power to prevent.

(2) "Bad Tendency" Test. [§719]

In a dissenting opinion, Justice Holmes argued that the government may punish speech only if it creates an imminent danger of some evil that the government has a right to prevent.

Abrams v. U.S., 250 U.S. 616 (1919). (Justice Holmes' dissent). The Court in *Abrams* affirmed convictions under amendments to the Espionage Act of 1917. The defendants had distributed leaflets criticizing President Wilson for sending troops to fight in Russia. The majority used a "bad tendency test," under which speech could be punished if it would tend to bring about some substantive evil. Justice Holmes, in dissent, said that only the present danger of immediate evil or an intent to bring it about warrants congressional punishment of speech.

(3) Specific Statutory Prohibition of Certain Speech. [§720]

The Court, in the 1920's, refused to apply the clear and present danger test, affirming the conviction of a speaker solely because he engaged in speech that was specifically prohibited by statute.

Gitlow v. New York, 268 U.S. 652 (1925). The Court, in applying the First Amendment against the states, affirmed a conviction under New York's Criminal Anarchy Law, which prohibited advocacy of the violent overthrow of the government. Gitlow was convicted for distributing 16,000 copies of a radical manifesto which urged strikes and other actions as methods of establishing socialism. The Court said that since the statute specifically prohibited certain language, the clear and present danger test was irrelevant, and the speech could be punished if its natural tendency and probable effect was to bring about a substantive evil. Justice Holmes dissented, saying Gitlow's speech was protected under clear and present danger principles.

(4) Specific Statutory Prohibition of Certain Speech. [§721]

The Court, in the 1920's, refused to apply the clear and present danger test, affirming the conviction of a speaker who engaged in allegedly subversive speech. The Court refused to review the jury finding that the speaker engaged in illegal speech activity.

Whitney v. California, 274 U.S. 357 (1927). The Court affirmed a conviction under California's Criminal Syndicalism Act, which prohibited advocating or teaching any doctrine which espouses crime, sabotage, or unlawful acts of force or violence as a means of bringing about economic or political change. The Act also criminalized organizing or belonging to any organization that advocates or teaches criminal syndicalism. Charlotte Whitney was convicted of joining and organizing the Communist Labor Party of California. The Court refused to review the finding of the jury that Ms. Whitney had engaged in activity contrary to the Act. Justice Brandeis, in a concurring opinion, argued that the clear and present danger test is required, even in a case like *Whitney*, when the statute specifically proscribes speech. Under the Brandeis approach, the Court has a serious role in reviewing these kinds of convictions, unlike the majority view, which basically rubber stamps the factfinding decision of the jury.

(5) "Gravity of the Evil" Version of the Clear and Present Danger Test. [§722]

In 1951, the Court applied a version of the clear and present danger test which asked whether the gravity of the evil, discounted by its improbability (the unlikelihood of its occurrence), justifies such invasion of free speech as is necessary to avoid the danger the government is trying to prevent.

Dennis v. U.S., 341 U.S. 494 (1951). The Court affirmed convictions under the Smith Act, a federal law which prohibited acting or conspiring to act to teach or advocate the duty or propriety of overthrowing the government by force or violence. The defendants were convicted of conspiring to organize the Communist Party of the United States, a group whose goals included the forceful overthrow of the United States government. Chief Justice Vinson, for a plurality, adopted a new version of the clear and present danger test: Whether the gravity of the evil, discounted by its improbability, justifies such invasion of free speech as is necessary to avoid the danger the government is trying to prevent. Compare this to the approach the Court used in *Schenck v. U.S.*, where the focus was on whether words are used in such circumstances and are of such a nature as to create a clear and present danger of an evil that Congress has the power to prevent.

(6) Present Advocacy of Future Violent Action May Be Punishable. [§723]

The government may punish the present advocacy of future violent action if the speech plus its surrounding circumstances make it highly likely that the evil will occur at some specific time in the future.

Yates v. U.S., 354 U.S. 298 (1957). The Court reversed convictions under the Smith Act for organizing the Communist Party and conspiring to bring about the forcible overthrow of the government. The Court, in an attempt to clarify *Dennis* (previous case), said that it would be constitutional for a government to punish the present advocacy of future violent action if a conspiracy is involved, the group is of sufficient size and cohesiveness, and is sufficiently oriented toward action, and other circumstances are such as to create a high probability that evil will occur. Advocacy of ideas is always protected; incitement of action may not be.

(7) Punishing Membership in the Communist Party. [§724]

The Government may not criminalize all membership in the Communist Party; active members may be punished if they intend to bring about illegal goals of the organization and they take some action to effectuate these goals.

Scales v. U.S., 367 U.S. 203 (1961). The Court affirmed convictions under the membership clause of the Smith Act which made it a crime to be a knowing member of any group which advocates the forcible overthrow of the government. The Court distinguished "active" from "passive" members, saying that not all membership in the Communist Party can be made a crime. Scales was Chairman of the North and South Carolina Districts of the Community Party and, as such, had knowledge of the party's illegal goals, and a specific intent to bring them about.

(8) Speech that Incites Imminent Lawless Action and is Likely to Produce it. [§725]

The government may punish speech if it is directed to inciting imminent lawless action and is likely to cause such action.

Brandenburg v. Ohio, 395 U.S. 444 (1969). The Court reversed the conviction of a Ku Klux Klan leader under the Ohio Criminal Syndicalism statute which prohibited assembling with others to advocate the duty or propriety of violent overthrow of the government. Brandenburg made some hateful but inconsequential statements at a Klan rally, and was arrested. The Court gives us the modern version of the clear and present danger test, which is that a state cannot proscribe advocacy of the use of force or of the violation of the law unless the advocacy is directed to inciting or producing imminent lawless action and is likely to incite or produce such action. The test is needed to ensure that the law only punishes incitement to illegal action, as opposed to advocacy of abstract ideas.

(9) Speech Must be Directed to a Specific Person or Group. [§726]

The Court has ruled that if speech is not directed to a specific person or group, it is not punishable under the clear and present danger doctrine because it is not likely to produce any imminent lawless action.

Hess v. Indiana, 414 U.S. 105 (1973). The Court reversed a conviction of an antiwar demonstrator who, after police had cleared a street during a rally on campus, said loudly, "We'll take the fucking street later (or again)." Hess was convicted under a disorderly conduct statute. The

Court applied *Brandenburg*, and concluded that Hess' speech was not directed to any specific person or group, so it was not intended to advocate any imminent lawless action, nor was it likely to produce any.

2. FIGHTING WORDS, OFFENSIVE SPEECH, HATE SPEECH. [§727]

These three kinds of speech have one common thread: each involves nasty, scurrilous language that is intended or likely to offend some people or inflict psychic trauma on the members of the audience. The constitutional question is when does this kind of speech cross the line and become regulable by the government. Remember that preventing hurt feelings, or psychic trauma, is not a legitimate government interest. There must be more, such as preventing a breach of the peace.

a. Definition of Fighting Words. [§728]

Fighting words are scurrilous epithets, delivered in person to the listener, which are likely to cause an average addressee to retaliate against the speaker. The theory is that fighting words are not essential to the expression of an idea, and are of such little social value that they may be prohibited, usually under breach-of-the-peace statutes. **Statutes which attempt to proscribe fighting words are very susceptible to attacks based on vagueness and overbreadth.**

(1) Probability of Violence. [§729]

A breach-of-the-peace conviction will not be upheld unless the speech creates a probability of violence.

Cantwell v. Connecticut, 310 U.S. 296 (1940). The Court reversed a breach-of-the-peace conviction of a Jehovah's Witness who stopped two men on the street and played for them an anti-Catholic phonograph record. One of the men told Cantwell to go away, and he did. The Court found that there was no assault, bodily threat, or personal abuse in Cantwell's message. Given the absence of any clear and present danger of a breach of the peace, the Court considered Cantwell's communication to be protected speech.

(2) Fighting Words As Unprotected Speech. [§730]

Fighting words are not protected by the First Amendment.

Chaplinsky v. New Hampshire, 315 U.S. 568 (1942). The Court unanimously affirmed the conviction of a Jehovah's Witness who called a city marshal a "God damned racketeer," and a "damned Fascist." The statute prohibited anyone from addressing any offensive, derisive, or annoying word to anyone lawfully in a public place, or calling anyone by any offensive or derisive name. The Court said there were certain categories of speech that were outside the concern of the First Amendment, including fighting words - words which by their very utterance inflict injury or tend to incite an immediate breach of the peace. **The first part of the test, words which by their very utterance inflict injury, is not used as an independent basis for regulating speech; the reason is that preventing psychological trauma or hurt feelings is not an evil the government has a right to prevent. The second test of *Chaplinsky*, words which tend to incite an immediate breach of the peace, is theoretically still a valid method of**

regulation. The fighting words doctrine requires a personally abusive epithet to be directed to the listener in such a manner as to provoke an average addressee to violence.

(3) Speech That Invites Dispute. [§731]
Speech cannot be punished merely because it invites dispute.

Terminiello v. Chicago, 337 U.S. 1 (1949). The Court reversed the breach-of-the-peace conviction of a speaker who made scurrilous comments about various political and racial groups. The statute prohibited speech which "stirs the public to anger, invites dispute, brings about a condition of unrest, or creates a disturbance." The statute was fatally overbroad in that the speaker could have been convicted for speech that "invited dispute," something the First Amendment clearly protects.

b. Offensive Speech. [§732]
Offensive speech is speech that is usually sexually oriented (but not obscene) and is offensive to mainstream sensibilities. The general rule in this category of cases is that government cannot regulate this speech just because it doesn't like it, or because it offends the sensibilities of adults. This speech may be regulated to protect children, or if it falls within one of the other proscribable categories (such as clear and present danger, or fighting words).

(1) Punishing Speech Because of Its Offensiveness. [§733]
Speech cannot be prohibited merely because it is offensive.

Cohen v. California, 403 U.S. 15 (1971). The Court reversed a breach-of-the-peace conviction for wearing into a public courthouse a jacket that said "Fuck the Draft." The speech was not obscene because it was not sexually oriented; it was not fighting words because it was not a personally abusive epithet directed to a specific listener; and it did not unduly invade the privacy interests of anyone in that public place. The Court recognized the emotive value of speech, saying that "one man's vulgarity is another's lyric."

(2) Restrictions on Offensive Speech. [§734]
The government may channel offensive speech away from children.

FCC v. Pacifica Foundation, 438 U.S. 726 (1978). The Court upheld the power of the FCC to order a radio station to play George Carlin's monologue, "Filthy Words," only later at night when children were not likely to be in the audience. The monologue was not obscene, but used explicit sexual and excretory language. Protecting the sensibilities of children was the significant government interest that justified this restriction on speech.

(3) Government Ban On Indecent Telephone Messages. [§735]
The government may not totally ban non-obscene sexually oriented speech.

Sable Communications v. Federal Communications Commission, 492 U.S. 115 (1989). The Court invalidated a provision of the Federal

OUTLINE

Communications Act which totally banned "indecent" interstate commercial telephone messages. The speech here was not obscene under prevailing federal standards, and this law (unlike the one in *Pacifica*, the prior case) totally prohibited the speech, rather than just channeling it to certain hours.

(4) Government Ban on Indecent Messages On the Internet. [§735.1]

The government may not criminalize transmission on the Internet of material that is indecent as to minors or that describes sexual or excretory activities in terms that are potentially offensive as to minors.

Reno v. American Civil Liberties Union, ___ S.Ct. ___ (1997). The Court invalidated two provisions of the Communications Decency Act of 1996 (CDA) which were designed to protect minors from harmful materials on the Internet. One provision prohibited the knowing transmission on the Internet of obscene or indecent messages to anyone under eighteen years of age. The other prohibited the transmission on the Internet to minors of patently offensive materials (as judged by contemporary community standards) that depict sexual or excretory activities or organs. The Court invalidated these provisions as content-based restrictions that swept within their scope a great deal of speech that adults have a constitutional right to send and receive on the Internet. The overbreadth of the CDA provisions meant that the law was not narrowly tailored to the government's interest in protecting minors from receiving harmful material on the Internet.

(5) Restrictions On Sexually Offensive Speech On Cable Television. [§736]

Congress may impose some restrictions on the ability of a cable television system operator to prohibit or channel non- obscene sexually offensive programming.

Denver Area Educational Telecommunications Consortium, Inc. v. FCC, ___ S.Ct. ___ (1996). The Court reviewed three provisions of a 1992 federal law which regulated the ability of cable television system operators to prohibit or channel sexually offensive programming. The Court upheld the provision of the law which permits cable television system operators to prohibit programming containing "patently offensive" sex-related material from being shown on "leased access channels" (these are channels reserved under federal law for commercial lease by parties unaffiliated with the cable television system operator). The Court invalidated the provision of the law which applied to leased access channels and which required cable television system operators who decided to carry "patently offensive" programming to segregate such programming on a single channel and to block access to that channel unless a subscriber consented in writing to receive the channel. The Court invalidated the provision of the law which allowed cable television system operators to prohibit the showing of sexually offensive programming on public, educational, or governmental use channels (these are channels required by local governments to be dedicated for these purposes).

c. Hate Speech. [§737]

Hate speech is offensive speech that is derogatory toward racial or ethnic groups. This speech is punishable under other established tests (clear and present danger, fighting words), but is not independently punishable based on the emotional injury it inflicts on the targeted group. However, the Court has held that a state may increase the sentence for an assaultive crime (a pre- existing, predicate offense) if the criminal chose his or her victim based on race or ethnicity.

(1) Content-Based Restrictions On Hate Speech. [§738]

The government cannot selectively ban certain categories of fighting words based on their content. In other words, the government cannot prohibit only those fighting words which it dislikes.

R.A.V. v. St. Paul, 112 S.Ct. 2538 (1992). The Court invalidated a "hate-speech" ordinance which made it a crime to place on public or private property any symbol or object, including a burning cross or Nazi swastika, which will cause anger, alarm, or resentment on the basis of race, color, creed, religion, or gender. R.A.V. and others burned a cross inside the fenced backyard of a black family. The Court, through Justice Scalia, invalidated this ordinance because it was a content-based restriction which failed strict scrutiny review because there were content-neutral alternatives that the city could have chosen to meet its compelling interest of eradicating racial hostility. The problem with the ordinance is that it reaches within the category of fighting words, and prohibits only those content- specific fighting words which the government dislikes.

(2) Hateful Beliefs. [§739]

A person cannot be punished for abstract beliefs, no matter how reprehensible or anti-social.

Dawson v. Delaware, 112 S.Ct. 1093 (1992). The Court excluded as irrelevant to the capital sentencing phase of a murder case evidence that Dawson was a member of the Ayran Brotherhood, a white racist prison gang. The victim in Dawson's case was white. The Court found that admission of the evidence might tend to punish Dawson for his abstract beliefs, which, while reprehensible and anti-social, had not been shown to be related to the murder of which Dawson was convicted.

(3) Sentence Enhancement. [§740]

A criminal defendant's sentence may be enhanced if the defendant chose his or her victim on the basis of race.

Wisconsin v. Mitchell, 113 S.Ct. 2194 (1993). The Court unanimously ruled that there was no First Amendment problem with a Wisconsin statute that increased the sentence for aggravated battery when the defendant selected the victim based on the victim's race. The Court characterized the law as punishing the conduct of selecting a victim, rather than punishing any abstract racist beliefs.

3. OBSCENITY. [§741]

Obscenity is sexually oriented speech that fails the test of *Miller v. California*, (below): 1) whether the average person, applying contemporary community standards, would find that the book or movie appeals to prurient interest; 2) whether the work depicts, in a patently offensive way, sexual conduct that is specifically defined by state law; and 3) using a reasonable person standard (not contemporary community standards), whether the work, taken as a whole, lacks serious literary, artistic, political, or scientific value. A state may not criminalize the private possession of obscenity by an adult, but may criminalize the private possession of child pornography by an adult. For a state to be able to criminalize the private possession of child pornography, the pornographic material must be defined as a videotape or film of children in explicit sex scenes. The state's interest in preventing child pornography is to stop sexual exploitation of children, an interest not present in the typical obscenity case. (Written descriptions of children engaged in sex do not fall within this analysis because no child is being forced to engage in any sexual activity, so the government interest in preventing sexual exploitation of children is not present.)

a. Development of the Obscenity Doctrine. [§742]

The Court has had an extremely difficult time figuring out obscenity law. That obviously says something about the nature of the speech being regulated, and the government's proffered reasons for its restrictions. **Think about why obscenity is unprotected. Does it lower the moral tone of the community? Does it degrade women? Does it contribute to or cause rape, sexual assault, child sexual abuse, or discrimination against women in private and public aspects of life?** How explicit must the sex be to be unprotected by the First Amendment? Consider these issues as we go through the obscenity cases.

(1) First Test for Obscenity Adopted by the Court. [§743]

The first test for obscenity adopted by the court was whether, to the average person applying contemporary community standards, the dominant theme of the material, taken as a whole, appeals to the prurient interest.

Roth v. U.S., 354 U.S. 476 (1957). The Court, in upholding the facial validity of two state statutes regulating obscenity, held that obscenity is not within the protection of the First Amendment. It said that all ideas having even the slightest redeeming social importance get the full protection of the Constitution, and that the test for judging obscenity is whether to the average person, applying contemporary community standards, the dominant theme of the material, taken as a whole, appeals to the prurient interest.

(2) The Court Clarifies the Obscenity Rules. [§744]

The Court ruled that, for a work to be obscene, it must be utterly without redeeming social value.

Memoirs v. Massachusetts, 383 U.S. 413 (1966). The Court reversed a state obscenity conviction, with Justice Brennan writing a plurality opinion for himself and two other Justices. According to Justice Brennan, a work could be deemed obscene only if the state could prove each of the following elements: 1) the dominant theme of the material, taken as a whole, appeals to prurient interest; 2) the work is patently offensive because if affronts contemporary community standards; and 3) the work is utterly without redeeming social value. This last prong created the biggest problem because, to secure a criminal conviction, the prosecutor had to show, beyond a reasonable doubt, that something did not exist.

(3) Modern Obscenity Test. [§745]

Today, for a work to be obscene, it must lack serious literary, artistic, political, or scientific value.

Miller v. California, 413 U.S. 15 (1973). A majority in *Miller* articulated a new obscenity standard: 1) whether the average person, applying contemporary community standards, would find that the work, taken as a whole, appeals to prurient interest; 2) whether the work depicts, in a patently offensive way, sexual conduct that is specifically defined by state law; and 3) whether the work, taken as a whole, lacks serious literary, artistic, political, or scientific value (SLAPS test). **Note that as we go from *Roth/Memoirs to Miller*, we go from the work having to be "utterly without redeeming social value," to the work "lacking serious literary, artistic, political, or scientific value." Theoretically, this new standard should be easier for prosecutors to meet.**

(4) Third Prong of *Miller* Judged By a Reasonable Person Standard. [§746]

The question of whether a work lacks serious literary, artistic, political, or scientific value is to be judged by a reasonable person (as opposed to contemporary community standards) test.

Pope v. Illinois, 481 U.S. 497 (1987). The Court emphasized that the third prong of *Miller* (SLAPS test) is to be judged by a reasonable person standard, rather than by contemporary community standards. The idea is to provide a more uniform standard throughout the country, thereby reducing regional differences in First Amendment interpretation.

b. Right to Possess Obscenity and Right to Receive Information. [§747]

A person has a constitutionally protected right to possess adult obscenity (no children as actors) in the privacy of his or her home. However, there is no constitutionally protected right to watch obscene movies in a theater, even if the theater very carefully restricts its clientele to consenting adults.

(1) Private Possession of Obscenity. [§748]

The government may not criminalize the private possession of obscenity in the home.

Stanley v. Georgia, 394 U.S. 557 (1969). The Court reversed a conviction for possession of obscenity in the privacy of the home. Stanley had three reels of obscene films in his home, but the Court, through Justice Marshall, said that the First Amendment protects the right to be let alone in one's home, at least so far as the books a person may read, or the films he may watch. The government may criminalize the importation, exportation, transportation, or sale of obscenity, but not its simple possession in the home.

(2) Commercial Exhibition of Obscenity to Consenting Adults. [§749]

The government may prohibit the showing of obscene films in a movie theater restricted to consenting adults.

Paris Adult Theatre I v. Slaton, 413 U.S. 49 (1973). The Court upheld a state court's injunction against the showing of obscene films in a movie theater restricted to consenting adults. The Court distinguished *Stanley* (previous case), saying that the privacy of the home that was controlling in *Stanley* was not present in the commercial exhibition of obscene movies in a theater.

c. Child Pornography - No Right to Sell or Privately Possess Child Pornography. [§750]

The Court has ruled that a state's interest in preventing the sexual exploitation of children is so great that it overrides a person's interest in the possession of child pornography. Note that in these cases, the states have defined child pornography as the use of children in explicit sex scenes. A written depiction of child sexual activity would have to be subjected to the *Miller* obscenity analysis.

(1) Sale of Child Pornography. [§751]

The government may prohibit the sale of child pornography, regardless of whether it is obscene under *Miller*.

New York v. Ferber, 458 U.S. 747 (1982). The Court upheld the state conviction of a seller of films showing young boys masturbating. The Court said that preventing the commercial sexual exploitation of children was a sufficiently compelling state interest to uphold the law. It is irrelevant whether these films meet the *Miller* obscenity standards; the state is regulating for an entirely different reason, and even non-obscene films could be subject to prosecution under the child pornography law.

(2) Private Possession of Child Pornography. [§752]

The government may prohibit all possession of child pornography, even in the privacy of the home.

Osborne v. Ohio, 495 U.S. 103 (1990). The Court upheld an Ohio statute that criminalized the private possession of child pornography. Osborne possessed photographs of a nude boy in a number of sexually explicit poses. *Stanley v. Georgia* (a state cannot criminalize the private possession of obscenity) was distinguished on the basis of the state interest advanced in each case. In *Stanley*, the state was trying to prevent obscenity from poisoning the minds of viewers; in *Osborne*, the state was trying to prevent sexual abuse and exploitation of children.

d. Factoring Children into the Obscenity Equation. [§753]

A state may not generally prohibit the sale of sexually- oriented material that is not suitable for consumption by children. The result would be that the adult population would have its reading or viewing choices reduced to a level appropriate for children. The Court also said that a state may prohibit the sale of material to minors if it is obscene *as to minors*, irrespective of whether it is obscene as to adults.

(1) Books That Are Unsuitable For Children. [§754]

The state cannot prohibit books merely because they are unfit for children.

Butler v. Michigan, 352 U.S. 380 (1957). The Court invalidated a Michigan law prohibiting the sale of books likely to have "a potentially deleterious influence on youth." Such a law would reduce the adult population to reading only what is fit for children.

(2) Defining the "Average Person." [§755]

Children may not be considered in determining the "average person."

Pinkus v. U.S., 436 U.S. 293 (1978). The Court ruled that when allegedly obscene works are distributed only to adults, children may not be considered when a jury is applying the standard of "the average person applying contemporary community standards." Including children in the mix would lower the average too greatly.

(3) Variable Definitions of Obscenity. [§756]

States may define obscenity differently for minors than for adults.

Ginsberg v. New York, 390 U.S. 629 (1968). The Court, using a doctrine of "variable" obscenity, held that a state could define obscenity differently as to minors (as compared to adults), and prohibit the sale to minors of works that would be non-obscene and therefore acceptable to adults.

e. Pornography as Sex Discrimination: The Feminist Perspective. [§757]

The government may not prohibit pornography merely because it depicts women in a certain way. In recent years, feminist scholars have tried to change the terms of the debate about pornography. **Rather than asking whether a given work, as a whole, violates the *Miller* standards for obscenity, Professor Catherine MacKinnon and author Andrea Dworkin have drafted a statute which is based on the premise that pornography *is* sex discrimination (it does not matter whether the work passes *Miller*).** Pornography is defined as the graphic, sexually **explicit subordination of women through pictures or words that depict women in a subordinated, degrading, or humiliating fashion.** The problems with this kind of ordinance are that it is viewpoint based, and does not fit into any traditional method of First Amendment analysis.

American Booksellers Association v. Hudnut, 771 F.2d 323 (7th Cir. 1985), affirmed 475 U.S. 1001 (1986). The Supreme Court summarily affirmed a decision of the Seventh Circuit Court of Appeals invalidating an Indianapolis anti-pornography statute. The ordinance asserted that pornography causes rape, battery, child sexual abuse, prostitution, and discrimination against women in education, jobs, and other important aspects of public and private life. Anyone injured by a person who has seen or read pornography has a cause of action against the maker or seller. Judge Easterbrook, for the court, ruled that the ordinance was viewpoint based because the city preferred certain kinds of depictions of women, but prohibited others. In addition, Judge Easterbrook was troubled by the slippery slope argument; if this ordinance is constitutional, what about ones that prohibit certain speech about racial, ethnic, or religious groups, or about homosexuals? The court also said that the evils described in the ordinance all took place after some sort of "mental intermediation" by the consumer of the pornography. This intervening mental step (between reading pornography and engaging in the evil act) breaks the chain of causation and injects some uncertainty regarding whether the evil will actually occur.

4. COMMERCIAL SPEECH. [§758]

Commercial speech is speech that advertises a product or service, usually for profit. To determine whether a restriction on commercial speech is permissible, first ask whether the commercial speech concerns a lawful activity, and whether it is misleading to consumers. If the commercial speech is not misleading, and is an advertisement for a lawful product or service, apply the following three-part test:

a) Does the government have a substantial (not compelling) reason for the regulation?;

b) Does the restriction directly advance the government interest?; and

c) Is the restriction narrowly tailored to achieve the government interest?

Remember that the main reason commercial speech is constitutionally protected is to benefit and protect consumers.

a. Development of Commercial Speech Doctrine. [§759]

Up until the mid-1970's, commercial speech was not protected under the First Amendment, but was simply a kind of economic transaction which a government could regulate for any rational reason. Today, commercial speech is protected under the First Amendment, but receives only an intermediate level of protection.

(1) Consumer's Right to Receive Information. [§760]

Commercial speech protects the consumer's right to receive information.

Virginia State Board of Pharmacy v. Virginia Citizens Consumer Council, 425 U.S. 748 (1976). The Court invalidated a Virginia statute which prohibited the advertising of prescription drug prices by pharmacists. The law was challenged by consumers who asserted a right to receive information about prescription drug prices. **Speech**

does not lose First Amendment protection because money is spent
to disseminate it, or because the advertiser has an economic interest
in the advertisement. The consumer also has a strong interest in the
free flow of commercial information. The Court said that certain
restrictions, such as time, place, or manner regulations would be
permissible, but it did not articulate any specific test by which to
analyze commercial speech.

(2) Prevailing Test in Commercial Speech Cases. [§761]

**The Court has adopted a four-part test to use in determining
whether commercial speech is entitled to constitutional protection.**

*Central Hudson Gas & Electric Corporation v. Public Service
Commission*, 447 U.S. 557 (1980). The Court invalidated a regulation
of the New York Public Service Commission which completely banned
promotional advertising by an electrical utility company. The Court
adopted what is the prevailing analysis in commercial speech cases.
First, for commercial speech to be protected by the First Amendment,
it must be for a lawful activity, and not be misleading. If the speech
meets both those requirements, a court will ask whether the government
has a substantial (not compelling) reason for the regulation, whether
the regulation directly advances the asserted government interest, and
whether the law is narrowly tailored to achieve the government interest.
This is a form of intermediate scrutiny which is similar to the rules for
time, place, or manner restrictions (See §688, above).

(3) Government Power to Channel Advertising. [§762]

**If the government has the power to prohibit an activity, it has the
power to channel its advertising.**

*Posadas de Puerto Rico Associates v. Tourism Company of Puerto
Rico*, 478 U.S. 328 (1986). The Court upheld regulations of the
Tourism Company of Puerto Rico which prohibited advertising of
casino gambling to Puerto Rican residents, but allowed it if aimed at
non-Puerto Rican residents. The purpose of the regulations was
basically to save the locals from themselves. The Court applied the
Central Hudson analysis (previous case) to uphold the regulations. In
dicta, Justice Rehnquist said that because the government could have
totally banned the activity of casino gambling, it must, as a less
intrusive matter, have the power to restrict advertising for the activity.
This doctrine has been disavowed or discredited by a majority of the
Court in *44 Liquormart, Inc. v. Rhode Island* (See §766)

(4) Distinctions Between Commercial and Noncommercial Speech. [§763]

**Restrictions that distinguish between commercial and
noncommercial speech must be narrowly tailored to further the
government's asserted interests.**

City of Cincinnati v. Discovery Network, Inc., 113 S.Ct. 1505 (1993).
The Court invalidated a Cincinnati ordinance that required the removal
from city streets of 62 newsracks containing commercial publications,
but allowed to remain on the streets 1,500 to 2,000 newsracks which

OUTLINE

sold newspapers which were devoted primarily to covering current events. Applying the *Central Hudson* analysis (see §761), the Court said that the city's distinction between commercial and noncommercial speech was not at all related to the asserted government interests (aesthetics and safety), and thus fails the "narrowly tailored means" requirement of *Central Hudson*.

(5) Restricting on Lottery Advertising. [§764]

The federal government may place restrictions on lottery advertising by broadcasters who are licensed by a state that does not have a lottery.

U.S. v. Edge Broadcasting Co., 113 S.Ct. 2696 (1993). The Court upheld a federal law which prohibits the broadcast of lottery advertising by a broadcaster who is licensed by a state that does not have a lottery. Edge Broadcasting was licensed by North Carolina, a state that does not have a lottery. Edge operated near the border of Virginia (a state which has a lottery), and had over 90% of its listening audience in Virginia. The Court applied the *Central Hudson* test (see §761) to uphold the law. Discussing the means analysis from *Central Hudson*, Justice White, for a majority, said that commercial speech doctrine requires a fit that is not necessarily perfect, but reasonable. Does this lower the standard for the last prong of *Central Hudson*?

(6) Advertising of Alcohol Content. [§765]

Congress cannot prohibit beer labels from displaying alcohol content.

Rubin v. Coors Brewing Co., 115 S.Ct. 1585 (1995). The Court invalidated a provision of the Federal Alcohol Administration Act (FAAA) which prohibited beer labels from displaying alcohol content. Coors Brewery sued when its application for approval of a proposed beer label was turned down by the Bureau of Alcohol, Tobacco, and Firearms. Applying the test of *Central Hudson* (see §761), the Court found that Congress did have a substantial interest underlying FAAA: protecting the interests of citizens by curbing "strength wars" — competition by brewers on the basis of the alcohol strength of their beers. The Court found that the provision of the FAAA at issue did not directly advance the asserted governmental interest because other provisions of federal law allowed statements of alcohol contents in certain beer advertisements, as well as required statements of alcohol content on the labels of wines and spirits.

(7) Advertising Liquor Prices. [§766]

A State cannot pass a law which prohibits the advertisement of retail liquor prices except at the place of sale. Such a law is not saved by the Twenty-First Amendment which repealed Prohibition and gave states extensive power to regulate the sale or use of alcoholic beverages.

44 Liquormart, Inc. v. Rhode Island, 116 S.Ct. 1495 (1996). The Court invalidated a Rhode Island statute which prohibited the advertising of retail liquor prices, except at the place of sale. A majority of the Court, in a fractionated set of opinions, applied the commercial speech analysis of *Central Hudson* (See §761) and found that Rhode Island could not completely ban advertisements that provide consumers with truthful, accurate information about retail liquor prices. The Court also ruled that the Twenty-First Amendment, which repealed Prohibition and gave states great power to regulate the sale and use of alcohol, does not qualify or diminish the First Amendment protections given to commercial speech. A majority of the Court also disavowed or discredited the doctrine from the *Posadas* case (See §762) that if a government has the power to prohibit an activity, it automatically has the power to channel the advertising for that activity.

b. Advertising by Lawyers And Certified Public Accountants. [§767]

The nature of the legal profession justifies greater restrictions on lawyer advertising than on that of other professions. How dangerous are we?

(1) In-Person Solicitation for Money by a Lawyer. [§768]

States may ban in-person solicitation for money by lawyers.

Ohralik v. Ohio State Bar Association, 436 U.S. 447 (1978). The Court upheld a state bar association's suspension of a lawyer for violating a ban on in-person solicitation of clients for money. Ohralik solicited one client when she was in traction in a hospital room following an accident. He used a hidden tape recorder while soliciting another accident victim on the day she got home from the hospital. The Court said that in-person solicitation by lawyers for economic gain created too great a risk of overreaching or overriding the will of the potential client. Compare *Ohralik* with the next case.

(2) In-Person Solicitation for Money by a Certified Public Accountant. [§769]

States may not ban in-person solicitation for money by Certified Public Accountants.

Edenfield v. Fane, 113 S.Ct. 1792 (1993). The Court held that, unlike lawyers, Certified Public Accountants could not be prohibited from engaging in in-person solicitation of clients for pecuniary gain. The Court said that a CPA, unlike a lawyer, is not trained in the art of persuasion, and is therefore not as dangerous when soliciting potential clients.

(3) Board of Accountancy Cannot Censure Truthful Advertising. [§770]

States cannot censure truthful advertising by lawyers concerning their qualifications as Certified Public Accountants.

Ibanez v. Florida Department of Business and Professional Regulation, Board of Accountancy, 114 S.Ct. 2084 (1994). The Court ruled that the Florida Board of Accountancy (Board) could not, consistent with the First Amendment, censure the truthful advertising by a lawyer of the fact that she was also a Certified Public Accountant (CPA) and a Certified Financial Planner (CFP). Ibanez, in her advertising as an attorney, indicated that she was a CPA and a CFP, both of which were true. The Board censured her for "false, deceptive, and misleading" advertising. The Court ruled that this was protected commercial speech, rejecting the assertions of the Board regarding the nature of Ibanez's speech.

(4) Solicitation by Mail. [§771]

States may not prohibit a lawyer from soliciting clients by mail to join a lawsuit to vindicate personal rights.

In re Primus 436 U.S. 412 (1978). The Court ruled that South Carolina could not discipline an ACLU lawyer who solicited female clients by mail to ask if they would like to join a class-action suit which claimed that women had been illegally sterilized as a condition of continued receipt of welfare money. There was no in-person solicitation here, and the lawyer was not soliciting for economic gain. The Court said that because political expression and association are implicated in this kind of case, the government would have a tougher time justifying this regulation than one directed at a proposed commercial transaction.

(5) Restrictions on Solicitation by Mail. [§772]

A state bar association can impose a thirty-day waiting period before a lawyer can send targeted direct mail solicitation to accident victims.

Florida Bar v. Went For It, 115 S.Ct. 2371 (1995). The Court upheld Florida Bar rules prohibiting lawyers from sending targeted direct-mail solicitations to victims and their relatives for thirty days following an accident or disaster. Applying *Central Hudson* (see §761), the Court ruled that the Florida Bar had two substantial reasons for its rules: protecting the privacy of injury victims and their families, and preventing the erosion of confidence in the legal profession resulting from such solicitation. The Florida Bar rule was also narrowly tailored to achieve its objective, being limited to a fairly brief thirty-day prohibition of solicitation.

(6) Use of Illustrations in Lawyer Advertising. [§773]

A state bar may not prohibit the use of accurate and nondeceptive illustrations in newspaper ads to solicit clients.

Zauderer v. Office of Disciplinary Counsel, 471 U.S. 626 (1985). The Court held that a state bar association may not discipline a lawyer who uses accurate and nondeceptive illustrations in newspaper ads to solicit clients. Zauderer placed ads soliciting clients who might have been injured by the use of the Dalkon Shield Intrauterine Device. The Court held that Zauderer could mention in the ads the fact that he had represented other women in similar litigation. The Court also ruled that a bar association could require a lawyer who advertises contingent-fee arrangements to disclose that a client may have to pay court costs, even though no actual "fee" may be owed to the lawyer.

(7) Targeted Mailing by Lawyers for Pecuniary Gain. [§774]

A state bar may not prohibit solicitation by mail for pecuniary gain to persons who might face specific legal problems.

Shapero v. Kentucky Bar Association, 486 U.S. 466 (1988). The Court invalidated a bar association rule that prohibited lawyers from engaging in targeted mailing for pecuniary gain. A lawyer was protected in mailing truthful letters to specific persons who might face specific legal problems. The Court found that this kind of targeted mailing created no greater danger to consumers than did the newspaper ads upheld in other cases.

5. DEFAMATION. [§775]

State common law rules pertaining to the torts of slander and libel are limited by the First Amendment guarantee of freedom of speech. The Court has attempted to balance the rights of free speech and press against the right of a person not to have his or her reputation injured. When a public official or public figure is allegedly defamed, the Court makes it relatively hard for that person to recover in a defamation action. The theory here is that a public person will usually have access to the media for a rebuttal that is unavailable to a private person who has been defamed. When the allegedly defamatory statement involves a matter of public concern, the Court has also imposed more stringent requirements on the plaintiff, whether a public or private person. The theory here is that if a matter of public concern is the subject of the statement in question, the public has a strong interest in knowing about it, and speakers must be given some breathing room so as to avoid the chilling effect flowing from slander or libel suits.

> **STUDY TIP:** If you see a defamation question in a Constitutional Law class, be very careful about whether the plaintiff (the allegedly defamed person) is a public official or public figure, or whether the allegedly defamatory statement involves a matter of public concern. If either is true, the Constitution imposes some very specific restrictions.

a. First Amendment Limitations On The Law Of Defamation. [§776]

The First Amendment limits a person's ability to recover damages for defamation. The Court tries to balance the need for open, robust debate on public matters against the First Amendment interest in protecting a person's reputation.

(1) Rules for Defamation of Public Officials. [§777]

The rules to be applied to the defamation of public officials relating to their performance of public duties are: **For a public official to be able to recover in a defamation action regarding his or her conduct in office, the public official must prove all the elements of defamation required by state law; must prove that the statement contains a false statement of fact; and must prove that the statement was made with actual malice (the speaker knew that it was false, or acted with reckless disregard of its truth or falsity). The plaintiff must show actual malice by clear and convincing evidence.** These rules were set forth in *New York Times v. Sullivan*.

New York Times v. Sullivan, 376 U.S. 254 (1964). The Court reversed a state court libel judgment against the New York Times, ruling that Alabama's defamation laws did not comport with the First Amendment, and, even if they did, the evidence was insufficient to meet constitutional standards. Sullivan, the police commissioner of

Montgomery, Alabama, alleged that he was libeled by a full-page ad placed in the New York Times. The ads described the civil rights struggle in the South, and, among other things, depicted Sullivan and the Alabama police as contributing to the racial tension in Montgomery. The Court also held that the "impersonal attack on governmental operations" in the ad could not be considered a libel of the individual in charge of the police conduct.

(2) Rules for Defamation of Public Figures (as opposed to public officials). [§778]

In *Curtis Publishing Co. v. Butts*, and *Associated Press v. Walker*, the Court extended the *New* York Times protections to defamation actions in which a public figure (as opposed to a public official) is the plaintiff.

(a) Football Coach as Public Figure. [§779]

A nationally known football coach may be considered a public figure.

Curtis Publishing Company v. Butts, 388 U.S. 130 (1967). Butts, the athletic director of the University of Georgia, and a nationally known ex-football coach, brought a libel action based on a Saturday Evening Post article which claimed that he had fixed a football game between Georgia and Alabama. The Court held that Butts was a "public figure," and that the *New York Times* rules must apply.

(b) Retired Military Officer as Public Figure. [§780]

A nationally known retired military officer may be considered a public figure.

Associated Press v. Walker, 389 U.S. 889 (1967). Walker was a retired general who had a distinguished military career, and was a nationally known figure. He brought a libel action against the Associated Press, asserting that it had issued a false news dispatch which said that he had led a violent crowd against federal marshals as they were attempting to enforce a desegregation decree at the University of Mississippi. The Court held that Walker was a "public figure," and that the *New York Times* rules must apply.

(3) Constitutional Limitations on Defamation Actions When a Private Individual is the Plaintiff. [§781]

If the allegedly defamatory speech is directed at a private individual (not a public official or public figure), the plaintiff must prove: a) all the elements of defamation required by state law; b) that the statement includes a false statement of fact (not opinion); and c) that the speaker was at least negligent in not determining the falsity of the allegedly defamatory statement. With a private-figure plaintiff, another very important issue is whether the speech is on a matter of public concern (public speech), or just has to do with private matters (private speech). **If the speech is on a matter of public concern, a private-figure plaintiff must show actual malice to be able to recover punitive or presumed damages. If the speech is about a purely private matter, a private-figure plaintiff does not need to show actual malice to be able to recover punitive** or presumed damages. The idea here is that public speech is more important, thus more protected, than private speech because of its relation to public issues and the democratic process. The Court has also said that, in addition to a person being a public figure for all purposes and in all contexts, he or she may voluntarily inject himself or herself into a particular controversy, or be drawn into such a controversy, as to be a public figure for purposes limited to that one event.

(4) Speech That Involves Matters of Public Concern. [§782]

When speech involves a matter of public concern, no punitive damages may be awarded without a showing of "actual malice."

Gertz v. Robert Welch, Inc., 418 U.S. 323 (1974). The Court refused to extend the *New York Times* rules to libel actions by private persons, even when a matter of public concern is involved. Gertz, a respected attorney, claimed that he was libeled by an article in *American Opinion*, a John Birch Society magazine. The article falsely stated that Gertz had a criminal record, and that he was behind a Communist frame-up of a police officer. The police officer had been convicted of murdering a young man whose family hired Gertz to represent them in a civil lawsuit against the police. **The Court held that a state may set its own standards for liability, as long as it does not impose liability without fault, and that a state may not permit the recovery of punitive or presumed damages unless there is a showing of "actual malice."** The Court, in a later case (*Dun & Bradstreet*, §783), characterized the speech in *Gertz* as involving a matter of public conern.

(5) Speech That Does Not Involve Matters of Public Concern. [§783]

When speech does not involve a matter of public concern, punitive damages may be awarded even without a showing of "actual malice."

Dun & Bradstreet, Inc. v. Greenmoss Builders, 472 U.S. 749 (1985). **The Court ruled that a state may provide for the recovery of presumed and punitive damages in defamation cases, even without a showing of "actual malice," when the defamatory statements do not involve matters of public concern.** Five Justices distinguished *Gertz* on the basis that the defamatory statement in that case involved a matter of public concern, whereas the defamatory statement in *Dun & Bradstreet* involved no public concerns, but were simply private speech. Dun & Bradstreet, a credit reporting agency, erroneously sent a credit report to five of its subscribers that Greenmoss had filed for bankruptcy. Greenmoss filed a defamation action, recovering $50,000 in compensatory damages, and $300,000 in punitive damages. The Court ruled for Greenmoss, reasoning that speech on matters of public concern is of more value than speech on purely private matters, and the private speech in this case (the false credit report) was not entitled to the full protection of the *New York Times* standard.

(6) Newsworthy Persons. [§784]

All newsworthy persons are not public figures for First Amendment purposes.

Time, Inc. v. Firestone, 424 U.S. 448 (1976). The Court refused to apply the "public figure" label to a wealthy, socially prominent woman whose divorce was extensively reported, including in her own press conference during the pendency of divorce proceedings. Ms. Firestone sued after Time magazine reported that the divorce was granted because of extreme cruelty and adultery, a basis never relied on by the state court. **The Court said that even such newsworthy persons are not "public figures" unless they "thrust themselves to the forefront of particular public controversies."**

(7) Defamation Actions by Private Figures Against Media Defendants for Statements of Public Concern. [§785]

A private-figure plaintiff who files a defamation action against a media defendant for statements of public concern has the burden of proving the falsity of those statements.

Philadelphia Newspapers, Inc. v. Hepps, 475 U.S. 767 (1986). The main stockholder of a chain of convenience stores sued the Philadelphia Inquirer for allegedly defamatory articles which linked the plaintiff to organized crime. Under state law, the plaintiff did not have to prove the falsity of the statements; the media defendant had to prove the truth of the statements if it wished to invoke truth as a defense. The Court reversed, holding that **a private-figure plaintiff has the burden of proving the falsity of the statements, at least when there is a media defendant and the statements deal with a matter of public concern.** The Court did not consider whether the same rule should apply with a non-media defendant, and has never resolved this question.

(8) Recovery For Intentional Infliction of Emotional Distress by Public Officials or Public Figures. [§786]

Public officials or public figures may not recover for intentional infliction of emotional distress unless they can show that the publication contains a false statement of fact and was made with knowledge of the falsity or with reckless disregard as to whether it was true. That is, a public figure cannot recover for intentional infliction of emotional distress unless he or she can show a false statement made with actual malice.

Hustler Magazine v. Falwell, 485 U.S. 46 (1988). *Hustler* magazine ran an ad parody which portrayed Jerry Falwell's first time having sex as involving "a drunken incestuous rendezvous with his mother in an outhouse." Falwell sued for intentional infliction of emotional distress, asserting that the truth or falsity of the statement was irrelevant. The Court ruled against Falwell, saying that **a public figure or public official could not recover for intentional infliction of emotional distress unless he or she could show a false statement of fact which was made with knowledge of its falsity, or with reckless disregard of whether it was true.**

(9) Erroneous Reports About Private Individuals Involved in a Matter of Public Interest. [§787]

The *New York Times* standard applies to an erroneous report about private individuals involved in a matter of public interest.

Time, Inc. v. Hill, 385 U.S. 374 (1967). After the Hill family was held hostage in their home by three ex-convicts, their story was turned into a play, and Life magazine ran a story that contained pictures of scenes from the play being reenacted in the Hills' former house. The play changed some of the facts of the hostage situation, thus creating a false picture of what actually happened. The Hills sued under a New York Right to Privacy statute which created a cause of action for a person who was the subject of a work containing material and substantial falsification. The Court reversed the judgment for the Hills, ruling that **the *New York Times* standard of actual malice must be met in cases involving false reports of matters of public interest. This standard applies even though the Hills did not voluntarily place themselves in a position of notoriety or celebrity.**

(10) Use of Quotation Marks to Attribute Words to a Speaker. [§788]

The use of quotation marks to attribute words to a speaker may constitute "actual malice" if the alteration results in a material change in the meaning of what the speaker actually said. Making up quotations does not always provide evidence of actual malice.

Masson v. New Yorker Magazine, Inc., 501 U.S. 496 (1991). Masson, a prominent psychoanalyst (and a public figure), was interviewed for an article in the New Yorker. The reporter allegedly made up some quotations and attributed them to Masson, who considered them defamatory. In his libel action, Masson claimed that the deliberate alteration or creation of quotations was evidence of "actual malice." The Court said that not every alteration of quotation marks meets the *New York Times* standard of knowledge of the falsity of the statement reported. **Alteration of words will be evidence of "actual malice" only if it results in a material change in the meaning of the words spoken.**

(11) No Defamation Exception For Statements Labeled "Opinions." [§789]

Speech is not necessarily exempt from a defamation action because it is phrased in terms of being an opinion.

Milkovich v. Lorain Journal Co., 497 U.S. 1 (1990). The Court ruled that there is no special privilege that limits the application of state defamation laws to speech that is labeled "opinion." Milkovich was a high school wrestling coach whose team was involved in an altercation with another team. He testified at an investigatory hearing and in court concerning the scuffle. A local newspaper columnist wrote that "Anyone who attended the meet . . . knows in his heart that Milkovich . . . lied at the hearing after . . . having given his solemn oath to tell the truth." The newspaper argued that the article was merely an "opinion" and, as such, protected by the First Amendment. The Court held that there is no automatic, wholesale exception from defamation laws for speech that is labeled "opinion." However, **some opinion statements will be protected if they are on a matter of public concern, and are purely statements of opinion that do not imply false or defamatory facts ("I think Mayor John lied" does contain an implicit defamatory fact - Mayor Jones is a liar.). If the opinion statement does imply false or defamatory facts, the rules of** *New York Times* **and** *Gertz* **apply.**

(12) Publication of Names of Rape Victims. [§790]

A newspaper cannot be held civilly liable for the publication of the name of a rape victim when the name was lawfully obtained.

Florida Star v. B.J.F., 491 U.S. 524 (1989). The Court held that a newspaper could not be held civilly liable for the publication of the name of a rape victim which it got from a publicly released police report. Under a Florida statute, it was unlawful to publish the name of a victim of a sexual offense in any medium of mass communication. The police department inadvertently included the victim's name in a report made available to the public. The Court held that a newspaper could not be punished for publishing truthful information that was lawfully acquired. The statute was faulty because it imposed liability in all cases of publications (even when the woman might want her name published), and because it was underinclusive in restricting speech only in instruments of mass communication (leaving legal the dissemination of the name through other channels).

(13) Lawsuits by Performers Against Television Stations for Copyright Infringement. [§791]

The First Amendment does not prohibit a performer from suing a television station for broadcasting his entire act. Airing a videotape of an entire act is actionable in the same sense as using a copyrighted work without the permission of the copyright owner.

Zacchini v. Scripps-Howard Broadcasting Co., 433 U.S. 562 (1977). Scripps-Howard ran a videotape of Zacchini's entire "human cannon ball" act in which he is shot from a cannon into a net 200 feet away. Zacchini alleged an unlawful appropriation of his professional property. The Court ruled that the First Amendment does not insulate the television station from having to compensate Zacchini for using his entire act on television, just as the First Amendment would not protect the airing a copyrighted work without the permission of the copyright owner.

b. First Amendment Limitations on Defamation of Groups. [§792]

The Court, in a case from 1952, upheld a group libel law - one which punished statements which defamed a group of people, rather than an individual. While this case has never been overruled, it is of virtually no precedential value after *New* **York Times v. Sullivan and the Court's later treatment of hate speech (see** *R.A.V. v. St. Paul*, **§738.**

Beauharnais v. Illinois, 343 U.S. 250 (1952). The Court upheld a state statute which criminalized the distribution in any public place of a publication which portrayed depravity, criminality, unchastity, or lack of virtue of any class of persons of any race, color, creed, or religion, which would expose the group to contempt, derision, or obloquy. The leaflets had racist, inflammatory statements about blacks. The Court held that speech which libels a group of persons is not within the protection of the First Amendment.

F. SYMBOLIC SPEECH. [§793]

Symbolic speech is communication effected through conduct; there are no words involved. Examples are draft card burning, flag burning, cross burning, nude dancing, and what happens when you cut in front of another driver on the highway. Symbolic speech always involves both a communicative element and a conduct element. **The argument is that the government has the power to regulate the conduct component of symbolic speech, and thereby impose some incidental burden on the communicative aspect of that conduct**. As with any other speech question, look to see whether the government is totally prohibiting the symbolic speech (usually by a criminal statute), or just moving it around (imposing a time, place or manner restriction). Be aware of the strong similarity between the analysis for prohibition of symbolic speech and the time, place, manner rules.

1. PROHIBITION OF SYMBOLIC SPEECH. [§794]

If a government is prohibiting symbolic speech, use the four-part test from _U.S. v. O'Brien_ (see §797) to determine the law's constitutionality: 1) Is the law within a constitutional power of the government?; 2) Does the law further an important or substantial government interest?; 3) Is the government interest unrelated to the suppression of free expression? (Is it content-neutral?); and 4) Is the incidental restriction on speech no greater than essential to furthering the government interest? (Are the means narrowly tailored?)

2. TIME, PLACE, OR MANNER RESTRICTIONS ON SYMBOLIC SPEECH. [§795]

If a government is simply trying to channel the symbolic speech in some way, use the four-part test for evaluating time, place, or manner restrictions (see _Renton v. Playtime Theatres, Inc._ §692 above): 1) Is the law content- neutral? (The government cannot regulate the speech just because it does not like it); 2) Does the government have a significant or important reason for the law?; 3) Are the means narrowly tailored to achieve the asserted interest; and 4) Are there ample alternative channels of communication available?

> **STUDY TIP:** The only difference between the _O'Brien_ and the time, place, manner analyses is that the latter has the requirement of "ample alternative channels." The existence of ample alternative channels of communication is relevant only when the government is simply moving speech around, but is irrelevant when the government is totally prohibiting the speech. This is because when the government decides to totally prohibit symbolic speech, it does not want there to be any alternative channels of communication. For example, if the government prohibits draft card burning, it does not want anyone to engage in that activity anywhere, anytime.

3. APPLICATION OF SYMBOLIC SPEECH ANALYSIS. [§796]

a. Draft-Card Burning. [§797]
The federal government may prohibit draft-card burning.

U.S. v. O'Brien, 391 U.S. 367 (1968). The Court upheld a conviction for burning a draft card in violation of a federal law which made it a crime to knowingly destroy or mutilate a draft card. O'Brien burned his draft card on the steps of the South Boston Courthouse to protest the Vietnam war. The Court ruled that when the government criminalizes symbolic speech (communication having both speech and non-speech elements), the law will be upheld if: 1) it is within the constitutional power of the government; 2) it furthers an important or substantial government interest; 3) the government interest is unrelated to the suppression of free expression; and 4) the incidental burden on speech is no greater than essential to the furtherance of the government interest. (Today, this prong is phrased in terms of whether the means are narrowly tailored to achieve the government goal.).

b. Flag Burning. [§798]
The government may not prohibit flag desecration merely because it is done in a manner that offends onlookers.

(1) *Texas v. Johnson*, 491 U.S. 397 (1989). [§799]
The Court invalidated Gregory Johnson's conviction for violating a Texas statute making it a crime to desecrate an American flag. Under the statute, a person could not desecrate a flag in such a way that he or she knows will seriously offend one or more persons likely to discover the act of desecration. Under prevailing federal law, the respectful burning of an American flag is an accepted method of disposing of a worn or tattered flag. Johnson's actions were symbolic speech, but the Court refused to use the *O'Brien* test (previous case) because the Texas law was content based (respectful burning is permissible, disrespectful burning is not). Content-based restrictions receive strict scrutiny, and the Texas law failed that standard because criminalizing flag burning was not narrowly tailored to achieve the State's interest of preserving the flag as an unalloyed symbol of our country.

(2) *U.S. v. Eichman*, 496 U.S. 310 (1990). [§800]
The Court invalidated the federal Flag Protection Act which prohibited the desecration of the American flag. The federal law was invalid for the same reason as the state law in *Texas v.* Johnson (previous case): it was content based because federal law provides that it is appropriate to dispose of a flag by burning it respectfully.

c. Nude Dancing. [§801]
A generally applicable public nudity statute may be applied to prohibit nude dancing.

Barnes v. Glen Theatre, Inc., 501 U.S. 560 (1991). The Court upheld an Indiana statute prohibiting public nudity as applied to nude dancing, which a majority of Justices considered entitled to at least some First Amendment protection. Chief Justice Rehnquist, for himself and Justices O'Connor and Kennedy, used the *O'Brien* test (see §797) to uphold the law. The state's prohibition on public nudity in general is not related to suppression of speech, and is narrowly tailored to achieve the significant government interests of order and morality. Justice Souter also used the *O'Brien* analysis to uphold the law. Justice Scalia asserted that no First Amendment scrutiny was called for because this was simply a generally applicable law directed at conduct, not speech. (For an interesting comparison, see the discussion of Justice Scalia's opinion for the Court in a leading Free Exercise Clause case, *Employment Division v. Smith*, 494 U.S. 872 (§975) below.)

d. Signs on Public Property. [§802]
A city may prohibit the placing of all signs on public property.

Los Angeles City Council v. Taxpayers for Vincent, 466 U.S. 789 (1984). The Court used the *O'Brien* analysis (earlier in this section) to uphold a Los Angeles ordinance which prohibited placing signs on public property, including political campaign signs. The ordinance was content-neutral because it applied to all signs, and was narrowly tailored to protect the city's interest in aesthetics.

e. Overnight Sleeping in National Parks. [§803]
The federal government may prohibit persons from sleeping overnight in national parks.

Clark v. Community for Creative Non-Violence (CCNV), 468 U.S. 288 (1984). The Court upheld a National Park Service regulation which prohibited overnight sleeping in national parks. CCNV wanted to erect a tent city and sleep overnight in Lafayette Park to protest the plight of the homeless. Conceding that symbolic speech was involved, the Court applied time, place, manner analysis, and concluded that the ban on overnight sleeping was narrowly tailored to advancing the content-neutral government interest in maintaining national parks in an intact and attractive condition.

G. SPEECH IN PUBLIC SCHOOLS. [§804]

Whenever you see a speech question in a public school setting asking you to analyze the constitutionality of a restriction on student speech, be very careful of the role the school authorities play in the communicative process. Are the school officials simply allowing students to come onto school grounds and express themselves, with no hint of the school authorizing or sponsoring the speech? Are the school authorities officially providing (paying for and sponsoring) the medium of communication (such as a school newspaper or assembly)? Are the school officials taking affirmative steps to decide which books shall be removed from (or placed in) the school library?

1. NON-SCHOOL-SPONSORED SPEECH. [§805]

If the school officials are simply allowing students to come in from the outside and speak, without school sponsorship of the speech, the test is whether the student's speech materially and substantially interferes with the functioning of the school or disrupts the discipline of the school.

Tinker v. Des Moines School District, 393 U.S. 503 (1969). The Court overturned the suspensions of high school students for wearing black armbands to school to protest the Vietnam war. The ban on armbands was enacted by the school specifically in response to the anticipation of such a protest. Other symbols, such as the Iron Cross, a symbol of Nazism, were allowed, making the armband ban content based. The Court said that neither students nor teachers shed their constitutional rights to free speech at the schoolhouse gate, and that the school could not punish these students based on an undifferentiated fear or apprehension of disturbance. Requiring a case-by-case analysis, the Court said that this kind of prohibition cannot be upheld unless there is some specific factual showing that the speech would materially and substantially interfere with the functioning of the school, or disrupt the discipline of the school.

2. SCHOOL-SPONSORED SPEECH. [§806]

If the school sponsors the student speech, such as a newspaper, yearbook, or assembly, content-neutral restrictions may be imposed if they are reasonably related to a legitimate educational or pedagogical interest, such as teaching students journalistic ethics, or the ability to engage in civil discourse in public.

a. *Bethel School District v. Fraser*, 478 U.S. 675 (1986). [§807]

The Court upheld the ability of a school board to discipline a student for delivering a lewd, suggestive speech at an officially sponsored school assembly. The Court did not rely on the *Tinker* test of whether the speech materially or substantially disrupted the functioning or discipline of the school. Rather, it upheld the suspension as a reasonable method of advancing the legitimate educational goal of teaching students to speak in a civil manner in public gatherings.

b. *Hazelwood School District v. Kuhlmeier*, 484 U.S. 260 (1988). [§808]

The Court upheld the ability of a high school principal to remove from the officially sponsored high school newspaper two articles, one dealing with the experiences of pregnant students at the school, the other with the impact of divorce on students at the school. The principal thought that some of the abortion article's references to sexual activity and birth control were inappropriate for some students, and that the identities of the students involved were not adequately protected. The principal also was concerned about the identities of the divorced parents being divulged, and that the parents had no chance to respond to the allegations in the article. **The Court ruled that educators may censor or edit school-sponsored expressive activities as long as their actions are reasonably related to legitimate pedagogical concerns.** Here, the concerns were with journalistic ethics (protecting identities), and ensuring grade and age appropriateness in the school newspaper's articles.

3. REMOVAL OF BOOKS FROM A SCHOOL LIBRARY. [§809]

If a school board removes books from a school library, its decisions will be upheld if content-neutral, and reasonably related to a legitimate educational or pedagogical goal such as ensuring that vulgar or grade-inappropriate books are not available to students.

Board of Education v. Pico, 457 U.S. 853 (1982). The Court dealt with the narrow question of whether and how the First Amendment limits the ability of a school board to remove books from (not acquire books for) junior high and high school libraries. Students brought a civil rights action to challenge a school board's decision to remove certain books from school libraries on the basis that the books were "anti-American, anti-Christian, anti-Semitic, and just plain filthy." Justice Brennan wrote a plurality opinion in which he said that it would violate the First Amendment for the school board to remove the books because they disagreed with the ideas expressed. However, if the school board removed the books because they were vulgar or not suitable for students of certain ages or maturity levels, the removal would be constitutionally permissible. Judge Brennan's main point is that a school board is not free to impose a political or religious orthodoxy on students, but it may act to protect the rights and sensibilities of students. This is obviously a very fine line to draw, especially because it focuses on the motivation of the school board members in removing the books.

OUTLINE

H. PUBLIC FORUM ANALYSIS. [§810]

Public forum analysis is called for whenever a person is speaking on or by means of public property. It may be a street, park, sidewalk, ublic phitheater, school mailbox system, or any other governmentally owned and operated property. **The goal of public forum analysis is to balance a person's right to use public property for speech purposes against the government's right to maintain the property for its intended use.** There are three ways that public forums may come into existence: 1) by tradition, some public places have become forums for speech purposes (streets, parks, sidewalks); 2) the government may designate publicly owned property to be a forum; and 3) speakers, usually protestors or demonstrators, may commandeer publicly owned property for use as a forum. The Court has set forth the following guidelines for each of these types of public forum.

1. TRADITIONAL PUBLIC FORUM. [§811]

A traditional public forum is government property which has historically been used for speech purposes. Public streets, sidewalks, parks, and public amphitheaters are examples of traditional public forums. In a traditional public forum, the government may not prohibit all communicative activity. In other words, **speakers have a presumptive right of access to traditional public forums for speech purposes. Given this presumptive right of access, what a government usually does is channel the speech in certain ways by employing a time, place, or manner restriction. (See section §688, above).** To be valid, a time, place or manner restriction must be content neutral, narrowly tailored to achieve a significant or important government interest, and leave open ample alternative channels of communication. If a government applies a content-based restriction, the law must be narrowly tailored to achieve a compelling government interest.

2. DESIGNATED PUBLIC FORUM. [§812]

A state may designate property to be a public forum. Once having done so, it may un-designate it as a public forum, returning the property to its prior, non-speech use.

a. Designated Open Forum. [§813]

If the government designates the property as an open, or unlimited public forum, the same rules apply as in the traditional public forum: guaranteed access exists during the duration of the designation as

an open forum; content-based restrictions get strict scrutiny; and properly drawn time, place, or manner restrictions are permissible.

b. Designated Limited Forum. [§814]

If the government designates the property as a limited or non-public forum, the following rules apply: properly drawn time, place, or manner restrictions are permissible; content-based restrictions get strict scrutiny; and total or selective restrictions (including exclusion) of speakers are permissible if they are rationally related to the legitimate government interest in maintaining the normal, non-speech use of the public property. Remember that these total or selective restrictions on speakers may not be based on government dislike of the speech; they must be justified by some content-neutral reason pertaining to the normal operation of the public place.

Greer v. Spock, 424 U.S. 828 (1976). The Court upheld regulations at Fort Dix which prohibited speeches and demonstrations of a partisan political nature, but allowed other civilian speakers and entertainers onto the base. Fort Dix is not a traditional public forum, so there is no presumptive right of access to the base for speech purposes. The regulation forbidding political speech was rationally related to the legitimate military objective of keeping military activities free from partisan politics. **If the base authorities had allowed Republican speakers in and kept Democratic speakers out (or vice-versa), that action would be viewpoint-based (preferring one kind of speech over another within a category of speakers), subject to strict scrutiny, and in all probability invalid.**

3. COMMANDEERED PUBLIC FORUM. [§815]

A speaker may go onto public property to speak even though the property is not a traditional public forum, and the government has not designated the property to be a forum for speech purposes. By definition, these speakers are trying to commandeer public property for speech purposes, regardless of the normal, non-speech function of the place. **In these cases, the Court has in the past (it is doubtful that a majority of the Court would do so today) looked to see if the manner of expression is basically incompatible with the normal activity of the government property at the time the speech is engaged in. If they are compatible, the government property will be considered a public forum; if not, the property will not be treated as a public forum, and reasonable restrictions on speech will be upheld.** The idea here is that the government should not have complete power to exclude speakers from public property by designating the property closed to speakers entirely, or open to only a small number of speakers whose speech the government deems compatible with the normal use of the place. **If the Court does not recognize the creation of new forums through the "commandeering" process, a government may designate all public property, other than traditional forums, to be off limits to speakers.**

Brown v. Louisiana, 447 U.S. 323 (1966). The Court reversed breach-of-the peace convictions of five black men who sat, in "silent and reproachful presence," in the reading room of a public library to protest the racial segregation of library facilities in the town of Clinton, Louisiana. Justice Fortas, writing for himself and two other Justices, said that this symbolic speech was protected by the First Amendment because there was no evidence that use of the library by others was disrupted by this silent protest. In other words, these protesters "commandeered" the public library for communicative purposes, and their speech was protected because of its compatibility with the normal use of the place.

> **STUDY TIP:** If you get a question where the speech has taken place on or by means of government property, determine which kind of forum the facts describe, then apply the applicable rules. To a large extent, the label controls the analysis.

4. APPLICATION OF PUBLIC FORUM ANALYSIS. [§816]

a. Government Power to Regulate Public Places. [§817]

The government does not have the same power to exclude speakers from public property that owners of private property enjoy.

Hague v. C.I.O., 307 U.S. 496 (1939). **The Court rejected the argument that a government's ownership of property confers on it the same power to exclude speakers as that enjoyed by the owner of private property.** Justice Roberts, in a plurality opinion, said: "Wherever the title of streets and parks may rest, they have immemorially been held in trust for the use of the public and, time out of mind, have been used for purposes of assembly, communicating thoughts between citizens, and discussing public questions Such use of the streets and public places has, from ancient times, been a part of the privileges, immunities, rights, and liberties of citizens."

b. Handbilling on Public Streets. [§818]

A city may not totally prohibit handbilling on public streets.

Schneider v. Irvington, 306 U.S. 628 (1939). The Court reversed convictions for violating city ordinances prohibiting the distribution of handbills in the streets or other public places. The Court said that a government may regulate the conduct of those using the streets, so long as their right to speak or distribute literature is not abridged. The city's interest in preventing litter was not sufficiently important to justify a total ban on distributing handbills; less drastic means, such as punishing litterers, were available.

c. Protesting on Jail Grounds. [§820]

A state may prohibit protesting on jail grounds.

Adderley v. Florida, 385 U.S. 39 (1966). The Court affirmed trespass convictions of students who protested on the grounds of a county jail that were reserved for jail uses. The Court said that, at least in this context, the state has the same right as the owner of private property to preserve its property for its intended use. The dissenting justices considered the jailhouse grounds to be every bit as much a seat of government, and therefore a public forum, as a statehouse, courthouse, or legislative chamber.

d. Picketing Near Schools. [§821]

A city may not selectively prohibit picketing near a school.

Chicago Police Department v. Mosley, 408 U.S. 92 (1972). The Court invalidated an ordinance which prohibited all picketing on a public sidewalk within 150 feet of a school building, from 30 minutes before school starts until 30 minutes after it ends, except for peaceful labor picketing, which was allowed during the school day. This was a content-based distinction, based on the message on a picket sign. The Court emphasized that selective exclusions from a public forum may not be based on content alone, nor may they be justified by reference to content alone.

e. Noise Near Schools. [§822]

A state may impose a generally applicable ban on noise near schools.

Grayned v. Rockford, 408 U.S. 104 (1972). The Court upheld convictions under an anti-noise ordinance which prohibited anyone on public or private property adjacent to a school from making any noise which disrupts the functioning of the school. About 200 persons were 100 feet away from a high school, protesting the administration's failure to act on complaints of black students at the school. In assessing the reasonableness of the ordinance, the Court said that the crucial question is whether the manner of expression is basically incompatible with the normal activity of a particular place at a particular time.

f. Access to School Mailbox Systems. [§823]

A school board may grant selective access to a school mailbox system.

Perry Educational Association v. Perry Local Educators' Association, 406 U.S. 37 (1983). The Court rejected Equal Protection and First Amendment challenges to an agreement between a school board and the union that represented the teachers in the district. Under the contract, the union had access to the school mailbox system (a designated limited forum), but another union, which lost the election to represent the teachers, did not have access. The Court said that the school district had not created an open public forum, so reasonable, content-neutral restrictions are permissible. The Court found that the loser union was not excluded because of any message it might convey, but because of its status, which was not being a member of the official school community. The Court upheld the ability of the school district to allow some outside groups (such as the Cub Scouts, YMCAs, and parochial schools) to use the mailbox system, because those decisions were based on the status or nature of the groups, not the content of their speech.

g. Signs Near Embassies. [§824]

The District of Columbia may not prohibit signs near embassies merely because the messages on the signs may be offensive to persons in the embassies.

Boos v. Barry, 485 U.S. 312 (1988). The Court invalidated a District of Columbia ordinance prohibiting the display of any sign within 500 feet of a foreign embassy if the sign tends to bring that foreign government into public odium or public disrepute. The Court considered this a content-based restriction on political speech in a public forum; the ordinance was directed only at the emotive impact of the speech on the listener - something that is not a "secondary effect" for purposes of free speech analysis. The Court upheld another part of the ordinance which, as narrowed by the Court of Appeals, prohibited congregating within 500 feet of an embassy when the police reasonably believe that the congregation of people poses a threat to the security or peace of the embassy. This regulation merely restricted the place and manner of speech in a public forum, and was related to achieving the significant government interest of preventing security threats to embassies.

h. Picketing in Front of a Residence. [§825]
A city can prohibit focused picketing in front of a residence.

Frisby v. Schultz, 487 U.S. 474 (1988). The Court upheld an ordinance which prohibited "focused picketing," which is picketing that takes place solely in front of and is directed at a particular residence. The ordinance was directed at anti-abortion protesters who picketed outside a doctor's home for an hour and a half. This ordinance was upheld as a valid place or manner restriction, advancing the significant government interest in protecting the privacy rights of residents, and leaving the picketers free to march up and down the street with their picket signs.

i. Fees for Use of Public Property. [§826]
A city cannot require payment of a fee to use public property.

Forsyth County v. The Nationalist Movement, 505 U.S. 123 (1992). The Court invalidated an ordinance that required an applicant for a permit to use public property for a parade, assembly, or any other use to pay a fee up to $1,000 per day, with the county administrator setting the amount to cover the cost of maintaining public order. In effect, the amount of the fee was determined by the content of the speech; the more controversial the speech, the more it would cost to police the area. The ordinance also gave the administrator too much discretion in deciding whether to charge any fee at all, or to determine its amount.

j. Airport Terminals. [§827]
Government-owned airport terminals are not public forums for speech purposes; therefore, the government may prohibit activities that are inconsistent with the use of the terminals.

International Society for Krishna Consciousness v. Lee, 505 U.S. 672 (1992). **The Court held that a government- owned airport terminal is not a public forum.** The Court upheld as reasonable a Port Authority regulation forbidding the repetitive solicitation of money within the terminals. It invalidated a regulation forbidding the distribution of literature in the airport terminals. Chief Justice Rehnquist said that publicly- owned airport terminals are not traditional public forums, nor did the Port Authority designate them as public forums. As a result, restrictions on speech will be analyzed to see if they are reasonably related to maintaining the normal use of the place. The ban on repetitive solicitation of money was rationally related to keeping the airport functioning; the ban on distribution of literature was not. The Court reasoned that repetitive solicitation of money is considerably more disruptive of pedestrian traffic within the terminals than is the simple distribution of literature.

5. DESIGNATED FORUMS AND RELIGIOUS SPEAKERS. [§828]

If a government entity, such as a university or a school district, opens its facilities to speakers, it may not exclude religious speakers from using the forum. It does not establish religion, in contravention of the First Amendment, to allow religious speech along with other kinds of speech.

a. Religious Student Groups at Universities. [§829]

A university may not exclude religious student groups from using its facilities when other student groups have been granted access to university buildings for speech purposes.

Widmar v. Vincent, 454 U.S. 263 (1981). The Court ruled that a state university could not exclude religious groups from using its facilities once the university opened its rooms to registered student groups for speech purposes. The Court rejected the argument that this content-based exclusion was justified by the state's interest in avoiding the establishment of religion that would result from allowing the religious group to speak. Simply permitting the religious groups to speak, along with numerous other student groups, does not equal endorsement or establishment of religion.

b. Religious Student Groups in High School. [§830]

Public schools may not exclude religious student groups from using school facilities when other high school groups have been granted access to school facilities for speech purposes.

Board of Education v. Mergens, 496 U.S. 226 (1990). The Court upheld the federal Equal Access Act, which prohibits public schools receiving federal funds from making content-based exclusions of students from school facilities which have been opened for speech purposes. The school allowed a number of non- curricular groups to use the facilities, but refused to allow the Christian Club to use a room. Following *Widmar* (previous case), the Court said that there is no establishment of religion effected by including the Christian Club with other student organizations.

c. Members of the Public Who Engage in Religious Speech. [§831]

A school may not exclude members of the public who engage in religious speech from using school facilities when other public groups have been granted access to school facilities for speech purposes.

Lamb's Chapel v. Center Moriches Union Free School District, 113 S.Ct. 2141 (1993). The Court ruled that a school which opened its facilities to the general public for speech purposes could not deny a church group access to the school property. The school had designated its property as a limited forum, but had denied access to the religious group because of the content of its speech. As in *Widmar*, the Court rejected the argument that the school had a compelling interest in avoiding the establishment of religion that would result from allowing the religious group to use the facilities. Inclusion of religious speakers along with numerous others does not violate the Establishment Clause.

d. Religious Student Publications. [§832]

A school may not deny funding to a religious student publication if it funds other student journals.

Rosenberger v. Rector and Visitors of the University of Virginia, 115 S.Ct. 2510 (1995). The Court ruled that the University of Virginia could not deny funding for the publication of a recognized student group's journal on the basis that the journal was religious in content. The university set up a program under which payments are made from a Student Activities Fund for the publication of student journals and magazines. When a religious student group, otherwise eligible for funding, applied for funding of its newspaper, Wide Awake: A Christian Perspective at the University of Virginia, the university turned it down, asserting that to fund a religious student publication would violate the Establishment Clause. The Court, relying on *Widmar* (see §829) and *Lamb's Chapel* (see §831), said that a university does not establish religion by granting access to its facilities to a wide spectrum of student groups, even if some of them are religious. The Court saw no difference between a university granting access to its facilities (*Widmar*) and a university funding the publication of student journals; both cases involved the university creating a limited forum for the purpose of enhancing diversity of student expression.

I. THE FIRST AMENDMENT AND THE ELECTORAL PROCESS: REGULATION OF BALLOT ACCESS, AND LIMITATIONS ON CONTRIBUTIONS AND EXPENDITURES. [§833]

Participation in the electoral process, by voting, becoming a candidate, or spending money to influence an election, involves the fundamental rights of free speech and freedom of political association. The government interests in regulating these activities are to enhance equality of access to the electoral system and to prevent corruption or the appearance of corruption in the electoral process.

1. RESTRICTIONS ON VOTING AND BECOMING A CANDIDATE. [§834]

The Court scrutinizes very carefully any state or local law which interferes with a person's right to become a candidate, or a political party's right to set the qualifications to participate in party primaries.

a. Filing Deadlines. [§835]

A state cannot have different filing deadlines for independent candidates and major-party candidates.

Anderson v. Celebrezze, 460 U.S. 780 (1983). The Court invalidated an Ohio statute which required independent candidates for President to file their nominating petitions in March to be able to appear on the general ballot in November. The March filing deadline preceded by a number of months the time when major parties chose their candidates for the general election ballot. **This requirement violated the First Amendment right of political association, and did not adequately advance the state's interest in political stability or voter awareness.**

b. Requirements to Vote In a Party Primary. [§836]

State law cannot require party membership to vote in a party primary.

Tashjian v. Republican Party of Connecticut, 479 U.S. 208 (1986). **The Court invalidated a Connecticut law which required voters in a party primary to be members of the party.** The law was challenged by the state Republican Party which had a rule allowing independent voters to vote in Republican primary elections for state and federal offices. **The Court ruled that the state law violated the First Amendment rights of political association of members of the Republican Party of Connecticut.** The Court rejected the state's asserted interests of avoiding administrative burdens, minimizing voter confusion, and protecting the integrity of the two-party system.

c. Political Parties Supporting Primary Candidates. [§837]

State law cannot prohibit political parties from supporting or opposing candidates in party primaries.

Eu v. San Francisco County Democratic Central Committee, 489 U.S. 214 (1989). The Court invalidated a state law which prohibited political parties from supporting or opposing candidates in party primaries. Applying strict scrutiny, **the Court ruled that there was no compelling state interest that justified the abridgment of the fundamental right of political association.**

2. LIMITATIONS ON CAMPAIGN CONTRIBUTIONS AND EXPENDITURES. [§838]

Be very careful to distinguish a direct monetary contribution to a candidate from an independent expenditure on the candidate's behalf. The rationale for the distinction is that even though you may spend your own money however you want to help someone get elected, the government has an important interest in avoiding the appearance of a contributor buying a candidate by contributing money to that candidate. Hence, the Court allows greater limitations on contributions to candidates than it does on expenditures.

The Court also distinguishes between contributions to a candidate (restrictions allowed) and contributions to a political action committee (PAC) supporting a ballot referendum such as lowering property taxes (restrictions not allowed). The rationale for this distinction is that while you can (appear to) own a candidate, you cannot own an idea.

a. Campaign Contributions. [§839]

The federal government may place limits on contributions to candidates for federal office.

Buckley v. Valeo, 424 U.S. 1 (1976). **The Court upheld provisions of the Federal Election Campaign Act which limited contributions to a candidate for federal office; it invalidated provisions of the Act which limited independent expenditures on behalf of a candidate.** Using First Amendment analysis, the Court said that the $1,000 limitation on expenditures for a candidate substantially restrains the quality and diversity of political speech, whereas the same limit on contributions to a candidate involves little direct restraint on political expression, and is necessary to achieve the government interest in preventing corruption and the appearance of corruption.

b. Ballot Referenda. [§840]

States cannot limit the ability of corporations to spend money to influence certain ballot referenda.

First National Bank v. Bellotti, 435 U.S. 765 (1978). The Court invalidated a Massachusetts law that criminalized certain expenditures by banks or business corporations to influence the vote on any referendum submitted to the voters, other than one materially affecting the property, business, or assets of the corporation. Asserting that the political speech of corporations is at the heart of the First Amendment, the Court found the state law to be content-based, and not supported by any compelling government interest.

c. Expenditure of Corporate or Union Funds for Political Purposes. [§841]

Federal law can require the use of segregated funds by corporations or unions for political purposes.

Federal Election Commission v. National Right To Work Committee, 459 U.S. 197 (1982). The Court upheld a federal law which prohibits corporations or labor unions from making contributions or expenditures to candidates in federal elections. However, the entities can set up segregated funds to be used for political purposes, but a corporation without capital stock can only solicit contributions to such funds from its members. This ban on outside solicitations was upheld as necessary to prevent corruption (or the appearance of corruption) resulting from large financial contributions to candidates. This case is different from *Bellotti* (previous case) in that *Bellotti* dealt with corporate contributions to support a ballot referendum rather than a candidate.

d. Campaign Expenditures By Political Action Committees. Federal law cannot limit expenditures by political action committees to support presidental candidates.

Federal Election Commission v. National Conservative Political Action Committee, 470 U.S. 480 (1985). **The Court invalidated a federal law which placed a $1,000 limit on expenditures by political action committees to support a presidential candidate.** Relying on the *Buckley v. Valeo* distinction between contributions and expenditures, the Court found no compelling government interest to justify this restriction on the political association rights of PAC members.

e. Campaign Expenditures By Ideological Corporations. [§842]

Federal law cannot limit political expenditures by non- profit, ideological corporations.

(1) *Federal Election Commission v. Massachusetts* Citizens for Life, 479 U.S. 238 (1986). The Court invalidated a federal law which prohibited corporations from using general treasury funds to make expenditures in relation to any election for public office. Under the law, expenditures by corporations must be made from separate, segregated funds. Massachusetts Citizens for Life (MCFL) is a nonprofit corporation dedicated solely to advancing pro-life positions and candidates. It has no connection to any business corporation. MCFL used general treasury funds to distribute a newsletter urging people to support pro-life candidates in an upcoming election. The Court said that the government could not restrict this kind of speech by a nonprofit, ideological corporation. **Three factors are important in immunizing MCFL's speech from government intrusion: 1) The corporation was formed solely to promote political ideas, and cannot engage in business activities; 2) no shareholders have a claim on the assets of the corporation; and 3) MCFL was not established by a business corporation or labor union, and it will not accept contributions from these entities.**

(2) *Austin v. Michigan State Chamber of Commerce*, **494 U.S. 652 (1990).** The Court rejected First and Fourteenth Amendment challenges to a Michigan law which prohibits corporations (with the exception of media corporations) from making contributions to candidates, or expenditures for or against candidates. Expenditures may be made from a segregated fund. The Michigan Chamber of Commerce (MCC), a corporation which served both political and business purposes, and whose membership is made up of primarily for-profit corporations, challenged the law. Using the three factors from *Massachusetts Citizens for Life* (MCFL) (previous case), the Court distinguished MCFL from the MCC, primarily on the basis that MCC serves business purposes and has business members. The government interest served by the law is to prevent huge corporate expenditures from skewing the political process, especially when the amount of money spent by a corporation is unrelated to the degree of political support that may exist among the members. The Court also rejected the argument that the exemption for media corporations violated the Equal Protection Clause. The Court reasoned that different treatment of media and non-media corporations is constitutional because they are not similarly situated. The state has a compelling reason to protect the news-gathering and editorial functions of media corporations, an interest not present with non-media corporations.

f. Campaign Expenditures By Political Parties. [§843]
Federal law cannot limit the expenditures of a political party in connection with the general election campaign of a congressional candidate.

Colorado Republican Federal Campaign Committee v. Federal Election Commission, ___ S.Ct. ___ (1996). The Court invalidated a provision of the Federal Election Campaign Act which imposed dollar limitations on political party expenditures made independently by the party to support the general election campaign of a congressional candidate. The Court ruled that the federal law could not be applied to limit the expenditures of a committee of the Colorado Republican Party which had bought radio advertisements attacking the likely candidate of the Democratic Party.

J. RESTRICTIONS ON SPEECH OF GOVERNMENT EMPLOYEES. [§845]

When a government restricts the speech of its employees, the Court must balance the free speech rights of the employee against the interest of the government as employer in maintaining the functioning of the workplace. Problems arise because the government is wearing two hats: it is an employer, just as any other entity might be, but it is also the sovereign, bound by constitutional limitations that do not apply to private employers. The fear is that the government, wearing its employer hat, may silence speech solely because that speech is critical of government policies or officials. **In this area, it is also important to distinguish between speech on matters of public concern and speech that is purely private. Speech of government employees that is on a matter of public concern is more important than purely private speech; disciplining or firing government employees for speech on a matter of public concern carries the danger of censorship.**

1. LOYALTY OATHS. [§846]

Loyalty oaths will be upheld as long as they simply require an affirmation by the employee to abide by the Constitution. They will be suspect if they are used to punish someone for membership in a subversive organization; that kind of oath would infringe upon the employee's freedom of political association.

a. Loyalty Oath as Violative of the Freedom of Association. [§847]

Loyalty oaths that punish a person solely for membership in a subversive organization violate the freedom of association.

Elfbrandt v. Russell, 384 U.S. 11 (1966). The Court invalidated an Arizona statute which required all state employees to take a loyalty oath, and which required the dismissal of any employee who took the oath and then remained or became a member of the Communist Party. **The statute violated an employee's freedom of association because it required the dismissal of any employee who was a member of a subversive group, even though the person had no specific intent to further the illegal goals of the organization.** A person cannot be punished for mere "passive" membership in a subversive organization.

b. Loyalty Oath to Uphold the Constitution. [§848]
Loyalty oaths to uphold the Constitution are permissible.

Cole v. Richardson, 405 U.S. 676 (1972). The Court upheld a loyalty oath which Massachusetts required its employees to sign. The oath bound the employee to uphold the Constitution, and to oppose the overthrow of the government by violence or any illegal or unconstitutional method. Richardson was fired from a job at a state hospital for refusing to sign the oath. The Court said that the oath simply required employees to abide by constitutional processes, and did not punish anyone for any membership or association.

2. POLITICAL ACTIVITY AND POLITICAL PATRONAGE IN PUBLIC EMPLOYMENT SITUATIONS. [§849]

Two issues run through the cases in this area: the ability of a government employer to make employment decisions based on the political affiliation of an employee; and the ability of a government employer to discipline employees for their speech. The Court tries to balance the rights of the employee to belong to the political party of his or her choice and to speak on the job, against the ability of the government to run the workplace. **A public employee's speech will be protected if it is on a matter of public concern, and does not disrupt the workplace. Speech on a matter of private concern will not be protected in the same**

manner; discipline or dismissal for private speech is simply an ordinary employment decision.

a. Politicial Activity of Government Employees. [§850]

The Court has upheld some restrictions on the political activity of government employees on the theory that such limitations are needed to prevent corruption or the appearance of corruption in government.

(1) Speech on Matters of Public Concern. [§851]

Government employees retain the right to speak on matters of public concern.

(a) *Pickering v. Board of Education*, 391 U.S. 563 (1968). [§852]

The Court ruled that a government employee does not give up First Amendment rights to comment on public issues by virtue of public employment. The Court balances the speech rights of public employees against the government's interests in the functioning of the workplace. In *Pickering*, a teacher published a letter in a newspaper that criticized school board policies. **The Court ruled that since the comments were on matters of public concern, and did not disrupt the functioning of the workplace, the teacher could not be punished for the speech.**

(b) *Connick v. Meyers*, 461 U.S. 138 (1983). [§853]

The Court upheld the firing of an assistant district attorney for circulating a questionnaire regarding office policy. The employee sued under 42 U.S.C. §1983, claiming that she was fired for exercising her right to free speech. **The Court held that when an employee does not speak on matters of public concern, but only on issues of personal interest, a federal court ordinarily should not intervene in the dispute.** To whatever limited extent the speech touched on public concern, Meyers' firing was justified by her supervisor's fear that her speech would disrupt the functioning of the office.

(c) *Rankin v. McPherson*, 483 U.S. 378 (1987). [§854]

The Court overturned the firing of a clerical employee in a constable's office when she remarked, after an assassination attempt on President Reagan, "If they go for him again, I hope they get him." The Court held that **this was speech on a matter of public concern, and that under the appropriate balancing approach, there was insufficient evidence that her comment disrupted the functioning of the office.**

(d) *Waters v. Churchill*, 114 S.Ct. 1878 (1993). [§855]

The Court upheld the firing of a nurse from a public hospital for comments she made to a co-worker criticizing her supervisor and hospital policies regarding the use of nursing personnel. There was some dispute about what was said, but the hospital investigated, thought the speech disruptive, and fired Churchill. The Court reiterated the *Connick* test that a public employee's speech is protected if it is on a matter of public concern, and does not unduly disrupt the functioning of the workplace. **The Court said that the** ***Connick*** **test should be applied to what the employer reasonably thought the employee said, rather then to what the trier-of-fact ultimately determines was said.**

(e) ***Board of County Commissioners v. Umbehr,*** **___ S.Ct. ___ (1996).** The Court ruled that **independent contractors may not have their government contracts terminated in retaliation for their speech on matters of public concern unless, under** *Pickering* **(See §852), that speech disrupts the functioning of the workplace.** In *Umbehr*, a trash hauler who criticized the Board of County Commissioners had his at-will contract terminated, and alleged that the termination was in retaliation for his speech. The Court applied *Pickering*, but adjusted the balance to reflect the fact that the government's and the individual's interests may be less strong in an independent contractor case than in the case of a regular employment relationship.

(2) Political Activity By Federal Employees. [§856]
Federal law can prohibit federal employees from engaging in political activity.

U.S. Civil Service Commission v. National Association of Letter Carriers, 413 U.S. 548 (1973). **The Court upheld a federal law which prohibited federal employees from taking an active part in political management or political campaigns. The prohibition is content neutral, applying equally to all partisan activities and all racial, ethnic, and religious groups.** Congress had overriding interests in removing the appearance of graft and corruption from the governmental process, and in ensuring that the operation of government is unaffected by partisan pressures.

(3) Honoraria for Speeches. [§857]
Congress cannot prohibit low-level federal employees from accepting honoraria for speeches that do not relate to their government employment.

U.S. v. National Treasury Employees Union, 115 S.Ct. 1003 (1995). The Court invalidated, as applied to low-level federal employees, a provision of the Ethics in Government Act which broadly prohibited federal employees from accepting any compensation for making speeches or writing articles. The speeches and articles to which the prohibition had been applied concerned matters totally unrelated to government employment or public concerns (religion, history, dance, the environment). The Court said that while there may be some evidence of actual or apparent impropriety by Senators, Representatives, and high-level executive officials, there was insufficient evidence to extend the honorarium-ban to low level federal employees (below the rank of GS-16) who had at best a negligible ability to misuse their power by conferring favors in return for being compensated for a speech or article.

b. Political Patronage in Government Employment. [§858]

Employment decisions based on political affiliation will be upheld if the government can show that they are necessary to the effective performance of the job.

(1) Dismissal From Government Employment Because of Political Affiliation. [§859]

Low-level public employees may not be dismissed merely because of their party affiliation.

(a) *Elrod v. Burns*, 427 U.S. 347 (1976). [§860]

The Court invalidated a system of political patronage under which a new sheriff (a Democrat) fired a number of employees because they were not Democrats. **These partisan dismissals violated the employee's First Amendment rights of free speech and political association.** Justice Brennan, in dicta, said that patronage dismissals from high-level policymaking positions may be permissible to advance the interest of political loyalty from high-level associates.

(b) *Branti v. Finkel*, 445 U.S. 507 (1980). [§861]

The Court ruled that two assistant public defenders could not be fired because they were of a different political party than the new Public Defender. **The Court conceded that party affiliation may be an acceptable requirement for some government positions, and said that the test is whether the hiring authority can show that party affiliation is an appropriate requirement for the effective performance of the public office involved.**

(c) *O'Hare Truck Service, Inc. v. Northlake*, ___ S.Ct. ___ (1996). [§862]

The Court extended the principles of *Elrod* and *Branti* (previous cases) to cover independent contractors (as opposed to regular employees). In this case, a city took a tow truck service off the list of companies hired by the city on a contract basis. The reason for the removal was that the company's owner refused to contribute to the mayor's reelection campaign, instead supporting the mayor's opponent. The Court reiterated the rule that **a government employee or contractor cannot be dismissed because of party affiliation unless the government can show that party affiliation is an appropriate requirement for the effective performance of the public office involved.**

(2) Political Affiliation Affecting Employment Decisions Other Than Dismissal. [§863]

Party affiliation may not be considered in any employment decision involving low-level employees.

Rutan v. Republican Party of Illinois, 497 U.S. 62 (1990). The Court held violative of the First Amendment a governor's executive order which imposed a political patronage system on promotion, transfer, recall, and hiring decisions of low-level government employees. **The Court extended the rule from the dismissal practices of *Elrod* and**

Branti (see §§860, 861) to all employment practices regarding low-level public employees.

K. THE RIGHT NOT TO SPEAK: FREEDOM FROM GOVERNMENT COERCION, SUBSIDIES, OR TAXES. [§864]

There is no enumerated constitutional right not to speak. However, in a number of cases, the Court has said that there is a right to be free from government compelled speech, whether compelled by a regulation, a subsidy, or a tax. One of the basic tenets of the First Amendment is that government cannot force anyone to speak, or to endorse any political, religious, or social orthodoxy. An essential part of the theory in these cases is that the First Amendment protects not only freedom of speech, but also freedom of belief and freedom of conscience. In the following cases, be aware of the methods a government may use to try to favor some speech over others.

1. THE RIGHT TO BE FREE FROM COMPELLED SPEECH. [§865]

The government may not force a person to speak, or to affirm any prescribed belief or idea. The unenumerated right not to speak is based in the free speech protections of the First Amendment. Be aware that if a person has religious objections to expressing a prescribed idea, the religion clauses of the First Amendment are also relevant. Compelled government speech may establish religion (being forced to recite an obviously sectarian prayer), or may violate the free exercise rights of a person who has religious scruples against expressing a particular message (see *Wooley v. Maynard*, §867).

a. Pledge of Allegiance. [§866]
A state cannot require students to recite the Pledge of Allegiance.

West Virginia State Board of Education v. Barnette, 319 U.S. 624 (1943). The Court invalidated a state law which required all students to salute and pledge allegiance to the flag of the United States. Failure to do so could result in expulsion from school. Asserting that the compulsory salute and pledge requires affirmation of a belief and an attitude of mind, the Court said that the Bill of Rights, which protects a person's right to speak his or her mind, cannot allow the government to compel a person to utter what is not on his or her mind.

b. State Motto On a License Plate. [§867]
A state cannot force someone to display the state motto on a license plate.

Wooley v. Maynard, 430 U.S. 705 (1977). The Court invalidated a New Hampshire law which required passenger vehicles to have license plates carrying the state motto, "Live Free or Die." The Court, through Chief Justice Burger, said that the freedom of thought protected by the First Amendment encompasses both the right to speak freely and the right to refrain from speaking at all. Private vehicles cannot be commandeered as mobile billboards for a state's ideological message.

c. Utility Companies. [§868]
A state cannot require a utility company to disseminate speech of a consumer group.

Pacific Gas & Electric Co. v. Public Utilities Commission, 475 U.S. 1 (1986). The Court ruled that a state may not require a private utility company to include in its billing envelopes speech of a

OUTLINE

consumer-advocacy group with which the utility disagrees. For years the utility company had sent a newsletter out with its bills. The newsletter included political editorials and information about utility services. The state Public Utilities Commission, in the interest of "equal access," required that an advocacy group be able to use the billing envelope four times a year to disseminate their message. The Court said this order would force the company to associate with speech with which it might disagree - a violation of the company's First Amendment rights.

d. Cable Television. [§869]

Federal law can require cable television systems to carry certain programming.

Turner Broadcasting System v. Federal Communications Commission I, 114 S.Ct. 2445 (1994). The Court reviewed the federal Cable Television Consumer Protection Act, under which Congress required cable television systems to devote a specified portion of their channels to the transmission of local commercial and public broadcast stations. The Court ruled that these "must-carry" provisions were content neutral, incidental burdens on speech, which should receive intermediate scrutiny. The Court refused to extend to cable television the less rigorous standard of review applicable to radio and over-the-air television broadcasting. The Court remanded the case to federal district court to allow the government to demonstrate that the must-carry provisions were necessary to protect the economic health of local broadcasting.

Turner Broadcasting System v. Federal Communications Commission II, 117 S.Ct. 1174 (1997). The Court affirmed the opinion of the District Court that there was substantial evidence supporting the judgment of Congress that the must-carry provisions further the following important governmental interests: 1) preserving the benefits of free, over-the-air local broadcast television, 2) promoting the dissemination of information from a multiplicity of sources, and 3) promoting fair competition in the television programming market. The Court also ruled that the must-carry provisions do not burden substantially more speech than is necessary to achieve the government's interests.

e. Private Parades. [§870]

A state cannot apply its public accommodations law to force parade organizers to include a group they do not wish to include.

Hurley v. Irish-American Gay, Lesbian and Bisexual Group of Boston, 115 S.Ct. 2338 (1995). The Court invalidated the application of Massachusetts' public accommodations law, which prohibits discrimination on the basis of sexual orientation, to private parade organizers who wanted to exclude from their parade a group who wished to proclaim pride in their homosexual and bisexual identities. The South Boston Allied War Veterans Council, a private group, was authorized by the City of Boston to organize the annual St. Patrick's Day parade. The Council refused to allow the Irish-American Gay, Lesbian and Bisexual Group of Boston (GLIB) to march in the parade. A state court found that the Council's refusal to allow GLIB to march in the parade violated a state law which prohibited discrimination based on sexual orientation in places of public accommodation. The Court ruled that parades are a form of expression protected under the First Amendment, and that application of the public accommodations law to the Council violated the parade organizers' right to choose the content of their message, as well as their right to decide what not to say.

2. GOVERNMENT SUBSIDIES OF SPEECH. [§871]

As a general matter, government subsidies (financial inducements) are constitutional if they are rationally related to a legitimate government interest. However, when a subsidy or condition on the receipt of money requires a person or entity to forego or waive a constitutional right to be eligible for the money, the Court will scrutinize those laws under appropriate First Amendment analysis. The idea here is that the government may not use its virtually unlimited economic power to require or control speech.

a. Tax Exempt Organizations. [§872]

The federal government may allow for selective deductibility of contributions to tax-exempt organizations as long as the deductions are not based on the content of the speech of those organizations.

Regan v. Taxation With Representation of Washington, 461 U.S. 540 (1983). The Court upheld a section of the Internal Revenue Code which made contributions to tax-exempt organizations deductible unless a substantial part of the organization's activities involve lobbying. Another section of the law made contributions to veterans' organizations deductible even if they engage in substantial lobbying. The Court said that this law was not directed at the content of speech of veterans' groups; it simply gave them a break because of the status of veterans in our country.

b. Public Broadcasting Station. [§873]

Federal law cannot prohibit public broadcasting stations from engaging in editorializing.

FCC v. League of Women Voters, 468 U.S. 364 (1984). The Court invalidated a federal law which prohibited any non- commercial educational station receiving a grant from the Corporation for Public Broadcasting from engaging in editorializing. The Court found this content-based restriction on the speech of publicly funded stations to be especially suspect because it was aimed at expression of public issues, speech which is at the core of the First Amendment.

c. Family Planning Clinics. [§874]

Federal law can prohibit federally-funded family planning clinics from discussing abortion as a method of family planning.

Rust v. Sullivan, 500 U.S. 173 (1991). The Court upheld a regulation of the Department of Health and Human Services which prohibited family planning clinics receiving federal money from discussing, within the confines of the federally-funded project, abortion as a method of family planning. The clinic could still advocate abortion through programs that are separate from those receiving federal funds. Medical personnel in the federally-funded clinics remain free to discuss abortion as family planning, as long as they do so on their own time.

3. TAX EXEMPTIONS AS DE FACTO SUBSIDIES FOR CERTAIN KINDS OF SPEECH. [§875]

A state may not grant a sales tax exemption to certain publications based on the content of their message. Government attempts to tax the press will also be dealt with in Chapter XVIII, Freedom of the Press.

Arkansas Writers' Project, Inc. v. Ragland, 481 U.S. 221 (1987). [§876]

The Court invalidated a state sales tax that taxed general interest magazines, but exempted newspapers and religious, professional, trade, and sports journals. This selective tax was content based, and not narrowly tailored to achieve a compelling government interest. The exemptions operated as a subsidy for the publications relieved of the sales tax.

Texas Monthly, Inc. v. Bullock, 489 U.S. 1 (1989). [§877]

The Court invalidated, on Establishment Clause grounds, a state sales tax exemption for religious books and periodicals. Justice Brennan, for a plurality, referred to the selective tax exemption as a "subsidy . . . targeted at writings that *promulgate* the teachings of religious faiths."

L. FREEDOM OF ASSOCIATION. [§878]

There is no right of association enumerated in the Constitution. However the Court has afforded constitutional protection to different kinds of associational rights. Be aware of the different theories that run through the following cases which deal with the right of association.

1. ASSOCIATION FOR BUSINESS PURPOSES. [§879]

If people associate for business or commercial purposes, no fundamental constitutional interest is being advanced, and a government regulation of such associations will be valid if rationally related to a legitimate government interest. The Court deals with these cases the same way it treats economic substantive due process cases. (See §475, above).

2. ASSOCIATION FOR PERSONAL REASONS. [§880]

If people associate for purely personal reasons, the Court may recognize a fundamental right of intimate association which protects the basic element of personal liberty relating to the ability of persons to enter into and maintain intimate human relationships. Under this theory, the issue is whether the association is sufficiently intimate to bring it within constitutional protections. The Court looks at three factors to decide this issue: 1) is it a relatively small group?; 2) is there a high degree of selectivity in decisions to begin and maintain the affiliation?; and 3) is there seclusion from others in critical aspects of the relationship (such as decisionmaking)?

3. ASSOCIATION FOR FIRST AMENDMENT PURPOSES. [§881]

If people associate for First Amendment purposes (speech or assembly), the Court may recognize a fundamental freedom of expressive association. This right is not absolute, and a government may abridge it to advance a compelling government interest.

4. RIGHT NOT TO ASSOCIATE, OR BE ASSOCIATED WITH, CERTAIN IDEAS. [§882]

The court has recognized a right not to be associated with certain ideas or speech. A typical case of this kind involves a union (or bar association) which uses members' dues for political purposes. The member has a right to not be associated with political speech with which he or she disagrees. The members may be forced to pay dues to cover the union's costs of performing labor representation functions, but may not be forced to contribute to the dissemination of speech that is extraneous to the union's function, as a bargaining agent.

5. CASES INVOLVING THE RIGHT OF ASSOCIATION, AND THE RIGHT NOT TO ASSOCIATE. [§883]

a. Membership Lists. [§884]

A state cannot compel the disclosure of the membership list of a political organization.

NAACP v. Alabama, 357 U.S. 449 (1958). The Court ruled that Alabama could not compel the NAACP to disclose the names of its members. The Court unanimously said that the freedom to engage in association for the advancement of beliefs and ideas is a protected liberty under the Due Process Clause. Compelled disclosure would violate the privacy interests of the members of the group.

b. Union Dues. [§885]

Union dues may not be spent to advance political views opposed by a union member.

Abood v. Detroit Board of Education, 433 U.S. 915 (1977). The Court upheld a Michigan statute which required local government employees represented by a union to pay union dues if a member of the union, or pay a service charge equal to the union dues if the employee is not a member. As long as the dues are used to pay for collective bargaining, contract administration, or grievance processing, they are constitutional. However, any expenditure by the union of dues from members, or fees from non- members, for purposes of expressing political views or electing candidates opposed by the employee violates the employee's First Amendment right not to be associated with certain causes or ideas.

c. Bar Association Dues. [§886]

Bar association dues may not be spent to advance political views opposed by a member of the bar.

Keller v. State Bar of California, 496 U.S. 1 (1990). The Court held that a state bar association may use compulsory dues for the purpose of regulating the legal profession or improving the quality of legal services available to the people of the state, but may not use them for political causes that the bar association members oppose.

d Contributions to Generic Advertising For an Industry. [§886.1]

Forced contributions to generic advertising for an entire industry do not implicate the First Amendment.

Glickman v. Wileman Brothers & Elliott, Inc, ___ S.Ct. ___ (1997). The Court, by a vote of 5-4 upheld marketing orders promulgated by the Secretary of Agriculture which required California tree fruit growers to contribute to the cost of generic advertising of the California tree fruit industry. The growers argued that such forced contributions violated their commercial speech rights under the *Central Hudson* test (See §761). The Court rejected the free speech argument entirely, relying on the following aspects of the generic advertising scheme: 1) the marketing orders do not limit a grower's ability to communicate any message to anyone; 2) the orders do not compel any grower to engage in any speech; and 3) the orders do not compel any grower to endorse or finance any political or ideological speech. Since the First Amendment did not apply, the Court upheld the marketing orders under the lenient rational basis test used to review economic legislation.

e. Privately Owned Shopping Centers. [§887]

A state constitution may confer a right of access to privately-owned shopping centers for speech purposes.

Pruneyard Shopping Center v. Robins, 447 U.S. 74 (1980). The Court upheld a California constitutional provision that gave speakers access to privately-owned shopping centers for speech purposes. The owner of the shopping center objected to being forced to provide the forum for speech that he might not agree with. The Court said that since there was little likelihood that the speech would be ascribed to the owner, no specific message was dictated by the State, and the owner could simply post signs disavowing the speech, the owner's right not to be associated with the speakers or their ideas was not violated.

f. Consumer Boycotts. [§888]

Consumer boycotts are protected as an aspect of the associational rights of an organization.

NAACP v. Clairborne Hardware Co. , 458 U.S. 886 (1982). The Court ruled that the NAACP and its members could not be held liable in tort for damages resulting from an organized consumer boycott which was intended to protest racial discrimination. The boycott was political speech, lying at the core of the First Amendment. The Court ruled that liability may be imposed only on a person whose unlawful conduct was the proximate cause of an injury. It is not permissible for a state to punish one member of an association simply because another member broke the law.

g. Gender Discrimination by Private Associations. [§889]

A state may require private associations to accept women as members.

Roberts v. U.S. Jaycees, 468 U.S. 609 (1984). The Court ruled that a state equal opportunity statute could be applied to force a state branch of the Jaycees to admit women as members, despite their policy of restricting membership to males between the ages of 18 and 35. The Court recognized two kinds of freedom of association: intimate and expressive.

- Freedom of intimate association has to do with starting and maintaining close personal relationships. This kind of association is

evidenced by relative smallness of the group, a high degree of selectivity in starting and maintaining the affiliation, and seclusion from others in important aspects of the association. The local chapters of the Jaycees failed to meet these criteria, and thus were not able to assert a right to intimate association as a defense to the state action of forcing the Jaycees to accept women as members.

- Freedom of expressive association has to do with associating for First Amendment purposes: speech, assembly, and petitioning for the redress of grievances. Freedom to associate for expressive purposes presupposes a freedom not to associate. Forced membership abridges the choice not to associate with certain people. The right to expressive association, while fundamental, is not absolute, and may be abridged to advance the state's compelling interest in eradicating gender discrimination.

h. Welfare Benefits. [§890]
The federal government can reduce the welfare benefits of family members of striking workers.

Lyng v. UAW, 485 U.S. 360 (1988). The Court upheld a provision of the federal Food Stamp Act providing that no family may become eligible for food stamps while any member of the household is on strike, nor shall any family receive increased food stamp allotments because the income of the striking family member had decreased. The Constitution's protection of associational rights included the right of workers to associate to better assert their lawful rights. However, the Court said that the law neither ordered nor prevented workers from associating. The government's decision not to subsidize the exercise of a right does not equal the government abridging that right.

i. Social Associations With Older Persons. [§891]
A city may prohibit persons over the age of 18 from using certain dance halls frequented by minors.

Dallas v. Stanglin, 490 U.S. 19 (1989). The Court upheld a city ordinance prohibiting persons over the age of 18 from using certain dance halls. The Court said there was no general right of social association that would protect the ability to go to a dance hall.

REVIEW PROBLEMS — FREEDOM OF SPEECH

PROBLEM 1. The City of Id has an ordinance which prohibits any "loud or boisterous" demonstrations or gatherings within 500 feet of any church, synagogue, temple, or any other house of worship while religious services are being held inside the building. Madeline O'Murray, a member of Atheists United, is arrested for violating this ordinance. Discuss her arguments against the ordinance. What is Id's best argument in support of the ordinance?

> **Answer:** Madeline's best argument is that the ordinance is vague; who knows what "loud and boisterous" means? The vagueness of the ordinance gives her no notice of what behavior is punishable, and it gives the Id police too much discretion in enforcing the law. She would also argue that the ordinance violates her free speech rights because a 500-foot buffer zone is not narrowly tailored to achieving the city's interests. Id will argue that this ordinance is a valid time, place, manner restriction. It is content neutral, and advances the significant government interest of protecting the privacy rights of worshippers. Id will argue that it is narrowly tailored, and that demonstrators still have ample alternative channels of communication. See §§668, 688 for further review.

PROBLEM 2. The State of Oz has a statute which provides that any sentence for an assaultive crime will be increased by a specified percentage if the victim was chosen based on his or her race or ethnicity. Mario Macho was convicted of aggravated assault for beating Zeb Smith. At trial, there was evidence that Mario chose Zeb as a victim because Zeb is of Mobanian descent. At sentencing, the judge increased Mario's sentence by one-third because his crime was motivated by hatred for Mobanians. Mario challenges Oz's enhanced-sentence statute on the basis that it violates his free speech rights. He claims that he received extra punishment because of what he believes and what he said about Mobanians. Will Mario win?

> **Answer:** No. The Court has upheld a statute which increases the penalty for an assaultive crime when the defendant selected his victim based on race. The Court said that the enhanced sentence punished the conduct of selecting a victim, not the abstract beliefs or utterances of the defendant. As a result, there is no constitutional infringement on the free speech rights of the criminal. See §740 for further review.

PROBLEM 3. Bob Barrister, an attorney licensed in the State of Oz, wrote letters to all persons with Mobanian surnames in the City of Id asking if they would like to join a class action lawsuit challenging allegedly discriminatory employment practices in the City of Id. The State Bar of Oz censures Bob for this solicitation. May the State Bar constitutionally discipline Bob?

> **Answer:** No. Targeted solicitation by mail is protected commercial speech. Mailing truthful letters to specific persons who might have specific legal problems creates no great danger to consumers. Also, Bob has the argument that, since this is a civil rights lawsuit, rights of political speech and association are involved, making this speech even more protected. See §771 for further review.

PROBLEM 4. Tyrell Toms is a resident of Oz, and had been an employee of the State Supreme Court Administrator's Office (SSCAO). Tyrell was fired after he uncovered some potentially illegal actions by the State Supreme Court Administrator, Angie Addlehooper. Tyrell found some documents indicating that Angie was violating SSCAO rules by assigning certain cases to judges who had reputations for being lenient on certain litigants. When Angie fired Tyrell, she made some defamatory comments about him and his performance at SSCAO, including the fact that Tyrell did not understand the case assignment system used at SSCAO. Under the laws of the State of Oz, a private plaintiff in a defamation action may recover punitive damages in any defamation action, even without showing actual malice. May Tyrell recover punitive damages from Angie even if he does not show actual malice?

Answer: No. If the allegedly defamatory speech is on a matter of public concern, a private-figure plaintiff may not recover punitive damages without showing actual malice on the part of the person who made the defamatory statement. The operation of the SSCAO is certainly a matter of public concern, and Tyrell must show actual malice to recover punitive damages. See §782 for further review.

PROBLEM 5. The principal of Id High School, a public school in the State of Oz, was perusing the page proofs of the high school yearbook when she saw some disturbing pictures: members of certain athletic teams had made obscene gestures on the team pictures. The principal decided to remove from the yearbook the pages on which the pictures appeared. Student editors of the yearbook sued, claiming censorship. Is the principal justified in her action?

Answer: Yes. In a case involving school-sponsored speech, a school official may impose restrictions on speech, including complete removal of certain stories or pictures, if the restrictions are rationally related to a legitimate educational purpose. The principal's actions here are rationally related to ensuring good taste and civility in student publications paid for by the school. See §808 for further review.

PROBLEM 6. The State of Oz owns and operates a large airport terminal. It has regulations which prohibit passing out leaflets inside the terminal, and in-person solicitation for money. Joan Camel, a member of Smokers Against Regulation (SAR), is arrested for passing out leaflets attacking government restrictions on smokers. She is also charged with violating the ban on soliciting money from people inside the terminal. Joan sues, alleging a violation of her free speech rights. Does she have a case?

Answer: Yes and No. A government-owned airport terminal is not a public forum, so the government may impose restrictions on speech that are reasonably related to keeping the terminal functioning for its intended purpose. The Court has upheld a ban on in-person solicitation within a terminal because of its disruptive effect on pedestrian traffic in the terminal. It has struck down a ban on leafletting, saying that no great disruption flows from simply passing out pieces of paper. See §827 for further review.

A. INTRODUCTION. [§892]

Under the First Amendment, neither Congress nor a state may pass a law abridging freedom of the press. The main purposes of a free press are to inform the public, and to serve as a check on government (obviously these overlap). Two big issues surrounding the press are whether it has any special immunity from laws that bind the rest of us, such as a right not to testify before a grand jury, (no, it does not), and whether the institutional status of the press confers any special privileges on it, such as a special right to attend trials, (no, again). Be aware of the tension between the freedom of the press and other constitutional concerns, such as the rights of litigants in civil or criminal trials. These tensions have been considered on numerous occasions by the Supreme Court.

B. FREEDOM OF THE PRESS AND THE RIGHT TO A FAIR TRIAL. [§893]

A recurrent problem involves the potential tension, if not conflict, between the right of the print and electronic media to gather and report news, and the right of a defendant to a fair trial. What steps may a judge take to ensure a fair trial, especially in a criminal case, while protecting the First Amendment interests of the press? Remember that prior restraints (See §677, above) are presumed unconstitutional, and the government has a heavy burden of justification for any such restriction on the press.

1. PRETRIAL PUBLICITY. [§894]

The Court reversed a murder conviction because the "carnival atmosphere" in the courtroom violated the defendant's right to a fair trial.

Sheppard v. Maxwell, 384 U.S. 333 (1966). The Court reversed a murder conviction on the basis of the extreme publicity surrounding the case, and the "carnival atmosphere" in the courtroom. The Court chastised the trial judge for not using available procedures to preserve the fairness and dignity of the trial. The judge can use voir dire to ensure that jurors have not been unduly influenced by pretrial publicity, can sequester the jurors as soon as they are chosen, or can grant a continuance or change of venue. The Court also indicated that a trial judge could have imposed gag orders on the attorneys and witnesses if necessary, although the press must be free to report events that happen in the courtroom.

2. PRIOR RESTRAINTS TO ENSURE FAIRNESS OF TRIALS. [§895]

Trial judges may not use prior restraints on the media to ensure the fairness of a trial if there are less drastic means available.

Nebraska Press Association v. Stuart, 427 U.S. 539 (1976). The Court struck down a state court pre-trial restraining order which prohibited the media from publishing any confessions made by the defendant (unless made to the press), and any other facts "strongly implicative" of the defendant's guilt. The state judge had also restrained the publication of any testimony or evidence given at the preliminary hearing. Using prior restraint analysis, the Court concluded that the trial judge had less drastic means available to preserve the defendant's right to a fair trial, such as a change of venue, postponing the trial, or sequestration of jurors.

C. ACCESS OF THE PRESS TO PRISONERS AND COURTROOMS. [§896]

Members of the media do not have any special right of access to courtrooms or jails. Their rights are the same as those of the general public. Members of the public have a presumptive First Amendment right to attend trials which may be overridden only if a judge articulates a compelling reason for closing the courtroom. Members of the public have no right to interview or visit with prisoners unless the prison authorities grant such a right.

1. ACCESS TO PRISONS OR INMATES. [§897]

Reporters have no special right of access to prisons or inmates whom they wish to interview.

Pell v. Procunier, 417 U.S. 817 (1974). The Court upheld a California prison regulation which prohibited face-to-face interviews between reporters and inmates they requested to interview. **The Court said that members of the press have no constitutional right of access to prisons or inmates beyond that afforded the general public.**

2. ACCESS TO JAILS. [§898]

Reporters have no special right of access to jails.

Houchins v. KQED, 429 U.S. 1341 (1978). The Court, in a very fragmented set of opinions, reversed a lower court order requiring a sheriff to grant reporters access to a jail facility. The seven members of the Court participating all agreed that the media have no greater right of access to jails than does the general public.

3. NO SIXTH AMENDMENT RIGHT OF ACCESS TO A CRIMINAL TRIAL. [§899]

Neither the public nor the press has a Sixth Amendment right of access to criminal trials; the Sixth Amendment right to a public trial belongs to the defendant.

Gannett Co., Inc. v. De Pasquale, 443 U.S. 368 (1979). The Court held that the Sixth Amendment's guarantee of a public trial belonged to the defendant, and was not assertable by the press or public as a basis for gaining access to a pretrial hearing in a murder case.

4. FIRST AMENDMENT RIGHT OF ACCESS TO CRIMINAL TRIALS. [§900]

There is a presumptive First Amendment right of the public and the press to attend criminal trials.

Richmond Newspapers, Inc. v. Virginia, 448 U.S. 555 (1980). **The Court ruled that the public and the press have a First Amendment right to attend criminal trials.** The right is not absolute, but to close a courtroom, a judge must state on the record some overriding reason justifying closure. The Court overturned the decision of a state trial judge, acting pursuant to a state statute, to close a murder trial.

5. CLOSED PROCEEDINGS INVOLVING MINORS. [§901]

A state may not close every proceeding involving testimony by a minor victim of a sexual assault.

Globe Newspapers Co. v. Superior Court, 457 U.S. 596 (1982). The Court invalidated a state statute requiring the exclusion of the press and public from a courtroom during the testimony of a minor victim of a sexual assault in a criminal case. The Court said that the press and public had a fundamental right to attend criminal trials, and that a judge could only close a trial if specific circumstances required it, and if the reasons for closure were placed in the record by the judge.

6. FIRST AMENDMENT RIGHT OF ACCESS TO VOIR DIRE. [§902]

There is a presumptive first amendment right of the public and the press to attend voir dire of potential jurors in a criminal case.

Press Enterprise Co. v. Superior Court, 464 U.S. 501 (1984). The Court held that the public and the press had a presumptive First Amendment right of access to the voir dire examination of potential jurors in a criminal trial. As with trials, closure of voir dire could only be justified by an overriding interest articulated on the record.

OUTLINE

D. NO REPORTER'S PRIVILEGE. [§903]

The general rule is that members of the media are no different from the rest of us in terms of being subject to generally applicable rules of law. If you want to know if a reporter must do something (or is prohibited from doing it), ask whether you must do it (or are prohibited from doing it). Whatever answer applies to you applies to reporters. Do you have to testify before a grand jury? Do you have to comply with a search warrant? If you do, so do reporters.

1. GRAND JURY TESTIMONY. [§904]

Reporters do not have any special privilege that exempts them from testifying before a grand jury.

Branzburg v. Hayes, 408 U.S. 665 (1972). The Court held that reporters do not have any First Amendment privilege that would immunize them from testifying before state or federal grand juries. In *Branzburg*, a reporter argued that a reporter's privilege was necessary because forcing reporters to testify before grand juries would result in confidential sources refusing to give information to reporters. In rejecting that argument, the Court said that the First Amendment does not guarantee the press a constitutional right of special access to information not available to the public generally.

2. SEARCH WARRANTS. [§905]

Members of the media have no special protection from search warrants. Acting pursuant to a valid search warrant, police officers may search the offices of a newspaper for evidence of a crime.

Zurcher v. Stanford Daily, 436 U.S. 547 (1978). The Court rejected the argument that newspapers have any special protection against complying with validly authorized search warrants. It also rejected the argument that when a newsroom is to be searched, a subpoena duces tecum, rather than a search warrant, must be used (a subpoena duces tecum is less intrusive than a search warrant because it does not authorize a wholesale search of the newspaper premises). The Court allowed a search of the offices of the Stanford Daily, a student newspaper, for pictures involving assaults on police officers during a demonstration at the Stanford University Hospital. The pictures were sought as a part of a police investigation of alleged crimes occurring at the demonstration.

3. DEPOSITION TESTIMONY. [§906]

Reporters do not have a special privilege that permits them to refuse to testify during a deposition.

Herbert v. Lando, 441 U.S. 153 (1979). The Court ruled that the producer of a television documentary has no privilege to refuse to answer questions during a deposition in a libel suit. A retired Army officer sued CBS, claiming that he was defamed during a documentary about the Vietnam war. During his deposition, the producer was asked questions about newsgathering and editorial conversations, the answers to which might have implicated the producer in the alleged defamation of the Army officer. It was necessary for the plaintiff officer, a public figure, to prove actual malice in the libel suit, making it imperative for him to inquire into the motivation of the producer. The Court reasoned that honoring legitimate discovery requests would not significantly discourage frank editorial discussions.

4. BREACH OF PROMISE OF CONFIDENTIALITY. [§907]

Members of the media have no special immunity from a civil suit against them for breach of a promise not to divulge the name of a source.

Cohen v. Cowles Media, Co., 501 U.S. 663 (1991). The Court ruled that a newspaper, just like any other entity, may be liable for damages under state promissory estoppel law if the newspaper breaches a promise not to print the name of a confidential source of information. Cohen was a Republican who provided information about a Democratic candidate to a newspaper on the condition that his (Cohen's) name not be published. The paper published Cohen's name, and was sued on a promissory estoppel theory, based on Cohen's detrimental reliance on the reporter's promise not to publish his name. The Court said that generally applicable laws do not offend the First Amendment simply because their enforcement against the press has incidental effects on its ability to gather and report the news.

E. ACCESS BY INDIVIDUALS TO THE MASS MEDIA. [§908]

A First Amendment issue arises as to when the government may require the media to disseminate certain messages. Be aware of the different treatment of print and electronic media. **With the broadcast media, there are only a finite number of frequencies available to broadcast radio and television (spectrum scarcity), so some government regulation is permissible to enhance equality of access and fairness of the range of ideas expressed. A government may not, however, require newspapers to give free reply space to political candidates.**

1. FEDERALLY-MANDATED REPLY TIME ON TELEVISION OR RADIO. [§909]

The federal government may require a radio or television station to give reply time to answer personal attacks or political editorials. The "fairness doctrine" is designed to prevent powerful corporations or wealthy individuals from controlling access to a medium of communication.

Red Lion Broadcasting Co. v. FCC, 395 U.S. 367 (1969). **The Court held that Congress and the FCC do not violate the First Amendment by requiring a radio or television station to give reply time to answer personal attacks or political editorials.** Focusing on the right of the public to receive information, the Court said that it is permissible for Congress and the FCC to try to ensure fairness in radio and television broadcasting because there were more persons who wanted to broadcast than there were frequencies available. Since the "marketplace" was limited, imposing fairness was constitutional.

2. NO RIGHT TO REPLY IN NEWSPAPERS. [§910]

Unlike the broadcast media, a newspaper may not be forced to provide a "right to reply."

Miami Herald Publishing Co. v. Tornillo, 418 U.S. 241 (1974). Distinguishing the press from the broadcast media, the Court invalidated a Florida "right to reply" statute which required a newspaper to give free reply space to any candidate whose personal character or official record had been attacked by the newspaper. The Court cited the economic cost to the newspaper of having to provide free reply space, plus the intrusion into editorial decisions as reasons for its holding. **Electronic media are different from newspapers because they enjoy a government- granted monopoly through the granting of licenses by the Federal Communications Commission. Hence, a government-required right of reply is permissible for radio and television, but not for newspapers.**

3. PAID EDITORIAL ADVERTISEMENTS. [§911]

Broadcasters may not be forced to accept paid editorial advertisements.

CBS v. Democratic National Committee, 412 U.S. 94 (1973). The Court held that neither federal statutes nor the First Amendment requires broadcasters to accept paid editorial advertisements. The Democratic National Committee and a group opposing the Vietnam war were turned down when they tried to buy time to broadcast their positions on issues that were clearly of public importance. The Court said that the public interest would best be served by leaving editorial decisions in the hands of the network editors, rather than at the mercy of the wealthiest applicants for broadcast time.

4. HELP-WANTED ADVERTISEMENTS. [§912]

A city can prohibit gender-specific help-wanted advertisements.

Pittsburgh Press Co. v. Pittsburgh Commission on Human Relations, 413 U.S. 376 (1973). The Court upheld a city ordinance prohibiting newspapers from carrying "help-wanted" advertisements in gender-designated columns. The National Organization for Women, Inc., filed a complaint with the Pittsburgh Commission on Human Relations, alleging that the Pittsburgh Press Co. was violating a city ordinance by running help-wanted advertisements in columns designated "Jobs-Male Interest," "Jobs-Female Interest," and "Male-Female." Relying on commercial speech analysis, the Court said that gender discrimination in employment is illegal commercial activity, and therefore regulable under such an ordinance.

5. CABLE TELEVISION FRANCHISES. [§913]

A city's refusal to grant a cable television franchise implicates the First Amendment.

Los Angeles v. Preferred Communications, Inc., 476 U.S. 488 (1986). The Court said that cable television partakes of some of the same aspects of speech and the communication of ideas as do newspapers and books. The Court remanded for an analysis of the First Amendment issues involved in a city's refusal to grant a franchise to a cable television company. The cable television company was refused the franchise because it failed to participate in an auction which would award the single cable franchise in the area. The company asserted that the auction process allowed the city to discriminate among applicants for the cable franchise, and that such discrimination violated the company's First Amendment rights.

F. SPECIAL TAXES ON THE PRESS. [§914]

Generally applicable laws, including taxes, may be imposed on the press. However, taxes which single out a certain segment of the press for discriminatory treatment will be invalidated.

1. DISCRIMINATORY TAXES ON THE PRESS. [§915]

A state may not impose a tax which targets specific members of the press for taxation, but exempts all others.

Minneapolis Star & Tribune Co. v. Minnesota Commissioner of Revenue, 460 U.S. 575 (1983). The Court invalidated a Minnesota tax scheme which targeted a small number of newspapers within the state. Under the Minnesota law, periodic publications were exempt from sales and use taxes until 1971, when the state applied the use tax to the cost of paper and ink used in producing periodic publications. In 1974, the state exempted the first $100,000 of paper and ink used by a publication in any one year, leaving the full tax burden to be borne by larger publications. The effect of the law was to exempt smaller publications from any tax burden. The Court objected to the law singling out larger periodicals for discriminatory treatment through selective taxation.

2. SALES TAX. [§916]

A state may impose a sales tax on the sale of cable television services while exempting receipts from newspaper sales and subscription magazine sales.

Leathers v. Medlock, 499 U.S. 439 (1991). The Court upheld an Arkansas sales tax which applied to cable television services, but exempted receipts from the sale of magazines and newspapers. The Court upheld the tax against a First Amendment challenge because the tax was not intended to create, nor did it have the effect of creating, a danger of suppressing particular ideas, and it did not discriminate on the basis of the content of speech. The Court also pointed out that the tax was not directed at a small group of speakers, but affected about 100 suppliers of cable television services, as well as sales of all tangible personal property and a broad range of other services. The imposition of the tax to a broad range of activities led the Court to conclude that the tax does not single out the press for discriminatory treatment and thus does not jeopardize the media's role as a watchdog of government activity.

3. CRIME VICTIM COMPENSATION. [§917]

The Court struck down a state law requiring that victims of crimes receive all proceeds from books written by the criminals who committed those crimes.

Simon & Schuster, Inc. v. New York State Crime Victims Board, 112 S.Ct. 501 (1991). The Court invalidated New York's "Son of Sam" law which required that all money received by an accused or convicted criminal for the rights to the story depicting his or her crime be given to the victims of the crime. The law covered not only criminals who were convicted in court, but also those who voluntarily (in the story) admitted a crime for which there has been no prosecution. The Court found this law to be presumptively unconstitutional (because content-based), and therefore subject to strict scrutiny. The state had compelling interests in ensuring that victims of crime are compensated by those who harm them, and in ensuring that criminals do not profit from their crimes. The means were not narrowly tailored, however, because the law was overinclusive, reaching works like the Autobiography of Malcolm X, which describes crimes committed by the civil rights leader before he became a public figure.

REVIEW PROBLEMS — FREEDOM OF THE PRESS

PROBLEM 1. Quenda Quinine is an investigative reporter for the Daily Bugle. Quenda has been writing a series of stories on drug trafficking in the City of Id. She has been subpoenaed to testify before a federal grand jury investigating the interstate drug trade. Quenda refuses to testify, citing the First Amendment. She claims that if she has to testify, her sources of information will dry up. Does Quenda have to testify?

> **Answer:** Yes. There is no reporter's privilege which exempts a journalist from testifying before a grand jury. Members of the media have no greater rights or protections than the general public. See §904 for further review.

PROBLEM 2. The State of Oz has a sales tax which is applied to the receipts from the sales of newspapers and magazines, but exempts receipts from the sale of cable television services. Is this tax constitutional?

> **Answer:** Yes. This tax is not directed at the content of speech, simply at certain media of communication. As a result, this content-neutral tax is not designed to, nor will it suppress particular ideas. See §916 for further review.

PROBLEM 3. Gregory Gridlock IV is a United States Senator from the State of Oz. Greg is running for re-election, and has been the target of some nasty, unflattering editorials in the Id Daily Bugle, a large metropolitan newspaper. Relying on a statute of the State of Oz which requires that newspapers give free reply space to targets of unfavorable editorials or articles, Greg demands space in the Daily Bugle to respond to the attacks on his character and record. Is the Oz statute constitutional?

> **Answer:** No. While the Court has upheld required reply time on radio and television, it has struck down such a requirement as to newspapers. The main difference is that radio and television stations operate pursuant to a government monopoly, whereas newspapers are privately owned and operated. See §§909, 910 for further review.

XIX. THE RELIGION CLAUSES OF THE FIRST AMENDMENT

A. INTRODUCTION. [§918]

The First Amendment says that, "Congress shall make no law respecting an establishment of religion, or prohibiting the free exercise thereof . . . ." These guarantees also apply to the states. While most books treat the religion clauses separately, remember that there is an unavoidable tension between them, and it may be necessary to consider and discuss both clauses when answering a question. For example, a tension between the clauses exists regarding prayer in public schools. On the one hand, it could be argued that allowing school prayer establishes religion. On the other hand, it could be argued that forbidding school prayer violates the free exercise rights of children who want to pray in school. When deciding a freedom of religion case, a court may be forced to choose between Establishment Clause and Free Exercise Clause principles.

B. THE ESTABLISHMENT CLAUSE. [§919]

The First Amendment says that Congress may not pass any law respecting the establishment of religion. This provision has been incorporated to apply against the states. **The Establishment Clause certainly prohibits a government from setting up or recognizing an official state church. It also prohibits government from forcing people to go to church or refrain from going to church. After these two extreme cases, the question is how much and what kind of government aid to religion is constitutionally permissible.**

1. ESTABLISHMENT CLAUSE TESTS. [§920]

The Court has set forth two tests to use in analyzing most Establishment Clause questions.

a. The *Lemon* Test. [§921]

The *Lemon* test (from *Lemon v. Kurtzman*, 403 U.S. 602 (1971)) is used when government acts in such a way as to prefer or advance religion over non-religion.

For a law to be valid under a *Lemon* analysis:

1. The law must have a secular legislative purpose;

2. Its principal or primary effect must be one that neither advances nor inhibits religion; and

3. It must not foster an excessive government entanglement with religion.

> **STUDY TIP:** Remember that the law must pass all three prongs of the *Lemon* test to be constitutional.

b. The *Larson* Test. [§922]

The *Larson* test (from *Larson v. Valente*, 456 U.S. 228 (1982)) is used when government prefers one religion over another. If that happens, the Court uses a compelling interest test to analyze the law. Strict scrutiny is called for because preferring one religion over another goes to the heart of Establishment Clause concerns.

> **STUDY TIP: THE "ADD OTHER STUFF" THEORY.** [§923] If a government does something that arguably advances religion, the way for the government to immunize its action from constitutional attack is to "add other stuff." (You will not see this terminology anywhere else - trust me.) The fancy way to say this is that **the government must secularize the program by making it apply to non-religious as well as religious beneficiaries, or it must include non-religious items or activities.** Want to have a constitutionally accepted Christmas display? Don't just set up a creche; add other stuff: Santa, presents, and lots of reindeer. Want to lend textbooks to parochial school students? Make sure public and non-sectarian private school students get them too. In other words, add other stuff. This is not a very elegant formulation, but it works in a great many cases.

2. RELIGION AND SCHOOLS. [§924]

The Court has been sensitive to the fact that school children are very impressionable, and are a captive audience. As a result, they are very susceptible to religious indoctrination, so the Court has been careful to maintain a clear separation of church and state in public school cases.

a. Financial Aid to Parochial School Students or Their Parents. [§925]

As a general matter, state financial aid to religious school students or parents will be upheld if the aid is also given to students or parents in non-religious schools.

(1) Transportation. [§926]

A state can reimburse parents for transportation to and from school.

Everson v. Board of Education, 330 U.S. 1 (1947). The Court upheld a local ordinance which reimbursed parents for the cost of sending their children on buses to public, parochial, and non-religious private schools. The class of beneficiaries was made up of religious and non-religious school parents. The secular purpose of the law was to provide safe transportation to and from school.

(2) Textbooks. [§927]

A state can loan textbooks to religious and private non- religious schools.

Board of Education v. Allen, 392 U.S. 236 (1968). The Court upheld the State of New York's program of lending state-approved secular textbooks to all secondary school children, including those in religious schools. The class of beneficiaries included students in religious and non-religious schools.

(3) Salaries. [§928]

A state cannot supplement the salaries of religious school teachers.

Lemon v. Kurtzman, 403 U.S. 602 (1971). The Court invalidated state statutes which supplemented salaries of teachers in parochial schools. Such supplements would result in excessive entanglement between government and religion because the religious school teachers would have to be monitored to make sure they did not sneak religion into the secular subjects that the government was paying them to teach.

> **STUDY TIP: The three-part test from *Lemon* is: the statute must have a secular legislative purpose; its principal or primary effect must be one that neither advances nor inhibits religion; and the law must not foster an excessive entanglement between government and religion.** The Court in *Lemon* also alluded to the possible problem of political divisiveness resulting from the legislature allocating money to certain religious groups. This is not a separate test, but is something that is discussed as part of the "entanglement" prong of *Lemon*.

(4) Maintenance Grants, Tuition Reimbursement, and Tax Benefits. [§928.1]

A State cannot grant money to nonpublic schools for maintenance and repair costs, cannot reimburse parents for tuition to nonpublic schools, and cannot grant tax benefits solely to parents who send their children to nonpublic schools. Since most nonpublic schools are religious, all of these measures unconstitutionally advance religion.

In *Committee for Public Education and Religious Liberty v. Nyquist*, 413 US 756 (1973), the Court struck down a New York law which provided financial assistance to nonpublic schools in the form of maintenance and repair grants, tuition reimbursement for parents, and tax benefits for parents. The Court held that, although the law was supported by legitimate secular purposes, all three measures failed to satisfy the second element of the *Lemon* test in that they had a primary effect of advancing religion. The maintenance and repair grants were a direct subsidy to nonpublic schools, with no mechanism by which to prevent the funds from being spent for the upkeep of facilities being used for religious purposes. The tuition reimbursement and tax benefit measures to parents operated to encourage and reward parents for sending children to nonpublic schools, most of which were religious.

(5) Special School Districts for Religious Groups. [§929]

A state cannot create a special school district for a religious group.

Board of Education of Kiryas Joel Village School District v. Grumet, 114 S.Ct. 2481 (1994). The Court invalidated, as violative of the Establishment Clause, a New York statute which created a public school district whose boundaries coincided with those of a neighborhood occupied by a discrete religious group. The district was created to provide services to the handicapped children of the Satmar Hasidic sect (practitioners of a strict form of Judaism). These services had already been available in surrounding community schools, to which the Satmar Hasidic parents refused to send their children. The creation of a special school district for one religious group crossed the line from permissible accommodation to impermissible establishment. This law also created the problems of government preferring one sect over another and excessive entanglement between government and religion.

> **STUDY TIP: Whenever the government gives financial aid that benefits religion, the grant or benefit will probably be constitutional if it goes to an individual who, in turn, makes the decision to direct the money or benefit to a religious institution.** The idea is that the person, not the government, is choosing to prefer religion. Also, the aid will probably be constitutional if both religious and non-religious entities are the ultimate beneficiaries.

(6) Aid for Handicapped Students. [§930]

States may provide money grants for handicapped students for use at religious institutions.

Witters v. Washington Department of Services for the Blind, 474 U.S. 481 (1986). The Court upheld a Washington state statute which provided funds for the education of blind students. Witters used his state grant to study at a Christian college to become a pastor, missionary, or youth director. The Court relied on the fact that this was a generally applicable aid program and any money that ultimately went to religious institutions did so as a result of the independent choices of private recipients.

(7) Sign-Language Interpreter. [§931]

States may provide sign language interpreters for religious school students.

Zobrest v. Catalina Foothills School District, 113 S.Ct. 2462 (1993). The Court upheld the practice of a school district providing a sign-language interpreter to a profoundly deaf student who chose to attend a parochial school. The Court held that this was a neutral, generally applicable benefit, and that the choice to place Jamie Zobrest (and his interpreter) in a parochial school was made by the parents, not the state. Also, the program did not relieve the parochial school of any cost it would otherwise have borne in educating Jamie Zobrest.

b. Released Time, Religious Instruction in Public Schools, and Enrichment Classes in Religious Schools. [§932]

Religious instruction in public school buildings violates the Establishment Clause because it has the effect of endorsing religion, and it creates a symbolic union between church and state.

(1) Religious Instruction in Public School Buildings. [§933]

Religious teachers cannot hold classes in a public school building.

McCollum v. Board of Education, 333 U.S. 203 (1948). The Court invalidated a released-time program in which religious teachers held classes in the public school building. Students who were not excused for religious study remained in the classroom. The Court objected to the use of the public building for religious purposes, and to the public school providing a captive audience from which the religious instructors could draw their students.

(2) Released-Time. [§934]
Public school students can <u>leave</u> school to go to religious education programs conducted in religious centers.

Zorach v. Clauson, 343 U.S. 306 (1952). The Court upheld a New York City program which allowed public school students to leave the school building to go to religious centers for instruction or devotional exercises. The public schools incurred no costs, unlike *McCollum* (previous case).

(3) Public School Teachers in Religious Schools. [§935]
Public school teachers cannot teach enrichment classes in religious schools. Public school teachers can provide supplemental remedial instruction on the premises of religious schools if safeguards are in place to prevent the endorsement of religion.

In two earlier cases, the Court invalidated programs in which public employees taught and provided guidance services on the premises of religious schools.

Grand Rapids School District v. Ball, 473 U.S. 373 (1985). The Court invalidated a program in which enrichment classes and adult education classes were taught by public school teachers in parochial school classrooms that were leased to the public school system. The parochial school classrooms were secularized by removing all religious symbols and posting a sign declaring the room to be a public school classroom. The Court said this arrangement violated the Establishment Clause because it had a primary effect of advancing religion, and it created a "symbolic union" between the school district and the religious schools.

Aguilar v. Felton, 473 U.S. 402 (1985). The Court invalidated a New York City program which used federal funds to pay the salaries of public employees who taught and provided guidance services in parochial schools. The program was designed to aid educationally deprived children from low-income families. The Court said this program violated the excessive entanglement prong of *Lemon*.

In *Agostini v. Felton*, ___ S.Ct. ___ (1997), the court reopened the *Aguilar* case and overruled it and the part of *Ball* allowing enrichment classes in parochial schools. The Court in *Agostini* held that a federally funded program providing supplemental remedial instruction to disadvantaged students on a neutral basis does not violate the Establishment Clause, even when the instruction is given in religious schools by government employees. To be constitutional, such a program must be secular, neutral, and non-ideological, and must supplement (not supplant) services already provided by the religious schools.

c. Prohibiting the Teaching of Evolution and the Teaching of Creation Science. [§937]

A state may not prohibit the teaching of evolution in public schools, nor may it require the teaching of creation science.

(1) Teaching of Evolution. [§938]

State law cannot prohibit the teaching of evolution in public schools.

Epperson v. Arkansas, 393 U.S. 97 (1968). The Court invalidated an Arkansas statute which prohibited teaching in public schools and universities the theory that "mankind ascended or descended from a lower order of animals." The Court said the law was purely motivated by the religious purpose of advancing fundamentalist Christian beliefs.

(2) Teaching of Creation Science. [§939]

State law cannot require the teaching of creation science whenever evolution is taught.

Edwards v. Aguillard, 482 U.S. 578 (1987). The Court invalidated a Louisiana statute which prohibited public schools from teaching the theory of evolution unless they also taught creation science. Ruling that the law had no secular purpose, the Court rejected the state's argument that it was trying to advance academic freedom by requiring a balanced treatment of the beginning of humankind.

d. Posting the Ten Commandments in Public Schools. [§940]
A state may not require the posting of the Ten Commandments in public school classrooms.

Stone v. Graham, 449 U.S. 39 (1980). The Court invalidated a Kentucky statute requiring the posting of the Ten Commandments in each public classroom in the state, even though the poster had to carry the disclaimer that the secular application of the Ten Commandments is seen in its adoption as the fundamental legal code of Western civilization and the Common Law of the United States. The Court said there was no secular purpose underlying the law.

NOTE: What if the school had added the Bill of Rights, the Magna Charta, the Code of Hammurabi, and the Declaration of Independence to the required display? Is that enough "other stuff" to save the law?

---

e. School Prayer, Moments of Silence, and Invocations at Graduation. [§941]

The Court has consistently invalidated any form of government sponsored or coerced prayer in public schools.

(1) Official School Prayer. [§942]

A state cannot require that an official school prayer be said in public school classrooms.

Engel v. Vitale, 370 U.S. 421 (1962). The Court invalidated the practice of a school board requiring a non- demoninational prayer to be said in public school classrooms each day. The fact that the prayer was written by the New York Board of Regents was tantamount to an establishment of an official state religion.

(2) Minute of Silence. [§943]

States may not require a minute of silence in public schools for meditation or voluntary prayer if the sole purpose is to endorse religion.

Wallace v. Jaffree, 472 U.S. 38 (1985). The Court invalidated an Alabama law which authorized a minute of silence in public schools for meditation or voluntary prayer. This law ran afoul of the purpose prong of *Lemon* because the state's sole purpose was to endorse religion.

(3) Graduation Ceremonies. [§944]

Clergy cannot offer the invocation and benediction at graduation ceremonies for junior and senior high school.

Lee v. Weisman, 505 U.S. 577 (1992). The Court invalidated the practice of public school principals inviting members of the clergy to offer invocation and benediction prayers at junior high and high school graduations. The principals also provided the clergy with a pamphlet containing guidelines on the content of the prayers to be given. The Court ruled that government involvement with religious activity was so pervasive as to create a state-sponsored and state-directed religious exercise in the public schools. The Court alluded to the subtle coercion that exists in such a setting, and said that a student attending graduation could not avoid the fact or appearance of participation in the religious exercise.

(4) Legislative Sessions. [§945]

A chaplain can open a legislative session with a prayer.

Marsh v. Chambers, 463 U.S. 783 (1983). The Court upheld the practice of a paid chaplain opening each session of the Nebraska legislature with a prayer. The Court did not rely on *Lemon*, but used a historical analysis, focusing on the fact that when Congress passed the First Amendment, a member of the clergy opened the session with a prayer. The difference between *Marsh* and *Weisman* (previous case) is that the legislators are adults who voted to have the chaplain, whereas the graduates are minors who had the prayer imposed on them by the school district.

f. Government Aid to Colleges and Universities. [§946]

Government financial aid to church-affiliated colleges and universities is analyzed under the *Lemon* standards. **The Court is usually willing to assume a secular purpose (educating as many students as possible), and there will not be a primary effect of advancing religion if there is a guarantee by the institution that the money will be used only for secular purposes.**

(1) Construction Grants. [§947]

It is constitutional for the government to offer construction grants to church-related colleges or universities for facilities to be used for non-sectarian instruction.

Tilton v. Richardson, 403 U.S. 672 (1971). The Court upheld federal construction grants to church-related colleges and universities for academic facilities that would be used only for non-sectarian instruction. The Court invalidated a provision of the law that would have allowed the buildings to be used for religious purposes after 20 years. In so holding, the Court noted that college students are far less impressionable than students in primary and secondary schools.

(2) Issuance of Revenue Bonds. [§948]

States may enact bond programs which will allow religious institutions to issue revenue bonds for the construction of college or university buildings.

Hunt v. McNair, 413 U.S. 734 (1973). The Court upheld a South Carolina construction assistance program which allowed colleges and universities to issue revenue bonds for the construction of buildings. The Court said that the primary effect prong of *Lemon* would be violated if aid went to an institution where religion thoroughly permeated all aspects of the educational program, or if the aid were used to fund a specifically religious activity.

(3) State Grants to Religious Colleges. [§949]

State grants to religious colleges are constitutional if not used for religious purposes.

Roemer v. Board of Public Works, 426 U.S. 736 (1976). The Court upheld a Maryland program which gave annual grants to religious colleges and universities, based on the number of full-time students enrolled each year. Under the grant system, the state would ensure that the institution was not pervasively religious, and that the money would not be used for religious purposes.

3. RELIGIOUS SYMBOLS DURING THE HOLIDAY SEASON. [§950]

When does government cross the line between merely recognizing Christmas as a traditional, historical holiday celebrated by a great many people, and endorsing Christmas as an official government holiday? Recognition of the "winter-holiday season" is constitutional, but endorsing a particular religious holy day is not. **Government-sponsored Christmas displays will be constitutional if they are sufficiently secular to avoid the appearance of the government endorsing religion.** These cases raise the burning constitutional question of "How many reindeer do you need to save the display from constitutional attack?"

a. Holiday Displays Including Non-Religious Symbols. [§951]

A Christmas holiday display will be deemed constitutional if it is secularized by the inclusion of non- religious symbols.

Lynch v. Donnelly, 465 U.S. 668 (1984). [§952] The Court held that it did not violate the Establishment Clause for a city to erect a Christmas display during the Christmas holiday season. The display included a creche with Jesus, Mary, and Joseph, along with reindeer, Santa, a Christmas tree, a clown, a teddy bear, and other festive stuff. The Court said that the display was simply a recognition of the winter holiday season, and that the inclusion of the creche did not "taint" the rest of the exhibit with excessive religiosity. (Is this the "fruit of the religious tree" doctrine?).

b. Holiday Displays With Only Religious Symbols. [§953]

A Christmas holiday display will be deemed unconstitutional if it is composed solely of religious symbols.

County of Allegheny v. ACLU, 492 U.S. 573 (1989). [§954] The Court dealt with two holiday displays. It said that the Establishment Clause was violated when a creche, along with animals, shepherds, wise men, and an angel with a banner proclaiming "Gloria in Excelsis Deo," were placed on the grand staircase of the Allegheny County Courthouse. There was nothing to detract from the religious message of the display (they didn't "add other stuff"), so the Court said this was government endorsement of religion.

The Court upheld another display which included a 45-foot Christmas tree at the center of the display, and an 18-foot menorah at the side. The Court's premise was that a Christmas tree is not a religious symbol, so the relative sizes and placements of the two symbols made this a non-religious display. If it had been a 45-foot menorah and an 18-foot Christmas tree, the county would have been in trouble. (A U.S. Court of Appeals judge later said that this kind of analysis was better suited to an interior decorator than a judge.)

4. TAX EXEMPTIONS AND DEDUCTIONS FOR RELIGIOUS ORGANIZATIONS. [§955]

State tax exemptions and deductions will be constitutional if both religious and non-religious taxpayers are able to claim them.

a. State Tax Exemptions. [§956]

State tax exemptions for religious, charitable, and educational institutions do not violate the establishment clause.

Walz v. Tax Commission, 397 U.S. 664 (1970). The Court upheld a state tax exemption for property used for religious, educational, or charitable purposes. The state merely included churches within a broad class of property owned by non-profit, quasi-public corporations. Any indirect financial benefit to churches was not enough to violate Establishment Clause standards.

b. State Tax Deductions for Educational Expenses. [§957]

State tax deductions for expenses of educating children are constitutional.

Mueller v. Allen, 463 U.S. 388 (1983). The Court upheld a state tax deduction for certain expenses incurred by taxpayers in educating their children. Applying *Lemon*, the Court found a secular purpose of educating all children in the state. There was no primary effect of advancing religion because taxpayers with children in non-sectarian private and public schools also benefited. Taking a deduction involved only minimal entanglement (no ongoing relationship).

5. DELEGATION OF SOVEREIGN POWER TO A CHURCH. [§958]

A state may not delegate a sovereign function to a church. Specifically, a state may not give to a church the power to veto the granting of a liquor license.

Larkin v. Grendel's Den, 459 U.S. 116 (1982). The Court invalidated a Massachusetts law which gave churches and schools the power to veto the grant of a liquor license to any establishment within 500 feet of the church or school. The Court said that a government cannot delegate discretionary governmental powers to religious bodies.

6. RESOLVING CHURCH DISPUTES ON THE BASIS OF CHURCH DOCTRINE. [§959]

Civil courts may not decide disputes on the basis of religious doctrine. A civil court may apply "neutral principles" of secular law to decide matters such as property or trust disputes, but it must not entangle itself with religious doctrine. To do so would implicate both the Free Exercise and Establishment Clauses.

Jones v. Wolf, 443 U.S. 595 (1979). The Court vacated a judgment of the Georgia Supreme Court involving a property dispute between factions of a Presbyterian church. The Court was not sure whether the state court relied solely on "neutral principles" of secular law in deciding the case. The Court reaffirmed that the First Amendment prohibits civil courts from resolving church property disputes on the basis of religious doctrine and practice, and that civil courts should defer to the resolution of issues of religious doctrine by the authoritative ecclesiastical body of the church. Given these limitations, a state may adopt any method of settling church property disputes, so long as it involves no consideration of doctrinal matters.

7. GRANTS TO RELIGIOUS SOCIAL WELFARE AGENCIES. [§960]

Religious entities (such as religious social-welfare agencies) may be recipients of governmental aid if they are not pervasively religious, and are among a group of beneficiaries which includes non-religious institutions.

Bowen v. Kendrick, 487 U.S. 589 (1988). The Court upheld a federal grant program which provided funding for services relating to adolescent sexuality and pregnancy. Recipients of the funds included public and private social welfare agencies including religious ones. The Court found a clearly secular purpose (helping adolescents through troubled times), and that there was no primary effect of advancing religion because the religious social welfare agencies were not pervasively sectarian institutions.

8. ESTABLISHMENT CLAUSE ISSUES IN A DESIGNATED PUBLIC FORUM. [§961]

If a government opens its property to a wide range of speakers, it does not violate the Establishment Clause to allow religious speakers to use the property. As a result, a government may not exclude religious speakers from a public forum.

> **STUDY TIP:** Be aware of how the Establishment Clause argument gets raised here. A government is excluding speakers from a forum based on the content of their speech. This requires strict scrutiny. The government says its compelling interest is to avoid the establishment of religion that would result from allowing the religious group to speak. The Court applies *Lemon* to see if inclusion of religious speakers would establish religion. It does not, so the government has no compelling interest in excluding the religious speakers.

OUTLINE

a. Religious Student Groups in a University. [§962]

A state university may not exclude a religious student group from a designated public forum.

Widmar v. Vincent, 454 U.S. 263 (1981). The Court ruled that a state university could not exclude religious groups from using its facilities once the university opened its rooms to registered student groups for speech purposes. The Court rejected the argument that this content-based exclusion was justified by the state's interest in avoiding the establishment of religion that would result from allowing the religious group to speak. Simply permitting the religious groups to speak, along with numerous other student groups, does not equal endorsement or establishment of religion.

b. Religious Student Groups in High School. [§963]

Public schools may not exclude a religious student group from a designated public forum.

Board of Education v. Mergens, 496 U.S. 226 (1990). The Court upheld the federal Equal Access Act, which prohibits public schools receiving federal funds from making content-based exclusions of students from school facilities which have been opened for speech purposes. The school allowed a number of non-curricular groups to use the facilities, but refused to allow the Christian Club to use a room. Following *Widmar* (previous case), the Court said that there is no establishment of religion effected by including the Christian Club along with other student organizations.

c. Religious Speakers. [§964]

A school may not exclude religious speakers from a designated public forum open to the public.

Lamb's Chapel v. Center Moriches Union Free School District, 113 S.Ct. 2141 (1993). The Court ruled that a school which opened its facilities to the general public for speech purposes could not deny a church group access to the school property. The school had designated its property as a limited forum, but had denied access to the religious group because of the content of its speech. As in *Widmar*, the Court rejected the argument that the school had a compelling interest in avoiding the establishment of religion that would result from allowing the religious group to use the facilities. Inclusion of religious speakers along with numerous others does not violate the Establishment Clause.

Sum & Substance QUICK REVIEW of Constitutional Law

277

d. Religious Student Publications. [§965]

A school may not deny funding to a religious student publication if it funds other student journals.

Rosenberger v. Rector and Visitors of the University of Virginia, 115 S.Ct. 2510 (1995). The Court ruled that the University of Virginia could not deny funding for the publication of a recognized student group's journal on the basis that the journal was religious in content. The university set up a program under which payments are made from a Student Activities Fund for the publication of student journals and magazines. When a religious student group, otherwise eligible for funding, applied for funding of its newspaper, Wide Awake: A Christian Perspective at the University of Virginia, the university turned them down, asserting that to fund a religious student publication would violate the Establishment Clause. The Court, relying on *Widmar* (See §829) and *Lamb's Chapel* (See §964), said that a university does not establish religion by granting access to its facilities to a wide spectrum of student groups, even if some of them are religious. The Court saw no difference between a university granting access to its facilities (*Widmar*) and a university funding the publication of student journals; both cases involved the university creating a limited forum for the purpose of enhancing diversity of student expression.

e. Display of Religious Symbols. [§966]

A state may not prohibit a private unattended display of a religious symbol in a public forum.

Capital Square Review and Advisory Board v. Pinette, 115 S.Ct. 2440 (1995). The Court ruled that a private, unattended display of a religious symbol in a public forum does not violate the Establishment Clause. In *Pinette*, the Ku Klux Klan applied to the Columbus, Ohio Capitol Square Review and Advisory Board for permission to place an unattended cross on the capitol square during the 1993 Christmas season. The Board denied the Klan permission to use the square which, under Ohio law, is a public forum. The Board asserted that it had a compelling interest in avoiding the establishment of religion which, it claimed, would occur if it permitted the Klan to erect a cross in the capitol square. The Court, relying on *Widmar* (See §829), ruled that it would not establish religion to allow an unattended religious symbol to be placed in a public forum that is generally open to the public for speech purposes. There was not government sponsorship or endorsement of religion when there was simply private religious expressions and the Klan had to go through the same application process as any other potential user of the capitol square.

9. GOVERNMENT PREFERENCE FOR ONE RELIGION OVER ANOTHER. [§967]

When a government takes action which prefers one religious group over another, the court uses the strict scrutiny, compelling interest balancing test.

Larson v. Valente, 456 U.S. 228 (1982). The Court invalidated a Minnesota law which imposed reporting and registration requirements only on those religious organizations that solicit more than fifty percent of their funds from nonmembers. The result of the law was to exempt mainstream religions with affiliated branches (like parishes) from the requirements, while burdening religions such as the Unification Church (which do not have organized affiliates). The Court applied strict scrutiny to this denominational preference, finding that the law was not narrowly tailored to any compelling government interest. **The Court noted that preference for some religions over others not only violates the Establishment Clause, but burdens the religious practices of other religions, creating a free exercise problem.**

C. THE FREE EXERCISE CLAUSE. [§968]

The First Amendment says that Congress shall make no law abridging the free exercise of religion. This is a fundamental right which applies against the states. Government may never regulate religious beliefs, just actions. Government may not regulate actions because they are religious; the impact on religion must be incidental to some legitimate governmental goal. Government may never inquire into the truth of a religious belief, but it may examine the sincerity with which a person claims to hold a religious belief.

1. OVERVIEW OF FREE EXERCISE ANALYSIS. [§969]

The Court has given us specific methods of analysis to use in different kinds of Free Exercise cases. **To identify the appropriate analysis, you must be very careful about two factors. First, is the law generally applicable? Laws that provide for individualized hearings or that have exceptions or exemptions built in (for example, apply only to certain religious groups) are not generally applicable. Second, is the challenge to the law based solely on the Free Exercise Clause, or on the Free Exercise Clause plus some other constitutional right such as freedom of speech, or the right to direct the education of your children?** Here is how the Court will analyze Free Exercise cases under constitutional principles.

a. Generally Applicable Laws. [§970]

Laws that apply equally to all persons (such as a criminal statute) are considered to be generally applicable.

(1) Challenges Based Solely on the Free Exercise Clause. [§971]

If a government has passed a generally applicable law, and the plaintiff's challenge to the law is based solely on the Free Exercise Clause, the law is good. There is no heightened scrutiny used.

(2) Challenges Based on the Free Exercise Clause Plus Some Other Constitutional Right. [§972]

If a government has passed a generally applicable law, and the plaintiff's challenge to the law is based on the Free Exercise Clause and some other constitutional right (free speech, rearing your children), strict scrutiny applies, and the government must show that the law is narrowly tailored to achieve a compelling government interest.

b. Laws That Are Not Generally Applicable. [§973]

Laws that provide for individualized hearings or that have exceptions or exemptions built in are not generally applicable.

If a government has passed a law that is not generally applicable, strict scrutiny applies, and the government must show that the law is narrowly tailored to achieve a compelling government interest. Look for two kinds of laws that are not generally applicable: unemployment compensation laws that provide individualized hearings on eligibility (*Sherbert, Hobbie* and *Thomas* cases, §§984, 985, 986); and laws which have built-in exceptions or exemptions (*Church of the Lukumi Babalu Aye* case, §988).

c. Types of Free Exercise Clause Analysis. [§974]

Employment Division v. Smith, 494 U.S. 872 (1990) is the leading Free Exercise case. Justice Scalia, for the Court, set forth the rules for the different kinds of cases.

Employment Division v. Smith, 494 U.S. 872 (1990). The Court upheld a state's power to criminalize the use of peyote, even when used by Native Americans as an essential part of their religion. Oregon had a generally applicable drug law (all uses of certain drugs were prohibited) which was challenged solely on the basis that it violated the Free Exercise rights of two drug counselors who had been fired for peyote use and then denied unemployment compensation because they were discharged for illegal conduct. The Court first said that a government may not regulate religious beliefs. It then set forth the rule that **a generally applicable law which has only an incidental effect of burdening religion does not offend the Free Exercise Clause. No heightened scrutiny is called for in such a case.**

In direct response to the *Smith* decision, Congress passed the Religious Freedom Restoration Act of 1993 Under the Act, a government could not substantially burden a person's free exercise of religion unless it had a compelling reason for the law and had chosen the least restrictive means of achieving that goal. The Religious Freedom Restoration Act was invalidated by the Court in ***Boerne v Flores***.

In *Boerne v. Flores*, cite (1997), the Court by a 6-3 vote, held that the Religious Freedom Restoration Act (RFRA) exceeded Congress' enforcement power under §5 of the Fourteenth Amendment. In *Boerne*, the Catholic Archbishop of San Antonio applied for a building permit to enlarge a church. The local zoning authorities denied the permit on the basis of a historic preservation ordinance which the zoning authorities said applied to the church. The Archbishop challenged the zoning ordinance, relying in part on RFRA, which would require the city to show a compelling reason for the permit denial and that it had chosen the least restrictive means to achieve the purposes of the historic preservation ordinance RFRA applied to any branch of federal or state government, to all federal or state officials, and to all federal or state laws. §5 of the Fourteenth Amendment gives Congress the power to enforce the equal protection and due process guarantee of the Fourteenth Amendment. The Court said that Congress does not have the power to define substantive rights under the Fourteenth Amendment; it only has the power to remedy violations of rights that have been defined by the Court under its power to interpret the Constitution. For Congress to define (not simply protect) substantive rights would violate separation-of-powers principles. The Court also said that RFRA, by defining substantive rights enforceable against states, violates the states' traditional prerogatives to regulate for the health and safety of its citizens.

(1) Examples of Generally Applicable Laws Challenged Solely on Free Exercise Grounds. [§976]

These laws receive no heightened scrutiny.

(a) Anti-Polygamy Laws. [§977]

A federal law prohibiting polygamy is constitutional.

Reynolds v. U.S., 80 S.Ct. 30 (1879). The Court upheld a federal law prohibiting polygamy as applied to a Mormon whose religion required polygamy. The Court said that the Congress could not regulate religious beliefs, but could reach actions that were violative of social duties or subversive of good order. This law applied generally and was challenged solely on Free Exercise grounds.

(b) Dress Codes. [§978]

An Air Force regulation prohibiting wearing a yarmulke on duty is constitutional.

Goldman v. Weinberger, 475 U.S. 503 (1986). The Court upheld an Air Force regulation which prohibited an Orthodox Jew from wearing his yarmulke while on duty. The Air Force regulations forbade all individualized headgear which was visible in public, a restriction which the Court thought sufficiently related to the military goals of unity and discipline.

(2) Examples of Generally Applicable Laws Challenged on the Basis of the Free Exercise Clause and Another Constitutional Right. [§979]

Strict scrutiny is used when a generally applicable law is challenged on the basis that it violates the Free Exercise Clause plus some other constitutional protection, such as freedom of speech or press, or the right of parents to direct the educational upbringing of their children.

(a) Mandatory Education Laws. [§980]

A state cannot apply a mandatory education law to the Old Order Amish.

Wisconsin v. Yoder, 406 U.S. 205 (1972). The Court upheld a state court's reversal of the convictions of members of the Old Order Amish community who refused to send their children to state-certified schools through the age of sixteen. The Amish children did go to school through the eighth grade. The Court applied strict scrutiny, asserting that the Wisconsin compulsory education law violated the Free Exercise rights of the Amish parents, as well as their unenumerated right to direct the educational upbringing of their children.

(b) State Laws Requiring a Motto on a License Plate. [§981]

A state may not force a person to use license plates which carry a message to which the person objects on religious grounds.

Wooley v. Maynard, 430 U.S. 705 (1977). The Court held that the state of New Hampshire could not require a Jehovah's Witness to display on his car a license plate with the state motto, "Live Free or Die." While the Court relied primarily on the plaintiff's "right to refrain from speaking," it also discussed his religious objections to being forced to disseminate such a message. The Court treated this challenge as one involving First Amendment rights of speech and religion.

(3) Examples of Laws That Are Not Generally Applicable. [§982]

In these cases, strict scrutiny applies, even though the law is challenged solely on Free Exercise grounds.

(a) Unemployment Compensation Cases. [§983]

Strict scrutiny is also used in unemployment compensation cases where benefits are denied to a person who has lost a job, but the government provides an individualized hearing to determine eligibility. The individualized hearing takes these cases out of the category of "generally applicable" laws.

(i) Refusal to Work on the Sabbath. [§984]

A state cannot deny benefits to a person who refuses to work on her Sabbath.

Sherbert v. Verner, 374 U.S. 398 (1963). The Court held that unemployment compensation benefits could not be denied to a Seventh Day Adventist who was fired because she would not work on Saturday, which was her Sabbath. The Court found that the State Employment Security Commission's refusal to grant Sherbert an exemption substantially burdened her exercise of religion, and that the state had no compelling reason to deny the exemption.

(ii) Religious Objection to Making Weapons. [§985]

A state cannot deny unemployment compensation benefits to a person who has religious reservations about making weapons.

Thomas v. Review Board, 450 U.S. 707 (1981). The Court reversed a state court's denial of unemployment compensation benefits to a Jehovah's Witness who quit his job because his religious beliefs would not allow him to participate in the production of armaments. He had been transferred to a department that made tank turrets. Relying on *Sherbert* (previous case), the Court found that the denial of benefits to Thomas substantially burdened the free exercise of his religion, and was not supported by any compelling government interest.

(iii) Post-Hiring Development of Religious Beliefs. [§986]

A state cannot deny benefits to a worker whose religious beliefs developed after she had been on the job.

Hobbie v. Unemployment Appeals Commission, 480 U.S. 136 (1987). The Court held violative of the Free Exercise Clause a state commission's refusal to grant unemployment benefits to a worker whose newly formed religious beliefs prohibited her from working from sundown Friday to sundown Saturday. Despite the fact that her religious beliefs had developed after she had been working awhile, the Court found that the denial of benefits substantially burdened her free exercise of religion, and was not justified by any compelling government interest.

(b) Example of a Law That Is Not Generally Applicable Because it Has Exceptions Built Into It. [§987]

If a law has exceptions or exemptions built into it, strict scrutiny will apply, even though the law is challenged solely on Free Exercise grounds.

(i) Activities of Specific Religious Groups. [§988]

A state cannot selectively prohibit activity engaged in by a specific religious group, while allowing other religious groups to engage in that activity.

Church of the Lukumi Babalu Aye, Inc. v. Hialeah, 113 S.Ct. 2217 (1993). The Court invalidated ordinances of the city of Hialeah which, when read together, prohibited animal slaughter by members of the Santeria religion, but allowed it by other religious and commercial slaughterhouses. The Court found the purpose of the ordinance to be to keep the Santeria religion from operating in town. The Court said that a neutral, generally applicable law will not receive strict scrutiny, even if it incidentally burdens a religious practice. However, a law which is not neutral and generally applicable (because of exceptions or exemptions) must be narrowly tailored to achieve a compelling government interest. In addition to the free exercise argument of the Santeria religion, it is also arguable that the government is establishing religion by allowing other religious groups to maintain slaughterhouses.

2. WHAT COUNTS AS "RELIGION" FOR FREE EXERCISE CLAUSE PURPOSES? [§989]

Obviously someone who is a believer in or a member of an accepted mainstream religion will be able to make a Free Exercise challenge to a law. An issue arises when someone belongs to a new or non-mainstream religion, or has a religious belief system that is purely personal.

a. Religious Belief as a Basis for Conscientious Objector Status. [§990]

The Court looks to the importance of religion in the life of a recognized, mainstream adherent to evaluate the religion claims of conscientious objectors.

(1) "Religion" for Purposes of Conscientious Objector Status. [§991]

"Religion" for purposes of conscientious objector status depends on whether a person's religious belief system fills the same place in his life as a mainstream religion does in the life of one of its adherents.

U.S. v. Seeger, 380 U.S. 163 (1965). The Court interpreted a federal law which exempted from combat a person who, by religious training and belief, is conscientiously opposed to participation in war in any form. The test of "belief in a relation to a Supreme Being" (statutory language) was whether a given belief that is sincere and meaningful occupies a place in the life of its possessor parallel to that filled by the orthodox belief in God of one who clearly qualifies for the exemption.

(2) Opposition to All War. [§992]
Conscientious objectors must oppose all war, not just specific ones.

Gillette v. U.S., 401 U.S. 437 (1971). The Court upheld a provision of federal law which allows Congress to draft persons who oppose a particular war (not war in general) on religious grounds. The Court rejected the argument that the law abridged the Free Exercise rights of those who religiously opposed only unjust wars; the government interest in an efficient draft system overrode this argument.

b. Sincerity of Religious Beliefs. [§993]
The government may not inquire into the truth or falsity of religious beliefs. It may, however, question the sincerity of a person's claimed religious belief. A government cannot declare some religious beliefs true and some false; that would be tantamount to establishment of religion.

(1) Jury Determination of Religious Beliefs. [§994]
A jury may not question the truth or falsity of religious beliefs.

U.S. v. Ballard, 322 U.S. 78 (1944). The Court ruled that a jury may not be given the question of whether particular religious beliefs are true. The defendants in this case, who had been charged with mail fraud, claimed to be divine messengers who had talked with Jesus, and who had the power to cure incurable diseases. The Court held that the First Amendment guarantees the protection of a person's chosen form of religion regardless of how incomprehensible those views may be to others.

(2) Exaggerated Claims of Religious Belief. [§995]
Some claims of religious belief just go too far.

U.S. v. Kuch, 288 F.Supp. 439 (D.D.C. 1968). The district court refused to rule that the Free Exercise claim of the defendant in a drug case was based on a religion within the meaning of the First Amendment. Judith Kuch claimed to be a minister of the Neo-American Church, and asserted that her religious beliefs immunized her from criminal prosecution for federal drug offenses. The Neo-American Church was founded in California, and its leader was Chief Boo Hoo. Kuch was the primate of the Potomac, and supervised the Boo Hoos in her area. To join the church, one had to subscribe to the principle that marijuana and LSD are not drugs, but the true Host of the church, and that it was the religious duty of all members to partake of the sacraments on a regular basis. The church symbol was a three- eyed toad, its bulletin was the "Divine Toad Sweat," and its motto was "Victory over Horseshit!" The district court did not take Kuch's Free Exercise claims seriously.

3. RELIGION AND POLITICAL OFFICE. [§996]

Religion may not be used to qualify or disqualify a person from holding political office. Article VI, clause 3 of the Constitution provides that "[N]o religious Test shall ever be required as a Qualification to any office or public Trust under the United States." The Court has applied this rule to protect the Free Exercise Clause rights of those seeking public office.

a. Belief in God. [§997]

Office-seekers may not be required to declare a belief in God.

Torcaso v. Watkins, 367 U.S. 488 (1961). The Court invalidated a Maryland law which required any person who wanted to hold public office to declare a belief in God. **A person's belief or non-belief in God cannot be the basis for granting or withholding access to government office or benefits.**

b. Clergy Members as Legislators. [§998]

Members of the clergy may not be prohibited from being legislators.

McDaniel v. Paty, 435 U.S. 618 (1978). The Court invalidated a Tennessee law which prohibited members of the clergy from serving as legislators. There was no majority opinion, but a majority of Justices thought there was a violation of the Free Exercise Clause. Justice Brennan, concurring, also thought the Establishment Clause was violated because the primary effect of the law was to inhibit religion (which is forbidden by *Lemon*).

4. TAXES ON RELIGIOUS INSTITUTIONS. [§999]

Generally applicable taxes may be imposed on religious institutions, but churches may not be singled out for discriminatory taxation.

a. Denial of Tax-Exempt Status. [§1000]

The federal government can deny tax-exempt status to schools that discriminate based on race.

Bob Jones University v. U.S., 461 U.S. 574 (1983). The Court upheld an Internal Revenue Service denial of tax exempt status to all schools that engaged in racial discrimination, even if the discrimination was the result of sincerely held religious beliefs. The government interest in eliminating racial discrimination outweighed any incidental impact on the Free Exercise rights of the schools, their students, and the parents of those students.

b. Denial of Tax-Exempt Status. [§1001]

The federal government can deny tax deductions for expenses for mandatory church programs.

Hernandez v. Commissioner of Internal Revenue, 490 U.S. 680 (1989). The Court found no violation of the Free Exercise Clause (or the Establishment Clause) as a result of the IRS denying a tax deduction to persons who make payments to the Church of Scientology for "auditing" and "training" sessions. The Church requires payment for these sessions, so the Court did not consider them "charitable contributions" that were deductible. The Court said that the government had an overriding interest in maintaining a sound tax system, free from numerous religious exceptions.

c. Sales and Use Taxes. [§1002]

Generally applicable sales and use taxes may be imposed on religious institutions.

Jimmy Swaggart Ministries v. Board of Equalization, 493 U.S. 378 (1990). The Court upheld the imposition of generally applicable sales and use taxes on the sale of religious goods and literature by a religious organization. The taxes, which were applied to all sales and uses of tangible personal property in the state, were challenged under both the Establishment Clause and the Free Exercise Clause.

d. Social Security Tax. [§1003]

The federal government can apply the social security tax system to those whose religion forbids participation.

U.S. v. Lee, 455 U.S. 252 (1992). The Court upheld the application of the Social Security tax system to members of the Old Order Amish religion, even though payment into the system and receipt of benefits were forbidden by the religion. The Court said that the government has an overriding interest in the fiscal integrity of the social security system, and mandatory participation is the only way to achieve it.

5. SUNDAY CLOSING LAWS. [§1004]

A state law which requires businesses to close on Sundays does not violate the First Amendment. Just because a law happens to coincide with the tenets of a religion does not mean that the law is unconstitutional.

a. Sunday Closing Laws and the Establishment Clause. [§1005]

Sunday closing laws do not violate the Establishment Clause.

McGowan v. Maryland, 366 U.S. 420 (1961). The Court upheld Maryland's Sunday Closing Law against both Free Exercise and Establishment Clause challenges. The purpose and effect of the law were secular (providing a uniform day of rest), so there was no establishment of religion. The law had no direct effect of burdening Free Exercise rights.

b. Sunday Closing Laws and the Free Exercise Clause. [§1006]

Sunday closing laws do not violate the Free Exercise Clause.

Braunfeld v. Brown, 366 U.S. 599 (1961). The Court upheld a Sunday closing law against a challenge by orthodox Jewish merchants who claimed a special injury because their religious beliefs prohibited work on Saturday, so they lost two workdays out of the week. As in *McGowan* (previous case), there was no direct burden on Free Exercise rights, and the state could not be expected to recognize exceptions for all whose religions required a day of rest other than Sunday.

6. LAWS AFFECTING THE FREE EXERCISE RIGHTS OF NATIVE AMERICANS. [§1007]

The Court has not been sympathetic to the Free Exercise claims of Native Americans. **Be aware of how government action frequently makes it** impossible for Native Americans to practice essential aspects of their religion.

a. Social Security Numbers. [§1008]

Forcing Native Americans to submit and use an identification number does not violate the Free Exercise Clause.

Bowen v. Roy, 476 U.S. 693 (1986). The Court held that it did not violate the Free Exercise rights of a Native American child and her parent for a state to require them to submit the child's Social Security number for the state to use to identify her. The child and her parent argued that the submission and use of such a number violated their sincerely held religious beliefs. The Court considered this only an incidental burden on Free Exercise rights, and one that was clearly outweighed by the interest in an efficient welfare system.

b. Destruction of Sacred Sites. [§1009]

Federal land may be used in a way that necessitates the destruction of sacred sites.

Lyng v. Northwest Indian Cemetery Protective Association, 485 U.S. 439 (1988). The Court held that the federal government did not violate the Free Exercise rights of Native Americans by building a road and allowing timber harvesting in a national forest which included sacred areas which were integral to the Native American religion. The Court said that the Free Exercise Clause cannot be read to require the federal government to conduct its own internal affairs in ways that comport with the religious beliefs of particular citizens.

c. Sacramental Use of Peyote. [§1010]

A state may criminalize the sacramental use of peyote by Native Americans.

Employment Division v. Smith, 494 U.S. 872 (1990). The Court upheld a state's power to criminalize the use of peyote, even when used by Native Americans as an essential part of their religion. Oregon had a generally applicable drug law (all uses of certain drugs were prohibited) which was challenged solely on the basis that it violated the Free Exercise rights of two Native American drug counselors who had been fired for peyote use and then denied unemployment compensation because they were discharged for illegal conduct. The Court first said that a government may not regulate religious beliefs. It then set forth the rule that **a generally applicable law which has only an incidental effect of burdening religion does not offend the Free Exercise Clause. No heightened scrutiny is called for in such a case.**

D. ACCOMMODATION BETWEEN THE RELIGIOUS BELIEFS OF EMPLOYEES AND THE INTERESTS OF EMPLOYERS: TENSION BETWEEN THE FREE EXERCISE CLAUSE AND THE ESTABLISHMENT CLAUSE. [§1011]

When a government accommodates the religious beliefs of employees (by forcing employers to recognize a chosen Sabbath), it runs the risk of establishing religion. The Court balances the religious beliefs of employees against the degree of hardship imposed on the employer by the accommodation.

1. Refusal to Work on the Sabbath. [§1012]

Employees have no absolute right to a day off on their chosen Sabbath.

Estate of Thornton v. Caldor, Inc., 472 U.S. 703 (1985). The Court invalidated a Connecticut law which required employers to give employees a day off work on the employee's chosen day of worship. This law violated the Establishment Clause because it had the primary effect of advancing the particular religious practice of any employee who demanded a certain day off. The state's attempt to accommodate religious beliefs crossed the line into establishment of religion.

2. Exemption of Religious Organizations from Laws Banning Discrimination Based on Religion. [§1013]

Congress may exempt religious organizations from laws banning discrimination based on religion.

Corporation of the Presiding Bishop of the Church of Jesus Christ of Latter-Day Saints v. Amos, 483 U.S. 327 (1987). The Court upheld Title VII's exemption of religious organizations from the statute's prohibition against discrimination in employment based on religion. The Mormon Church fired a building engineer because he failed to qualify for a certificate that he was a member of the Church, and eligible to attend its temples. The Court applied the *Lemon* analysis, and found that the Title VII exemption for religious organizations met the purpose, effect, and entanglement prongs, thus avoiding any establishment of religion.

REVIEW PROBLEMS — THE RELIGION CLAUSES OF THE FIRST AMENDMENT

PROBLEM 1. The State of Oz has a program of providing computerized "readers" for visually impaired students in its public schools. A student simply puts any printed material on the scanner of the reader, and a computerized voice reads what is on the page. Jamie Jaynes is a ninth-grader in the Id School District (in the State of Oz), and has been blind from birth. She applies for and is given the use of a computerized reader to help her with her schoolwork. Jamie attends St. Matthew's Catholic High School. A group called Keep Religion Out of Schools (KROOS) sues, arguing that providing Jamie with a reader violates the Establishment Clause. Will KROOS prevail?

> **Answer:** No. Providing the computerized reader is a neutral, generally applicable benefit which the state gives to students in public, non-religious private, and parochial schools. Also, it is Jamie's decision, not the state's to use the reader in a parochial school. See §931 for further review.

PROBLEM 2. The School District of the City of Id allows high school graduates to decide if they would want a prayer at their graduation ceremony. If they do, the students choose a classmate to deliver the prayer, and the class advisor makes sure that the prayer is non-sectarian. Is this practice constitutional?

> **Answer:** Maybe. In *Lee v. Weisman*, 505 U.S. 577 (1992), see §944, the Court invalidated the practice of a principal choosing a member of the clergy to deliver an invocation or benediction at a junior high school graduation. This case is different because the students decide whether or not to have a prayer, and they choose a student to deliver it. At least one lower federal court has approved this kind of arrangement. See *Jones v. Clear Creek Independent School District*, 930 F.2d 416 (5th Cir. 1991).

PROBLEM 3. Id High School, a public school in the State of Oz, opens its gymnasium to members of the general public for speech purposes. All groups are admitted unless they are engaged in illegal activity. The Church of the Sublime Essence (CSE) applies for permission to use the school facilities for its meetings. CSE admits that there will be praying, singing, and discussion of spiritual matters. The principal of Id High School, who is in charge of granting permission to speakers, denies CSE's request on the basis that allowing them to use the gym would establish religion, in violation of the First Amendment. Does CSE have a right to use the public school gym for its meetings?

> **ANSWER:** Yes. Id High School has created a designated public forum. Any content-based exclusions from that forum receive strict scrutiny. The principal will argue that the government has a compelling interest in not establishing religion. The problem with this argument is that allowing religious speakers to have access to this kind of forum does not establish religion, so there is no compelling reason for the school to exclude them. As long as a number of different kinds of speakers have access, religious speakers must also be allowed to use the government property. See §964 for further review.

PROBLEM 4. The State of Oz has a law which requires that an autopsy be performed anytime a death occurs under certain, statutorily-defined circumstances. One of these circumstances is when a person's death is caused by or related to police activity. Gene Attroman belongs to a religion which prohibits autopsies as a desecration of the body of a deceased person. The religion also requires, as a matter of scriptural interpretation, that parents have control and dominion over the bodies of their deceased children. Gene's son, Jake, was killed in a high-speed chase with police. The state has Jake's body and wants to perform an autopsy as required by state law. Gene sues, claiming that the autopsy would violate his Free Exercise rights. Will Gene prevail?

Answer: Under *Employment Division v. Smith*, 494 U.S. 872 (1990), Gene will lose if he is challenging the mandatory autopsy law solely on free exercise grounds. A neutral, generally applicable law trumps free exercise claims. If Gene can inject another fundamental right into his argument, a court will use strict scrutiny, and may very well invalidate the application of the law to Gene. Remember that under the Religious Freedom Restoration Act of 1993, a court would use strict scrutiny to analyze Gene's case even if he is asserting only a free exercise argument. See §974 for further review.

PROBLEM 5. Holy Harry's Divine Discount Emporium is a large retail store in the State of Oz that sells only religious items and literature. The State of Oz imposes its sales tax on all retail establishments in the state, including Holy Harry's. Harry challenges the imposition of this tax on his business, arguing that it violates his free exercise rights. Will Harry win?

Answer: No. A generally applicable sales tax, applied in a neutral fashion to all retail stores in the state, would not violate Harry's free exercise rights. If religious stores were singled out for special taxation, then there would be a problem. See §1002 for further review.

XX. CRUEL AND UNUSUAL PUNISHMENT: THE DEATH PENALTY AND PROPORTIONALITY OF PUNISHMENT TO THE CRIME COMMITTED

A. INTRODUCTION. [§1014]

The Eighth Amendment prohibits the infliction of cruel and unusual punishments. This protection has been incorporated to apply to the states through the Fourteenth Amendment. The prohibition against cruel and unusual punishments has resulted in very specific judge-made rules regarding the imposition of the death penalty. It has also caused the Court to inquire into the proportionality between the offense committed and the penalty imposed. **Remember that the Constitution prohibits only those punishments that are cruel <u>and</u> unusual.** "Unusual" means the punishment has not often been used throughout history - it is not common."Cruel" means the forms or modes of punishment go beyond evolving standards of decency in a civilized society (caning, drawing and quartering, the rack).

B. DEATH PENALTY CASES. [§1015]

The death penalty is not intrinsically unconstitutional; the Due Process Clauses refer to the deprivation of life, so the Constitution clearly contemplates the use of the death penalty. The constitutional question in death penalty cases is the manner in which the death penalty is imposed. Be aware of the specific rules articulated by the Court, as well as the underlying concerns of fairness and equality of application.

1. FOUNDATION CASES DEALING WITH THE DEATH PENALTY. [§1016]

Since 1972 (when the Court essentially invalidated the death penalty as it was then being applied), the Court has been struggling with the issue of potential unfairness in imposing the death penalty. **The main focus of its jurisprudence in this area has been to try to erect procedural safeguards to alleviate problems of arbitrary imposition of the death penalty, including discrimination in its application. One of the main safeguards required by the Court is that a sentencing judge must consider aggravating and mitigating circumstances of the crime before imposing the death penalty.**

a. Imposition of the Death Penalty. [§1017]
Arbitrary imposition of the death penalty violates the Eighth Amendment.

Furman v. Georgia, 408 U.S. 238 (1972). The Court overturned three death sentences from Georgia and Texas, holding that **the random and arbitrary method of imposing the death penalty was cruel and unusual punishment under the Eighth Amendment.** In *Furman* and its two companion cases, one of the death sentences was imposed for murder, the other two for rape. In each of the cases, the determination whether the penalty should be death or some lighter sentence was, by state statute, left to the unguided discretion of a jury. In reversing the imposition of the death penalty in these cases, the Justices cited the infrequency with which Georgia and Texas imposed the death penalty (the death penalty was disproportionately imposed on the poor, and on members of racial minority groups), as well as the lack of procedural safeguards provided by the states.

b. Procedural Aspects of Imposing the Death Penalty. [§1018]

States may impose the death penalty as long as bifurcated trials are used, and aggravating and mitigating circumstances are considered.

Gregg v. Georgia, 428 U.S. 153 (1976). The Court upheld the death penalty procedures implemented by Georgia after the *Furman* case. A majority of Justices agreed that the death penalty is a constitutionally permissible punishment if imposed fairly. The Court upheld Georgia's system of a bifurcated trial, at which the issues of guilt and sentence are considered separately. **The Georgia law also required that, before a jury may impose the death penalty, it must find at least one of the statutorily listed aggravating circumstances beyond a reasonable doubt.** The jury must also consider any mitigating circumstances that may lead it to recommend a penalty other than death.

c. Mandatory Death Sentences. [§1019]

States may not impose mandatory death sentences for certain crimes.

Woodson v. North Carolina, 428 U.S. 280 (1976) and *Roberts v. Louisiana*, 428 U.S. 325 (1976). The Court invalidated mandatory death sentences for specified crimes. Mandatory death statutes did not allow for individualized consideration of relevant aspects of the character and record of each defendant (no specific aggravating or mitigating circumstances were considered). The rigidity and harshness of such sentences may invite juries to disregard the law so as to avoid imposing the death penalty.

d. Mitigating Circumstances. [§1020]

The trial judge must be able to consider all possible mitigating circumstances.

(1) *Lockett v. Ohio*, 438 U.S. 586 (1978). [§1021]

The Court invalidated a statute which limited a judge in a capital sentencing case to the consideration of only three narrowly defined mitigating circumstances. The Court ruled that the sentencer must be allowed to consider all possible mitigating circumstances that pertain to a defendant's character or record, or to the circumstances surrounding the particular crime at issue. The Court has ruled in a later case (*Walton v. Arizona*, 497 U.S. 639 (1990)) that it is permissible for a state to allow a judge, rather than a jury, to decide whether to impose the death penalty, and that a trial judge may impose the death penalty even if an advisory jury has recommended a prison sentence (*Spaziano v. Florida*, 468 U.S. 447 (1984)).

(2) *Eddings v. Oklahoma*, 455 U.S. 104 (1982). [§1022]

The Court vacated the death penalty of a defendant who was 16 years old at the time of the murder. The sentencing judge refused to consider as a mitigating circumstance the fact that the defendant had been brutally beaten by his father, and had a history of emotional problems.

The Court reiterated the rule that all mitigating factors must be considered before imposing the death penalty.

e. Advisory Jury Verdicts. [§1023]

Capital sentencing statutes that require the sentencing judge to consider an advisory jury verdict need not specify the weight the judge must give to the advisory verdict.

Harris v. Alabama, 115 S.Ct. 1031 (1995). The Court upheld an Alabama law which vested capital sentencing authority in the trial judge and required the judge to consider an advisory jury verdict as to whether the death penalty should be imposed, but did not specify how much weight the judge is to give to the advisory verdict. The Court said that because the Constitution permits a trial judge, acting alone, to impose the death penalty, there is no problem under the Cruel and Unusual Punishment Clause with a state entrusting to the judge the decision of how much weight to give to the advisory verdict of the jury.

f. Vagueness Challenge to Aggravating Factors. [§1024]

The Court rejected a vagueness challenge to a state law that allowed a judge to impose the death sentence for crimes committed in an especially "heinous, cruel, or depraved manner."

Walton v. Arizona, 497 U.S. 639 (1990). The Court upheld against a vagueness challenge an Arizona law that allowed a judge to impose the death penalty if she finds that the crime was committed in an especially "heinous, cruel, or depraved manner." The Court ruled that the Arizona statute did not give judges an excessive amount of discretion in sentencing.

g. Vagueness Challenge to Jury Instructions. [§1025]

Reviewing courts should give deference to state-court jury instructions regarding the conditions under which the death penalty should be imposed.

Tuilaepa v. California, 114 S.Ct. 2630 (1994). The Court held that certain jury instructions given during the penalty phase of a death penalty case were not so vague as to violate the Eighth Amendment (the argument was that the jury instructions were not clear enough to provide specific guidance to the jurors in their deliberations whether or not to impose the death penalty). The challenged instructions required the jurors to consider the circumstances of the crime, the existence of any special circumstances, and the presence or absence of prior criminal activity involving the use or attempted use of force or violence. In finding that the instructions were not unconstitutionally vague, the Court reiterated the rule that vagueness review is very deferential, and that a sentencing factor will be upheld so long as it has some common sense core of meaning which juries should be able to understand.

2. MENTAL STATE OF DEFENDANTS IN DEATH PENALTY CASES. [§1026]

The mental state of a defendant must be considered before the death penalty may be imposed.

a. Execution of Insane Defendants. [§1027]

The Eighth Amendment prohibits the execution of a defendant who is insane at the time of the scheduled execution. *Ford v. Wainwright*, 477 U.S. 399 (1986).

b. Use of Anti-Psychotic Medication. [§1028]

Anti-psychotic medication may be given to a prisoner involuntarily under certain circumstances, making that prisoner eligible for the death penalty (a psychotic defendant would fall within the legal definition of insanity, and thus be ineligible for execution). In relation to the rule that an insane defendant cannot be executed, consider *Washington v. Harper*, 494 U.S. 210 (1990), in which the Court held that **as long as proper administrative procedures are in place, a mentally ill inmate may be given anti-psychotic medication against his or her will.** In that case, officials of a state correctional institution were able to administer anti-psychotic medication to an inmate who suffered from a manic-depressive disorder.

c. Execution of Mentally Retarded Defendants. [§1029]

It is not a per se violation of the Eighth Amendment to execute a mentally retarded defendant. The Eighth Amendment does not prohibit the execution of a mildly or moderately retarded defendant, as long as the retarded defendant has the ability to prove mitigating circumstances pertaining to his or her character record, or circumstances of the offense. *Penry v. Lynaugh*, 492 U.S. 302 (1989).

3. EXECUTION OF JUVENILES. [§1030]

The Eighth Amendment prohibits the execution of a defendant who was fifteen years old or younger at the time of committing the offense. (*Thompson v. Oklahoma*, 487 U.S. 815 (1988)). It does not prohibit the execution of a defendant who was sixteen years old or older at the time of committing the offense (*Stanford v. Kentucky*, 492 U.S. 361 (1989)). In drawing this line, the Court considered factors such as the degree of moral culpability of juvenile offenders (to what extent can society hold juveniles morally responsible for their acts?), a minor's capacity for growth, society's obligation to care for its children, and the practices in different jurisdictions regarding imposing the death penalty on juveniles.

4. STATISTICAL EVIDENCE OF RACIAL DISPARITY IN IMPOSING THE DEATH PENALTY IS NOT ENOUGH TO PROVE AN EIGHTH AMENDMENT VIOLATION. [§1031]

The Court rejected the argument that an Eighth Amendment violation can be proven by presenting statistical evidence that black defendants who murder white victims are more likely to receive the death penalty than other defendants.

McCleskey v. Kemp, 481 U.S. 279 (1987). The Court rejected the Eighth Amendment argument of a defendant sentenced to death who offered a study showing that defendants who murder white victims are 4.3 times as likely to receive the death penalty as those charged with killing black victims. Given the protections built into the Georgia capital sentencing system, the Court held that the study was not sufficient to prove a constitutionally significant risk of racial bias in capital- sentencing cases.

5. VICTIM IMPACT STATEMENTS. [§1032]

The Eighth Amendment does not erect any <u>per se</u> bar to the introduction of "victim impact evidence" in a capital sentencing proceeding. This evidence involves the impact of the crime on the victim's family, friends, and professional associates, as well as the effect of the crime on the community.

Payne v. Tennessee, 501 U.S. 808 (1991). The Court overruled two recent cases in holding that the Eighth Amendment imposed no **per se** rule against the use of "victim impact evidence" and prosecutorial discussion of that evidence in a capital sentencing proceeding. The Court rejected the argument that the introduction of "victim-impact evidence" allows a jury to conclude that defendants whose victims were assets to the community deserve greater punishment than defendants whose victims are not as highly regarded in the community.

6. JURY INSTRUCTIONS REGARDING INELIGIBILITY FOR PAROLE FROM A LIFE SENTENCE. [§1033]

A jury cannot sentence a defendant to death unless it is apprised of the fact that, under state law, the defendant would be ineligible for parole if he or she received a life sentence. It would be unfair for a jury to sentence a defendant to death on the assumption that he or she may get out on parole and create a future danger to society.

Simmons v. South Carolina, 114 S.Ct. 2187 (1994). A majority of the Court ruled that when a defendant's future dangerousness is a potential aggravating factor during the penalty phase of a capital case, and state law prohibits the defendant's release on parole, due process requires that the jury be told that the defendant is ineligible for parole. A defendant may not be sentenced to death on the possibility that the jury thought its choices were between the death penalty and a limited prison term. There was no Eighth Amendment issue in this case.

7. EVIDENCE OF A PRIOR DEATH SENTENCE. [§1034]

Even though irrelevant under state rules of evidence, **it is not an Eighth Amendment violation for a sentencing jury to learn that the defendant had received the death penalty in a prior case.**

Romano v. Oklahoma, 114 S.Ct. 2004 (1994). The Court held that it did not violate the Eighth Amendment or the Due Process Clause for the state, during the penalty phase of a capital trial, to introduce evidence that the defendant had received the death penalty during an earlier trial for another murder. Even though evidence of a prior death penalty may have been irrelevant under state law, it does not follow that its admission amounted to federal constitutional error. The Court ruled that, even though the evidence in question was irrelevant, the jury's consideration of it did not render the sentencing phase of the capital trial so unreliable as to violate the Eighth Amendment.

C. PROPORTIONALITY. [§1035]

The Court has said that the Eighth Amendment includes a proportionality requirement that should be applied in both capital and non-capital cases. This is a judicially created doctrine requiring that the harshness of the sentence be proportionate to the gravity of the offense.

1. Proportionality in Capital Cases. [§1036]

The Court has used the proportionality principle to overturn certain death sentences.

a. Rape. [§1037]

The death penalty may not be imposed for rape.

Coker v. Georgia, 433 U.S. 584 (1977). The Court held that it was disproportionate to impose the death penalty for rape, a crime that did not involve the death of the victim. The Court said that in terms of moral depravity and injury to the victim, rape does not compare with murder, so the Eighth Amendment bars the death penalty in such cases.

b. Accomplice Not Present at a Murder. [§1038]

The death penalty may not be imposed on an accomplice who was not present at the murder.

Enmund v. Florida, 458 U.S. 782 (1982). The Court used proportionality analysis to rule that the death penalty may not be imposed on a defendant who is an accomplice to a murder (waited outside in the getaway car), but did not himself kill, attempt to kill, or intend that a killing take place or that lethal force be used.

c. Accomplice Present at a Murder. [§1039]

The death penalty may be imposed on an accomplice who was present at the murder.

Tison v. Arizona, 481 U.S. 137 (1987). The Court ruled that the proportionality requirement of the Eighth Amendment does not bar the imposition of the death penalty on a defendant who was present at the murders of a family of four, but made no move to stop the murders. Even though the defendant neither killed, nor intended to kill, the victims, his participation in the killings was major, and his mental state was one of reckless indifference to human life.

2. Proportionality in Non-Capital Cases. [§1040]

The Court also uses proportionality analysis in non-capital cases. **The Court will look at the gravity of the offense and the harshness of the penalty; the sentences imposed on other criminals in the same jurisdiction; and sentences imposed for the same crime in other jurisdictions.**

a. Factors in Applying Proportionality Analysis. [§1041]

The Court has identified three factors to use in applying proportionality analysis.

Solem v. Helm, 463 U.S. 277 (1983). The Court used proportionality analysis to overturn a life sentence with no possibility of parole under a South Dakota recidivist statute. The defendant had committed seven non-violent felonies. **Asserting that proportionality analysis is applicable in non-capital cases, the Court set forth three factors to consider: the gravity of the offense and the harshness of the penalty; the sentences imposed on other criminals in the same jurisdiction; and sentences imposed for the same crime in other jurisdictions.**

b. Life Sentence Under Recidivist Statute. [§1042]

States may impose a life sentence under recidivist statutes, even for fairly minor crimes.

Rummel v. Estelle, 445 U.S. 263 (1980). The Court rejected the proportionality argument in a case where the defendant received a life sentence under a recidivist statute for three fairly minor crimes. The Court emphasized that proportionality analysis was especially appropriate in death penalty cases because of the unique and final nature of that punishment. In *Rummel*, the defendant received only a life sentence, and might become eligible for parole. These factors led the Court to reject proportionality analysis.

c. Mandatory Life Sentence For Cocaine Possession. [§1043]

A state may impose a mandatory life sentence for possession of cocaine.

Harmelin v. Michigan, 501 U.S. 957 (1991). The Court upheld a Michigan law imposing a mandatory life sentence without parole for possession of 650 or more grams of cocaine. The Court rejected the defendant's arguments that the law violated the Eighth Amendment because the penalty was disproportionate to the crime, and because the sentencing judge was not able to consider the defendant's character, record, and the circumstances of the offense. On the issue of proportionality, Justice Scalia and Chief Justice Rehnquist said there was no such requirement in the Eighth Amendment. However, a majority of Justices concluded that the Eighth Amendment does have a proportionality principle that applies even in non-capital cases.

OUTLINE

PROBLEM 1. The State of Oz is a death penalty state. Under its statutes, the death penalty is mandatory for certain crimes, including a homicide committed during or resulting from a kidnapping of a child. Jebediah Joons was convicted of killing a child after he had kidnapped her. Jeb is sentenced to death. Is his sentence constitutional?

> **Answer:** No. Mandatory death sentences for specific crimes are unconstitutional because they do not allow for consideration of mitigating factors. See §1019 for further review.

PROBLEM 2. Jebediah Joons has been convicted of a capital offense in the State of Oz. The jury's sentencing options are the death penalty or life imprisonment. Under state law, Jeb is ineligible for parole from a life sentence. The jury finds the statutorily prescribed aggravating circumstance of future dangerousness, and sentences Jeb to death. Jeb requested, but was denied, a jury instruction that he was not eligible for parole. Is his death sentence constitutional?

> **Answer:** No. Due process requires that, before a jury imposes the death penalty, it must be apprised of the defendant's ineligibility for parole from a life sentence. It is not fair for a jury to impose the death penalty on the assumption that the alternative is that the defendant will be out on parole in a few years. See §1033 for further review.

PROBLEM 3. Sam Spade was convicted of first degree criminal sexual conduct in the State of Id. Under state law, first degree criminal sexual conduct was a crime involving serious physical injury to the victim. The jury was presented with various aggravating factors, including the fact that the victim was a 14-year old girl, and sentenced Spade to death. Is Spade's death sentence constitutional?

> **ANSWER:** No. The Eighth Amendment contains a proportionality requirement in death penalty cases. Despite the heinous nature of the crime of rape, the Court has held that because it is not a crime involving the death of the victim, the death penalty would be a disproportionate penalty. See §1037 for further review.

XXI. PRACTICE MULTIPLE CHOICE QUESTIONS

Question 1

In an attempt to balance the budget, Congress has passed a comprehensive tax program. Under one provision, Congress imposed a special tax on all transportation activities in the ten largest transportation centers in the country. The law contains detailed procedures for determining which cities will be on the list. Transportation activities in other cities will not be taxed under the law.

Joe Jones, the Director of Transportation in the second largest transportation center in the country, sues to challenge this tax. The tax is probably:

(A) Constitutional, because a tax is valid as long as it raises money.

(B) Constitutional under Congress' General Welfare power.

(C) Unconstitutional under the Equal Protection Clause of the Fourteenth Amendment.

(D) Unconstitutional as a taking of private property.

Question 2

Dr. Jack Manoogian has made it a personal crusade to help long-suffering, terminally ill persons end their lives. The "suicide doctor" has helped over thirty people die. Even though the State of Oz, where Dr. Manoogian practices, has no law prohibiting assisted suicide, the local prosecutor has prosecuted Dr. Manoogian five times. Each of the five times, a court has dismissed the charges because no law is being violated. Despite this history, the prosecutor brings charges a sixth time against Dr. Manoogian. While this criminal case is pending, Dr. Manoogian goes to federal court to enjoin further state prosecution. The federal district court should:

(A) Abstain because a state criminal case is pending.

(B) Abstain because the state law is ambiguous, and state courts should clarify it.

(C) Issue the injunction because the latest state prosecution is brought in bad faith.

(D) Issue the injunction because state courts are not capable of resolving the issue of assisted suicide.

Question 3

Within the boundaries of State of Oz, there is a federal wildlife refuge. The Secretary of the Interior has issued regulations prohibiting the killing of any wildlife on federal land. The regulations also prohibit the killing of animals that have wandered off the federal land onto land under the jurisdiction of the state.

Jane Kleppe is a hunter who has a license from the State of Oz to kill deer. She watches a deer walk off the federal land, and shoots it. Jane is arrested by a federal game warden who watched the entire chain of events. Jane is prosecuted in federal court for violating the federal law. The strongest argument in favor of the federal law is:

(A) The police power of Congress includes protecting wild animals.

(B) The Secretary's regulations were enacted pursuant to a delegation of Congress' Property Power.

(C) Wildlife are in interstate commerce.

(D) The Supremacy Clause authorizes this federal law.

Question 4

Congress passes a law which provides that any dispute between a state and the federal government over specified aspects of nuclear power production (safety, disposal, economics) must be settled by the filing of a lawsuit in the federal district court of the District of Columbia. According to the law, that court shall render an opinion which shall be transmitted to the Secretary of Energy who, if satisfied with the court's opinion, shall take steps to insure that the federal government will comply with the court order. The strongest argument against this law is:

(A) It intrudes upon Congress' power to regulate interstate commerce.

(B) It violates the Eleventh Amendment immunity of states.

(C) It authorizes federal courts to issue advisory opinions.

(D) Congress has no power to set the jurisdiction of lower federal courts.

Question 5

A United States Supreme Court Justice was convicted of bribery and sentenced to 25 years in prison. Upon this event, the House of Representatives started impeachment proceedings against the Justice. Following an affirmative vote to impeach, a special subcommittee of the United States Senate started its own proceedings, pursuant to its constitutional duty to try all impeachments. After all of the pertinent evidence was gathered by this subcommittee, it presented its findings to the full Senate. The Senate voted to revoke all benefits and privileges for this Justice and to remove him from office. This Justice files a lawsuit in the Federal District Court claiming that the Senate did not follow the correct procedure to impeach him; specifically, Article I, section 3, clause 6 which states that the "Senate shall have the sole power to try all impeachments." The Justice's argument is that the entire Senate must participate in all aspects of the proceedings, including factfinding.

The District Court should:

(A) Not hear this case because it is moot.

(B) Not hear this case because it is a political question and the court does not have any manageable standards for resolving this dispute.

(C) Not hear this case because it is impossible for a court to decide this case without having an initial policy decision by some other co-equal branch of government.

(D) Not hear this case because the court lacks personal jurisdiction of the subject matter of this dispute because there are no minimum contacts.

Questions 6 and 7 are based on the following fact pattern.

Congress is very concerned about the disposal of toxic and nuclear waste, especially the fact that states keep trying to keep out-of-staters from dumping their waste instate. As part of a compromise package of legislation, Congress has authorized states, upon meeting certain requirements, to charge out-of-state toxic and nuclear waste disposal companies a special surcharge that is not applied to instate disposal companies. The State of Oz imposes the added surcharge on Gilda's Garbage Haulers, an out-of-state disposal company.

6.   If Gilda challenges the state law on the basis that it violates commerce clause principles, the court should:

(A) Uphold the state law because Congress may delegate to a state the power to discriminate against out-of-staters.

(B) Uphold the state law because a state has the right to keep out-of-staters from dumping waste instate.

(C) Invalidate the state law because it violates dormant commerce clause principles.

(D) Invalidate the state law as outside the Tenth Amendment police powers of the state.

7.   If Gilda challenges the state law on the basis that it violates the Equal Protection Clause, a court should:

(A) Uphold the state law because Congress may delegate to a state the power to discriminate against out-of-staters.

(B) Uphold the state law because a state has the right to keep out-of-staters from dumping waste in-state.

(C) Invalidate the state law because it violates the Equal Protection Clause.

(D) Invalidate the state law as outside the Tenth Amendment police powers of the state.

Question 8

Kid Nation is a corporation that builds and operates indoor play facilities for children. Kid Nation operates only in the State of Oz. It refurbishes old warehouses and installs all sorts of equipment for climbing and other activities for children. Kid Nation purchases all its climbing equipment from Cindy's Climbing Equipment, an out-of-state company. Cindy's is one of the two biggest manufacturers of children's play equipment. The other major manufacturer, Pat's Playthings, is an Oz company. The legislature of the State of Oz is concerned about the number of accidents in indoor children's play facilities. As a result, it is considering a law which would require all indoor play facilities within the state to meet very specific safety standards. The only equipment available that meets those standards is the "Hold-Fast" brand of play equipment. "Hold-Fast" has been tested and proven to be the safest play equipment available. Pat's Playthings, the instate company is a supplier of "Hold-Fast" equipment. Cindy's Climbing Equipment, the out-of-state company, sells another brand. To comply with this law, Kid Nation would have to switch its business from Cindy to Pat. If Cindy were to challenge this law, a court would:

(A) Invalidate this law because it discriminates against instate commerce.

(B) Invalidate this law because it imposes too great a burden on interstate commerce.

(C) Uphold the law as a valid exercise of the state's police power.

(D) Invalidate the law because it violates the Equal Protection Clause.

Questions 9-11 are based on the following fact pattern.

The legislature of the State of Oz is concerned about the growing shortage of landfill space in the state available for dumping garbage. The legislators know that they cannot simply pass a law prohibiting instate landfill operators from accepting solid waste from out of state. Instead, the State of Oz uses its power of eminent domain to acquire all the landfill space in the state, and begins to operate the State of Oz Landfill Company. The State, in the operation of its company, prohibits out-of-staters from bringing any solid waste into the state. The state asserts safety, health, and ecological reasons for its law. Gilda's Garbage Haulers, Inc., an out-of-state corporation, files suit challenging this law.

9. If the Gilda's Garbage Haulers, Inc., lawsuit is based on the argument that the Oz practice of refusing out-of-state waste violates dormant commerce clause principles, a court should rule for:

(A) Gilda because Oz is facially discriminating against out-of-state commerce.

(B) Gilda, because this practice creates a great risk of multiple burdens.

(C) Oz, because as a market participant, it is not bound by the dormant commerce clause.

(D) Oz, because it has significant reasons for the discrimination.

10. If the Gilda's Garbage Haulers, Inc., lawsuit is based on the argument that the Oz practice violates the Privileges and Immunities Clause of Particle IV, a court should rule for:

(A) Gilda, because Oz is facially discriminating against out-of-staters.

(B) Gilda, because her basic right to pursue an occupation is being abridged.

(C) Oz, because as a market participant, it is not bound by the Privileges and Immunities Clause of Article IV.

(D) Oz, because the Privileges and Immunities Clause of Article IV does not apply to these facts.

11. If the Gilda's Garbage Haulers, Inc., lawsuit is based on the argument that the Oz practice violates the Equal Protection Clause, a court should rule for:

(A) Gilda, because Oz is facially discriminating against out-of-staters.

(B) Gilda, because there is no legitimate reason for this law.

(C) Oz, because the Equal Protection Clause does not protect corporations.

(D) Oz, because it does have a legitimate reason for this practice, and its means are rationally related.

Question 12

The legislature of the State of Oz passes a law which prohibits any state money from being spent to pay for abortions. The law is challenged by a proper plaintiff as violating the Fourteenth Amendment Equal Protection Clause and the equal protection clause of the State Constitution. The State Supreme Court strikes down the state law, relying on the state equal protection clause which it says "is informed by the Equal Protection Clause of the Fourteenth Amendment." The State of Oz appeals to the U.S. Supreme Court. The Court should:

(A) Hear the case because a federal question is involved.

(B) Hear the case because the State Supreme Court did not make it clear that it was relying solely on state law.

(C) Not hear the case because it rests on adequate and independent state grounds.

(D) Not hear the case because no federal question is involved.

Question 13

The legislature of the State of Oz, succumbing to pressure from lobbyists for trial lawyers, recently raised the permissible percentage lawyers may charge in contingent fee cases from 30% to 40%. Lawyers were ecstatic, but a group of citizens known as People Against Lawyers (PAL) was furious. While there are thousands of contingent-fee cases pending in the state, no member of PAL is involved in any contingent fee case. Nonetheless, PAL sues in federal court, claiming that this new law effects an unconstitutional deprivation of property. The court should:

(A) Uphold the law because it is rationally related to a legitimate state interest.

(B) Dismiss the action because there is no dispute that is ripe.

(C) Uphold the law because this group has suffered a specific injury from this law.

(D) Dismiss the action because PAL has no standing.

Question 14

The federal government hired Bob's Construction Company to build a new federal building in the State of Oz. Oz has a very specific ordinance requiring handicapper access to all public buildings in the state. The plans for the federal building do not have handicapper access that comes close to meeting the Oz standards. Bob builds the federal building, and is cited by Oz authorities for violation of the state law. Bob's best argument against the application of the state law to him is:

(A) Supremacy Clause.

(B) Commerce Clause.

(C) Privileges and Immunities clause.

(D) The Tenth Amendment.

Question 15

A number of congressional committees are holding hearings on the "Blackwater Affair," involving real estate transactions of the President of the United States before she was elected. Not satisfied with the response of presidential aides, a Senate subcommittee subpoenas documents and other materials from a number of executive branch officials. The President, citing "executive privilege," orders the subpoenaed officials to refuse to turn over the requested documents and materials. What best describes the President's claim of executive privilege?

(A) The subpoena violates the constitutional principle of separation of powers.

(B) The President's executive privilege is absolute, except in cases of impeachment.

(C) The presidential papers are presumptively privileged, but the privilege must yield to a demonstrated specific need for evidence in a pending legislative proceeding.

(D) The President's executive privilege applies to proceedings by the Congress, but not to proceedings by the courts.

Questions 16 and 17 are based on the following fact pattern.

The President of the United States entered into an executive agreement with the Prime Minister of Canada regarding riverboat casino gambling on all waterways separating the two countries. Under this agreement, riverboat casino gambling would be allowed under certain conditions, on both the Canadian and American sides of the waterways. The State of Michigan passes a law prohibiting all riverboat casino gambling on any waters adjoining the state of Michigan.

16. The executive agreement between the President of the United States and the Prime Minister of Canada is:

(A) Valid, because even though executive agreements are not provided for in the Constitution, they have become an accepted practice.

(B) Valid, even if it conflicts with existing federal law.

(C) Invalid, because the President has, in effect, made a treaty which requires approval of two-thirds of the Senate.

(D) Invalid, because the power of the President to make an executive agreement must be delegated to him by an act of Congress.

17. The state statute is:

(A) Constitutional, because a state law takes precedence over any conflicting executive agreement.

(B) Constitutional, because the Michigan statute falls within the state's police power, and there is no superseding federal action.

(C) Unconstitutional, because state law for all states that are bounded by international waters is deemed to have terminated at the point of high tide.

(D) Unconstitutional, because an executive agreement is the law of the land and any act by the state inconsistent therewith is null and void.

Question 18

The President recently signed a treaty with the President of Ruritania, and the Senate promptly ratified it. Congress quickly passed legislation to implement the treaty. The treaty sets new rules and procedures for all aspects of trade between the two countries. There is tremendous opposition to certain provisions of this treaty from the largest energy producing companies in the United States. To appease them, Congress passes a law which provides that any lawsuit challenging provisions of the treaty, or of its implementing legislation, shall be filed directly in the Supreme Court of the United States, so that any litigation could be quickly resolved. The legislation allowing these suits to be filed directly in the Supreme Court is:

(A) Unconstitutional, because Congress may not enlarge or restrict the original jurisdiction of the Supreme Court.

(B) Unconstitutional, because the jurisdiction of the federal courts is established by Article III of the federal constitution.

(C)   Constitutional, because it is a "necessary and proper" means of implementing a treaty of the United States.

(D)   Constitutional, because Congress is empowered to make exceptions to and regulations governing the jurisdiction of the courts of the United States.

Question 19

Joe and Jane lived in the City of Id, which had a very large Mobanian population. Joe was Mobanian, Jane was not. Jane sued Joe in state court, alleging that he tortiously injured her when he left his car running and it smashed into her truck. During jury selection, Jane's attorney used all ten of her peremptory challenges to excuse Mobanians jurors. Joe objects, arguing that his Fourteenth Amendment right to equal protection has been violated by the use of peremptory challenges to exclude Mobanians from the jury. Joe's argument is:

(A)   Incorrect, because the Fourteenth Amendment does not apply when an attorney for a private litigant in a civil case exercises peremptory challenges.

(B)   Incorrect, because there is no right to a jury made up of a certain racial or ethnic group.

(C)   Correct, because the Fourteenth Amendment does apply to the exercise of peremptory challenges.

(D)   Correct, because Joe is entitled to the same percentage of Mobanians on his jury as there are in the general population.

Question 20 and 21 are based on the following fact pattern.

The legislature of the State of Oz is concerned about the number of illegitimate births in the state, especially to young, uneducated mothers. It passes a law which requires any female under the age of 19 to get an "Affidavit of Fitness to Parent" from a designated state agency. Any woman who has not applied for such an Affidavit, or who has applied and was turned down, must have an abortion before her fetus is viable. Any child born to a woman without a proper Affidavit must be put up for adoption. Breanda is an 18 year-old pregnant woman who dropped out of high school, and is presently on welfare. She does not want to apply for an Affidavit, so she files suit challenging this law. The state's best defense to Breanda's lawsuit is:

20.   The state's best defense to Breanda's law suit is:

(A)   The state interest in reducing welfare payments justifies this law.

(B)   The lawsuit is not ripe, because Breanda has not applied for an Affidavit.

(C)   The Tenth Amendment police power of a state allows this kind of restriction.

(D)   The law is rationally related to a legitimate government interest.

21.   Breanda's best argument is:

(A)   The law discriminates against her because of her age.

(B)   The law abridges her fundamental right to decide whether or not to terminate her pregnancy, and is not narrowly tailored to achieving a compelling government interest.

(C)   The law creates an unconstitutional irrebuttable presumption.

(D)   The law violates her rights under the privileges and immunities clause.

Question 22

The School Board of the City of Oz was running out of money, and decided to implement a "pay to play" requirement for high school sports. To play any sport, a student must pay a set fee ($200 for football, $100 for basketball, $50 for track, etc.). This requirement most severely affected poorer students who, statistically, were members of racial and ethnic minorities. A group of parents sues, asserting that the school board regulation discriminates on the basis of race and ethnicity. Which of the following statements is most correct?

(A)   The School Board will have to show a compelling interest and narrowly tailored means.

(B)   The School Board will have to show a legitimate interest and rationally related means.

(C)   The parents will have to show that the requirement is irrational.

(D)   The parents will have to show that the school board has no compelling interest underlying the requirement.

Question 23

Princess Myrna Maruba, a self-proclaimed priestess, has declared herself the leader of the Church of the Exalted Goddess. Princess Myrna was recently convicted of prostitution. She acknowledged exchanging sex for money, but claims that her sex partners were members of her church, and that the money was simply a "church offering." She was arrested after soliciting an undercover police officer to engage in sex for money. If Princess Myrna challenges her conviction on Free Exercise grounds, she will probably:

(A) Win, because her Free Exercise rights have been violated.

(B) Win, because the law discriminates against her religion.

(C) Lose, because her religious beliefs are not true.

(D) Lose, because even if her religious beliefs are sincere, a generally applicable prostitution law may be applied to her.

Question 24

The State of Oz was hard hit by a number of economic problems. Interest rates were soaring, construction was down, and the number of small businesses in the state was dropping. To help combat these problems, the legislature set up a Small Business Loans Association (SBLA), which would help small businesses get started through a system of loans, tax breaks, and other incentives. The SBLA limited its help and programs to United States citizens. Erin Smith was not a citizen of the United States, and was turned down for a loan by the SBLA. She sues to challenge the exclusion of aliens from this program. Which of the following best describes the standard to be applied in Erin's case?

(A) Erin must prove that this citizenship requirement is not rationally related to a legitimate government interest.

(B) The State must prove that this citizenship requirement is rationally related to a legitimate government interest.

(C) The State must prove that this citizenship requirement is substantially related to a significant or important government interest.

(D) The State must prove that this citizenship requirement is narrowly tailored to a compelling government interest.

Question 25

In an effort to reduce the state deficit, the State of Oz imposed a 2% sales tax on all food. The Sanctified Church of Cosmic Oneness (SCCO) took personal offense to this state law. For the past 10 years the SCCO has solicited contributions at churches, in airports, and in parks to purchase groceries and distribute food to the poor. Many church groups had lobbied against the imposition of this tax, alleging that this tax would reduce the amount of food purchased and distributed to the people who really need it. Once this law was enacted, Minister Mooney, a high official of SCCO, filed an action in district court challenging the constitutionality of the food tax. The federal court should find the tax:

(A) Constitutional, because Minister Mooney has no standing to file an action.

(B) Constitutional, because the tax is equally implemented, was not designed to benefit or burden religion, and its effect on religious organizations is merely incidental.

(C) Unconstitutional, because the law is facially discriminatory, and the State cannot show any compelling governmental interest and narrowly tailored means.

(D) Unconstitutional, because the tax obstructs the free exercise of religion.

Question 26

The State of Oz has fallen upon some financial difficulties and is looking for a way to increase revenues. The legislature enacts a law that would allow river boat casino gambling within its state borders. The policy behind this law is that the legislature hopes these boats will bring in out-of-staters and thus increase state revenues. However, the State is concerned that their state residents may be drawn to these gambling boats also. To prevent this from happening, the State legislature passes another law prohibiting the gambling establishments form targeting local residents in their advertising. The advertising law is probably:

(A) Unconstitutional, because this is a content-based restriction, and the state does not have a compelling interest or narrowly tailored means.

(B) Constitutional, because a state has limited power to regulate commercial speech.

(C) Unconstitutional, because once a state allows gambling there is no significant interest in protecting its citizens from gambling advertisement.

(D) Constitutional, because if the state may completely prohibit the activity, it may channel the advertising for that activity.

Question 27

The State of Oz recently passed new health care reform legislation. Since then, the government office building is getting hundreds and maybe thousands of phone calls per day regarding the new legislation. The State of Blue decided to have a "What You Ever Wanted To Know About Health Care Day". All members of the public were invited. Government employees would be on hand to answer as many questions as they could regarding health care reform. Chapter 32 of the Mobanian Supremacy Society (MSS), located in the State of Oz, has the lowest membership of any MSS chapter in the United States. Thus, MSS decided to come to the Health Care Question Day and hand out leaflets to increase its membership. Police officers at the government office building asked the members to stop because they were violating a local ordinance prohibiting all leafletting in the government office building except that done by government employees and related to their work. The MSS members refused to stop and were arrested. Which of the following is most correct:

(A) The office building was transformed into a public forum for the day.

(B) The government has discretion in formulating reasonable rules regarding who has access to governmental buildings.

(C) The local ordinance violates the MSS's right to freedom of expression.

(D) The ordinance is valid since it leaves open ample alternative channels of communications.

Question 28

The Town of Id has been overwhelmed with adult bookstores. Many residents were complaining about a decrease in property values, and an increase in crime. In response to all of these complaints the Town Council amended its zoning ordinances to ban adult bookstores in all areas zoned "residential" or "commercial." The bookstores would still be allowed in all areas zoned industrial. In the Town of Id there were numerous areas zoned industrial; however, none was located near any major streets. Mr. Renton, owner and operator of a chain of adult bookstores in the town of Id, files a suit in federal court, alleging that the statute is unconstitutional. The court is likely to rule in favor of:

(A) The Town, because its zoning code allowed ample alternative avenues for adult bookstores to operate.

(B) Mr. Renton, because the amended zoning code will deprive him of his constitutional right to make a living.

(C) The Town, because this is a justifiable prior restraint.

(D) Mr. Renton, because this time, place, manner, restriction must be content neutral, and it is not.

Question 29

The State of Oz has had a huge population growth since the last time it drew the boundaries of congressional voting districts. Due to the increase in population, plus shifting housing patterns, the legislature has redrawn the lines of its seven congressional districts. After redistricting, each of the districts had a population within 1% of that of any other district. Norm Nostrum, a citizen in one of the new districts, files a lawsuit challenging the new district boundaries. Norm will:

(A) Win, if the redistricting was done for political reasons.

(B) Win, because any disparity in the number of people in congressional districts is an equal protection violation.

(C) Lose, if the state can provide a compelling reason for its new district boundaries.

(D) Lose, because a 1% differential is within the constitutionally acceptable range for congressional districts.

Questions 30 and 31 are based on the following fact pattern.

The State of Oz just amended its Probate Code. Section 700.272 states that any unacknowledged illegitimate child may not inherit his or her biological father's property. The order of intestate property distribution is as follows: (1) the then living spouse; (2) any other blood relative not explicitly excluded in this section; and (3) if 1 or 2 is not met, then all funds shall escheat to the state.

30. Mariah was an illegitimate unacknowledged child of Mike Boosweather. Mike dies intestate, without any living spouse or blood relatives except Mariah. Mariah files an action with the Probate Court in the State of Oz alleging that Section 700.272 is unconstitutional, and that she should be declared the lawful heir of the Boosweather fortune. Mariah's strongest argument in challenging the constitutionality of this statute is:

(A) There is not an important governmental reason why the state favors more distant relatives and, ultimately, the state, over any unacknowledged illegitimate children, thus this statute violates the Equal Protection Clause.

(B) Mariah has been deprived of her property without due process of law, and therefore the effect of this law is similar to a taking without any reasonable compensation.

(C) This statute violates Mariah's procedural due process rights because no hearing is provided to prove paternity.

(D) This statute violates the Due Process clause of the Fifth Amendment.

31. The State's strongest defense of the statute would be that:

(A) Under the Tenth Amendment, all powers not specifically reserved for the federal government are left to the states.

(B) Inheritance under intestate succession laws is not a constitutionally protected right. It is a privilege, and not covered under the Due Process Clause.

(C) Many times an unacknowledged illegitimate child is very difficult to locate and the State has a legitimate governmental interest in closing a probated estate. Thus this interest is rationally related to Section 700.272 of the Probate Code.

(D) The State has a significant governmental interest in encouraging family harmony, and in encouraging the formal acknowledgement of children, and Section 700.272 substantially achieves that governmental interest.

Question 32

The City of Discreet enacted legislation that prohibits the display of movies on television if those movies are found to be obscene as to children. The policy behind this legislation is to protect minors from the sexually explicit messages of these films. The legislation specifically defines the criteria for these films in conformance with Supreme Court precedent.

Motel 666, a nationwide motel chain, wishes to show some of these films to its customers. Motel 666 has two locations in the State of Discreet. Motel 666's best argument against this law is:

(A) This legislation is unconstitutionally applied to Motel 666 because the legislature must apply a contemporary national standard as opposed to a contemporary community standard.

(B) The legislature can only prohibit obscene materials as judged by an adult standard.

(C) The legislation is not narrowly drawn as to the stated purpose of preventing minors' access to this material.

(D) The legislation lacks the constitutionally mandated exception of supplying obscene material to consenting adults.

Question 33

The State of Oz passed a new abortion statute. The statute provides for legal abortions. However, the state will only pay for abortions of indigent women when two licensed physicians can substantiate that the life of the mother is in imminent danger. A pro-choice group found an indigent mother who was raped and wanted an abortion, but lacked the necessary funds. This mother files suit in the federal district court challenging the statute. The court should rule that this statute is:

(A) Constitutional, because the fetus has all the protections of the Fourteenth Amendment, and therefore the state may protect the fetus's interest in life.

(B) Unconstitutional, because this statute deprives women of their constitutional right to decide whether or not to terminate their pregnancies.

(C) Constitutional, because the statute does not prevent women from having abortions; it just refuses to pay for them.

(D) Unconstitutional, because wealth is a suspect class and the state does not have a compelling interest in refusing to fund abortions.

Question 34

The State of Oz decided that the state needed a new Hall of Justice to house its state Supreme Court and Court of Appeals. The legislature passed a statute authorizing the governor to enter into a contract for a new building, and directing the expenditure of $40 million for construction. The governor entered into the construction contract with Bob's Construction Company. After the contract was signed, a recession hit the state, and the legislature passed a statute cancelling the contract, and withdrawing the authorization to spend money for the new Hall of Justice. Bob's Construction Company files suit in federal court to enforce the contract. In ruling on the statute cancelling the contract, a court should hold that the statute is:

(A) Invalid as an unconstitutional impairment of an existing contract.

(B) Valid, because a legislature can always repeal a law.

(C) Valid, because a state cannot be sued in federal court.

(D) Invalid, if Bob's Construction Company can show detrimental reliance.

Question 35

The State of Oz has a law which requires all state employees to retire at age 70. However, state police officers must retire at age 50. The state argues that, as a general matter, the reflexes and physical abilities of people decline at age 50, so this is a reasonable age at which to force police to retire. The state says the mandatory retirement age protects the police officer, other officers, and the public. Ryan Nolan, 50 years old, and every bit as fit as any of the younger officers, sues in federal court, challenging the mandatory retirement law. The court will:

(A) Invalidate the law as not being substantially related to any important government issue.

(B) Uphold the law because a state has plenary power to regulate its police force.

(C) Invalidate the law because Ryan has a fundamental right to pursue the occupation of police officer.

(D) Uphold the law because age classifications receive only rational basis review.

Question 36

The National Rotisserie Football League (NRFL) is a nationwide organization of men who drink beer, wear official football jerseys, and play an entire schedule of football games on computers The men also conduct mock player drafts, pretend to trade players, and do whatever else real football executives and coaches do. NRFL is incorporated in the State of Oz. Oz has a law that prohibits all membership organizations above a certain size from excluding persons from membership because of their race or gender. Louella Bodine applied to be a member of NRFL. She was refused because no women were allowed. Louella sues NRFL on the basis of the Oz statute. NRFL claims that the Oz statute is unconstitutional. NRFL will:

(A) Prevail, because the statute forces it to accept women as members, thereby violating the associational rights of its members.

(B) Prevail, because the statute impairs the obligations of contracts of NRFL members.

(C) Lose, because the state's interest in eradicating gender discrimination outweighs the associational rights of NRFL members.

(D) Lose, because NRFL has no associational rights to assert.

Question 37

The State of Oz enacted a statute requiring the parents of every child to have the child vaccinated for smallpox before the child's third birthday. Failure to comply is a misdemeanor punishable by a fine of $500. Joe and Jane Jones object to the application of the statute to their infant children on the ground that any injections or vaccinations violate the tenets and beliefs of their religion, and interfere with their right to raise their children. What best describes the burden of proof if the Joneses file suit challenging this state law?

(A) The Joneses must prove that the state has no legitimate reason for passing this law.

(B) The Joneses must prove that the state has no compelling interest in passing this law.

(C) The state must show a compelling interest underlying this law.

(D) The state must show that this is a law of general applicability that only incidentally burdens religion.

Question 38

The State of Oz imposed a sales tax on cable television services, but did not similarly tax the print media. Karen's Kablevision brought suit challenging this law on the basis that a discriminatory tax against one medium of mass communication violates the First Amendment guarantee of freedom of the press, as well as the Equal Protection Clause. The court should rule that the Oz sales tax is:

(A) Unconstitutional as a discriminatory tax against one medium of communication.

(B) Unconstitutional because there is no rational basis for this discrimination.

(C) Constitutional, because the tax is content neutral, and does not threaten to suppress the expression of particular ideas or viewpoints.

(D) Constitutional, because there is no First Amendment protection afforded cable television.

Question 39

Jane Jones was a reporter for the Daily Bugle, the largest newspaper in the City of Id. Jane was doing a series of stories on corruption and crime in local government. Edna Edwards was a member of the Id City Council who was supplying Jane with information about other government officials. Edna only provided information on the condition that Jane never use her name in a story. In Jane's last story of the series, she divulged Edna's name. Edna sued Jane for breach of contract. The court should:

(A) Rule for Jane because reporters have a First Amendment privilege which immunizes them from a civil suit for printing the name of sources.

(B) Rule for Jane because if civil liability were imposed on reporters, it would have a chilling effect on their speech.

(C) Rule for Edna because she is a public official whose career has been ruined by the story.

(D) Rule for Edna because reporters have no special First Amendment privilege, and may be sued just like anyone else.

Question 40

The State of Oz is a death penalty state. Jeffrey Doomer has been convicted of multiple murders, and is sentenced to die on September 1st. During the summer preceding his scheduled execution, Doomer becomes increasingly psychotic, to the point where he is completely out of touch with reality, and is suffering from delusions and hallucinations. Every mental health professional who has seen him has declared him severely mentally ill. The Director of Corrections of the State of Oz intends to go ahead with the scheduled execution. Doomer's lawyer sues to block the impending execution. The court should rule for:

(A)   The State, because Doomer was sane at the time he committed the crime.

(B)   The State, because it complied with all procedural due process requirements, and should be able to carry out its sentence.

(C)   Doomer, because executing an insane person violates the Eighth Amendment's ban on cruel and unusual punishment.

(D)   Doomer, because executing an insane person violates his due process rights.

ANSWERS TO THE MULTIPLE CHOICE QUESTIONS

Answer to Question 1.

(A) is the right answer.

A tax is valid if it raises money, or is a means of achieving a legitimate government goal. This tax, even though selective, raises money. (B) is incorrect because Congress has no "General Welfare power." It only has the power to spend for the general welfare. (C) is wrong for two reasons: the Fourteenth Amendment has nothing to do with Congress, and the discrimination would pass rationality review in any event. (D) is wrong because taxes are not analyzed under the Takings Clause. [See Text §173]

Answer to Question 2.

(C) is the right answer.

(A) is wrong, although it reflects the general rule that a federal court will usually abstain from enjoining a pending criminal case in state court. However, if there is no chance of a conviction, a federal court may enjoin the state proceeding. On the facts, there is no state law prohibiting what Dr. Manoogian is doing, plus five courts have already thrown out charges against him. (B) is wrong because there is no state law, so there is nothing to be ambiguous. (D) is wrong because it's beside the point - the issue is not a court's ability to resolve this question, it is the ability to continue to prosecute someone with no chance of success. [See Text §118]

Answer to Question 3.

(B) is the right answer.

The Property Power gives Congress the power to make rules for federal property, including wildlife on federal lands. This law is probably valid because it is a necessary and proper means of protecting federal property. (A) is wrong because Congress has no general police power (it has a specific one for the District of Columbia). (C) is not the best answer. You could make an argument that, in the aggregate, wildlife affect interstate commerce, but that is not as strong as the Property Power argument. (D) is a premature argument because before you get to the issue of preemption, you must have a valid federal law. In other words, the law must be independently justified under a congressional power before it is able to trump an existing state law. [See Text §202]

Answer to Question 4.

(C) is the right answer.

Under Article III, federal courts may not issue advisory opinions; they are not within federal judicial power. Since a court may not issue one, Congress may not authorize one. (A) is wrong because it gets to the merits when there is a fatal justiciability problem, and because if properly done, a court may limit Congress' Commerce Power. (B) is wrong because Congress may, if it clearly says so, abrogate a state's Eleventh Amendment immunity under its Commerce Power. (D) is wrong because under Articles I and III, Congress may set the jurisdiction of lower federal courts, as long as it complies with other constitutional requirements. [See Text §36]

Answer to Question 5.

(B) is the right answer.

The Court should not hear this case because it is a political question which is constitutionally committed to another branch for resolution, and there are no judicially manageable standards to use in resolving this case. (A) is wrong because the case is not moot; the Justice has an ongoing injury-in-fact. (C) is the wrong rationale for not hearing this case. Although this answer refers to one kind of political question, it is not the one at issue here. (D) is wrong because there is clearly jurisdiction over this case, but for the political question problem. [See Text §37]

Answer to Question 6.

(A) is the right answer.

Under *Prudential Insurance Co. v. Benjamin*, Congress may give to a state the power to discriminate against out-of-staters, as long as the challenge is solely based on Commerce Clause principles. Congress may discriminate against certain segments of interstate commerce, so it may allow states to do so. (B) is wrong because, without congressional authorization, a state does not have the power to exclude out-of-state dumping. See *Philadelphia v. New Jersey*. (C) is wrong because this is not a dormant commerce clause case; Congress has acted, which is not true if we are doing a dormant commerce clause analysis. (D) is wrong because it has the wrong result - the law is good. [See Text §305]

Answer to Question 7.

(C) is the right answer.

Under *Metropolitan Life Insurance Co. v. Ward*, a state's discriminatory treatment of out- of-staters violates equal protection even if there is an attempted congressional delegation of the power to discriminate. Congress does not have the power to violate equal protection, so it may not give that power to a state. Even under rationality review, it is not a legitimate government interest to prefer local economic interests. (A) is wrong because Congress cannot authorize states to violate equal protection. (B) is wrong because a state does not possess that power in general, or in relation to an equal protection challenge. (D) is not as good an answer as (C). This law may be outside the state's police power, but the focus of this question is on equal protection. [See Text §305]

Answer to Question 8.

(C) is the right answer.

This law does not discriminate against out-of-staters. Because the State has a valid interest in protecting the safety of its citizens, it may determine what kind of equipment may be used in the State, regardless of where that equipment is manufactured. (A) is wrong. It distinguishes between kinds of play equipment, based on the safety features of the equipment. The state's safety interests outweigh any burden on interstate commerce, so (B) is wrong. (D) is wrong because under equal protection, rationality review applies, and the state's safety interests clearly qualify as a legitimate state interest. [See Text §277]

Answer to Question 9.

(C) is the right answer.

If a state is a market participant, rather than a market regulator, it is totally free from any dormant commerce clause restraints; it may discriminate against out-of-staters for any reason, including economic protectionism. Since that is true, (A) and (B) are wrong, since they both reflect dormant commerce clause rules. (D) is irrelevant. If the dormant commerce clause does not even apply, who cares if the state has significant reasons for its discrimination? [See Text §288]

Answer to Question 10.

(D) is the right answer.

The Privileges and Immunities Clause of Article IV does not protect corporations, only real people. Therefore Gilda's Garbage Haulers, Inc. is out of luck. Since the clause does not apply, (A) and (B) are irrelevant. (C) is wrong because there is no market participant exception to the Privileges and Immunities Clause of Article IV - only to the dormant commerce clause. [See Text §294]

Answer to Question 11.

(D) is the right answer.

Under rationality review, a state must have a legitimate reason for its law or practice. Here, Oz asserts safety, health, and ecology, enough to meet rational basis standards. (A) is wrong because discrimination is not necessarily fatal; it may be justified, as in this case. (B) is wrong - the state asserted three legitimate interests. (C) is wrong because corporations are protected by the Equal Protection Clause. [See Text §305]

Answer to Question 12.

(B) is the right answer.

Under *Michigan v. Long*, if a state court wants to insulate its decision from U.S. Supreme Court review, it must make a plain and clear statement that its decision was based solely on state law. If there is any ambiguity about the basis of the state court's decision, the Supreme Court will take the case. Here, the state court failed to make it clear that the state equal protection clause operates independently of the Fourteenth Amendment. (A) is not dispositive if a state question is the sole basis of the state court's decision. (C) is wrong because of the rule from *Michigan v. Long*. (D) is wrong on the facts - there is a Fourteenth Amendment issue here. [See Text §46]

Answer to Question 13.

(D) is the right answer.

The Court has said that a do-gooder group with no specific injury does not have standing to challenge a law. There is no general citizen standing to try to get government to do the right thing. (A) is wrong because the court will not even get to the merits of the case. (B) is wrong because there are a number of concrete disputes in existence; it's just that no PAL member is a party to one. (C) is wrong because, on the facts, this group has suffered no injury. [See Text §53]

Answer to Question 14.

(A) is the right answer.

Under the Supremacy Clause, the federal government wins if there is a conflict between federal and state law. A state may not impose direct regulations on an agent of the federal government. (B) only gives half the picture. Congress may invoke the Commerce Clause to justify building the federal building, but the issue here comes up when the state acts in contravention of the federal requirements. The real issue is supremacy. (C) is wrong a couple of ways. First, it is unclear which Privileges and Immunities Clause (C) is referring to. Second, whichever one it refers to is the wrong answer. The Fourteenth Amendment clause is a virtual nullity, and the Article IV one only applies if instaters and out-of-staters are treated differently. (D) is the state's argument, not Bob's. [See Text §332]

Answer to Question 15.

(C) is the right answer.

Once the President asserts executive privilege, a court must balance the specific reasons for non-disclosure against the reasons for disclosure. Here, a Senate subcommittee's need for information for an investigation would be balanced against whatever assertions the President would make. (A) is wrong because, under *U.S. v. Nixon*, a subpoena may be directed to a sitting President. (B) is wrong, again under *Nixon*. The privilege is only a presumptive one. (D) is wrong. The privilege may be invoked anytime anyone requests information, documents, or materials from the President. [See Text §238]

Answer to Question 16.

(A) is the right answer.

Executive agreements have become an accepted practice. Remember that they only trump conflicting state laws; they lose to conflicting treaties or federal statutes. (B) is wrong because federal law trumps an executive agreement. (C) is wrong because executive agreements and treaties are two different kinds of enactments, each of which is presumptively constitutional. (D) is wrong because the Court has never imposed this requirement, primarily because of congressional acquiescence in executive agreements. [See Text §193]

Answer to Question 17.

(D) is the right answer.

Under the Supremacy Clause, an executive agreement trumps a conflicting state law. (A) is wrong because it's backwards. (B) is wrong because the executive agreement is the superseding federal action. (C) is wrong because it's goofy, and because the real basis of a finding of unconstitutionality is the Supremacy Clause. [See Text §329]

Answer to Question 18.

(A) is the right answer.

(A) is correct under *Marbury v. Madison*. The Constitution specifies the original jurisdiction of the Court, and Congress may not enlarge that jurisdiction. (B) is wrong because it is phrased too broadly. The question focuses on the jurisdiction of the Supreme Court, not federal courts in general. (C) is wrong because treaties and their implementing legislation cannot alter the Constitution. (D) is wrong because the "Exceptions and Regulations Clause" applies only to the appellate jurisdiction of the Supreme Court. [See Text §21]

Answer to Question 19.

(C) is the right answer.

This question is answered by *Edmonson v. Leesville Concrete Co.*. There is state action whenever an attorney exercises peremptory challenges. The Court relies on both the "exclusive government function" and "significant state involvement" theories. Since there is state action, the Fourteenth Amendment applies. (A) is wrong for the reasons just mentioned. (B) and (D) are wrong for the same reasons: while there is no right to a certain racial or ethnic composition of a jury, that whole issue is beside the point, which is that the Equal Protection Clause applies to the **process** of picking a jury, irrespective of the result. [See Text §356]

Answer to Question 20.

(B) is the right answer.

(B) is the best answer because if the court rules on the basis of ripeness, it never gets to the merits of Breanda's argument, and the law continues to be applied. (A) is wrong on the facts - the state interest would not justify a forced abortion or adoption. (C) is also wrong on the facts. (D) is wrong because it uses rationality review language, when this is a strict scrutiny case. [See Text §50]

Answer to Question 21.

(B) is the right answer.

(B) is right because it identifies both the right that Breanda is asserting, and the correct level of review - strict scrutiny. Remember that the best argument of a person challenging a law is always that strict scrutiny applies - the burden of proof shifts to the government to prove a compelling interest and narrowly tailored means. (A) is not her best argument. Age is a non-suspect classification, and the scrutiny does not go up. (C) is wrong on the facts; the presumption of unfitness is rebuttable. (D) is wrong because you don't know which privileges and immunities clause it refers to (Fourteenth Amendment or Article IV), plus each of them is a wrong answer. The Fourteenth Amendment Privileges or Immunities Clause is always a wrong answer on a multiple choice question, and the Article IV Privileges and Immunities Clause is irrelevant because there is no discrimination against out-of-staters. [See Text §490]

Answer to Question 22.

(C) is the right answer.

(B) and (D) are always wrong because the plaintiff, not the government, has the burden of proof at rational basis review, and the government, not the plaintiff has the burden of proof at strict scrutiny. (A) is wrong because the parents did not make out a prima facie case of an equal protection violation; there is no intent to discriminate on the basis of race. As a result, the burden of proof never shifts to the government. [See Text §645]

Answer to Question 23.

(D) is the right answer.

(D) is right because, under *Employment Division v. Smith*, a generally applicable law trumps a free exercise argument. Myrna is not asserting any other constitutional interest here. Therefore, (A) is the wrong answer. (B) is wrong because the government is not singling out her religion for regulation; it is simply trying to deal with the problem of prostitution. (C) is wrong because a government may never inquire into the truth or falsity of someone's religious beliefs. [See Text §974]

Answer to Question 24.

(D) is the right answer.

When a state discriminates against aliens, strict scrutiny applies unless the exclusion is from a politically sensitive position; then rationality review applies. Exclusion from a loan program does not involve the political function exception, so strict scrutiny applies, and the state has the burden of proof. (B) is always wrong - the state never has to prove rationality. (C) has the wrong level of scrutiny - intermediate, rather than strict. (A) is wrong because it has the wrong level of scrutiny; rationality review would apply if Erin fell within the political function exception - she doesn't. [See Text §594]

Answer to Question 25.

(B) is the right answer.

(B) is correct because this is a generally applicable tax, with no indication that it was intended to or does discriminate against religion. (A) is wrong because Minister Mooney is an officer of an organization that has suffered a direct injury-in-fact from the tax. (C) is wrong because the tax is not discriminatory, so strict scrutiny does not apply. (D) is wrong because a non-discriminatory, generally applicable tax may be imposed on religious groups without any free exercise violation. [See Text §1000]

Answer to Question 26.

(D) is the right answer.

Under *Posadas de Puerto Rico Associates v. Tourism Company of Puerto Rico*, if a state may ban an activity altogether, it may restrict the advertising for that activity. This law would also be constitutional under the test enunciated in *Central Hudson Gas & Electric Corporation v. Public Service Commission*. Remember that under the *Central Hudson* test for commercial speech, even if the commercial speech is for a lawful activity and is not misleading, the government can regulate it if: (1) it has a substantial reason for the regulation; (2) the regulation directly advances the asserted government interest; and (3) the law is narrowly tailored to achieve the government interest. (A) is wrong because it is not the analysis used in commercial speech cases. (B) is too broad; be careful of answers phrased this broadly - there are usually exceptions. (C) is wrong because of *Posadas*; a state may have a significant interest in protecting its citizens from themselves. [See Text §758]

Answer to Question 27.

(B) is the correct answer.

This is not an open public forum, so reasonable, content-neutral restrictions are permissible. Leafletting is only permitted by government employees on issues related to their work. Under the cases of *Perry Educational Association v. Perry Local Educators' Association* and *Cornelius v. NAACP Legal Defense and Educational Fund, Inc.*, this regulation is constitutional. (A) is wrong because an open public forum was not created - the offices were opened for a specific, limited purpose. (C) is wrong because MSS does not have a First Amendment right of access to these offices. (D) is wrong because there is no such requirement here; reasonable exclusions from non-public forums, irrespective of alternative methods of communication, are constitutional. [See Text §810]

Answer to Question 28.

(A) is the right answer.

Under *Young v. American Mini Theatres, Inc.* and *Renton v. Playtime Theatres, Inc.*, a city may regulate the secondary effects of adult movie theaters being concentrated in one area. This restriction is a valid time, place, or manner restriction because there are numerous areas where Mr. Renton could have adult bookstores. (B) is wrong because Mr. Renton is not being deprived of any constitutional right - he can still operate bookstores. (C) is wrong because the presence of alternative channels of communication means this is not a prior restraint. (D) is wrong because the law is content neutral - it goes after the secondary effects of the speech. [See Text §688]

Answer to Question 29.

(D) is the right answer.

A 1% disparity between congressional districts is constitutionally permissible, and the state does not have to offer any justification. (This assumes no problems of racial discrimination.) (A) is wrong because that's how redistricting gets done, and with only a 1% disparity, no one's right to vote is diluted. (B) is wrong because there could never be absolute mathematical equality; 1% is close enough. (C) is wrong because 1% is acceptable, so the state does not have to prove anything. [See Text §523]

Answer to Question 30.

(A) is the right answer.

(A) is correct because illegitimacy is a quasi-suspect classification, calling for intermediate scrutiny. This is certainly Mariah's strongest argument. (B) is wrong because there is no property interest in an inheritance you are not entitled to under state law. (C) is wrong because there is no rule that a person who might inherit property is entitled to a paternity hearing. There is no constitutionally-based right to inherit, so there is no right to a hearing. (D) is wrong because this is a state law, and the Fifth Amendment is irrelevant; any argument gets made under the Fourteenth Amendment. [See Text §622]

Answer to Question 31.

(D) is the right answer.

(D) is correct because it is phrased in terms of the appropriate level of scrutiny (intermediate). If the court buys these arguments, the state wins. (A) and (B) are wrong because even though a state has the power, as a general matter, to regulate intestate succession, it must do so in conformance with other constitutional provisions, such as the Equal Protection Clause. (C) is wrong because it includes the wrong buzzwords - it is phrased in terms of rationality review, whereas this is an intermediate scrutiny case. [See Text §622]

Answer to Question 32.

(C) is the right answer.

A state cannot prohibit adults from having access to material that is obscene as to children, but protected as to adults. As a result, this statute is overbroad. (A) is wrong because it doesn't make any sense. It uses some obscenity terminology, but in a very vague manner. (B) is wrong because it is too broad. Certainly a state can prohibit materials that are obscene as to children, but the law must be narrowly tailored so as to avoid burdening too much speech. (D) is wrong as a matter of law. There is no such exception. [See Text §673]

Answer to Question 33.

(C) is the right answer.

Under the cases of *Maher v. Roe* and *Harris v. McRae*, a government does not have to pay for the abortions of indigent women. The Court's theory is that the government is creating no obstacle to a poor woman getting an abortion - her poverty is. This rule will probably remain after *Planned Parenthood of Southeastern Pennsylvania v. Casey*. (A) is wrong because under *Roe v. Wade* and subsequent cases, a fetus is not a person for Fourteenth Amendment purposes. (B) is wrong because women may still have abortions, even though the state will not pay for them. (D) is wrong because wealth is a non-suspect classification, requiring only rationality review. [See Text §512]

Answer to Question 34.

(A) is the right answer.

Under the Impairment of Contracts Clause, a state may not impair the obligations of an existing contract unless it has a substantial reason for doing so. Here, to make matters worse, the state is a party to the contract, raising the issue of the impairment being solely for the economic benefit of the state. (B) is a correct statement of the general rule, but here the repeal contravenes a specific constitutional provision. (C) is wrong because a state official may be sued in federal court for violating someone's federal rights, and injunctive relief may issue. (D) is a nice common-law rule, but not as good an answer as (A), which implicates a clear constitutional prohibition. [See Text §403]

Answer to Question 35.

(D) is the right answer.

Age is a non-suspect classification, and under rational basis review, a classification may be extremely over-inclusive (it may disadvantage people who do not possess the evil trait). Any rational explanation is enough to uphold a law such as this one. (A) is wrong because it uses intermediate scrutiny language, when only rationality review is called for. (B) is too broad an answer. A state may not regulate its police force in violation of a constitutional right. (C) is wrong because there is no fundamental right to pursue an occupation. [See Text §636]

Answer to Question 36.

(C) is the right answer.

The Court upheld this kind of law in *Roberts v. Jaycees*. The NRFL members may have a right of association here, but it is outweighed by the strong state interest in preventing discrimination based on race or gender. (A) is wrong for the reasons just mentioned. (B) is wrong because even if there were a contracts clause issue, the state has a substantial reason for its law, thereby meeting its burden under Contracts Clause analysis. (D) is wrong because there probably are associational rights at issue here, but NRFL members lose because of the overriding state interest underlying the law. [See Text §878]

Answer to Question 37.

(C) is the right answer.

This case involves both a free exercise argument, and a claim based on the right to rear one's child. This hybrid kind of case would invoke strict scrutiny under *Employment Division v. Smith*. There is an obvious Free Exercise Clause issue, and parents have at least a presumptive right to control medical decisions regarding their children. (A) is wrong because it is phrased in rationality review terms. (B) is always wrong. A plaintiff never has to show a compelling interest; that is the state's job at strict scrutiny. (D) is wrong because this is a case involving free exercise plus another right, so the burden of proof is higher for the state. [See Text §979]

Answer to Question 38.

(C) is the right answer.

The Court, in *Leathers v. Medlock*, upheld this kind of tax. Even though regulation of cable television does implicate the First Amendment (so (D) is wrong), this law has neither the purpose nor effect of suppressing particular ideas. (A) is wrong under *Leathers*. (B) is wrong because a selective tax is permissible, unless it is selectively based on the content of the speech taxed. [See Text §914]

Answer to Question 39.

(D) is the right answer.

The general rule with members of the media is that they have no special protections or rights over and above those of the general public. Jane can be sued for breach of contract, just like anyone else. (A) is wrong for the reasons just stated. (B) is wrong because any alleged "chilling effect" on speech is not enough to immunize reporters from generally applicable laws. (C) is wrong because it has nothing to do with a breach of contract action. [See Text §903]

(C) is the right answer.

In *Ford v. Wainwright*, the Court ruled that executing an insane person violated the Eighth Amendment's ban on cruel and unusual punishment. (A) is wrong because it is irrelevant that Doomer was sane when he committed the crimes. The Eighth Amendment focuses on the punishment phase of the process. (B) is wrong because compliance with procedural requirements cannot override individual rights guaranteed under the Eighth Amendment. (D) is wrong because there were no procedural due process problems here, and Doomer's substantive right is anchored in the Eighth Amendment, not in some notion of substantive due process. [See Text §1026]

XXII. PRACTICE ESSAY QUESTIONS

> **Study Tip: Questions 1-5 cover material usually studied in Constitutional Law I classes. Questions 6-10 cover material usually studied in Constitutional Law II classes.**

Question 1

The State of Oz has passed a law which requires that the last car on any train over 1000 feet long operating in the state be a manned caboose. Violation of this law can result in criminal prosecution. Red Railway (RR) sought to have the statute declared unconstitutional and its enforcement enjoined.

In defense of its statute, State Oz argued in federal court that there were unique safety concerns within the state. Basically, the state argued that its topography resulted in longer trains traveling frequently in open country where fires and accidents, if not detected by a caboose crew, could go undetected for a long time, resulting in loss of life and property. The state also argued that it had an important concern with rail-highway crossing accidents. The legislature felt that caboose crews are in a position to spot accidents occurring towards the rear portion of long trains out of view of the locomotive crew. Finally, the state argued that they had a specific concern with train derailments, which caused personal and property injury. Their argument was that the role of a caboose crew in derailments consists largely of spotting defective equipment and other mechanical problems which usually cannot be spotted by the locomotive crew.

Red Railway, on the other hand, argued that this manned-caboose requirement imposed too great a burden on interstate commerce. It pointed out that no other states in the immediate area had such a requirement.

Discuss the constitutional issues in Red Railway's challenge to this law.

Question 2

Congress passed a law establishing a federal agency to regulate the disposal of nuclear waste throughout the country. A five-member board of commissioners was to govern the agency. The commissioners would have investigative, regulatory, and enforcement powers. Congress passed a statute giving the President the power to appoint the five commissioners.

Congress became disenchanted with the conservative, states-rights orientation of the commission, and decided to try to change the direction of its work. Congress increased the number of commissioners to fifteen, and provided that the President still got to appoint five commissioners, and that the chairpersons of the Senate and the House Energy Committees each got to appoint five commissioners.

The Commission was still charged with investigative, regulatory, and enforcement functions.

Discuss the constitutionality of the commission as presently set up.

Question 3

Under the Federal Salary Act, Congress authorized the President to adjust judicial salaries every fourth year. According to the Act, the President was to submit recommendations on salary changes to Congress which would become effective automatically within a specified time, but only to the extent that:

(A) No statute has been enacted which establishes rates of pay other than those proposed by the President;

(B) Neither House of Congress has passed a resolution which specifically disapproves all or part of such recommendations; or

(C) Both.

Assume proper plaintiffs challenge this law.

Discuss the constitutional arguments against the validity of the Act.

Question 4

Joe Jones is an indigent person who lives in the State of Oz. For the last six years, Joe has been receiving welfare payments from the state. Recently, Joe's cousin Jane Jones, an accountant, looked over Joe's papers and concluded that the State Welfare Department (SWD) had been shortchanging Joe in his welfare payments, to the tune of about $4,000 over the six years. Joe contacted Bob Smith, the Director of SWD, but Bob told Joe that nothing could be done at this point, and that Joe was not going to get any increase in his welfare payments.

Joe wants to sue the state in federal court to get the $4,000 to which he feels he is entitled, and to force it to increase his payments in the future. Joe believes that the state is violating its own welfare laws, as well as federal statutes regarding acceptable methods of computation.

Assuming that Joe has standing. What constitutional issues exist regarding the filing of his lawsuit in federal court? Discuss the relief Joe may get from a federal court.

Question 5

Congress delegated to the Secretary of the Air Force the power to dispose of any outdated surplus equipment, including helicopters and airplanes. The Secretary set up a system under which the various pieces of surplus property would be advertised, and persons or groups could get on a list to be considered as recipients. Under this system, the Secretary gave a helicopter worth one million dollars to a hospital owned and operated by a church. The church plans to use the helicopter to transport emergency cases from accident scenes to the hospital.

Harry Hardcase is a federal taxpayer who vehemently objects to any governmental aid to religion. He hears about the gift to the church hospital, and decides to sue in federal court to put a stop to this practice of helping religious institutions.

Will Harry have standing, as a federal taxpayer, to challenge the practice of the Secretary of the Air Force making huge gifts to religious institutions?

Question 6

The City of Oz is experiencing serious problems with Ackthian males dropping out of high school. A study commissioned by the city showed that 61% of Ackthian male students have dropped out of high school during the preceding five-year period.

The study also indicated that a major cause of the very high dropout rate is the absence of strong male role models in many Ackthian households in certain areas of the city. A disproportionately high percentage of inner-city Ackthian households are one-parent households, with the one parent overwhelmingly being the mother.

To try to remedy this situation, the city has set up three all-male, all-Ackthian high schools in which all the teachers are Ackthian males. The purpose of these schools is to provide a rigorous education being delivered by Ackthian male teachers who provide valuable role models.

The program works. The dropout-rate of the students in these schools is now 12%, and the achievement test scores of these students have risen dramatically. Parents and educators alike regard these schools as an unqualified success.

Discuss the constitutionality of these schools.

Question 7

The City of Oz appropriates funds to provide day-care for the children of needy parents. The city sets up a system under which any licensed day-care provider can submit a bid to become the city's day-care provider. The system of submitting bids is widely published in all the local news media.

The Reformed United Druid Evangelical Church (RUDE) is the only entity to submit a bid to be the day-care provider. RUDE is a licensed day-care provider, and meets all state requirements to provide such services.

RUDE is a pantheistic religion whose tenets include the belief that God is all around us, in everything, and is equally manifested in humans, animals, and all other living creatures. Its catechism teaches that religion must be incorporated into every aspect of one's life.

The city's contract, naming the RUDE day-care center as the city's official day-care provider, is challenged by Citizens Against Religious Indoctrination (CARI) a group of taxpayers opposed to government endorsement of religion.

Discuss the religion issues in CARI's challenge to the contract. Do not worry about any problems of justiciability.

Question 8

The State Supreme Court of the State of Oz has an official policy of not hiring non-U.S. citizens as law clerks. Justice Karen Ortiz was forced to dismiss two well-qualified Mobanian law clerks because of their status as aliens. The former clerks sue the Chief Justice of the Supreme court, challenging the policy of excluding aliens from positions as law clerks.

Assuming that there are no Eleventh Amendment or sovereign immunity problems in suing the Chief Justice, discuss the constitutional issues involved in this lawsuit.

Question 9

The State of Oz has passed a statute which requires that all pregnant women who are known to be currently using certain drugs must have their pregnancies terminated. The purpose of the statute is to prevent the birth of drug-addicted babies.

Jane Jones is pregnant with her third child. The first two children were removed from her custody because she abused them and allowed others to abuse them in exchange for crack cocaine. Crack cocaine is one of the drugs covered under the involuntary termination of pregnancy statute passed by the State of Oz. Jane is currently addicted to crack cocaine, and is seeing a doctor who is unable to get her off the drug.

The State takes appropriate measures to terminate Jane's pregnancy. She files suit in federal court challenging the statute on its face and as applied to her.

Discuss the constitutional issues in Jane's lawsuit.

Question 10

While driving down the main street of the City of Oz, Mayor Ed Smith saw a most disturbing sight - a bumper sticker displaying a very offensive and vulgar message. Enraged by this affront to civility and decency, Mayor Smith contacted the City Attorney to see if anything could be done about the increase in the number of bumper stickers containing offensive language. Upon the City Attorney's recommendation, the City decided not to try to ban this kind of speech. Instead, the City Council made a list of offensive words, and passed an ordinance which said that these offending words may appear on bumper stickers, but may not be more than 1/8 inch high. Edna Edwards was stopped by a police officer for having on her car a bumper sticker with one of the offending words in large letters.

Edna challenges the ordinance as a violation of her free speech rights. Discuss the constitutional issues in her lawsuit.

Answer to Question 1

This is a dormant commerce clause question. This law applies to all trains operating in the state, so there is no discrimination against interstate commerce. That means that the proper analysis is the balancing approach of *Pike v. Bruce Church*. You should discuss the state's interests advanced by the law, and balance them against the law's adverse impact on interstate commerce. Here, the state has legitimate safety concerns, and the question boils down to whether requiring a person to be in the caboose interferes too greatly with interstate transportation. You should also discuss the issue of whether this requirement creates too great a risk of multiple burdens (what if a number of states have conflicting laws?). It is a bother to comply with this law, but the impact on commerce is slight compared to a case like *Bibb v. Navajo Freight Lines*, where all trucks operating in the state had to have contoured mudguards, which had to be welded onto the trucks. [See Text §277]

Answer to Question 2

There is an Appointments Clause question, based on *Buckley v. Valeo*. Under the Appointments Clause, Congress may vest the appointment of inferior officers in the President alone, courts of law, or heads of departments. The first thing to establish is that these commissioners are inferior officers. In *Buckley*, members of the Federal Election Commission were held to be inferior officers, so these commissioners would also fall in that category. The President may be given the power to appoint inferior officers, so the five presidential appointees are appropriately appointed, and may perform all functions of the commission. The problem here is that Congress may not give itself the power to appoint officers to fill positions on executive-branch agencies. As a result, the ten appointees of the Senate and House chairpersons are not able to do anything more than a legislative aide could do — investigate, and inform Congress of the results of the investigation. They are not able to perform any discretionary, executive functions such as regulation or enforcement. [See Text §227]

Answer to Question 3

This is a legislative veto question. Congress may delegate certain powers to the President or other executive branch officials or entities, but it may not retain control over the delegation.

Remember that any time Congress passes a law, or takes an action that has the effect of law, it must meet **both** the bicameralism and presentment requirements of Article I, Section 7. Bicameralism means both the House and the Senate must pass the law, and presentment means that the bill must be presented to the President for signature. The Federal Salary Act effects a delegation to the President of the power to set judicial salaries. No problem so far. Under A., Congress may change the President's recommendations by passing a statute which has met the bicameralism and presentment requirements. No problem with A. B is the issue — it builds a legislative veto into the delegation. Either house of Congress may disapprove (veto) the President's recommendation, violating the bicameralism and presentment requirements. See the discussion of *INS v. Chadha*, at §224.

Answer to Question 4

This is an Eleventh Amendment question (see §100). The Eleventh Amendment prohibits an individual from suing a state in federal court. To get around the Eleventh Amendment bar, a plaintiff must name an individual state official, and assert that the state official acted outside the scope of his or her authority and violated the plaintiff's federal (not state) rights. Here, Joe would name Bob Smith as the Defendant, and claim that Bob acted outside the scope of his authority to violate Joe's federal statutory rights. Once Joe has done that, he is in court.

As far as relief is concerned, *Edelman v. Jordan* tells us that retroactive money damages are not recoverable if they are to be paid out of state funds. Joe can kiss his $4,000 goodbye. However, prospective injunctive relief is permissible, as well as any money the state would have to spend to comply with the injunction. The court could order Bob to press the right buttons on the calculator in the future, even if that would result in the state spending more welfare money to pay Joe the correct amount. [See Text §103]

Answer to Question 5

This is a federal taxpayer standing question. Remember that a federal taxpayer can always challenge a tax as being improperly calculated, or otherwise unconstitutional. A problem comes up when a federal taxpayer wants to challenge a spending measure by Congress. The general rule is that a federal taxpayer has no standing to challenge a congressional spending measure. The one exception, from *Flast v. Cohen*, is that a federal taxpayer will have standing to challenge a congressional action, under the spending power, which establishes religion. Remember that the taxpayer must go three-for-three to have standing to challenge a congressional spending measure. To have standing, the taxpayer must show: 1.) Congress is acting; 2.) Spending Power; and 3.) To establish religion. Harry will lose here because it is the Secretary of the Air Force (not Congress), acting under the Property Power (not the Spending Power), to establish religion. Harry's only one-for-three - which is not good enough under *Flast v. Cohen*. See *Valley Forge Christian College v. Americans United for Separation of Church and State* [See Text §73].

Answer to Question 6

This question deals with a local race-based affirmative action program, plus discrimination against female students. Federal, state and local race-based affirmative action plans all receive strict scrutiny under *Richmond v. J.A. Croson Co.*, and *Adarand v. Pena* (federal). The city would have to show that this program is narrowly tailored to achieve a compelling government interest. Under *Croson* and *Adarand*, remedying societal discrimination does not qualify as a compelling government interest. The city would at least have to show that it had been a passive participant in some prior discrimination against Ackthian male students. Without such a showing, the plan would fail strict scrutiny. Also, in *Wygant v. Jackson Board of Education*, the Court rejected the idea that providing role models for students was a compelling government interest. This program is also subject to an attack based on gender discrimination. Females are excluded from these schools, thus calling for intermediate scrutiny review: can the government show that the program is substantially related to a significant or important government interest? [See Text §§574, 605]

Answer to Question 7

This question involves the Establishment Clause, and is similar to *Bowen v. Kendrick*, where the Court upheld a federal program that provided funds to various public and private social welfare agencies (including religious) for services relating to adolescent sexuality and pregnancy. The three-part test from *Lemon v. Kurtzman* applies here: (1) the statute must have a secular legislative purpose; (2) its principal or primary effect must be one that neither advances nor inhibits religion; (3) the law must not foster excessive entanglement between government and religion. First of all, the bidding system was open to all bidders - religious and non-religious. Thus, there was no intent by the city to establish religion - just to provide day-care. Under *Lemon*, there may be problems with effect and entanglement. RUDE is a religion whose beliefs include the duty to incorporate religion into every aspect of life (unlike *Bowen*, where the welfare agencies were not pervasively sectarian institutions). Also, RUDE is the only day-care provider (unlike *Bowen*, where there were a number of social welfare agencies), and it will be dealing with children, an especially vulnerable group. There may also be entanglement problems if the city decides to monitor RUDE's performance to make sure there is no religious indoctrination. [See Text §960]

Answer to Question 8

This question deals with an alienage classification imposed by a state. The general rule is that state discrimination against aliens receives strict scrutiny, and the government must show that the exclusion is narrowly tailored to achieving a compelling government interest. However, if the position from which the alien is excluded is politically sensitive (goes to the heart of representative government, involves the formulation or implementation of public policy), rational basis scrutiny is appropriate.

All elected, and important non-elected positions fall within this "political function" exception, as do police officers, probation or parole officers, and public school teachers. The factual issue in this case is whether the position of law clerk to a state Supreme Court Justice falls within the political function exception. If it does, rationality review applies, and the policy will be upheld. If it does not, strict scrutiny applies, and the policy will be struck down. You would have to discuss (or make some assumptions about) the functions of a law clerk to be able to place that position in the appropriate category. [See Text §594]

Answer to Question 9

This question involves the right to procreate, the right to decide not to terminate a pregnancy, and the right of bodily integrity. First of all, Jane has an unenumerated, but fundamental privacy interest at stake here. In *Skinner v. Oklahoma*, the Court said there is a right to marry and procreate. Subsequent cases have reemphasized the fundamental nature of this right: the cases, from *Roe v. Wade* through *Planned Parenthood of Southeastern Pennsylvania v. Casey*, say that a woman has a fundamental right to decide not to terminate her pregnancy. In addition, any forced abortion would violate Jane's right to be free from involuntary bodily intrusions. Although the state has a compelling interest in preventing the birth of drug addicted babies, the means that it chose to effectuate that interest impinge too greatly on Jane's individual rights. [See Text §502]

Answer to Question 10

This is a free speech question, with the issue being whether the city has imposed a prior restraint on Edna's speech, or whether it has it simply passed a time, place, or manner regulation. To be constitutional, a time, place, or manner regulation must be content neutral, narrowly tailored to achieve a significant government interest, and leave open ample alternative channels of communication. A law can be content neutral in one of two ways: the government does not look at content at all, or the government is trying to regulate the secondary effects of the speech. Obviously, the city looked at content here, but it will argue that it is concerned with the secondary effects of these words corrupting children, and lowering the moral tone of the community. The other problem is whether it is an adequate alternative method of communication to limit speech to letters that are 1/8 inch high. If it is not, this law becomes a prior restraint, and is probably invalid under strict scrutiny. [See Text §§677, 688]

XXIII. THE CONSTITUTION OF THE UNITED STATES

PREAMBLE

We the People of the United States, in Order to form a more perfect Union, establish Justice, insure domestic Tranquility, provide for the common defence, promote the general Welfare, and secure the Blessings of Liberty to ourselves and our Posterity, do ordain and establish this Constitution for the United States of America.

ARTICLE I

Section 1. All legislative Powers herein granted shall be vested in a Congress of the United States, which shall consist of a Senate and House of Representatives.

Section 2. [1] The House of Representatives shall be composed of Members chosen every second Year by the People of the several States, and the Electors in each State shall have the Qualifications requisite for Electors of the most numerous Branch of the State Legislature.

[2] No Person shall be a Representative who shall not have attained to the Age of twenty five Years, and been seven Years a Citizen of the United States, and who shall not, when elected, be an Inhabitant of that State in which he shall be chosen.

[3] Representatives and direct Taxes shall be apportioned among the several States which may be included within this Union, according to their respective Numbers, which shall be determined by adding to the whole Number of free Persons, including those bound to Service for a Term of Years, and excluding Indians not taxed, three fifths of all other Persons. The actual Enumeration shall be made within three Years after the first Meeting of the Congress of the United States, and within every subsequent Term of ten Years, in such Manner as they shall by Law direct. The Number of Representatives shall not exceed one for every thirty Thousand, but each State shall have at Least one Representative; and until such enumeration shall be made, the State of New Hampshire shall be entitled to chuse three, Massachusetts eight, Rhode Island and Providence Plantations one, Connecticut five, New York six, New Jersey four, Pennsylvania eight, Delaware one, Maryland six, Virginia ten, North Carolina five, South Carolina five, and Georgia three.

[4] When vacancies happen in the Representation from any State, the Executive Authority thereof shall issue Writs of Election to fill such Vacancies.

[5] The House of Representatives shall chuse their Speaker and other Officers; and shall have the sole Power of Impeachment.

Section 3. [1] The Senate of the United States shall be composed of two Senators from each State, chosen by the Legislature thereof, for six Years; and each Senator shall have one Vote.

[2] Immediately after they shall be assembled in Consequence of the first Election, they shall be divided as equally as may be into three Classes. The Seats of the Senators of the first Class shall be vacated at the Expiration of the Second Year, of the second Class at the Expiration of the fourth year, and of the third Class at the Expiration of the sixth Year, so that one third may be chosen every second Year; and if Vacancies happen by Resignation, or otherwise, during the Recess of the Legislature of any State, the Executive thereof may make temporary Appointments until the next Meeting of the Legislature, which shall then fill such Vacancies.

[3] No Person shall be a Senator who shall not have attained to the Age of thirty Years, and been nine years a Citizen of the United States, and who shall not, when elected, by an Inhabitant of that State for which he shall be chosen.

[4] The Vice President of the United States shall be President of the Senate, but shall have no Vote, unless they be equally divided.

[5] The Senate shall chuse their other Officers, and also a President pro tempore, in the Absence of the Vice President, or when he shall exercise the Office of President of the United States.

[6] The Senate shall have the sole Power to try all Impeachments. When sitting for that Purpose, they shall be on Oath or Affirmation. When the President of the United States is tried, the Chief Justice shall preside: And no Person shall be convicted without the Concurrence of two thirds of the Members present.

[7] Judgment in Cases of Impeachment shall not extend further than to removal from Office, and disqualification to hold and enjoy any Office of honor, Trust, or Profit under the United States: but the Party convicted shall nevertheless be liable and subject to Indictment, Trial, Judgment, and Punishment, according to Law.

Section 4. [1] The Times, Places and Manner of holding Elections for Senators and Representatives, shall be prescribed in each State by the Legislature thereof; but the Congress may at any time by Law make or alter such Regulations, except as to the Places of chusing Senators.

[2] The Congress shall assemble at least once in every Year, and such Meeting shall be on the first Monday in December, unless they shall by Law appoint a different Day.

Section 5. [1] Each House shall be the Judge of the Elections, Returns, and Qualifications of its own Members, and a Majority of each shall constitute a Quorum to do Business; but a smaller Number may adjourn from day to day, and may be authorized to compel the Attendance of absent Members, in such Manner, and under such Penalties as each House may provide.

[2] Each House may determine the Rules of its Proceedings, punish its Members for disorderly Behavior, and, with the Concurrence of two thirds, expel a Member.

[3] Each House shall keep a Journal of its Proceedings, and from time to time publish the same, excepting such Parts as may in their Judgment require Secrecy; and the Yeas and Nays of the Members of either House on any question shall, at the Desire of one fifth of those Present, be entered on the Journal.

[4] Neither House, during the Session of Congress, shall without the Consent of the other, adjourn for more than three days, nor to any other Place than that in which the two Houses shall be sitting.

Section 6. [1] The Senators and Representatives shall receive a Compensation for their Services, to be ascertained by law, and paid out of the Treasury of the United States. They shall in all Cases, except Treason, Felony and Breach of the Peace, be privileged from Arrest during their Attendance at the Session of their respective Houses, and in going to and returning from the same; and for any Speech or Debate in either House, they shall not be questioned in any other Place.

[2] No Senator or Representative shall, during the Time for which he was elected, be appointed to any civil Office under the Authority of the United States, which shall have been created, or the Emoluments whereof shall have been increased during such time; and no Person holding any Office under the United States, shall be a Member of either House during his Continuance in Office.

Section 7. [1] All Bills for raising Revenue shall originate in the House of Representatives; but the Senate may propose or concur with Amendments as on other Bills.

[2] Every Bill which shall have passed the House of Representatives and the Senate, shall, before it become a Law, be presented to the President of the United States; If he approve he shall sign it, but if not he shall return it, with his Objections to the House in which it shall have originated, who shall enter the Objections at large on their Journal, and proceed to reconsider it. If after such Reconsideration two thirds of that House shall agree to pass the Bill, it shall be sent together with the Objections, to the other House, by which it shall likewise be reconsidered, and if approved by two thirds of that House, it shall become a Law. But in all such Cases the Votes of both Houses shall be determined by yeas and Nays, and the Names of the Persons voting for and against the Bill shall be entered on the Journal of each house respectively. If any Bill shall not be returned by the President within ten Days (Sundays excepted) after it shall have been presented to him, the Same shall be a Law, in like Manner as if he had signed it, unless the Congress by their Adjournment prevent its Return in which Case it shall not be a Law.

[3] Every Order, Resolution, or Vote, to Which the Concurrence of the Senate and House of Representatives may be necessary (except on a question of Adjournment) shall be presented to the President of the United States; and before the Same shall take Effect, shall be approved by him, or being disapproved by him, shall be repassed by two thirds of the Senate and House of Representatives, according to the Rules and Limitations prescribed in the Case of a Bill.

Section 8. [1] The Congress shall have Power To lay and collect Taxes, Duties, Imposts, and Excises, to pay the Debts and provide for the common Defence and general Welfare of the United States; but all Duties, Imposts and Excises shall be uniform throughout the United States;

[2] To borrow money on the credit of the United States;

[3] To regulate Commerce with foreign Nations, and among the several States, and with the Indian Tribes;

[4] To establish an uniform Rule of Naturalization, and uniform Laws on the subject of Bankruptcies throughout the United States;

[5] To coin Money, regulate the Value thereof, and of foreign Coin, and fix the Standard of Weights and Measures;

[6] To provide for the Punishment of counterfeiting the Securities and current Coin of the United States;

[7] To Establish Post Offices and Post Roads;

[8] To promote the Progress of Science and useful Arts, by securing for limited Times to Authors and Inventors the exclusive Right to their respective Writings and Discoveries;

[9] To constitute Tribunals inferior to the supreme Court;

[10] To define and punish Piracies and Felonies committed on the high Seas, and Offenses against the Law of Nations;

[11] To declare War, grant Letters of Marque and Reprisal, and make Rules concerning Captures on Land and Water;

[12] To raise and support Armies, but no Appropriation of Money to that Use shall be for a longer Term than two Years;

[13] To provide and maintain a Navy;

[14] To make Rules for the Government and Regulation of the land and naval Forces;

[15] To provide for calling forth the Militia to execute the Laws of the Union, suppress Insurrections and repel Invasions;

[16] To provide for organizing, arming, and disciplining, the Militia, and for governing such Part of them as may be employed in the Service of the United States, reserving to the States respectively, the Appointment of the Officers, and the Authority of training the Militia according to the discipline prescribed by Congress;

[17] To exercise exclusive Legislation in all Cases whatsoever, over such District (not exceeding ten Miles square) as may, by Cession of particular States, and the Acceptance of Congress, become the Seat of the Government of the United States, and to exercise like Authority over all Places purchased by the Consent of the Legislature of the State in which the Same shall be, for the Erection of Forts, Magazines, Arsenals, dock-Yards, and other needful Buildings; — And

[18] To make all laws which shall be necessary and proper for carrying into Execution the foregoing Powers, and all other Powers vested by this Constitution in the Government of the United States, or in any Department or Officer thereof.

Section 9. [1] The Migration of Importation of Such Persons as any of the States now existing shall think proper to admit, shall not be prohibited by the Congress prior to the Year one thousand eight hundred and eight, but a Tax or duty may be imposed on such Importation, not exceeding ten dollars for each Person.

[2] The privilege of the Writ of Habeas Corpus shall not be suspended, unless when in Cases of Rebellion or Invasion the public Safety may require it.

[3] No Bill of Attainder or ex post facto Law shall be passed.

[4] No Capitation, or other direct, Tax shall be laid, unless in Proportion to the Census or Enumeration herein before directed to be taken.

Sum & Substance QUICK REVIEW of Constitutional Law

[5] No Tax or Duty shall be laid on Articles exported from any State.

[6] No Preference shall be given by any Regulation of Commerce or Revenue to the Ports of one State over those of another: nor shall Vessels bound to, or from, one State be obliged to enter, clear, or pay Duties in another.

[7] No money shall be drawn from the Treasury, but in Consequence of Appropriations made by Law; and a regular Statement and Account of the Receipts and Expenditures of all public Money shall be published from time to time.

[8] No Title of Nobility shall be granted by the United States: And no Person holding any Office of Profit or Trust under them, shall, without the Consent of the Congress, accept of any present, Emolument, Office, or Title, of any kind whatever, from any King, Prince, or foreign State.

Section 10. [1] No State shall enter into any Treaty, Alliance, or Confederation; grant Letters of Marque and Reprisal; coin Money; emit Bills of Credit; make any Thing but gold and silver Coin a Tender in Payment of Debts; pass any Bill of Attainder, ex post facto Law, or Law impairing the Obligation of Contracts, or grant any Title of Nobility.

[2] No State shall, without the Consent of the Congress, lay any Imposts or Duties on Imports or Exports, except what may be absolutely necessary for executing it's inspection Laws: and the net Produce of all Duties and Imposts, laid by any State on Imports or Exports, shall be for the Use of the Treasury of the United States; and all such laws shall be subject to the Revision and Controul of the Congress.

[3] No State shall, without the Consent of Congress, lay any Duty of Tonnage, keep Troops, or Ships of War in time of Peace, enter into any Agreement or Compact with another State, or with a foreign Power, or engage in War, unless actually invaded, or in such imminent Danger as will not admit of delay.

ARTICLE II

Section 1. [1] The executive Power shall be vested in a President of the United States of America. He shall hold his Office during the Term of four Years, and, together with the Vice President, chosen for the same Term, be elected, as follows:

[2] Each State shall appoint, in such Manner as the Legislature thereof may direct, a Number of Electors, equal to the whole Number of Senators and Representatives to which the State may be entitled in the Congress; but no Senator or Representative, or Person holding an Office of Trust or Profit under the United States, shall be appointed an Elector.

[3] The Electors shall meet in their respective States, and vote by Ballot for two Persons, of whom one at least shall not be an Inhabitant of the same State with themselves. And they shall make a List of all the Persons voted for, and of the Number of Votes for each; which List they shall sign and certify, and transmit sealed to the Seat of the Government of the United States, directed to the President of the Senate. The President of the Senate shall, in the Presence of the Senate and House of Representatives, open all the Certificates, and the Votes shall then be counted. The Person having the greatest Number of Votes shall be the President, if such Number be a Majority of the whole Number of Electors appointed; and if there be more than one who have such Majority, and have an equal Number of Votes, then the House of Representatives shall immediately chuse by Ballot one of them for President; and if

no Person have a majority, then from the five highest on the List the said House shall in like Manner chuse the President. But in chusing the President, the Votes shall be taken by States the Representation from each State having one Vote; A quorum for this Purpose shall consist of a member or Members from two thirds of the States, and a Majority of all the States shall be necessary to a Choice. In every Case, after the Choice of the President, the Person having the greater Number of Votes of the Electors shall be the Vice President. But if there should remain two or more who have equal Votes, the Senate shall chuse from them by Ballot the Vice President.

[4] The Congress may determine the Time of chusing the Electors, and the Day on which they shall give their Votes; which Day shall be the same throughout the United States.

[5] No person except a natural born Citizen, or a Citizen of the United States, at the time of the Adoption of this Constitution, shall be eligible to the Office of President; neither shall any Person be eligible to that Office who shall not have attained to the Age of thirty five Years, and been fourteen Years a Resident within the United States.

[6] In case of the removal of the President from Office, or of his Death, Resignation or Inability to discharge the Powers and Duties of the said Office, the Same shall devolve on the Vice President, and the Congress may by Law provide for the Case of Removal, Death, Resignation or Inability, both of the President and Vice President, declaring what Officer shall then act as President, and such Officer shall act accordingly, until the Disability be removed, or a President shall be elected.

[7] The President shall, at stated Times, receive for his Services, a Compensation, which shall neither be increased nor diminished during the Period for which he shall have been elected, and he shall not receive within that Period any other Emolument from the United States, or any of them.

[8] Before he enter on the Execution of his Office, he shall take the following oath or Affirmation: "I do solemnly swear (or affirm) that I will faithfully execute the Office of President of the United States, and will to the best of my Ability, preserve, protect and defend the Constitution of the United States."

Section 2. [1] The President shall be Commander in Chief of the Army and Navy of the United States, and of the militia of the several States, when called into the actual Service of the United States; he may require the Opinion, in writing, of the principal Officer in each of the Executive Departments, upon any Subject relating to the Duties of their respective Offices, and he shall have Power to grant Reprieves and Pardons for Offenses against the United States, except in Cases of Impeachment.

[2] He shall have Power, by and with the Advice and Consent of the Senate to make Treaties, provided two thirds of the Senators present concur; and he shall nominate, and by and with the Advice and Consent of the Senate, shall appoint Ambassadors, other public Ministers and Consuls, Judges of the supreme Court, and all other Officers of the United States, whose Appointments are not herein otherwise provided for, and which shall be established by Law; but the Congress may by Law vest the Appointment of such inferior Officers, as they think proper, in the President alone, in the Courts of Law, or in the Heads of Departments.

[3] The President shall have Power to fill up all Vacancies that may happen during the Recess of the Senate, by granting Commissions which shall expire at the End of their next Session.

Section 3. He shall from time to time give to the Congress Information of the State of the Union, and recommend to their Consideration such Measures as he shall judge necessary and expedient; he may, on extraordinary Occasions, convene both Houses, or either of them, and in Case of Disagreement between them, with Respect to the Time of Adjournment, he may adjourn them to such Time as he shall think proper; he shall receive Ambassadors and other public Ministers; he shall take Care that the Laws be faithfully executed, and shall Commission all the Officers of the United States.

Section 4. The President, Vice President and all civil Officers of the United States, shall be removed from Office on Impeachment for, and Conviction of, Treason, Bribery, or other high Crimes and Misdemeanors.

ARTICLE III

Section 1. The judicial Power of the United States, shall be vested in one supreme Court, and in such inferior Courts as the Congress may from time to time ordain and establish. The Judges, both of the supreme and inferior Courts, shall hold their Offices during good Behaviour, and shall, at stated Times, receive for their Services a Compensation, which shall not be diminished during their Continuance in Office.

Section 2. [1] The judicial Power shall extend to all Cases, in Law and Equity, arising under this Constitution, the Laws of the United States, and Treaties made, or which shall be made, under their Authority; — to all Cases affecting Ambassadors, other public Ministers and Consuls; — to all Cases of admiralty and maritime Jurisdiction; — to Controversies to which the United States shall be a Party; — to Controversies between two or more States; — between a State and Citizens of another State; — between Citizens of different States; — between Citizens of the same State claiming Lands under the Grants of different States, and between a State, or the Citizens thereof, and foreign States, Citizens or Subjects.

[2] In all Cases affecting Ambassadors, other public Ministers and Consuls, and those in which a State shall be a Party, the supreme Court shall have original Jurisdiction. In all the other Cases before mentioned, the supreme Court shall have appellate Jurisdiction, both as to Law and Fact, with such Exceptions, and under such Regulations as the Congress shall make.

[3] The trial of all Crimes, except in Cases of Impeachment, shall be by Jury; and such Trial shall be held in the State where the said Crimes shall have been committed; but when not committed within any State, the Trial shall be at such Place or Places as the Congress may by Law have directed.

Section 3. [1] Treason against the United States, shall consist only in levying War against them, or, in adhering to their Enemies, giving them Aid and Comfort. No Person shall be convicted of Treason unless on the Testimony of two Witnesses to the same overt Act, or on Confession in open Court.

[2] The Congress shall have Power to declare the Punishment of Treason, but no Attainder of Treason shall work Corruption of Blood, or Forfeiture except during the Life of the Person attainted.

ARTICLE IV

Section 1. Full Faith and Credit shall be given in each State to the public Acts, Records, and judicial Proceedings of every other State. And the Congress may by general Laws prescribe the Manner in which such Acts, Records and Proceedings shall be proved, and the Effect thereof.

U.S. CONSTITUTION

Section 2. [1] The Citizens of each State shall be entitled to all Privileges and Immunities of Citizens in the several States.

[2] A Person charged in any State with Treason, Felony, or other Crime, who shall flee from Justice, and be found in another State, shall on demand of the executive Authority of the State from which he fled, be delivered up, to be removed to the State having Jurisdiction of the Crime.

[3] No Person held to Service or Labour in one State, under the Laws thereof, escaping into another, shall, in Consequence of any Law or Regulation therein, be discharged from such Service or Labour, but shall be delivered up on Claim of the Party to whom such Service or Labour may be due.

Section 3. [1] New States may be admitted by the Congress into this Union; but no new State shall be formed or erected within the Jurisdiction of any other State; nor any State be formed by the Junction of two or more States, or Parts of States, without the Consent of the Legislatures of the States concerned as well as of the Congress.

[2] The Congress shall have Power to dispose of and make all needful Rules and Regulations respecting the Territory or other Property belonging to the United States; and nothing in this Constitution shall be so construed as to Prejudice any Claims of the United States, or of any particular State.

Section 4. The United States shall guarantee to every State in this Union a Republican Form of Government, and shall protect each of them against Invasion; and on Application of the Legislature, or of the Executive (when the Legislature cannot be convened) against domestic Violence.

ARTICLE V

The Congress, whenever two thirds of both Houses shall deem it necessary, shall propose Amendments to this Constitution, or, on the Application of the Legislatures of two thirds of the several States, shall call a Convention for proposing Amendments, which, in either Case, shall be valid to all Intents and Purposes, as part of this Constitution, when ratified by the Legislatures of three fourths of the several States, or by Conventions in three fourths thereof, as the one or the other Mode of Ratification may be proposed by the Congress; Provided that no Amendment which may be made prior to the Year One thousand eight hundred and eight shall in any Manner affect the first and fourth Clauses in the Ninth Section of the first Article; and that no State, without its Consent, shall be deprived of its equal Suffrage in the Senate.

ARTICLE VI

[1] All Debts contracted and Engagements entered into, before the Adoption of this Constitution shall be as valid against the United States under this Constitution, as under the Confederation.

[2] This Constitution, and the Laws of the United States which shall be made in Pursuance thereof; and all Treaties made, or which shall be made, under the Authority of the United States, shall be the supreme Law of the Land; and the Judges in every State shall be bound thereby, any Thing in the Constitution or Laws of any State to the Contrary notwithstanding.

[3] The Senators and Representatives before mentioned, and the Members of the several State Legislatures, and all executive and judicial Officers, both of the United States and of the several States, shall be bound by Oath or Affirmation, to support this Constitution; but no religious Test shall ever be required as a Qualification to any Office or public Trust under the United States.

Sum & Substance QUICK REVIEW of Constitutional Law

ARTICLE VII

The Ratification of the Conventions of nine States shall be sufficient for the Establishment of this Constitution between the States so ratifying the Same.

ARTICLES IN ADDITION TO, AND AMENDMENT OF, THE CONSTITUTION OF THE UNITED STATES OF AMERICA, PROPOSED BY CONGRESS, AND RATIFIED BY THE LEGISLATURES OF THE SEVERAL STATES PURSUANT TO THE FIFTH ARTICLE OF THE ORIGINAL CONSTITUTION.

AMENDMENT I [1791]

Congress shall make no law respecting an establishment of religion, or prohibiting the free exercise thereof, or abridging the freedom of speech, or of the press; or the right of the people peaceably to assemble, and to petition the Government for a redress of grievances.

AMENDMENT II [1791]

A well regulated Militia, being necessary to the security of a free State, the right of the people to keep and bear Arms, shall not be infringed.

AMENDMENT III [1791]

No Soldier shall, in time of peace be quartered in any house, without the consent of the Owner, nor in time of war, but in a manner to be prescribed by law.

AMENDMENT IV [1791]

The right of the people to be secure in their persons, houses, papers, and effects, against unreasonable searches and seizures, shall not be violated, and no Warrants shall issue, but upon probable cause, supported by Oath or affirmation and particularly describing the place to be searched, and the persons or things to be seized.

AMENDMENT V [1791]

No person shall be held to answer for a capital, or otherwise infamous crime, unless on a presentment or indictment of a Grand Jury, except in cases arising in the land or naval forces, or in the Militia, when in actual service in time of War or public danger; nor shall any person be subject for the same offence to be twice put in jeopardy of life or limb; nor shall be compelled in any criminal case to be a witness against himself, nor be deprived of life, liberty, or property, without due process of law; nor shall private property be taken for public use, without just compensation.

AMENDMENT VI [1791]

In all criminal prosecutions, the accused shall enjoy the right to a speedy and public trial, by an impartial jury of the State and district wherein the crime shall have been committed, which district shall have been previously ascertained by law, and to be informed of the nature and cause of the accusation; to be confronted with the witnesses against him; to have compulsory process for obtaining witnesses in his favor, and to have the Assistance of Counsel for his defence.

AMENDMENT VII [1791]

In Suits at common law, where the value in controversy shall exceed twenty dollars, the right of trial by jury shall be preserved, and no fact tried by jury, shall be otherwise re- examined in any Court of the United States, than according to the rules of the common law.

AMENDMENT VIII [1791]

Excessive bail shall not be required, nor excessive fines imposed, nor cruel and unusual punishments inflicted.

AMENDMENT IX [1791]

The enumeration in the Constitution, of certain rights, shall not be construed to deny or disparage others retained by the people.

AMENDMENT X [1791]

The powers not delegated to the United States by the Constitution, nor prohibited by it to the States, are reserved to the States respectively, or to the people.

AMENDMENT XI [1798]

The Judicial power of the United States shall not be construed to extend to any suit in law or equity, commenced or prosecuted against one of the United States by Citizens of another State, or by Citizens or Subjects of any Foreign State.

AMENDMENT XII [1804]

The Electors shall meet in their respective states and vote by ballot for President and Vice-President, one of whom, at least, shall not be an inhabitant of the same state with themselves; they shall name in their ballots the person voted for as President, and in distinct ballots the person voted for as Vice-President, and they shall make distinct lists of all persons voted for as President, and of all persons voted for as Vice-President, and of the number of votes for each, which lists they shall sign and certify, and transmit sealed to the seat of the government of the United States, directed to the President of the Senate; — The President of the Senate shall, in the presence of the Senate and House of Representatives, open all the certificates and the votes shall then be counted; — The person having the greatest number of votes for President, shall be the President, if such number be a majority of the whole number of Electors appointed; and if no person have such majority, then from the persons having the highest numbers not exceeding three on the list of those voted for as President, the House of Representatives shall choose immediately, by ballot, the President. But in choosing the President, the votes shall be taken by states, the representation from each state having one vote; a quorum for this purpose shall consist of a member or members from two-thirds of the states, and a majority of all the states shall be necessary to a choice. And if the House of Representatives shall not choose a President whenever the right of choice shall devolve upon them before the fourth day of March next following, then the Vice-President shall act as President, as in the case of the death or other constitutional disability of the President. — The person having the greatest number of votes as Vice-President, shall be the Vice-President, if such number be a majority of the whole number of Electors appointed, and if no person have a majority, then from the two highest numbers on the list, the Senate shall choose the Vice-President; a quorum for the purpose shall consist of two-thirds of the whole number of Senators, and a majority of the whole number shall be necessary to a choice. But no person constitutionally ineligible to the office of President shall be eligible to that of Vice-President of the United States.

AMENDMENT XIII [1865]

Section 1. Neither slavery nor involuntary servitude, except as a punishment for crime whereof the party shall have been duly convicted, shall exist within the United States, or any place subject to their jurisdiction.

Section 2. Congress shall have power to enforce this article by appropriate legislation.

AMENDMENT XIV [1868]

Section 1. All persons born or naturalized in the United States, and subject to the jurisdiction thereof, are citizens of the United States and of the State wherein they reside. No State shall make or enforce any law which shall abridge the privileges or immunities of citizens of the United States; nor shall any State deprive any person of life, liberty, or property, without due process of law; nor deny to any person within its jurisdiction the equal protection of the laws.

Section 2. Representatives shall be apportioned among the several States according to their respective numbers, counting the whole number of persons in each State, excluding Indians not taxed. But when the right to vote at any election for the choice of electors for President and Vice President of the United States, Representatives in Congress, the Executive and Judicial officers of a State, or the members of the Legislature thereof, is denied to any of the male inhabitants of such State, being twenty-one years of age, and citizens of the United States, or in any way abridged, except for participation in rebellion, or other crime, the basis of representation therein shall be reduced in the proportion which the number of such male citizens shall bear to the whole number of male citizens twenty- one years of age in such State.

Section 3. No person shall be a Senator or Representative in Congress, or elector of President and Vice President, or hold any office, civil or military, under the United States, or under any State, who having previously taken an oath, as a member of Congress, or as an officer of the United States, or as a member of any State legislature, or as an executive or judicial officer of any State, to support the Constitution of the United States, shall have engaged in insurrection or rebellion against the same, or given aid or comfort to the enemies thereof. But Congress may by a vote of two-thirds of each House, remove such disability.

Section 4. The validity of the public debt of the United States, authorized by law, including debts incurred for payment of pensions and bounties for services in suppressing insurrection or rebellion, shall not be questioned. But neither the United States nor any State shall assume or pay any debt or obligation incurred in aid of insurrection or rebellion against the United States, or any claim for the loss or emancipation of any slave; but all such debts, obligations and claims shall be held illegal and void.

Section 5. The Congress shall have power to enforce, by appropriate legislation, the provisions of this article.

AMENDMENT XV [1870]

Section 1. The right of citizens of the United States to vote shall not be denied or abridged by the United States or by any State on account of race, color, or previous condition of servitude.

Section 2. The Congress shall have power to enforce this article by appropriate legislation.

AMENDMENT XVI [1913]

The Congress shall have power to lay and collect taxes on incomes, from whatever source derived, without apportionment among the several States, and without regard to any census or enumeration.

AMENDMENT XVII [1913]

[1] The Senate of the United States shall be composed of two Senators from each State, elected by the people thereof, for six years; and each Senator shall have one vote. The electors in each State shall have the qualifications requisite for electors of the most numerous branch of the State legislatures.

[2]When vacancies happen in the representation of any State in the Senate, the executive authority of such State shall issue writs of election to fill such vacancies: *Provided*, That the legislature of any State may empower the executive thereof to make temporary appointments until the people fill the vacancies by election as the legislature may direct.

[3] This amendment shall not be so construed as to affect the election or term of any Senator chosen before it becomes valid as part of the Constitution.

AMENDMENT XVIII [1919]

Section 1. After one year from the ratification of this article the manufacture, sale, or transportation of intoxicating liquors within, the importation thereof into, or the exportation thereof from the United States and all territory subject to the jurisdiction thereof for beverage purposes is hereby prohibited.

Section 2. The Congress and the several States shall have concurrent power to enforce this article by appropriate legislation.

Section 3. This article shall be inoperative unless it shall have been ratified as an amendment to the Constitution by the legislatures of the several States, as provided in the Constitution, within seven years from the date of the submission hereof to the States by the Congress.

AMENDMENT XIX [1920]

[1] The right of citizens of the United States to vote shall not be denied or abridged by the United States or by any State on account of sex.

[2] Congress shall have power to enforce this article by appropriate legislation.

Section 1. The terms of the President and Vice President shall end at noon on the 20th day of January, and the terms of Senators and Representatives at noon on the 3d day of January, of the years in which such terms would have ended if this article had not been ratified; and the terms of their successors shall then begin.

Section 2. The Congress shall assemble at least once in every year, and such meeting shall begin at noon on the 3d day of January, unless they shall by law appoint a different day.

Section 3. If, at the time fixed for the beginning of the term of the President, the President elect shall have died, the Vice President elect shall become President. If the President shall not have been chosen before the time fixed for the beginning of his term, or if the President elect shall have failed to qualify, then the Vice President elect shall act as President until a President shall have qualified; and the Congress may by law provide for the case wherein neither a President elect nor a Vice President elect shall have qualified, declaring who shall then act as President, or the manner in which one who is to act shall be selected, and such person shall act accordingly until a President or Vice President shall have qualified.

Section 4. The Congress may by law provide for the case of the death of any of the persons from whom the House of Representatives may choose a President whenever the right of choice shall have devolved upon them, and for the case of the death of any of the persons from whom the Senate may choose a Vice President whenever the right of choice shall have devolved upon them.

Section 5. Sections 1 and 2 shall take effect on the 15th day of October following the ratification of this article.

Section 6. This article shall be inoperative unless it shall have been ratified as an amendment to the Constitution by the legislatures of three-fourths of the several States within seven years from the date of its submission.

AMENDMENT XXI [1933]

Section 1. The eighteenth article of amendment to the Constitution of the United States is hereby repealed.

Section 2. The transportation or importation into any State, Territory, or possession of the United States for delivery or use therein of intoxicating liquors, in violation of the laws thereof, is hereby prohibited.

Section 3. This article shall be inoperative unless it shall have been ratified as an amendment to the Constitution by conventions in the several States, as provided in the Constitution, within seven years from the date of the submission hereof to the States by the Congress.

U.S. CONSTITUTION

AMENDMENT XXII [1951]

Section 1. No person shall be elected to the office of the President more than twice, and no person who has held the office of President, or acted as President, for more than two years of a term to which some other person was elected President shall be elected to the office of President more than once. But this Article shall not apply to any person holding the office of President when this Article was proposed by the Congress, and shall not prevent any person who may be holding the office of President, or acting as President, during the term within which this Article becomes operative from holding the office of President or acting as President during the remainder of such term.

Section 2. This article shall be inoperative unless it shall have been ratified as an amendment to the Constitution by the legislatures of three-fourths of the several States within seven years from the date of its submission to the States by the Congress.

AMENDMENT XXIII [1961]

Section 1. The District constituting the seat of Government of the United States shall appoint in such manner as the Congress may direct:

A number of electors of President and Vice President equal to the whole number of Senators and Representatives in Congress to which the District would be entitled if it were a State, but in no event more than the least populous state; they shall be in addition to those appointed by the states, but they shall be considered, for the purposes of the election of President and Vice President, to be electors appointed by a state; and they shall meet in the District and perform such duties as provided by the twelfth article of amendment.

Section 2. The Congress shall have power to enforce this article by appropriate legislation.

AMENDMENT XXIV [1964]

Section 1. The right of citizens of the United States to vote in any primary or other election for President or Vice President, for electors for President or Vice President, or for Senator or Representative in Congress, shall not be denied or abridged by the United States or any State by reason of failure to pay any poll tax or other tax.

Section 2. The Congress shall have power to enforce this article by appropriate legislation.

AMENDMENT XXV [1967]

Section 1. In case of the removal of the President from office or of his death or resignation, the Vice President shall become President.

Section 2. Whenever there is a vacancy in the office of the Vice President, the President shall nominate a Vice President who shall take office upon confirmation by a majority vote of both Houses of Congress.

Section 3. Whenever the President transmits to the President pro tempore of the Senate and the Speaker of the House of Representatives his written declaration that he is unable to discharge the powers and duties of his office, and until he transmits to them a written declaration to the contrary, such powers and duties shall be discharged by the Vice President as Acting President.

Section 4. Whenever the Vice President and a majority of either the principal officers of the executive departments or of such other body as Congress may by law provide, transmit to the President pro tempore of the Senate and the Speaker of the House of Representatives their written declaration that the President is unable to discharge the powers and duties of his office, the Vice President shall immediately assume the powers and duties of the office as Acting President.

Thereafter, when the President transmits to the President pro tempore of the Senate and the Speaker of the House of Representatives his written declaration that no inability exists, he shall resume the powers and duties of his office unless the Vice President and a majority of either the principal officers of the executive department or of such other body as Congress may by law provide, transmit within four days to the President pro tempore of the Senate and the Speaker of the House of Representatives their written declaration that the President is unable to discharge the powers and duties of his office. Thereupon Congress shall decide the issue, assembling within forty-eight hours for that purpose if not in session. If the Congress, within twenty-one days after receipt of the latter written declaration, or, if Congress is not in session, within twenty-one days after Congress is required to assemble, determines by two-thirds vote of both Houses that the President is unable to discharge the powers and duties of his office, the Vice President shall continue to discharge the same as Acting President; otherwise, the President shall resume the powers and duties of his office.

Section 1. The right of citizens of the United States, who are eighteen years of age or older, to vote shall not be denied or abridged by the United States or by any State on account of age.

Section 2. The Congress shall have power to enforce this article by appropriate legislation.

No law, varying compensation for the services of Senators and Representatives, shall take effect, until an election of Representatives shall have intervened.

U.S. CONSTITUTION

XXIV. TABLE OF CASES

TABLE OF CASES

TABLE OF CASES

TABLE OF CASES

TABLE OF
CASES

TABLE OF
CASES

TABLE OF
CASES

TABLE OF CASES

TABLE OF
CASES

United States v. (see opposing party)

TABLE OF CASES

XXV. INDEX

References are to section numbers

Sum & Substance QUICK REVIEW of Constitutional Law